THE DEFLATION OF 1930

ITS CAUSES AND PERNICIOUS EFFECTS

Volume II of

The Great Deleverage Series

The Story of 1929-33

John C. Harvey & Mary Keil

FOUR DIRECTIONS PRESS
RHINEBECK NEW YORK

Published in the United States by Four Directions Press,
P. O. Box 417, Rhinebeck, New York, 12572.

ISBN 979-8-9910734-1-7
Library of Congress Control Number 2025907710

Printed by KDP, an Amazon company

Published May 2025
First Edition

Book and cover design by Sean McCarthy

Dedicated to the late Professor Irving Fisher of Yale University

whose eloquent and insightful explanation of deflation
is herein statistically demonstrated and confirmed.

Acknowledgements:

First and foremost, we acknowledge and express deep gratitude to our spouses for the countless ways they supported us and contributed to our ability to reach this point in *The Great Deleverage Series.*

Our Editor with a capital "E," of both volumes, Sally V. Keil, holds a special position on the list of those to be thankful for as a perceptive, wise and steady presence to both authors over the years. In her unwavering quest for clarity, she edited for ever more verbal precision, hopefully enabling our brave readers to understand clearly our approach, explanations and conclusions.

We are additionally grateful to colleagues Matthew Sambor, Donald Hill, Michael McCormick and Julie Saxton for their help and support; as well as to Sean McCarthy of Four Directions Press, our publisher, for his well-honed skills, ongoing encouragement and skill in getting us over the finish line.

CONTENTS

Acknowledgements iv
Transitional Introduction 1
1: Irving Fisher's Debt Factor Approach 18
2: Problems Caused by Deflation (Late 1929-1933) 48
3: Liquidity Panic & the Beginnings of Deflation (Late 1929) 66
4: Year-End Reckoning for 1929: Meet the Speculators and Investors. 93
5: Over-indebedness Recognized: From Growing Consumption to Net Repayment 134
6: Speculation Renewed and Hoover's Stabilization Plan Launched (Late 1929 through First Quarter 1930) 161
7: Prospects Dim Then Darken (Second Quarter of 1930) 196
8: Thoughts of a Quick Recovery Vanish (Third Quarter of 1930) 228
9: Pausing in October 1930 260
10: Friedman & Schwartz's First "Banking Crisis" (November and December 1930) 281
11: Retrospective & Look Forward for Americans as Individuals 310
12: Retrospective & a Brief Look Forward: American Corporations and Business (Year-End 1930) 341
13: American Farmers: Speculation, Indebtedness and the Shrugged-off IRS (Year-End 1930) 389
14: An Overview of 1931 in the U.S.: Repayments of Over-Indebtedness Accelerate 412
15: Incipient Conclusions: Interim Thoughts about Deflation 439
About Appendices 446
References 447
Index 455
Regarding Perrmissions 475
About the Authors 476

List of Tables and Charts

Tables Title Page Number

TI.1 Rates of Change 1929-1933 3

TI.2 Gross National Product Annually 1929-1934 4

2.1A Aggregate Price Indexes 1919-39 52

2.1B Change in Price Indexes from Year Earlier 53

2.2 Annual Totals of Credit Sought/ Granted. 54

3.1 Prices of Specified Commodities. 71

3.2 Changes in U. S. Prices of Selected Commodities. 72

3.3 Indexes of Velocity of Bank Deposits .80

3.4 Two Measures of Friedman's Income Velocity. 82

3.5 Statistics of U.S. Economic Activity 91

4.1 Summary Stastics 97

4.2 Simple Distribution of Individual Tax Returns 1929 98

4.3 Simple Distribution of Individual Tax Returns 1928 98

4.4 Sources of Income and Deductions in Individual Returns . . . 102

4.5 Percentage Distribution of Income Individual Returns 1928. . 103

4.6 Percentage Distribution of Income Individual Returns 1929 . 104

4.7 Short and Long-term Gains 1928-1929. 111

4.8 Comparison of Sources of Income for 1928 and 1929. 113

4.9 Average 1928 Income per Filer 114

4.10 Average 1929 Income per Filer 114

4.11 Short and Long-term Profit for 1928-1929 127

4.12 Call Loan Statistics & Rates in 1929 131

5.1 Aggregate U. S. Corporate Sources & Uses of Funds 139

5.2 Spreading the Repayments of $7,135 Million over 1930 142

5SB.1 Quarters of Member Banks Borrowing Decline 145

5.3 Rebalancing of Debt Maturities by Corporations 146

5.4 Repayment of Notes & Accounts Receivable in 1930 148

5A Results Estimated Assignment of "Others" 150

5.5 Derivation of Monthly Debt Repayment Averages 160

Tables Title Page Number

6.1 Percentage of New York Stock Exchange Loans 166
6.2 Installment Credit Granted and Rate of Change 190
6.3 Statistics of U.S. Economic Activity 194
7.1 Percent of New York Stock Exchange Loans 201
7.2 Installment Credit Granted and Rate of Change. 204
7.3 Installment Credit Granted and Rate of Change 2nd Qtr. . . . 206
7.4 Cars and Trucks Produced 216
7.5 Statistics of U.S. Economic Activity 226
8.1 Price Index: All Urban Consumers 1930 232
8.2 Number of Homes Forclosed 246
8.3 Yield Curves: Jan 1930–Mar 1931 254
8.4 Statistics of U.S. Economic Activity 258
9.1 Commercial Banks: Loans, Investments, Deposits 1928-34 . . 269
9.2 Statistics of U.S. Economic Activity 280
10.1 Bank Suspensions and Deposits in Closed Banks 287
10.2 Changes in M-1 and M-2 (Aug 1929-Apr 1931) 297
10.3 Statistics of U.S. Economic Activity 309
11.1 Gross National Product & Aggregate Price Indexes. 312
11.2 Estimates of Labor Force, Employment and Unemployment. 316
11.3 Estimates of Unemployment in the U.S. 1929 to 1940 317
11.4 Summary Statistics 321
11.5 Sources of Income and Deductions 322
11.6 Speculation in 1930 326
11.7 Sources of Income by Net Income Class 329
11.8 Returns from Asset Sales by Net Income Class 330
11.9 Distribution of Total Income in Individual Returns 332
11.10 Demographic Ups and Downs 334
11.11 Short-Term Profits & Long-Term Net Gains 335
11.12 Average Income by Net Income Class 336
11.13 Downward Movement of Net Income Classes. 337
11.14 Results of Downward Movement by Income Classes. 338

Tables Title Page Number

11.15 Percent of New York Stock Exchange Loans. 340
12.1 All Sectors: Gross Income 1918-1930 .347
12.2 All Manufacturing, Gross Income 1918-1930. 349
12.3 Comparing Depression Downturns of 1920-22 and 1930. . . .361
12.3A Changes in Price Indexes from Year Earlier. 363
12.3B Consumer Price Index: All Urban Consumers 1919-1923 . . .363
12.3C Commercial Paper rates 1919-1923 .365
12.3D Quarters of Member Bank Borrowing Change 1919-1923 . .366
12.4 All Sectors: Net Income Less Deficit 1918-1930 373
12.5 Manufacturing Subsections: Net Income Less Deficit. 375
12.6 Finance Net Income Less Deficit from 1928-1930 377
12.7 Finance Gross Income from 1929 to 1930. 378
12.8 Metal Products and Processes Changes in Gross Income 380
12.9 Metal Products and Processes Changes in Net Income 382
12.10 Net Profit from Business for 1929 and 1930. 386
12.11 Net Income of Profitable Corporations for 1930 387
13.1 Farmer Otto Opitz's Balance Sheet 1928 and 1932 409
14.Deflation Consumer Price Index: AllUrban Consumers 1931 . . 415
14.1 1931 Aggregate U.S. Corporate Sources and Uses of Funds . .420
14.2 Spreading the Repayment of $11.008 Million over 1931 425
14.3 Repayment of Notes & Accounts Receivable in 1931 428
14.A Results Estimate Assignment of "Others" at End of 1931 432
14.4 Statistics of U.S. Economic Activity .438

Charts

Chart TI.1 Total Loans and Investments 15
Chart 3.1 The Stock of Money and Its Proximate Determinates 67
Chart 3.2 Fisher's View of Velocity of Bank Deposits 79
Chart 7.1 Stock Price Indexes. 222
Chart 9.1 The Stock of Money and Its Proximate Determinants . . .275
Chart 10.1 Prices, Personal Income and Industrial Production 1929-33. 302
Chart 12.1 Historical Statistics Cycle Expansions and Contractions 1914-33 354

Figures

Figure 3.1 Passenger Car Output Adjusted to Domestic & Foreign Sales 1925-29. 87
Figure 3.2 Passenger Car Output Adjusted to Domestic & Foreign Sales 1925-30. 89
Figure 7.1 Passenger Car Output Adjusted to Domestic & Foreign Sales 1925-30. 217
Figure 8.1 Mortgage Commitments of Mortgage Lenders 239
Figure 9.2 Friedman and Schwartz Money Supply Equation. 274

Transitional Introduction

"...The General Attitude Which is Called 'Deflation'"[1]

In *How the Crash of 1929 Caused the Great Depression*, our first volume in *The Great Deleverage Series*, we explored in-depth the economic factors up to late 1929 that propelled the country into the Great Depression. We also developed our thesis (one that Yale's Irving Fisher had posited in 1932) that over-indebtedness — speculative margin stock purchases, installment credit, mortgage debt by consumers, etc — was a primary underlying cause. In this second volume in *The Great Deleverage Series*, we offer an equally thorough and compelling look at another primary cause of the distress of 1930 and 1931 that accompanied the issue of over-indebtedness, namely deflation. Deflation, a far less explored condition, developed with the Crash, then worsened consistently thereafter, persisting throughout the country — and weakening it like a slow-acting poison with no antidote.

Many see the events of the Great Depression as beginning with the Crash and then descending a year later into depression via a "banking crisis" in the last two months of 1930. That assumption — in our considered view, a significant mistake — skips almost completely over what else happened in 1930. As this volume will document, 1930 was an eventful, in fact pivotal year in which the dynamic of the Great Depression, with its accompanying deflation, settled in as a series of economic factors took hold of the imagination of the American psyche and dramatically changed their economic behavior.

---

1 Gilbert Seldes, *The Years of the Locust (America 1929-1932)*, Little, Brown, 1933, p. 63.

We make use of cultural critic Gilbert Seldes's words in the title of this introduction because his description of deflation in his 1933 book *The Years of the Locust* resonated. He called deflation an "attitude," one that prevailed as a crucial, yet poorly understood part of the zeitgeist in the country throughout the time period of this second volume in our series. With the Crash, Americans quickly fell from feeling the possibility-fueled rush of speculative riches to its opposite, as they succumbed to Seldes's "general attitude of deflation" that blanketed the outlook of "the American people, lulled to sleep by promises and fairy tales," as Seldes observed, under a layer of caution.[2] In 1930, that caution decisively changed economic conditions.

Reflections on the Historian's Approach and Helpful Data

For readers of *How the Crash Caused*, it may already be clear that we consider historians tasked with using their skills and tools to explore as many paths as appear to them as they research the terrain of the historical time period and events they study. Again, the emphasis in this second volume is on exploring statistical records and other research on post-Crash realities widely and not limiting explorations to any preconceived pathways, especially along paths that may be novel and unfamiliar to readers. As is attributed to Yogi Berra, "When you come to a fork in the road, take it." Our approach to our subject was first to explore it, and time and again, when we were faced with alternative forks, to consider each before establishing our point of view. Obviously, historians also aim to report their findings, which may mean, to some extent, reporting on counterfactuals. Along the way, historians may change their minds when presented with new information. What is important, of course, is that historians convey their findings, occasionally discuss what they don't or can't find and always explain their conclusions and their reasoning.

---

2 Ibid.

What is also clear is that we view data as key to providing the compelling support needed in order to reach insightful conclusions, even novel ones, about this period to which we and many others—historians and economists predominating before us—have devoted so much time and attention. Appropriately, then, we begin our Introduction to the second volume in *The Great Deleverage Series* with two illuminating tables of macro-level data that also appeared early in *How the Crash Caused.*

Table TI.1

Rates of Change - 1929-1933

(Assumes **100%** of corporate payables are owed to corporations)

($ million in current dollars)

1929	1930	1931	1932	1933	% Change from 1929
Fall in GNP					
103,420	90,700				-12.3
		76,073			-26.4
			58,280		-43.6
				55,818	-46.0
Fall in personal consumption expenditures					
77,251	69,916				-9.5
		60,482			-21.7
			48,591		-37.1
				45,811	-40.7
Fall in fixed Investment					
14,483	10,601				-26.8
		6,768			-53.3
			3,445		-76.2
				2,970	-79.5
Decline from prior year					
	-3,882	-3,833	-3,323	-475	
Fall in notes and accounts receivable **held** by U.S Corporations					
66,810	59,675				-10.7
		48,667			-27.2
			39,564		-40.8
				35,835	-46.4
Fall in notes and accounts payable **owed** by U.S. Corporations					
29,453	26,870				-8.8
		23,251			-21.1
			20,562		-30.2
				19,362	-34.3
Fall in debt — due and payable within one year — owed by non-corporations to U.S. Corporations					
37,358	32,805				-12.2
		25,416			-32.0
			19,002		-49.1
				16,473	-55.9
Decline from prior year					
	-4,553	-7,389	-6,414	-2,529	

Source: Commerce Department; IRS *Statistics of Income 1929-1933*

Table TI.2

Gross National Product: Annually, 1929-1934

($ million)

	1929	1930	1931	1932	1933	1934
Gross national product	**103,420**	**90,700**	**76,073**	**58,280**	**55,818**	**65,291**
Personal consumption expenditures	**77,251**	**69,916**	**60,482**	**48,591**	**45,811**	**51,344**
Durable goods	9,243	7,166	5,483	3,641	3,464	4,219
Nondurable goods	37,686	34,022	28,956	22,741	22,257	26,691
Services	30,322	28,728	26,043	22,209	20,090	20,434
Gross private domestic investment	**16,197**	**10,249**	**5,620**	**965**	**1,406**	**3,328**
Fixed investment	14,483	10,601	6,768	3,445	2,970	4,063
Non residential	10,610	8,325	5,031	2,705	2,390	3,177
Structures	5,118	4,145	2,388	1,245	954	1,079
Producers' durable equipment	5,492	4,180	2,643	1,460	1,436	2,098
Residential	3,873	2,276	1,737	740	580	886
Nonfarm structures	3,620	2,078	1,602	667	497	783
Farm structures	175	131	78	38	43	52
Producers' durable equipment	78	67	57	35	40	51
Change in business inventories	1,714	-352	-1,148	-2,480	-1,564	-735
Nonfarm	1,836	-83	-1,608	-2,590	-1,370	195
Farm	-122	-269	460	110	-194	-930
Net exports of goods and services	**1,149**	**1,032**	**516**	**407**	**358**	**601**
Exports	7,035	5,448	3,641	2,474	2,402	2,975
Imports	5,886	4,416	3,125	2,067	2,044	2,374
Government purchase of goods and services	**8,823**	**9,503**	**9,455**	**8,317**	**8,243**	**10,018**
Federal	1,441	1,552	1,613	1,578	2,122	3,123
National defense	----------	----------	----------	----------	----------	----------
Nondefense	----------	----------	----------	----------	----------	----------
State and local	7,382	7,951	7,842	6,739	6,121	6,895

Source: *The National Income & Product Accounts of the United States 1929-76; Table 1.1*, p.1.

Each table offers a different overview of the dramatic rates of change of key economic indicators from our period of focus. The specific purpose of Table TI.1 (prior page) (Table Introduction.1 in *How the Crash Caused*) is to draw attention to the size of debt repayments made by non-corporations (i.e., individuals/consumers, in particular) to corporations (e.g., retailers and banks) and to the urgency with which the payments were made. Table TI.2 (above) (Table 1.1 in *How the Crash Caused*) shows how components of Gross National Product evolved over the years 1929-1934. We repeat these important fundamentals here to keep them right at hand as we proceed with our narrative singling out deflation as a defining aspect of American life from the Crash through 1930 into 1931 (and beyond to 1933).

In addition, we provide a condensed version of our Cast of Characters, our take on the period's key economic players, discussed in depth in Chapter 12 of *How the Crash Caused.* As historians, we found this way of classifying U.S. citizens extremely helpful in refining our understanding and in considering the challenging forks in the road each category faced. We will continue referring to them throughout the chapters ahead. Some cast members played multiple roles, compounding their possible woes.

Cast of Characters

Our Cast of Characters in 1930 follows with a brief description of each group. See the full discussion in Chapter 12 of *How the Crash Caused.*

• Repentant Ex-Speculators (post-Crash). By far the unhappiest group of people, many had considered themselves well-to-do. Now they faced a new reality of financial loss and the need to deal with major debt obligations.

• Wall Street Professionals. These brokers, dealers and bankers were beset by great concerns and regrets, exhausted from the intensity and demands of market events, including personally losing significant sums and facing increased debts having responded to margin calls themselves. In addition, they had their firms and colleagues to worry about, including the branch managers of the roughly 1400 branch offices of Wall Street brokerage firms around the country.

• Debtors (in general). Common to all debtors, whether businesses or individuals, is that they owe principal and interest payments (together called "debt service") to their various creditors. Post-Crash, this category — whether proprietors or consumers — found themselves on edge. Consumer debtors understood the losses they would suffer if they stopped repaying: repossession of items purchased on installments and all prior payments. This fear ranked high and led to rapid changes in consumption behavior.

• Businessmen. Businessmen (as was the going term in 1929) who managed still-profitable businesses tended to take longer term outlooks, while those managing unprofitable businesses became more focused on short-term objectives like obtaining loans to tide their businesses over or laying workers off. Post-Crash, businessmen likely spent many sleepless nights wondering what lay ahead for them and their firm.

• Corporate Financial Executives. Corporate financial executives concentrated especially on minimizing financial risk. In challenging times of great uncertainty, they especially focused on minimizing the risks of insolvency for the company (which means running out of cash) and at worst, bankruptcy.

• Public Officials. Public officials managed the "public good" — the government functions at federal, state and local levels. Many public officials who took their responsibilities seriously and performed them conscientiously were apprehensive about tax revenue losses, budget cuts, layoffs or even, as ultimately occurred, the inability to pay essential salaries, such as for teachers. Yet, even in crises, elected public officials are motivated by an overall desire to be reelected, and appointed officials want to be reappointed.

• Consumers. In the "boom times" of the 1920s, consumers had become motivated by aggressively marketed "easy" credit that enabled them to improve their comfort, happiness, not to mention their status. With increasingly widespread electrification, households had been busy buying the many appealing, newly invented and manufactured household goods as well as securing services such as insurance to cover their homes and cars. The Crash led many to rethink their priorities.

• Successful Speculators (post-Crash). By November 1929, successful speculators had realized wealth and were materially out of the stock market. The really successful speculators among them had divested by early September 1929 and were proud of their good judgment and prowess, although some still had hopes of repeating their earlier investing success. Given that they had realized gains and gotten out of the market before the Crash, those funds may—or may not — have been "burning holes in their pockets" in late 1929.

• Workers. This diverse group of working Americans earned wages and salaries, motivated by making enough to provide comfortable lifestyles for themselves and their families. Many aspired to achieve the fabled American Dream. Among this category were also many people classified as self-employed, including professionals — doctors, lawyers, architects, etc. — and sole proprietors of small businesses.

• Insider Speculator Instigators. This small group of Wall Street insiders had been stoking the fires of speculation by promoting a particular stock they themselves had already purchased. Their behavior stimulated demand in that stock by non-insider speculators who responded to the rumors, bought in and bid up the per share prices. The Insider Speculator Instigators rode the stock prices up to pre-determined levels, then sold their holdings and pocketed the gains before outsiders learned of their sales and began selling as the stock prices fell. As a rule, Insider Speculator Instigators had made fortunes in the late 1920s and wanted to keep those fortunes.

• The Unemployed. Only as the Depression set in and progressed did involuntary unemployment become apparent and, in fact, a serious and growing problem. Counted or not, the involuntarily unemployed or those laid off, many of whom had families to support, were motivated by the increasingly desperate need for income to keep meeting their debt obligations and buy the basics.

• Voters. Elections became an important means for voters to express their anger or despair. Voters at all levels of the economic ladder were in assessment mode, depending on their circumstances.

Some Thoughts About Deflation as Fleshed Out in This Volume

A common thumb-nail phrase describing inflation is that it occurs when "too much money is chasing goods." Under these circumstances, prices rise. The analogous phrase describes deflation as occurring when "too little money is chasing goods." In this case, prices fall. This sounds simple, but in considering the period from late 1929 through 1933, we repeatedly found ourselves confronted with a number of wide-ranging, complex and painful problems associated with deflation—a defining condition of the time.

Finding answers to two key questions became primary motivators as we wrote *The Deflation of 1930*:

1) What causes deflation?

and

2) What does deflation cause?

In this volume, we pursue both of these questions within the context of what is likely *the* textbook examples from our country's history of deflationary processes unleashed, from their incipient causes to their final relevance. In the first and more momentous example, 1929-33, deflation arose with the Crash of 1929, which sent stock prices and commodities prices plummeting with greatest power in 1931-32, and ended in March of 1933 with deflation as a largely spent force. We also highlight another case, 1920-21, when deflation had a very different profile. In this impactful though briefer period, depression began with the Fed raising the discount rate in stair-step fashion to curb inflation as businesses converted from the sale of wartime goods to peacetime products. This caused deflation to evolve along a bifurcated pathway of wholesale prices and consumer prices. When the bifurcation ended and the evolution returned to normality, a rapid segue into prosperity developed. Manufacturers produced peacetime goods. Consumers eagerly bought them. Prices stabilized.

As we approached each notable aspect of deflation playing out primarily in 1929-33, and secondarily in the earlier depression of 1920-21 considered ahead in Chapter 12, we formed further questions that we deemed important to address and answer, including:

- Could deflation be "a monetary force" as Friedman and Schwartz meant those terms? Indeed, could deflation be "an inescapable monetary force"? Why does that matter?

- When did deflation begin in 1929-1930? In 1920-21?

• How quickly did deflation develop in both time periods?

• Were any countervailing forces evident in 1929-31? In 1920-21?

• What caused the U.S. to move so rapidly and confidently to prosperity after the Depression of 1920-21 and not in 1930-31??

This volume is our attempt to answer these questions and many others. Within our narrative of 1929-33, we will look at the rapid rise in the general attitude and practical functioning of deflation and what deflation caused, not just at its onset in the final two months of 1929, but also throughout 1930 and into 1931. Throughout 1930, deflation settled in and accelerated, bringing with it a growing number of damaging repercussions, including the momentum to repay debt, falling demand for goods and growing unemployment as employers cut back—all sliding in one slippery downward spiral. We hope the journey taken here through the early years of 1929-33 brings readers to a new level of understanding of deflation and the damage it can do to a nation's economy.

A Guide to This Volume's Approach

This volume follows a chronological narrative similar to that of *How the Crash Caused*, along with chapters providing summaries of noteworthy factors and influences. Chapter 1 presents Irving Fisher's deconstruction of how rising debt grew into over-indebtedness, a concept that he was unable to find the data to prove, that quickly motivated the indebted to pivot from debt-enabled consumption to net debt repayment causing the money supply to shrink and in-turn causing deflation to develop. Chapter 2 discusses significant problems caused by deflation. In Chapter 3, economist and historian Charles

P. Kindleberger helps us show how significant evidences of deflation developed in the period that began with the Crash and persisted through the end of 1929 and into what he called the "baffling second quarter of 1930." Chapter 4 uses IRS statistics to explain the economic reckoning for 1929 and focuses in particular on what tax returns revealed about speculators and investors. Chapter 5 concentrates on estimating the amount of over-indebtedness that was repaid in 1930 and concludes that $4+ billion was repaid to U.S. corporations by non-corporations through consumer "belt-tightening".

Chapters 6 through 10 provide a chronological view of the economy in 1930. Chapter 6 explains the optimistic first quarter as the Little Bull Market developed, but also shows that demand for installment credit was already slowing as a consequence of the Crash, though this was unobserved at the time. Chapter 7 describes how that falling demand for installment credit brought the Great Depression to full force in May 1930 and how the Little Bull Market collapsed in the late spring. Chapter 8 discusses how debt payment delinquencies began to grow in the third quarter of 1930, especially in mortgage markets. Chapter 9 summarizes statistics on monetary decline by the end of October. Chapter 10 explores how the "first liquidity crisis" that Friedman and Schwartz claimed changed the character of our nation's economic decline from non-monetary to monetary in fact had, in their own words, "no clear imprint."[3]

Using the extensive treasure trove of data from the Internal Revenue Service, we zero in on what was happening in 1930 with American individual taxfilers in Chapter 11 and with U.S. corporations in Chapter 12. Chapter 12 also takes a useful look at the Depression of 1920-21 and what factors caused that depression to turn itself around and evolve into prosperity, unlike the later Great Depression. Chapter 13 dives into the critical sector of farming and how farmers shared indebtedness with non-farmers, and it also discusses a peculiar phenomenon among farmers in 1930 regarding the IRS, as well as showing the painful reality in one Iowa farmer's

3 Friedman and Schwartz (1963a), p. 313.

account books. Chapter 14 provides an "Overview of 1931," estimating the amount of over-indebtedness that was repaid to U.S. corporations in 1931 by individuals/consumers as $7+ billion — 75% greater than was repaid in 1930. Consumers achieved this staggering level of debt repayment by further "belt-tightening" (aka, yet *further* reduction in consumption). Chapter 14 also introduces the earnest voice of Youngstown, Ohio, lawyer Ben Roth, then in his thirties, who started a diary in 1931 to record what was happening and to try to understand why. His honest observations put a human face on the conditions of the times. Finally, Chapter 15 constitutes our "Incipient Conclusions" about the deflation of 1930 and offers a glimpse into a possible approach to mitigating its effects.

Economic Stability: A Call for Monetarism AND Keynesianism

Our aim in *The Great Deleverage Series*, as we wrote in the Preface in *How the Crash Caused*, is a United States that has "a more stable economy with less political friction." In our view, to achieve this worthy aim requires utilizing the tools offered by both monetarism and the Keynesian approach. And in point of fact, this volume presents an amalgam of influences, both monetary and Keynesian in orientation.

It became clear to us as our statistical research deepened that deflation was a monetary phenomenon with monetary causes, but with potent Keynesian aspects materially impacting the demand side and absolutely necessitating governmental response and action to reverse the course. As we described in Chapter 12 of *How the Crash Caused* and will discuss again in Chapter 2, we have found dramatic evidence of an immediate decrease in purchases, particularly on readily available credit, following the Crash. Demand was falling.

Meanwhile, for esteemed New York banker Paul Warburg, the runaway stock speculation of the late 1920s sounded a warning of trouble ahead— and we see speculation clearly as a *monetary phenomenon.* As early as March 1929, Warburg wrote in his International Acceptance Bank's 1929 annual report that speculation was creating inflated purchasing power and unless speculation was brought under control, an "ultimate collapse" would take place.[4] Of Warburg's urgent warnings, *New York Times* financial editor Alexander Dana Noyes accurately summed them up in his excellent 1938 memoir *The Market Place*:

> This was plain language; it came from a high source, and the longer sequel proved it to be *perhaps the most accurate prediction in that strange era.* But, except for a brief reaction on the Stock exchange, the sober warning had no visible effect. Professional Wall Street's usual comment on the speech ranged from characterization of Warburg's arguments as "obsolete" to description of his public warnings as "sandbagging American prosperity," or to the suggestion that anyone who talked like that must have some ulterior purpose of his own. To the speculating public Warburg's warnings first caused alarm, then indignation, and presently, when the stock market resumed its upward rush, expression of supercilious contempt.[5] (emphasis ours)

As Warburg suggested and our data confirm, in the process of indulging in speculation, speculators created inflated purchasing power which was very real and substantial in amount. When it vanished with the Crash, that inflated purchasing power was not replaced. Instead, the immediate reaction—an overreaction—to such a shocking financial event was to repay debt. In lockstep, purchasing power vanished, the money supply shrank and prices dropped. The result was deflation, a significant economic, and we say monetary

---

4 *The Commercial & Financial Chronicle,* Vol. 128, March 9, 1929, pp. 1443-4.

5 Noyes (1938), p. 324.

phenomenon that quickly became salient throughout our research.

Tragically for the country and the world, despite Warburg's sterling reputation and prescience, his sobering words had no impact on the actions of the Federal Reserve System, the federal government with Hoover newly in charge or the leaders and participants of Wall Street and corporate America.

Absent corrective action, the prevailing advice—if it can be called advice at all—was to permit the situation "to work itself out." In late October, the Crash took place. The shock and magnitude of the Crash led consumers—autonomously and in aggregate— to stop buying on installment credit. As installment credit began to drop, loan repayments began, both trends caused by the Crash. (We revealed these occurrences in *How the Crash Caused* and will revisit them in more detail in the chapters ahead.) The broad dynamic of the Great Depression became fully operative across the broad spectrum of consumer installment sales in May 1930, just seven months after the Crash. In sum, deflation commenced immediately with the Crash along with plunging commodity prices, the vaporization of inflated purchasing power in brokerage house margin accounts and the loss of roughly $15 billion of market value of shares listed on the NYSE between October 1 and November 1, 1929.

Throughout 1930, as we will show, something was happening that wasn't seen or understood, certainly not at the time nor, in fact, since. We are told that Milton Friedman's core aspiration was to have the Fed manage the money supply to grow at a steady rate rather than adjusting it up and down with open market operations, but in the Great Depression the money supply shrank. Why? Consumers who had enthusiastically embraced installment debt to acquire what they wanted became debt-averse overnight and focused on repaying their existing indebtedness as quickly as possible to retailers and other creditors who, in turn, repaid it mostly to banks. The aggregate amount of these repayments became a monetary force sufficient to shrink the money supply, thus causing deflation to develop, throwing the national economy into a downward spiraling depression.

In a complex modern economy, a steady rate of money supply growth requires an ongoing level of growth in bank borrowing. But almost immediately after the Crash of 1929, borrowing from banks and other lending institutions began to decline and then to decline at an accelerating rate that became precipitous. Not only was there the vast monetary phenomenon of American consumers, in aggregate, repaying the debts they had assumed during the boom times of the 1920s, they went further by refusing to borrow more for purchases. Bank borrowing plunged.

Chart TI.1

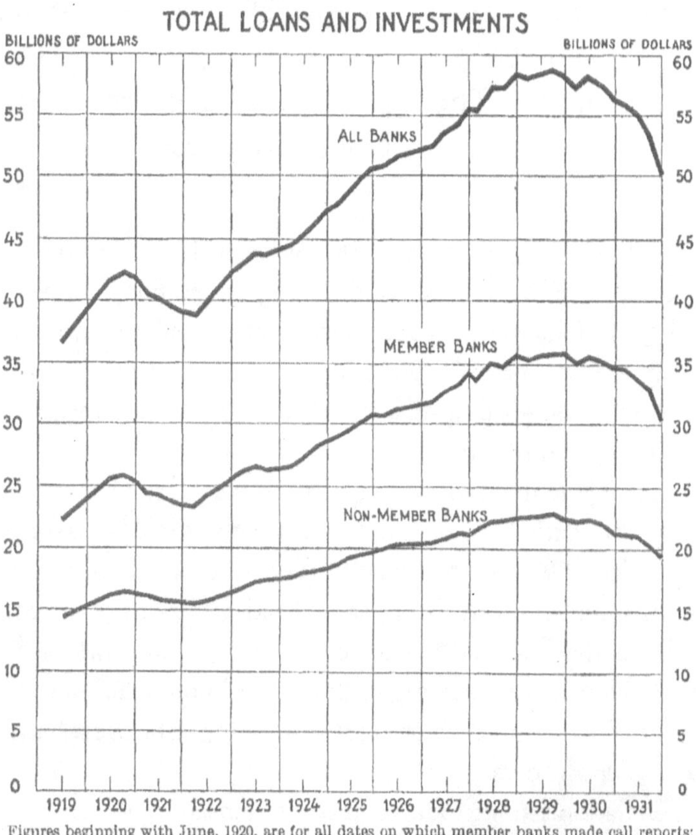

Figures beginning with June, 1920, are for all dates on which member banks made call reports; for earlier period they are for June only

Source: ARBG 1931, p. 5

It is a fundamental monetary idea that the volume of bank loans determines the size of the money supply, as we discussed in Chapter 4 of *How the Crash Caused*. In fact, a bellwether indicator of deflation is a dropping volume of bank loans. *The Annual Report of the Board of Governors of the Federal Reserve 1931* described the conditions regarding the pronounced, rapid and continuous reduction in the volume of bank loans that prevailed from the autumn of 1929 through the end of 1931.[6] With the volume of bank loans falling and even accelerating, it can be no surprise that the U.S. experienced deflation also accelerating in this period. In times of uncertainty when, in response, bank loans are repaid, deflation sets in, as happened in 1920-21 and again following the Crash of 1929.

Further Thoughts About Deflation: What Does Deflation Cause?

Deflation is not inflation in reverse. It is its own powerfully damaging force that erases wealth in *large gulps*. For example, as we will show in Chapter 8, the total value of all real estate in the U.S. fell 35.3% from April 1, 1930 to January 1, 1934. On a straight-line basis, over those 45 monthly months, deflation swallowed $2.458 *billion in value each month.*

We devote much of this volume to examining the pernicious impacts of deflation. For example, for members of our Cast of Characters called "Debtors (in general)," deflation raises the real cost of repaying debt significantly. To stay ahead of the curve by reducing debt faster than normal would require even more work, at a time when employers were cutting back workers' hours and not offering overtime. Furthermore, these costs of repaying debt affect businesses as well as consumers.

Deflation also introduces imperfections and inefficiencies into

6 Federal Reserve Board, *Annual Report of the Board of Governors 1931*, pp. 4-5.

business management, particularly by distorting appearances which may lead to poor management decisions. Examples of management challenges in a deflationary environment include interpreting falling revenues and taking appropriate steps, such as reducing production, laying off workers and delaying or canceling fixed investments. Misappraisals of asset values might lead to poorly timed or unwisely priced asset sales. Cash management decisions become critical. Deflation leads to an erosion of confidence in the economy's future, which leads to persistent economic downturn and downward spirals of business activity.

As to governmental functions, deflation causes tax revenues to fall as incomes and business profits decline, especially where tax rates are progressive, thereby weakening the ability of governments to provide essential services and stimulate economic recovery. Finally, deflation in one country can have adverse international impacts, especially where "beggar thy neighbor" policies are pursued, thereby fostering global economic adversity.

This book tells the story of deflation's costly effects that have left multi-generational scars and traumas. We, the authors, as children of parents for whom the Great Depression altered life views, bear witness and offer, through these volumes, the clarity understanding provides, and we end this book proposing a possible way out should the need arise in the future, the topic of our third volume in *The Great Deleverage Series.*

CHAPTER 1

Irving Fisher's Debt Factor Approach

In our Transitional Introduction, we presented our "Cast of Characters," a breakdown of Americans as to the pivotal roles they played in response to the times. We first described the various cast members in *How the Crash Caused the Great Depression* (see Chapter 12) in context of 1929's momentous final quarter. In the chapters ahead, as we embark on the economic events of 1930 and beyond, we will put special focus on particular cast members: Successful Speculators (post-Crash), Insider Speculator Instigators, Repentant Ex-Speculators (post-Crash), Debtors (in general)and Corporate Financial Executives. The collective shock of the Crash, regardless of an individual's direct participation in stock market speculation, reverberated from business to customer, neighbor to neighbor, in urban and rural settings alike. Each person, with newly widened eyes and some level of fear about what lay ahead, came to a decision as to how to modify his or her behavior. Finances likely became the first concern, and focus on indebtedness went from blurry to 20-20 sharp overnight. Repaying debt as quickly as possible became the top monetary priority.

One economist of the time, Yale's Irving Fisher, stands out in the development of an explanation and theory about the influence of debt, specifically what he called over-indebtedness. Economics professor, inventor and widely quoted pundit, Fisher had gained considerable respect early in the 20th century. Fisher's world turned upside down in 1929 when he fell from his pedestal of high professional regard and financial comfort and landed onto a hard new reality. As we introduced in *How the Crash Caused* (Chapter 11), Fisher suffered ruinous speculative losses on top of the ignominy of ill-timed public comments that badly missed the Crash. But, true to his character and resilience, he turned his personal reversal of fortune to scholarship—pondering deeply just what was causing his and the country's ongoing nationwide suffering.

Fisher's explorations resulted in two seminal publications that focused on the role indebtedness plays during depressions. First in his book, *Booms and Depressions: Some First Principles* (1932) and then in his paper, "The Debt-Deflation Theory of Great Depressions" (1933), both published by the Econometric Society, Fisher articulated his groundbreaking account and theory about causes of economic cycles that we have chosen to call the "Debt Factor Approach." According to Fisher, the debt factor is the condition of over-indebtedness in businesses and for individuals that can initiate a complex cycle of economic swings. As we have found key statistics to enable examination of those swings in 1929-33, we endeavor in this chapter to give due credit to Fisher and to explore the Debt Factor Approach, while also providing an historical account of those eventful years. We posit that his ideas could have moved out of the realm of the theoretical and into the practical as Fisher desired, had he made use of these statistics, some of which were, in fact, available at the time. These data would have confirmed his theory, as they do today, thereby providing an accurate description of what was actually happening at the very time he was writing.

Professor Schumpeter's Memorial to Irving Fisher

Shortly after Irving Fisher's death in 1947, a laudatory paper appeared in *Econometrica* written by political economist and Harvard professor Joseph Schumpeter entitled "Irving Fisher's Econometrics." The paper began:

> The great American who has departed from us was much more than an economist.... For whatever else Fisher may have been—social philosopher, economic engineer, passionate crusader in many causes that he believed to be essential to the welfare of humanity, teacher, inventor, businessman—I venture to predict that his name will stand in history principally as the name of this country's greatest scientific economist.[1]

In his tribute, Schumpeter chose to focus on Fisher as a theorist, but as Schumpeter described it, Fisher's goal was also practical—to develop "a theory that would be statistically operative." Schumpeter explained:

> It is the theorist only, not the statistician, who will be considered in what is to follow. Nevertheless, the statistician cannot be entirely eliminated even from the section of Fisher's activities with which I propose to deal. For throughout and from the start, Fisher aimed at a *theory that would be statistically operative,* in other words, at not merely quantitative but also numerical results.[2] (emphasis ours)

In 1930, when already in his sixties, Fisher wrote *The Theory of Interest,* about which Schumpeter commented, "[T]he book is a wonderful performance, the peak achievement, so far as perfection within its own frame is concerned, of the literature of interest."[3] In a burst of creative contemplation indicating he was certainly not past his prime, Fisher segued from that respected effort to *Booms*

1 Joseph A. Schumpeter, "Irving Fisher's Econometrics," *Econometrica*, Vol. 16, No. 3 (July, 1948), p. 219.

2 Ibid.

3 Ibid., p. 225.

and Depressions in 1932 and then to his follow-up paper in 1933, "The Debt-Deflation Theory of Great Depressions." But unlike *The Theory of Interest,* neither subsequent work presented a theory that Fisher knew to be "statistically operative," to use Schumpeter's words, because Fisher apparently couldn't find statistics that would prove his case to his satisfaction. Our intention has been to delve into that missing statistical evidence.

The Question of Dates of Maturity

Early in *Booms and Depressions* Fisher laid out the essentials of his concept that over-indebtedness is "largely a question of dates of maturity." Reflecting his financial management acumen and careful thinking, he wrote:

> Chance is inseparable from life. Every transaction is a taking of chances, and over-indebtedness is whatever degree of indebtedness multiplies *unduly* the chances of becoming insolvent. Everyone who is not a gambler provides himself with a margin of safety. He puts a buffer between his debts and the collector. This buffer is the difference between assets and liabilities. Corporations call it "capital and surplus." But the sufficiency of the buffer is not solely a matter of quantity. It must be varied according to the quality of the liabilities. Slow assets and quick liabilities (such as call loans) require a larger buffer than quick assets and slow liabilities. The quickest asset, and therefore the safest when pressure comes, is cash. The quickest liability, and therefore the most unsafe in times of pressure, is the call-loan. Over-indebtedness is largely a question of dates of maturity. The entire set-up of assets and liabilities, therefore, has to be considered—and not only the ratio between the two sides of the capital account, and between current assets and current liabilities, but the ratio between the two sides of the income account; the ratio

> between the income and assets, between the income and the debts, between the income and the balancing item of capital and surplus. A balance sheet is the result of anxious efforts to weigh correctly these and many other considerations.[4]

Fisher emphasized the word *unduly* to stress the reality that there is a limit to the amount of debt that any individual or enterprise can handle, specifically: "Over-indebtedness is whatever degree of indebtedness multiplies *unduly* the chances of becoming insolvent." Further, he identified the most important characteristic of indebtedness, maturity dates. He drew on his years of experience as an entrepreneur—unusual for an economist—to focus on the particular type of statistics that he felt would be important in order to estimate over-indebtedness and to determine when over-indebtedness has been reached. He knew balance sheets contained such statistics.

In the "The Debt-Deflation Theory," Fisher, recognizing the inadequacy of his proof, did something else unusual—he set forth his "creed" and then, like the good scientist Schumpeter pronounced him to be, Fisher clearly set forth his challenge to readers to improve on his ideas:

> I am offering this paper as embodying, in brief, my present "creed" on the whole subject of so-called "cycle theory." My "creed" consists of 49 "articles" some of which are old and some new. I say "creed" because, for brevity, it is purposely expressed dogmatically and without proof. It is not a creed in the sense that my faith in it does not rest on evidence and that I am not ready to modify it on presentation of new evidence. On the contrary, it is quite tentative. It may serve as a challenge to others and as the raw material to help them work out a better product.[5]

4 Irving Fisher, *Booms and Depressions: Some First Principles*, Adelphi Company, (1932), p. 9.

5 Irving Fisher, "The Debt Deflation Theory of Great Depressions," Econometric Society, *Econometrica*, 1933, p. 337.

Here we are, some nine decades later, taking up that challenge and attempting to contribute to making Fisher's product better.[6] In exploring the IRS statistics on aggregate U.S. corporate balance sheets for the years 1929-33, we may have had an advantage in responding to Fisher in that ours is a work of history examining a particular period of time and not claiming to offer economic theory. While we are examining conditions of long-ago, Fisher began his discussion in *Booms and Depressions* acknowledging that he was writing "at the crest of the wave, with a state of over-indebtedness presupposed."[7] Living in the midst of such a difficult economic crisis he took great pains to distinguish an historical cycle from a theoretical cycle:

> The main point, however, is to acknowledge the distinction between cycle as a fact and cycle as a tendency. It is one thing to say that, under certain simplified conditions, business *would* oscillate according to a certain repeating curve. It is quite another thing to say that business *did* actually oscillate on that curve in the years 1929-32, or any other historical case...[8] For these reasons, I deprecate the use of the term "cycle" as applied to any actual historical event. I would reserve the cycle concept for a tendency, or

6 As we describe in *How the Crash Caused* (Chapter 6), the first step towards our taking up the challenge came about with our discovery of the in-plain-sight IRS archive—especially the IRS statistics on aggregate U.S. corporate balance sheets for the years 1929-33—which gave us a view of the Crash and post-Crash period as if from 50,000 feet. This annual data provided a statistical means of accepting Professor Fisher's invitation, enabled us to follow Fisher's trail and especially to focus attention on what we, and all those in finance know, are, by definition, the "quickest" debt obligations on balance sheets—notes and accounts payable due year-by-year.

7 Fisher (1932), p. 44.

8 Our statistics show 1929-33 as spiraling downwards rather than oscillating on a curve.

at utmost a specified number of tendencies.[9]

In his tribute to Fisher, Schumpeter posited that over-indebtedness in *Booms and Depressions* was a theory in which "everything is being reduced to a mechanically controllable surface phenomenon with the result that Fisher actually deprecated the use of the term 'cycle' as applied to any actual historical event."[10] In our view, what Schumpeter described as "a mechanically controllable surface phenomenon" was not intended as a theory, but rather was Fisher's account of what he was convinced actually happened since 1929. Fisher's view was historical, not theoretical, but he simply lacked the statistics to prove it. Schumpeter obviously gave Fisher credit for his perspective from within the very depression that was raging around him, even while finding it "imperfectly sketched" theoretically:

> [W]e find in Part III of *Booms and Depressions* (entitled Factual) a simple and popularly worded survey of means of monetary control in which hardly any economist will find much matter for disagreement and which includes practically all the policies of "reflation" that were either adopted or proposed in the subsequent years. I do not want to belittle the merit or to question the wisdom of almost everything Fisher wrote there. On the contrary, considering the date of publication, I believe him to be entitled to much more credit than he received. But I do wish to emphasize that this was not the only merit of the book and that, though but imperfectly sketched, something much larger and deeper looms behind the façade.[11]

---

9 Fisher (1932), p. 58.

10 Schumpeter (1948), p. 230.

11 Ibid.

Whether as history or imperfectly sketched theory, Fisher's ideas about over-indebtedness, especially from today's perspective, clearly merit further discussion.

Fisher's Overall Scheme and First Main Factor—Over-Indebtedness

Fisher, whose work on the quantity theory of money established the school of macroeconomic thought known as monetarism, nonetheless undertook an income/expenditure or demand-side approach in his post-Crash and early Great Depression works, specifically in his focus on the debt factor as a general cycling process of over-indebtedness leading to under-indebtedness returning to over-indebtedness.

In this chapter, we have intentionally chosen to make extensive use of Fisher's own words. The experience of reading Fisher's works convinced us that his explanations could not be clearer or more meticulous, yet we also found in Fisher's tone a distinct hint of empathy for the times that befitted his own newly constrained circumstances and those of many around him. Fisher organized his ideas in a straightforward, somewhat unusual outline format that draws attention to the succinct presentation of his main points. Not wanting to risk losing Fisher's admirable verbal precision and singular use of language, we have offered a selection of quotes from *Booms and Depressions* and his follow-up journal article, "The Debt-Deflation Theory," interspersed with our own observations. We point out that Fisher made use of italics for emphasis, as do we. While our italics are noted at the end of quotes, all other italicized words and phrases were in Fisher's original work.

Economic Downswing into Depression Conditions

We begin with Fisher's 1932 *Booms and Depressions* by focusing on the downswing into depression—pertinent, of course, because that was the country's economic condition when he wrote the book. To take this historical depression downswing through its full process, Fisher delineated nine main cycling tendencies which, as he described movingly, "carry in their vitals much of the tragedy of economic life."[12] Fisher began:

> The nine are listed here, and each will be discussed on its downswing to depression, for the first task is to see how the debt-structure, once erected, may topple into the trough of depression and take us with it.
>
> Following are the nine oscillating factors to which reference has just been made:
>
> 1. The Debt Factor [initially called, in the downswing, "over-indebtedness"]
> 2. The Currency-Volume Factor
> 3. The Price-Level Factor
> 4. The Net-Worth Factor
> 5. The Profit Factor
> 6. The Production Factor
> 7. The Psychological Factor
> 8. The Currency-Turnover Factor
> 9. Rates of Interest[13]

We now cover Debts, Currency-Volume, and Price-Level—the first three of Fisher's factors—which are closely linked together by what he called "distress selling." We regard Fisher's description of

12 Fisher (1932), p. 12.

13 Ibid., pp. 12-13.

distress selling as seminal to understanding how an economy moves downwards towards and then into economic depression:

> When over-indebtedness, whether by sheer bulk or by rashness as to maturity dates, is discovered and attempts are made to correct it, distress selling is likely to arise. That is, in order to protect the creditors, some of the possessions of the debtor may have to be sold—his stocks, his bonds, his farmlands, or whatever his available assets may be. The debtor may choose, on his own responsibility, to facilitate *liquidation* by selling some of his property, even though he never pledged any of it for the debt; or his bank or his broker may cash in on the debtor's collateral; or the mortgagee may foreclose the mortgage; or the debtor may go into bankruptcy, and the trustee in bankruptcy may then auction off his assets. In short, the debtor becomes the victim of *distress selling* either on his own initiative or on the initiative of his creditors.[14] (emphasis ours)

In the above quote, we italicized both *liquidation*—the liquidation of debts when over-indebtedness occurs—and *distress selling* to emphasize, as did Fisher, that both are inherent results of the first factor, the Debt Factor, on the depression/downswing side.

Next, Fisher described more fully the effect of distress selling on a community, particularly on how, as he forcefully described, "Distress selling perverts the operation of the law of supply and demand."[15] Fisher said:

> Normally, sales are made because supply-and-demand has worked out a price attractive to the seller; but when the seller is in distress, the sale is made for precisely the opposite reason; not the attraction of a high price, but the compulsion

14 Ibid., pp. 13-14.

15 Ibid., p. 14.

of the low price, which threatens his solvency. The danger or the fact of insolvency is the all-important consideration in distress selling.... When a whole community is involved in distress selling, the effect is to lower the general price level.[16]

In Fisher's summary of the key aspects of the first and initiating factor of over-indebtedness, he stressed liquidation of debts as a key result or outcome of that initial debt factor:

We have now mentioned, on their *depression* side, the cycle tendencies of the [first] three of our [nine main] factors.

1. Debts (their *liquidation)*

2. Volume of Currency (its contraction)

3. The Dollar (its swelling...)[17] (emphasis ours)

Fisher's Second Main Factor—Volume of Currency

Fisher next addressed his Second Main Factor, the Volume of Currency:

This excessive eagerness on the selling side of a market may seem enough to explain how distress selling tends to lower the price level, but it is not the fundamental influence. In fact, the buyer largely gains the spending power which the seller loses, and spending power is what sustains prices. But the *stampede liquidation* involved in distress selling has a radical effect on the price level, by actually shrinking the volume of the currency—that is, of "deposit currency."[18]

16 Ibid.

17 Ibid., p. 26.

18 Ibid., p. 14.

Here we see that Fisher's own characterization and emphasis on stampede liquidation was an important aspect of distress selling *en masse*. Fisher continued to describe the process entailed in mass selling to achieve debt liquidation and how it reduces the money supply:

> Deposits are the balances on the stubs of check books—the "money" which people have in banks and which they transfer by check. A typical depositor deposits neither gold nor silver nor any other money but merely his promissory note. What he thus accomplishes is to trade his debt to the bank for a debt from the bank to himself; the object being that he may get something which will circulate. His own note will not circulate, but the bank's deposit-liability to him will. Against this, he can draw checks which, in his own business circle, will be accepted almost as freely is legal-tender money. In short, he converts his own non-circulating credit into the bank's circulating credit. New "money" is thereby created, not by the mint nor the Bureau of Engraving, but merely by the pen and ink of the banker and his customer. But when the customer *pays* his note, he undoes the whole transaction; that is, he wipes out an equal amount of circulating credit. In this respect, the payment of a business debt owing to a commercial bank involves consequences different from those involved in the payment of a debt owing from one individual to another. *A man-to-man debt may be paid without affecting the volume of outstanding currency; for whatever currency is paid by one, whether it be legal tender or deposit currency transferred by check, is received by the other, and is still outstanding.* [emphasis ours] But when a debt to a commercial bank it is paid by check *out of a deposit balance*,[emphasis Fisher's] that amount of deposit currency simply disappears.[19]

19 Ibid.

Fisher's description benefits from explication. First of all, Fisher referred only to demand deposits in commercial banks. He excluded time deposits since depositors didn't write checks against time deposits, and thus those deposits didn't create new money (via the bank multiplier effect). Banks routinely required borrowers—either corporate or sole proprietors, for example—to maintain a certain percentage of any borrowings as compensating balances. To break down such a borrowing and how it adds to the money supply: when a corporate customer borrows against, say, a line of credit, its bank credits the borrowing to the customer's demand deposit account. While the customer may have spending needs for some of the funds, the compensating balance portion is not available to the bank for re-lending because it is already lent to the bank borrower into whose account it is credited, where it sits idle. In contrast, we emphasized Fisher's passage regarding the payment of "man-to-man debt" in order to show that, while "man-to-man" transactions might involve debt payments, no credit currency is expanded or contracted as a result. In this type of transaction, banks are neither making loans—the mechanism by which the money supply grows—nor receiving repayments—the mechanism by which the money supply contracts. If both borrower and lender are customers of that bank, the bank is simply debiting one account and crediting another. If two banks are involved, one bank is receiving a new deposit, and the other is debiting a deposit.

We focus in on a pivotal day for banks, October 24, 1929—Black Thursday—and what happened in brokerage firms that impacted banks. As stock prices declined, brokers issued margin calls to margin account customers requiring them to come up with more cash to maintain their margin requirements. In response to those margin calls, many margin account customers came up with the cash. For those customers who couldn't come up with more cash to maintain margins, brokers liquidated margined shares. Given the reduction in margin account holdings because of the lower market close, most brokerage firms required fewer call market loans by the end of Black Thursday. This led most brokerage firms to call or repay—liquidate—some portion of their outstanding call market loans on October 25. Not surprisingly this also came at a time when the historical data show that a large number of call market lenders instructed their New York agent banks to call their call market loans, thus exiting the market. These various transfers of cash from brokers and, ultimately, to banks occurred quickly considering the technology of the time. The pace of transactions being uncertain and undocumented, however, we don't know what quantity of funds called by call market lenders in the week ending October 30 actually reached banks before October 31, the end of the month when data were reported. But what is important from the banks' viewpoint is that bank loans were repaid. From our viewpoint what is important is that these steps contract the money supply.

We will revisit this analysis shortly, but we consider Fisher's explanation of what happens to the money supply or "credit currency" when bank loans are repaid useful for further understanding of the implications:

> Thus to pay a debt at the bank tends to contract the circulating medium. But this tendency is, in normal times, neutralized by a counter-tendency. For generally, as fast as some bank debtors pay off their debts, the extinguished currency is replaced by new depositors who obtain new credits. When, however, by reason of a general state of over-indebtedness, there is a stampede of liquidation, then the new borrowings will by no means suffice to restore the balance, and there must follow a net shrinkage of deposits, or "credit currency."[20]

As we described in *How the Crash Caused* (Chapter 10), the stock market's implosion led immediately to what the Fed described as a "drastic liquidation of security loans," and what Fisher vividly

20 Ibid., p. 15.

described as "stampede liquidation." Fisher elaborated further on the cascading effects of the huge volume of transactions that took place:

> Credit currency is recorded in the statistics of the Controller's Office, under the heading, "Individual deposits subject to check without notice." Its shrinkage is of vast importance; for, in the United States at least, credit currency is the most important kind of Twentieth Century currency. It transacts nine-tenths of the country's business, and, when it is deflated, the general price level tends to fall because, with less funds, less buying can be accomplished.[21]

Fisher's Third Main Factor—The Price Level and Signs of Deflation Ahead

We now approach Fisher's view of what causes the crucial phenomenon of deflation, which is an important theme of this second volume and one we'll cover again in detail in the next chapter. A textbook example of Fisher's Third Main Factor was the distress selling on Black Thursday when a lowering of the general price level—that is, deflation— took place. To convey the climate induced by distress selling on Wall Street on that infamous day, we leave Professor Fisher briefly to offer John Kenneth Galbraith's words regarding the morning of Black Thursday:

> The panic...was a phenomenon of the morning hours. The market opening itself was unspectacular, and for a while prices were firm. Volume, however, was very large, and soon prices began to sag. Once again the ticker dropped behind. Prices fell farther and faster, and the ticker lagged more and more. By eleven o'clock the market had degenerated into a wild, mad scramble to sell. In the crowded boardrooms

21 Ibid., p. 16.

> across the country the ticker told of a frightful collapse. But the selected quotations coming in over the bond ticker also showed that current prices were far below the ancient history of the tape. The uncertainty led more and more people to try to sell. *Others, no longer able to respond to margin calls, were sold out.* By eleven-thirty the market had surrendered to blind, relentless fear. This, indeed, was panic.[22] (emphasis ours)

This quote described a deflationary process clearly—distress selling *en masse*. Certainly stock prices were falling, and forced selling followed in its wake, which led us to ask if, after years of relatively stable prices on all goods and services, deflation didn't begin on that fateful day, October 24, 1929, or perhaps even earlier.

Black Thursday, in Fisher's view, demonstrated not only distress selling *en masse* but also "*stampede liquidation,*" conditions that spoke loudly of deflationary forces underway. Those who were actively selling shares that morning included investors (who sold large blocks of stock), speculators (who individually tended to sell smaller, short-term, speculative positions) and, of particular significance to a deflationary process, brokers. This third group had at first received cash from margin customers, who were desperately trying to maintain their portfolios by meeting margin calls amidst falling stock prices and the declining value of their margin accounts. Soon, however, many brokers had to sell out some or all of the positions that had only that morning been owned by customers who became, over the course of the day, unable to meet margin calls.

By the end of Black Thursday, another sign of deflation became clear. This took place in the call money market. Brokers' exhausted accountants, after assessing the day's carnage, likely determined that the quantity of the brokers' loans they offered to their margin customers had, in aggregate, also declined. This meant brokers could repay an analogous portion of their call market loans on those no-longer-needed loan funds, thus reducing the interest they were

22 Galbraith (1954), p. 99.

paying on those loans, another deflationary sign. We will return to this analysis shortly, but first we continue with Fisher's main factors.

From Fisher's concluding statement that "[w]ith less funds less buying can be accomplished," we discuss his Third Main Factor, the Price Level and of the deflationary effects of a general debt liquidation:

> Thus, the volume of the most important circulating medium is tied to the volume of debts, *especially debts at banks*, one of the most important kinds; so that a sudden disturbance of this debt-volume is passed on to the currency-volume and consequently passed on to the general price level; for, as all authorities agree, an increase in the volume of currency tends, in some degree at least, to raise the price level and a decrease, to lower it. What we now have to consider is the way in which a changed price level *changes the burdensomeness of all outstanding debts* — in a word, changes *real* debts as distinguished from nominal or money debts.[23]

In this passage, Professor Fisher launched a teaching session to help people wrap their minds around the idea that already burdensome debts become even more burdensome as the repayment of those debts causes more deflation to occur, which elevates the debt burden further, sometimes much further, an idea we explore in the pages ahead.

By 1932, when *Booms and Depressions* was published, Fisher had become perhaps the foremost American expert on deflation and inflation. He explored both extensively in his earlier books: *The Purchasing Power of Money* (1911); *Stabilizing the Dollar* (1920); and *The Money Illusion* (1928), to name just three. Much, of course, had transpired both personally for Fisher and societally even since 1928, but he brought this expertise—and his own difficulties and

---

23 Fisher (1932), p. 17. Emphasis ours, except for "*real,*" which Fisher emphasized.

observations—to bear in grappling with the concepts of debt and what he called "real debt."

In order to consider the influence of Americans' accumulated levels of debt and their ensuing repayment beginning at the onset of the Depression, we offer these highly readable and relevant quotes from *Booms and Depressions* written in the midst of the Depression era:

> There are few people today who do not grasp the difference between nominal or money wages, on the one hand, and "real" wages, on the other. Let money and wages remain unchanged, and we all acknowledge that, if the cost-of-living rises, real wages fall; or, if the cost-of-living falls, real wages rise. We know that money wages may rise and yet real wages fall, as in the case of Germany's postwar inflation. For real wages are the budget of goods—the composite of commodities — the "living" — which the money wages will buy. Only by translating money wages into real wages can we express the true economic state of the nation.
>
> This same principle applies to debts. Though a debt be paid with the same number of the money dollars, yet *these dollars, when prices are falling, will cost the debtor more goods.* To earn them, he must sell more goods. In other words, when the price level falls, each dollar, to all intents and purposes, is a bigger dollar. (emphasis ours)
>
> For instance, suppose a farmer contracts a debt when wheat is $1.00 a bushel, and pays it when wheat is 50 cents a bushel. Obviously, to him the dollar has doubled in terms of wheat; he must use twice as much wheat to pay each dollar of his debt. That is, when the price of wheat is halved, the farmer's *real* debt is doubled. Likewise, if the general price

> level is halved, the *real* debt of the average man is doubled.
>
> And this is but half of the debtor's predicament; for first, he gets fewer of these bigger dollars for his goods (while owing the same number of them on his debts); and second, his security is worth fewer of these bigger dollars in the market, and therefore worth less in the eyes of his creditor. The creditor is unaware of receiving more than he is properly entitled to, and the debtor is unaware of paying more than he properly owes. One gains and the other suffers—but both suffer from what it is about to be discussed as the Money Illusion.[24]

While Chapter 2 delves deeply into deflation and its effects on people, we make the general point here that, as deflation continued, those with accumulated debt, whether individual wage earners or business owners needing to sell goods or services, felt the growing burden of those debts as they dealt with factors that negatively impacted their incomes.

Fisher proceeded with a worthwhile examination of what money actually is, especially the concept of "real" money and the impact of inflation and deflation on the value of money, by examining this phenomenon that he called "The Money Illusion."

> Few people look at money for their explanations, because most people simply look *through* money, think in terms of money, take money for granted, assume that a dollar is always a dollar. Since we measure everything else in dollars, it does not readily occur to us to measure the dollar itself. Few people realize, for instance, that the depression dollar of 1932, as compared with the pre-depression dollar of 1929, became really a dollar and two thirds; and still fewer realize the tremendous significance of this fact. Yet its significance

24 Ibid., pp. 17-18.

> is all the greater just because it is not clearly realized.
>
> The real meaning of the unit of money is the goods which that unit will buy. Instead of measuring goods by dollars, the economist is accustomed to measure dollars by goods—not by any one article of goods such as bread, but by the general budget of goods such as food-stuffs, clothing and cloth, furniture and houses, building materials, services, amusements and so on. When the price of bread alone changes, this is presumably due to some change in the quantity or quality of wheat, and not to any change in the dollar. But when a thousand other prices change at the same time, and all change in the same direction, or all change *on the average* in the same direction, we are, in general, justified in saying that the dollar has changed in the *opposite* direction.
>
> Nevertheless, the Money Illusion goes on telling us that the dollar stands still while other things move. This Money Illusion is analogous to the illusion of a passenger on a train who seems to see the landscape rushing past him. It is analogous to the illusion of sun-rise and sun-set, which makes the earth appear fixed with the sun swinging 'round it once a day. So when prices change, we forget the money on which we ride and ascribe the change to something outside—the goods, the merchant, the consumer, the producer, the fertility of the earth—anything at all except the money in terms of which we think. [25]

After World War I, a hyperinflation occurred in Germany as the German government paid off its war debts by printing marks in very rapidly rising denominations. Fisher studied this situation closely:

> German money, after the [First] World War, furnished a good example. We in America, measuring everything in

25 Ibid., p. 18-20.

dollars, said that the mark had fallen. But the Germans, measuring everything in marks, said the dollar had risen. In 1922, I visited Germany and took particular pains to learn from many representative citizens how they accounted for the skyrocketing of German prices. Practically all ascribed it to some misbehavior on the part of commodities, or to the after-effects of the war, or to the Allied blockade, or to the wastefulness of the new German government, or to almost any cause but the important one; which was, of course, that the German government was paying its debts and other expenses with new paper money manufactured for the purpose.

Yet Germans are no more prone to the money illusion than others. Over a generation ago, when England was on the gold standard and India was on the silver standard, General Keating, in conversation with an Indian merchant, mentioned the then recent fall in the value of the silver rupee. The Indian merchant was non-plussed. He said that he had never heard of any fall of the rupee, although he had agents all over India. After a pause, he added, "But my agents have mentioned the rise of the pound sterling. Perhaps that is what you are thinking of."

Sometimes both observers (even if one be an American) are equally deluded. Before the [First] World War, an American woman owed money on a mortgage in Germany. After the war, she went to the German bank and offered the amount which she conceived to be due--$7,000. "But," said the banker, "The debt is in marks, not dollars—it is 28,000 marks; and today that comes to about $250."

"Oh!" she said, "I am not going to take advantage of the fall of the mark. I will pay the full $7,000." The banker,

> thinking in terms of marks, could not see the point. Indeed, the fair-minded American lady only half saw it, and "cheated" her creditor after all; for even American money was worth less than when the debt had been contracted. To pay the full amount in terms not of marks, or dollars, but in terms of the purchasing power which she had borrowed, the lady should have paid not $7,000 but $12,000. Yet, had the German banker known this and suggested it, the lady's indignation at such an "unfair" suggestion would doubtless have exceeded the banker's astonishment at receiving 28 times as much as he thought was due.[26]

Fisher's point was that the "money illusion" deceives people because they "simply look through" the dollar and "assume the dollar is always a dollar."

Index Numbers Tell the Story of Change

We move now in Fisher's account to index numbers, not a widely contemplated concept but an important one when working with statistical changes over time. Index numbers allow us to estimate general levels of prices at any given time, thereby enabling us to assess how prices change from time to time. This, too, was a subject matter in which Fisher had developed extensive expertise. Galbraith, in *The Great Crash 1929*, praised Fisher's contributions to this topic:

> Irving Fisher was one of the most original economists.—[T]here are better things—his contributions to index numbers, technical economic theory, and monetary theory—for which he is remembered.[27]

26 Ibid., pp. 19-20.

27 Galbraith (1954), pp. 70-71.

The following paragraphs offer an abbreviated version of Fisher's anecdotal discussion about index numbers from his trip to Germany after World War I and how they make sense of the "money illusion":

> There is now available a statistical measure which ought to go far toward dispelling the money illusion. This measure is the "index number" of prices. Its function is to measure the *average percentage change* in prices; that is, the change in the *general price level*, or the *general scale of prices*.... What the index number has done... is to show up (to an unfortunately limited number of observers) the difference between a mass movement of the prices and the individual price movements.
>
> Changes in the price level and changes in the dollar are reciprocal. For instance, if a new price level (or scale) is double the old price level (or scale), the new dollar is half the old dollar—or has lost 50 per cent of its purchasing power. This scale-principle was never better illustrated than in German hotels during that period of the greatest post-war inflation. A so-called "multiplicator" was supplied by the hotel; and by means of it, each guest could translate the printed prices on his bill of fare. He found that the price of his dinner listed as, say, "6 marks," and the price of his room as "9 marks"; but, before he paid his bill, these figures had to be multiplied by the "multiplicator." This was a factor, or index, representing the price level, or scale of prices, and varied from day to day, going up as the mark went down. It had nothing to do with the real price of the dinner, either in terms of labor, or relatively to the price of the room. Whether the multiplicator was 100,000 or 1,000,000 made no difference to these relations, but only changed the dinner and room from 600,000 and 900,000 to 6,000,000 and 9,000,000. The multiplicator, or index, saved the trouble of too frequently reprinting the

price lists when the price level was changing so fast.

> The almost universal failure to distinguish between a price and a price *level*, or *scale* of prices, is responsible for untold confusion of mind on the subject of this book.... The concept of a price level, its measurement by an index number, and its reciprocal, the purchasing power of the dollar, are pre-requisites for understanding what happened in 1932.[28]

Thus, index numbers such as the wholesale price index and the consumer price index, enable us to estimate that wholesale prices fell 9.3% from 1929 to 1930 and 30.8% from 1929 to 1933, and consumer prices fell 2.5% from 1929 to 1930 and 24.6% from 1929 to 1933.[29] We then have an elegantly sharp snapshot of how things changed—in this case, declined—during these critical years.

The Dollar Disease in a Time of Deflation

Fisher's account turned next to American's experience in the on-going Depression and his thoughts on what he called "the dollar disease." The following paragraphs cite Fisher in a section he graphically titled, "The vicious spiral downward":

> When a whole community is in a state of over-indebtedness, the dollar reacts in such way that the very act of liquidation may sometimes *enlarge the real debts instead of reducing them!* Nominally, of course, any liquidation must reduce debts, but really (by swelling the worth of every dollar in the country) it may swell the unpaid balance of every debt in the country, because the dollar which has to be paid may increase in size faster than the number of dollars in the debt decreases. And when this process starts, it may go on and on, much

28 Fisher (1932), pp. 22-24.

29 U. S. Commerce Department, U.S. Census Bureau, *Historical Statistics of the United States, 1789-1945,* pp. 233 and 236 respectively.

> after the fashion of a vicious circle. First, mass payment by the weaker debtors swells the whole community's dollar, and so weakens the financial position of stronger debtors; whereupon, many of these rush to liquidate too, thus further swelling the dollar, till it weakens the position of still stronger debtors; whereupon many of these in turn rush to liquidate, thus further swelling the dollar and weakening still other debtors—and so on in a vicious circle; or, rather, in a vicious spiral *downward*—a tail spin—into the trough of depression.[30]

Fisher's use of the expression "tail spin" says it all. A mad rush to liquidate can worsen and, indeed, become a vicious downward spiral with no end in sight.

Fortunately, for those who want to read Fisher's complete account, his works, including *Booms and Depressions* and his paper, "The Debt-Deflation Theory of Great Depressions," are available in their entirety online. Meanwhile, recognizing that this is not our last opportunity to bring Fisher back in whenever we need to, we offer what is, for us, the core of Fisher's thinking. Here is Fisher's own summary of the first three tendencies of what we call the Debt Factor Approach to understanding economic tendencies, along with some important concluding thoughts:

> We have now mentioned, on their depression side, the cycle tendencies of the three of our [nine main] factors.
>
> 1. Debts (their liquidation)
>
> 2. Volume of Currency (its contraction)
>
> 3. The Dollar (its swelling—usually considered in terms of a shrinking scale of prices).

30 Fisher (1932), p. 25.

> Of these three depression tendencies, the second (currency contraction) is important only as a connective process between the other two—which two should be called
>
> *The Debt Disease* (too much debt)
>
> *The Dollar Disease* (a swelling dollar)
>
> (T)he mere fact that the debt disease may lead to the dollar disease does not prove that it must do so. The dollar disease will be unavoidable only "if other things remain equal."
>
> And it should be equally clear that deflation, or dollar bulging, is not an "Act of God" with a special mandate to baffle the human race. We need not wait for a happy accident to neutralize deflation. We ourselves may frustrate it by design. Man has, or should have, control of his own currency....
>
> In a word, if we *must* suffer from the debt disease, why also catch the dollar disease? If we catch cold, why let it lead to pneumonia?[31]

While in Fisher's summary of the first three tendencies, he devoted little attention to the second, calling it simply currency contraction, we should add that Fisher did address remedies in *Booms and Depressions* (Chapter X). Early in this chapter he wrote in a section entitled: "Reflating and Stabilizing the Price Level":

> Suppose that the price scale has recently jumped up or down so as to impoverish lenders to the advantage borrowers, or borrowers to the advantage of lenders. In that case, the price level should be first *corrected* by reflation and thenceforward safeguarded. How much reflation is right?.... The

31 Ibid., pp. 26-28.

> answer is: far enough back to repair, as nearly as possible. the injustice to the creditor or the debtor, as the case may be.[32]

Fisher also included in *Booms and Depressions* two appendixes that addressed reflation and stabilization in detail.[33]

As we know, Friedman and Schwartz focused on what they called monetary contraction at length; however, they shifted responsibility to the Fed without offering solutions that were in the Fed's purview.

How Academic Economists Received *Booms and Depressions*

In his 1993 book *Irving Fisher: A Biography*, professor Robert Loring Allen, himself an academic economist, indicated that response to *Booms and Depressions* was lukewarm at best. For instance, in the December 1932 *Economic Journal*, an unnamed reviewer wrote, "From the pen of Prof. Fisher this book cannot but be something of a disappointment. What little theory it contains is in no way novel."[34] In its March 1933 issue, *The American Economic Review* flatly declared, "In the reviewer's opinion, this book is of little use to the lay reader and of even smaller value to the technical investigator of business cycle phenomena."[35]

Clearly, what these reviewers were anticipating from Fisher was a work of theory in the vein of his earlier publications. Instead, Fisher's book focused on a nuts-and-bolts framework for what he

---

32 Fisher (1932), pp. 121-142 and especially p. 125.

33 Ibid., pp. 212-243.

34 *Economic Journal,* 43 (December 1932), p. 681.

35 *American Economic Review* 23, Issue 1 (March 1933), pp. 127-128. Of course, this comment came at a time when such technical investigators considered business cycles to originate in the business realm and not in terms of, in particular, consumer debt repayment. As we saw above, Schumpeter, who would certainly qualify as such a technical investigator, did view Fisher's book favorably, insisting that "though but imperfectly sketched, something much larger and deeper looms behind the façade."

regarded as the "very practical task" ahead of solving the "greatest of all economic problems" confronting the nation.[36] From our vantage point, we see Fisher as seeking proof of actual events in order to solve problems, not articulating a new theory detached from reality. For him, theory was trying hard to meet the practical.

The situation Fisher found himself in with his reviewers provides an example of that ongoing to-and-fro between theoretical and practical solutions to important economic problems. This tension has long occupied—and divided—the economics profession well before 1929 and up to the present day. In 1976, Peter Temin wrote of how most views about the Depression lacked credible statistical proof—that "[m]ost of the literature on the Depression—is replete with assertions about unobserved and unpredictable magnitudes."[37] A decade earlier, University of Pennsylvania Professor Lawrence Klein offered his feeling (his chosen word) about theoretical versus practical arguments as related to Keynes's *General Theory*, especially the absence of statistics, when he concluded in *The Keynesian Revolution*, "My feeling now is that the General Theory is an intellectual breakthrough, but that it is too simple for judging the real world."[38] Furthermore, MIT Professor Paul Samuelson stated, also in 1966, in a source often referred to as simply *Papers*:

> [T]he first duty of an economist is to describe correctly what is out there: a valid description without a deeper explanation is worth a thousand times more than a clever explanation of nonexistent facts.[39]

It seems clear to us that Fisher was seeking existing facts to provide more than a clever explanation. What is less clear is how

---

36 Fisher (1932), p. viii.

37 Peter Temin, *Did Monetary Forces Cause the Great Depression*, W. W. Norton & Company, 1976, p. 174.

38 Lawrence R. Klein, *The Keynesian Revolution*, The Macmillan Company, 1966, p. 197.

39 Paul Samuelson, *The Collected Scientific Papers of Paul Samuelson,* The MIT Press, 1966, p. 1543.

the IRS corporate balance sheet statistics, available at the time, escaped Fisher's notice. Fisher himself had experience with the IRS as both a personal and corporate tax filer, but, despite his business experience, he evidently didn't regard the IRS as a data-collecting entity or possible data resource. And most trained economists, either contemporaries or later, lacked the perspective of business managers accustomed to working with financial management tools (such as balance sheets, income statements and sources and uses of funds statements). Bringing such tools into the picture might have led Fisher and other economists—as they led us—to the IRS archives within which indeed that deeper explanation lay.[40]

Contrary to his contemporary reviewers, we contend that Fisher, rather than offering a work of theory in *Booms and Depressions*, was trying to initiate a dialogue within his profession about what he called a "very practical task." In his Preface, he elaborated on the urgent invitation he was making to his fellow economists to tackle what had emerged as the "greatest of all practical economic problems":

> In my opinion, no time should...be lost in grappling with the practical measures necessary...to free the world from such needless suffering as it has endured since 1929.
>
> If this very practical task is not soon undertaken in earnest, nor brought to a successful conclusion before another such disaster overwhelms the world, we may expect that a great body of informed public opinion will then hold specific individuals responsible. In short, ignorance cannot much longer serve as an excuse for neglecting this greatest of all practical economic problems.[41]

40 We are, of course well aware of how the Internet has made our kind of research possible as massive databases readily unfold with a few clicks and only a few trips to the esteemed New York Public Library called for.

41 Fisher (1932), p. vii.

We sense the earnestness and gravity in Fisher's words because of what he saw all around him and experienced personally. It is not hard to imagine Fisher's frustration at not being able to provide statistical evidence, especially since by the time either of his works appeared, the country was in its third year of depression with dire conditions nationwide, both monetary and fiscal.

In this book, as we have reiterated, we have undertaken the task of scouring what looks to us like almost entirely unexplored turf—the archives of the Internal Revenue Service—to provide the quintessential "well-documented statistical base" to which Professor Klein referred and which Irving Fisher urged his colleagues— contemporary and future—to find. In the course of doing so, we have also found significant evidence that Fisher was onto explanations of a very practical kind.[42] We have likewise seen that money indeed matters. But in the Great Depression, it did not matter in quite the way Milton Friedman and Anna Schwartz thought.

42 Fisher (1932), pp. 212-13.

CHAPTER 2

Problems Caused by Deflation (Late 1929-1933)

THE LATE 1920s had been a period of remarkably stable prices, but with the Crash, widespread distress selling occurred, and prices and demand in general fell as consumers pivoted from years of rapidly growing borrowing to a years-long process of net debt repayment during which deflation appeared and grew. In this chapter, we cover the unfolding implications of this deleterious process of growing deflation on businesses, individuals and governments, supported, once again, by powerful statistics. In the next chapter we deal with the specifics of liquidity panic and the development of deflation in the last two months of 1929.

An Introduction to the Problems of Deflation

As explained in the prior chapter, the dollar disease brings about contraction of the money supply, which is due to bank loan repayments and the lack of demand for new loans. This contraction process results in the expansion or swelling of the value of the dollar, and those fewer dollars in circulation are each able to purchase more. Stated simply, less money is chasing goods, even as sellers of goods lower prices in order try to attract buyers. The swelling value of the dollar causes the difficult problems of deflation.

It is important, however, to distinguish carefully the unfavorable business and financial problems of 1929-33 from the effects of deflation by itself. The business and financial conditions of 1929-33 *and* deflation were both contractionary, but they were also additive, with deflation compounding the effects of already difficult business conditions. We know that, with the mounting seriousness of the adverse business and financial problems, including the fall in demand for goods and mounting unemployment, the U.S. embarked on a contractionary period beginning in 1929. But contraction gained momentum because three problems manifested. The first problem was that the two processes of weak business conditions and deflation compounded each other. Deflation made the adverse business conditions *look and feel* worse. The second problem was that deflation grew rapidly with no counterbalancing forces in sight. The third problem was simply that, because no one understood the dynamics of what they were looking at or, importantly, the root causes, business managers, individuals, even government leaders reacted to the problems they experienced with actions that actually made the situation worse. In this chapter, we endeavor to discuss the enormous impact of this lack of understanding within business and the various levels of government, as well as its effect on individuals.

The Problem of Deflation "By Itself"

Focusing on the business sector first, professional experience in one particular area of corporate management at a particular point in time enabled us to contemplate the effects of a sustained level of price change. This opportunity presented itself in the "stagflationary" period of the 1970s when many businesses hired cash managers. The specific task for cash managers at that time was to adopt procedures that minimized the amount of cash the company held because, with painful and disturbing levels of inflation, the value of cash was *falling*. Every idle dollar lost value.

In the early 1930s, the opposite condition existed. With deflation, the dollar swelled, and the value of cash *rose*. Thus, for businesses operating in a deflationary period, business bank depositors endeavored to *increase* the quantity of cash deposits they held because their deposits would increase in value over time. In other words, deflation encouraged holding increasing quantities of money—what Irving Fisher called hoarding. But as Fisher recognized, hoarding goes beyond the idea of *hiding* money somewhere, which some individuals did when they feared their bank would fail. Hoarding by businesses occurred in plain sight as money was deposited *and held idle*, for example, in time deposits or savings accounts or to meet the compensating balance requirements of corporate bank loans. (Friedman and Schwartz included the value of such time deposits in their measure of the quantity of the money supply—M-2.) Simply put, a dollar hoarded today would be worth more—and purchase more—tomorrow.

Hoarding, however, whether by businesses or individuals, caused a reduction in an important measure of economic health, the velocity of money. The higher the velocity, or turnover, of money, the more robust the economy. The lower the velocity, the less commerce is underway. Whether money sits idle in accounts, or as we contend, is not used in "commerce" by indebted individuals but instead to repay their indebtedness, velocity slows. For businesses, in a period of liquidity panic such as the aftermath of the Crash, velocity also slowed because the logical thing for a financial manager to do was to slow payments to creditors so as to retain cash for as long as possible. For example, rather than paying within 30 days after receiving invoices, the manager might pay 45 days later. This strategy not only slowed the velocity of money in circulation but also put stress on the supplier, who may have needed the invoice paid in a timely manner in order to meet its own payables obligations. It is important to point out that this particular strategy is only relevant to businesses. Indebted individuals did not have the leeway to extend due dates as they were contractually obligated to make payments by a certain date or risk repossession and loss of all prior payments.[1]

---

1 In Chapter 15, we suggest that broadscale renegotiation of the maturity dates of consumer loans by banks, thus reducing monthly debt obligations, would have helped mitigate deflation if consumers used the freed-up income for consumption, not to repay further debt.

Statistics of Inflation and Deflation

Table 2.1A

Aggregate Price Indexes, 1919-39

Year	Wholesale Price Index (WPI) (1947-49=100)	Consumer Price Index (CPI) (1947-49=100)	Implicit GNP Price Deflator (1929=100)
1919	90.1	74.0	106
1920	100.3	85.7	121
1921	63.4	76.4	103
1922	62.8	71.6	98
1923	65.4	72.9	100
1924	63.8	73.1	99
1925	67.3	75.0	101
1926	65.0	75.6	101
1927	62.0	74.2	99
1928	62.9	73.3	100
1929	61.9	73.3	100
1930	56.1	71.4	96
1931	47.4	65.0	85
1932	42.1	58.4	77
1933	42.8	55.3	75
1934	48.7	57.2	80
1935	52.0	58.7	79
1936	52.5	59.3	82
1937	56.1	61.4	83
1938	51.1	60.3	83
1939	50.1	59.4	82

Source: *Historical Statistics of the United States: Colonial Times to 1957*, Series E25, E113, F5, pp. 117, 125, 139.

Table 2.1A shows familiar price indexes that serve as the basis for determining rates of inflation and deflation. The Wholesale Price

Index (WPI) tracks the prices of goods and services purchased by businesses. The Consumer Price Index (CPI) tracks the prices of goods and services purchased by consumers. The Implicit GNP Price Deflator is the weighted measure of the prices of goods and services purchased each year and measured in the Gross National Product.

Table 2.1B

Change in Price Indexes from Year Earlier

Year	Wholesale Price Index (WPI)	Consumer Price Index (CPI)	Implicit GNP Price Deflator
1929	-1.6%	0.0%	0.0%
1930	-9.4%	-2.6%	-4.0%
1931	-15.5%	-9.0%	-11.5%
1932	-11.2%	-10.2%	-9.4%
1933	1.7%	-5.3%	-2.6%
1934	13.8%	3.4%	6.7%

Source: Authors' calculations.

Table 2.1B reflects the rates at which prices changed year by year in the Table 2.1A indexes and provides the bases for determining the annual rates at which inflation or deflation occurred. In 1929, the WPI fell slightly, reflecting modest deflation that affected business purchases. Meanwhile the CPI and GNP Price Deflator were both unchanged in 1929. By 1933, wholesale prices rose slightly while the CPI and GNP Price Deflator reflected aggressive deflation. In 1930-32 deflation occurred in all three categories, although at lower rates in 1930 than in 1931-32. Only in 1934 did consumer prices rise.

Significant Business Statistics for 1929-33

Table 2.2

Annual Totals of Installment Credit Sought/Granted, Repayments, Net Credit Change, and Total Outstanding for Dealers in New and Used Automobiles[1], 1928-33

($ million)

Full Year	Credit sought/granted	Repay-ments	Net credit change[2]	Total outstanding[3]
1928	1,915.2	1,557.9	357.3	1,078.4
1929	2,382.3	2,143.2	239.1	1,317.5
1930	1,715.6	2,104.8	-389.2	928.3
1931	1,166.7	1,458.3	-291.6	636.7
1932	577.2	892.2	-315.0	321.7
1933	748.6	611.6	137.0	458.7

Same as above for Five Types of Retail Establishments Combined[4], 1929-34

($ million)

Full Year	Credit sought/granted	Repay-ments	Net credit change[2]	Total outstanding[3]
1929	4,001.8	3,669.8	332.0	2,441.8
1930	3,077.9	3,573.5	-495.6	1,946.2
1931	2,234.0	2,681.3	-447.3	1,498.9
1932	1,210.0	1,793.2	-583.2	915.7
1933	1,426.0	1,283.2	142.8	1,058.5
1934	1,761.9	1,592.4	169.5	1,228.0

[1]Passenger cars only.

[2]Minus sign indicates a decrease on net credit; otherwise an increase is to be understood.

[3]End of year.

[4]Includes dealers in new and used (passenger) automobiles, department stores, furniture stores, household appliance stores and jewelry stores.

Source: "The Volume of Consumer Instalment Credit, 1929-1938," NBER, Feb 1940, pp. 2, 8, 9 & 10 of Appendix A.

Table 2.2 reveals the cost to the economy of reductions in sales of certain products financed with installment loans during the Great Depression. New and used automobiles were the most important, and the upper half of Table 2.2 focuses on automobile sales financed with installment loans. The lower half of Table 2.2 focuses on sales financed with installment loans not only at automobile dealers, but also department stores, furniture stores, household appliance stores and jewelry stores.

Two factors impacted, at least in part, installment sales, one of which arose from the new wariness on the part of all consumers post-Crash. Speculators, of course, were no longer thought of themselves as getting rich through speculation, but consumers, in general, whether or not they had speculated, caught the cautionary fever and reduced their demand for consumption, certainly purchases funded by installment loans.[2]

The second dynamic resulted from consumers' tendency to make provisions for their debts due and payable each month, then to decide how they would spend any remaining income. In both groupings, 1929 showed the highest volume of sales in current dollars and 1932 its lowest volume. In the case of automobile dealers, sales dropped -75.8% from $2,382.3 million in 1929 to $577.2 million in 1932. As to the five types of retail establishments (including auto dealers), sales dropped -69.8% from $4,001.8 million in 1929 to $1,210.0 million in 1932.

These two rates of decline in sales were notably larger than the -43.6% overall fall in Gross National Product for 1929-32, as shown in Table TI.1 (page 3). In fact, both rates of decline rivaled the -76.2% rate of fall in fixed investment in the business realm, the oft-stated principal cause of the Great Depression. The -$11,038 million fall in fixed investment by business in those years far overshadowed the -$2,791.8 million fall of installment sales in the five types of retail establishments for the years 1929-32. However, the really significant causative drop in 1929-32 was -$28,660 million in Personal consumption expenditures of which the -$2,791.8 million fall of installment sales at the five establishments was a dynamic part.

---

2 Table 2.2 shows the annual numbers based on the monthly numbers in Tables 12.3 and 12.4 in *How the Crash Caused.* To help us recognize that the credit "granted" by retailers actually measured the credit sought by purchasers, we labeled the headings of the first columns in the upper and lower halves of Table 2.2 "Credit sought/granted."

Deflation Begins to Hurt

When economists focus on inflation and deflation, they generally discuss "real" rates as distinguished from "nominal" or "current rates." Over a period of years such as 1929-32, "real" rates are the prices over those years with the effects of inflation or deflation "abstracted out" through the use of appropriate indexes. Nominal or current rates constitute the prices that were in effect at the time when sales took place.

For example, we can calculate the rate of deflation for the years 1929-32 by selecting an index—for instance, the CPI that relates to a "market basket of consumer goods." Dividing its 1932 value by its 1929 value (58.4 ÷ 73.3 = 0.7967) and subtracting that amount from 1.0 yields a decline over four years of -0.2033—or -20.3 %—the amount of deflation that affected the CPI from 1929-32.

But consumers do not "abstract out" prices. They pay prices, and falling prices affect them.

If we look at the period of 1929-1932 as presented in current dollars in Table TI.1 on page 3, we see that Personal consumption expenditures fell from $77,251 billion in 1929 to $48,591 billion in 1932. Dividing the 1932 value by the 1929 value (48.6/77.3 = 0.6287) and subtracting that amount from 1.0 leads to a nominal decline in Personal consumpton expenditures of -0.37128 or -37.1% over these years. Thus, with the nominal decline of -37.1% and the deflationary decline of -20.3%, we have a "real" decline of -16.8% in a "deflationary spiral" over three years. This level of "real" decline can (and did) result in a very high and worsening level of unemployment. Furthermore, as the time passed, deflation made things *look* worse and worse. But they *were* worse and worse! The downward force of falling nominal and real demand readily caused awful unemployment. But as we will consider in Chapter 8, they also caused all kinds of financial problems, for example, falling financial values—especially of mortages leading to "open", unresolved mortgage issues as foreclosures rose.

Overall, despite lower prices, the problems of deflation far outweigh its benefits to most individuals, businesses and government units, and each is affected differently and at different times. As we consider these differences using data, one impact becomes evident quickly. Prices, generally speaking, collapsed first in broad markets—for example, stock markets and commodities markets—then reached down to local community venues like farmers' markets and garage sales. One clear thing—evident in Table 2.1A (page 52)—is that with passing time, the Wholesale Price Index fell first, then the downturn went on to affect the CPI and the GNP price deflator more slowly.

Table 2.1A also suggests that after the experience of relatively stable prices in the late 1920s, executives and business owners responded by considering various cost-cutting measures as business conditions worsened. One of these necessarily was cutting production. Certainly, the implications of falling production concerned the Hoover administration, especially the impact on workers, and, as described in Chapter 2 of *How the Crash Caused*, Hoover held many meetings at the White House with business leaders to try and persuade them not to cut wages or lay off workers. But the time would come, and soon, that those harmful options had to be on the table for a business to keep its doors open.

Furthermore, declining revenues inevitably led businesses to reduce prices in response to a decline in orders from users of basic commodities. Early on in the post-Crash environment, this downward trend was most obvious at companies whose products were commodities, such as agriculture, mining & quarrying and natural resources (e.g., lumber). However, in practice, before manufacturers took actions such as reducing production, laying off workers and lowering prices, they first needed to examine their inventories and assess retail selling behavior throughout their industries. (As we discussed in Chapter 12 of *How the Crash Caused*, even before the Crash, automobile manufacturers were already cutting production, and after the Crash, radio retailers practically ceased ordering radio sets from manufacturers.) Even though many businesses saw lower costs for raw materials and semi-finished goods as commodity prices fell toward the end of 1929, considering the slowdown in sales, making yet more radios to sit in a warehouse, for instance, was not a sound management decision, no matter how much the manufacturer might save on raw materials. Multiply one business owner's decision times thousands and people started to feel the impact in multiple ways.

What role did peoples' expectations play with regards to deflation? Once people expected deflation to continue, that in and of itself became an important, albeit difficult-to-measure factor that Irving Fisher discussed. The reality as 1929 ended was that those in business needed time to learn (or relearn) the implications of deflation for their business, their industry and society at large. Certainly those who had experienced deflation during the Depression of 1920-1921 took such signs of deflation as the drop in commodities prices as indicators that deflation, with the attendant fall in demand for goods and services, could grow.

Moreover, many argued that earlier investment in property, plant and equipment by manufacturers committed to during high-demand years, such as had occurred in the radio industry, was actually one of the factors leading to the downturn. Indeed, some of that earlier investment came to be regarded as *over*-investment. Under the circumstances that prevailed, business managers certainly understood that they could stop making further fixed investments in property, plant and equipment, but such decisions added to the issue of deflation.

The Economic Impact of This Consumer-Sector Core Depression Dynamic

The growing real cost to the economy of the increasing volume of consumer debt repayment, laudable as debt repayment may have seemed to each debtor, was a core dynamic of the Great Depression. We get clear examples of the economic consequences of this core depression dynamic in the Consumer Installment Sales statistics in Table 2.2. (page 54) It is particularly instructive how these complex economic consequences affected the bellwether automobile industry. As we saw in Table 8.2 in *How the Crash Caused*, car and truck production experienced big swings over the course of 1929, with a significant decline over the last months. Production, having peaked in April at 663,200 vehicles, fell to 512,600 by August, then plunged to 131,900 by year end 1929, reflecting the dramatic shift in sales expectations after the Crash. With these steep production cuts, reduced shifts, layoffs and involuntary unemployment undoubtedly occurred in the automobile industry by the end of 1929 and rose to numbers of some size.

Table 2.2 also reveals that total (credit) outstanding for new and used vehicle dealers annually rose over 18% from the end of December 1928 to the end of December 1929. But it took a closer look at monthly statistics for 1929 for a more telling story (see Table 12.3 in *How the Crash Caused*, and Table 12.4,). For the first eight months of 1929, total (credit) outstanding rose over 26% or $377.8 million from $1,078.4 million at the end of December 1928 to $1,456.2 million at the end of August 1929. Then, for the last four months of 1929, total (credit) outstanding fell -9.5% or $138.7 million to $1,317.5 million. Thus, although monthly data confirm that total (credit) outstanding in 1929 still rose +$239.1 million in full-year 1929 overall, by the fourth quarter, consumer appetite for purchasing new or used vehicles using debt had diminished, and that trend continued, stair-stepping down into 1933 as we discuss below.

For emphasis, we reiterate that these effects reflect their origin in the consumer realm. The statistics certainly show the pivot described in Chapter 12 of *How The Crash Caused* from growing borrowing by consumers throughout most of 1929 to growing repayment of debts, accompanied by falling consumption and rising unemployment.[3] All this is to say that, while the pivot in the final months of 1929 and

3 We should also note that a month-by-month visual comparison of credit granted in the last four months of 1929 with the last four months of 1928 does not reveal demand to have fallen in late 1929 from 12 months earlier (i.e., from 1928), but we consider demand to have fallen from six months earlier (i.e., earlier in 1929).

early 1930 definitely took place, the small downward numbers at the end of August or in September 1929 when the net credit change first went negative were not only harbingers of the Crash, as we described them. These downward credit change numbers were the first signs of that significant pivot in behavior which, as it developed more fully, we have attributed to the shock and magnitude of the Crash.

In 1930, the automobile industry continued to lead the way down as credit repayments exceeded credit granted, again the result of consumers' decisions. The amount of credit granted by automobile dealers to buyers using installment credit was down -28% from 1929 to \$1,715.7 million in 1930. Further, credit repayments to dealers totaled \$2,104.8 million (down 1.8% from 1929), a net credit change of -\$389.1 million in 1930, when total (credit) outstanding fell -29.5% from \$1,317.5 million at year end 1929 to \$928.3 million at year end 1930.

How could repayments in 1930 be down only -1.8% when credit granted was down almost -28%? The answer is that, unlike credit granted, which immediately funded purchases in the month it was granted, repayments were based on sequences of ten or twelve earlier months when credit conditions were more robust. Thus, as economic contraction took place, diminished new credit sought/granted fell short of accumulated repayment obligations due on credit granted and spent in earlier expansionary periods.[4]

In 1931, the amount of credit granted by automobile dealers to buyers was down almost -32.0%, or \$1,166.7 million from 1930. Credit repayments to dealers in 1931 were down -30.7% from 1930, a net credit change in 1929 of -\$291.5 million. Thus total (credit) outstanding fell -31.4% from \$928.3 million at year end 1930 to \$636.7 million at year end 1931.

Then, as table 2.2 (page 53) shows, in 1932, the amount of credit sought by buyers and granted to them by automobile dealers was down -50.5% or \$577.2 million from 1931. Credit repayments to

4 Though diminishing sales hurt, dealers were receiving swelled dollars in repayment.

dealers were down -38.8% from 1931, a net credit change in 1932 of -$315.0 million. Thus total (credit) outstanding fell a further -49.5%, from $636.7 million at the end of 1931 to $321.7 million at the end of 1932. The implications of this downward trajectory in one of the country's key industries were significant.

How Deflation Benefitted One Group of Individuals

In spite of everything we have discussed so far, deflation did offer *some* benefits, principally to the well-to-do who, for instance, owned investments with fixed payment obligations, the value of which rose as the dollar swelled.[5] The most obvious of such investments were bonds with contractually fixed coupon rates. As deflation worsened, the spendable values of those bond coupon payments rose at the rate at which the dollar swelled, thus allowing the recipient to purchase more goods, services and even assets such as real estate at deflated prices. Similarly, owners of real estate with fixed rental obligations—e.g., leases—benefited from deflation. We also add the point that when interest rates in financial markets fell, the saleable values in secondary markets of such properties as bonds could increase in some relation to deflation. In addition, stocks that continued to pay high dividends, also benefitted shareholders.

Indeed, those fortunate individuals who kept and held onto incomes and cash were able to weather deflationary times, some quite comfortably. For much of working America, however, especially those carrying mortgage and installment debt and those unemployed or underemployed already or fearing unemployment, these advantages had either never pertained to them or had come to represent painful reminders of a life they had once aspired to. For them—a far larger group—deflation hurt.

5 The rate at which the dollar swelled was the inverse of the rate of deflation—1/(1-R)—or 1/0.9 if the rate of deflation was 10.0%.

Problems of Deflation for Indebted Working Americans

It is our assessment that working Americans and their families experienced the most burdensome and painful problems of deflation in 1929-33. As we know well by this point, many working Americans were in debt. As an example of deflation's impact, an American working consumer, who had financed purchases in a time of stable prices and wages, had doubtless signed on the dotted line and incurred fixed financial obligations while looking ahead with confidence in the ability to make those payments. When times were good, an aspiring consumer could opt to work extra hours to acquire things and achieve his and his family's desired lifestyle. He might work five extra hours above his normal work week and use the five extra hours of earnings to pay debt obligations—an example in microcosm of Irving Fisher's personal overindebtedness. Deflation frequently threatened that option.

Falling prices were very real and had consequences. Tables 2.1A and B (pages 52 and 53) show that the CPI dropped -2.6% in 1930, -9.0% in 1931, and -10.2% in 1932. Lower prices for eggs, butter, bread, milk, cornflakes, Maxwell House coffee, coal and other household items would have helped if the extra dollars a worker could earn to pay debts had remained stable in this period. Had this been the case, to repay increasingly swelled dollars, the worker would have needed to work 2.7% longer in 1930 than 1929, 9.9% longer in 1931 than 1930, and 11.3% longer in 1932 than in 1931.[6] In other words, because the dollar was swelling, our debtor needed to work a quantity of time in 1932 that was 23.9% greater than he had worked in 1929 just to keep even with his payment obligations.

However, reality for almost all workers was that they were laboring in workplaces that were experiencing falling revenues and reductions in hours worked, certainly alarming to the many who

6 The equation used to determine these figures is: The % worked = 1 / (1 – R) where R equals the annual rate of deflation as a positive number.

faced reduced income and ongoing fixed installment payments. In that case, workers couldn't work those extra five hours they had counted on; they had to scale back both their aspirations and lifestyle via belt-tightening to continue to pay the fixed monthly payments on any existing installment contracts. In this case, the real costs of their debts swelled relative to their ability to earn and became much more onerous.

The implications of becoming unemployed cast an ever-larger shadow. As Table 11.2 (page 316) shows, unemployment as a percentage of the civilian labor force, a normal 3.1% in 1929, rose to 8.8% in 1930, 16.1% in 1931 and climbed rapidly thereafter. By 1931, many of those who had entered into installment loan agreements earlier were either unemployed or working reduced hours, with no opportunity to work additional hours to service their existing debts.

Many of these same people were also mortgagors, adding another significant source of fear, as we shall see ahead. Mortgagors with fixed mortgage payments and a relatively short mortgage term, now found themselves contemplating the very real possibility of foreclosure as their incomes—and the value of their homes—dropped.

Things grew perceptibly worse, and, while few people understood what caused deflation in 1930, 1931 and 1932, nearly everyone recognized how the overall situation negatively impacted them, their families and their neighborhoods. In 1932, the CPI fell -10.2% from 65.0 to 58.4, and unemployment reached 24.0%. For many workers, fixed debt payments took up more and more of their (remaining) income, causing them to eschew entering into additional consumer installment sales contracts. This reluctance changed their expectations regarding achieving some alluring lifestyle target and altered their consumption pattern often for the rest of their lives. Meanwhile, to avoid repossessions and foreclosures, Americans had to keep paying their debt obligations in a fashion that at least tried to approach timeliness. The result for the many indebted individuals was almost certainly painfully reduced spending on consumer goods in general. As real consumption declined—falling quantities of money "chased goods" in the CPI "market basket"—deflation worsened, and the situation nationwide deteriorated.

As the expression goes, hindsight is golden. Americans might have found some consolation—and understanding— had they been able to take in the implications of what statistics now show (see Table 6.3 in *How the Crash Caused*). By the end of 1932 indebted consumers had repaid almost half ($18.4 billion) of the $37.4 billion they owed U.S. corporations (including banks) at the end of 1929.

Problems of Deflation for Federal, State, and Local Governments

Deflation also had a negative impact on state and local governments as tax revenues fell due to reduced earnings by both individual and business taxpayers. Newly enacted sales taxes failed to provide sufficient revenue due to scaled back consumption, and, over time, real estate tax revenues decreased due to lower property valuations. These revenue losses greatly weakened the ability of local governments to provide even essential services. Especially when tax rates were progressive, deflation, by itself, can result in taxpayers falling into lower tax brackets.

In the case of the federal government, deflation created other problems, and these highlighted the limitations on what was viewed as appropriate federal actions at the time. Today, we would expect elected federal government leaders to lead us out of deflationary situations, to understand the causes and effects of deflation and to take appropriate actions to reinflate the economy. Unfortunately, as we have seen, the causes and effects of deflation were easily misunderstood in a period Irving Fisher described as "full of tangles and crosscurrents."

Reconsidering Irving Fisher's Efforts

In our view, it is a considerable misfortune that the efforts of Irving Fisher, who wrote so effectively and eloquently about deflation and the "dollar disease," stopped short of success. It was not for want of trying but, in our opinion, for want of statistical proof. It was also because Fisher bumped up against his profession's bias against argument absent a theory. Unlike Keynes who addressed theory aggressively from the very first paragraph of *General Theory*, Fisher described what he called his "creed." According to Nobel Prize-winning Yale economist James Tobin:

> Fisher did not provide a formal model of his latter-day cycle theory, as he probably would have at a younger age. The point here is that he came to recognize *important...sources of disturbance*. His practical message in the early 1930s was "Reflation!" He was right.[7] (emphasis ours)

7 James Tobin, "Neoclassical Theory in America: J. B. Clark and Fisher," *American Economic Review*, December 1985, p. 36.

CHAPTER 3

Liquidity Panic and the Beginnings of Deflation (Late 1929)

IN THE PRIOR CHAPTER we covered the major implications of the deleterious process of growing deflation for businesses, individuals and governments, supported, once again, by powerful statistics. In this chapter we tell the story of the liquidity panic in the last two months of 1929 and the development of deflation that began in late 1929, immediately following the Crash.

Reconsidering Price Levels

Tables 2.1A and 2.1B (pages 52-53) focused on the development of deflation in 1929-33 by looking at three price indexes over the period of 1919-39 and determining how the three changed from the year earlier in 1929-34. The Wholesale Price Index (WPI), which addresses prices paid by businesses, fell in 1929 nearly 1.6 % from its value in 1928, though in doing so it returned to its 1927 value and was even slightly lower than its values in the mid-1920s. The Consumer Price Index (CPI), which considers prices paid by consumers, was unchanged in 1929 from 1928 and slightly lower than its values in the mid-1920s. The Implicit GNP Price Deflator, which deals with prices reflected in the Gross National Product, was also unchanged in 1929 from 1928 and within one point of its values in the mid-1920s. All three registered single-digit deflation in 1930 and double-digit deflation in 1931 and 1932. In 1933, the WPI was up 1.7% while the other two indexes registered single-digit deflation. All three indexes rose in 1934. As Barrie Wigmore wrote in *The Crash and Its Aftermath* about prices in the period leading up to the end of 1929:

> The overall impact of price trends in the boom years was in neutral. There were a few rising prices, and a slight trend to declining prices, but this trend was not significant enough to affect business and financial decisions. Increased

Chart 3.1

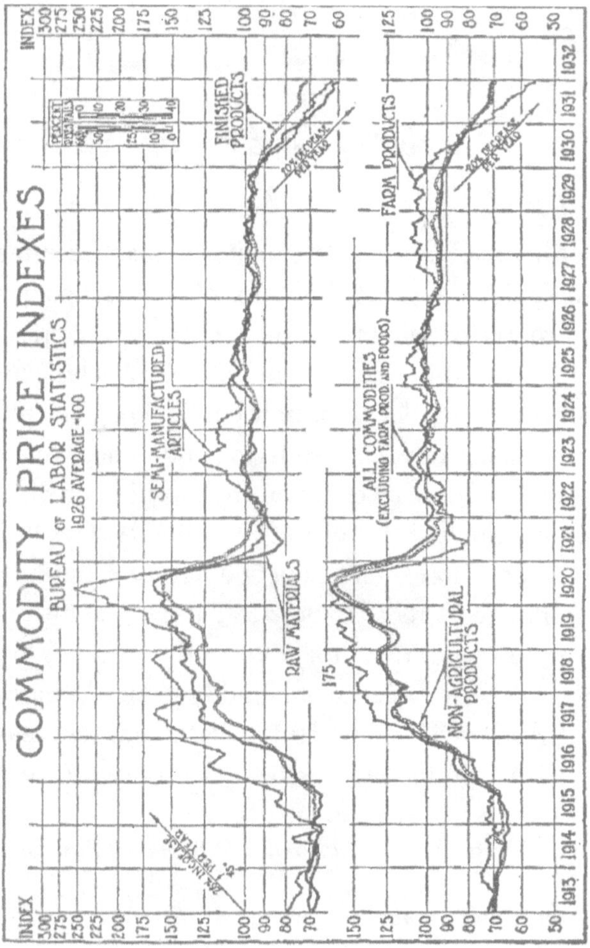

productivity and expanded output and capacity overcame the slight deleterious effects of a declining price level.[1]

Chart 3.1 (previous page) , as it appeared in Irving Fisher's *Booms and Depressions,* shows his view of prices over the longer period of 1913-1931.[2] There were wide swings in prices during World War I and for a brief time in its aftermath. Thereafter in the 1920s, prices were basically stable, trending only slightly downwards, until 1929. Close examination of Fisher's statistics reveals that deflation began in the last quarter of 1929 when prices fell significantly and then fell at an accelerating rate in 1930. However, this statistical evidence on the crucial factor of price levels did not, in and of itself, portend what lay just ahead.

Liquidity Panic in Late 1929

With the Crash, stable conditions changed rapidly with regards to liquidity — a key indicator of how easily an asset can be sold and converted into cash without effecting the price of the asset. The panic affected businesses and individuals who confronted the reality of insolvency due to insufficient liquidity, i.e., too few liquid assets. In Chapter 1, we covered Irving Fisher's account of "stampede liquidation" and saw its effect on the morning of Black Thursday, October 24, the first day of the stock market Crash. In fact, the Crash suddenly inaugurated a period of severe liquidity panic that lasted from late October to year-end 1929. The distress selling of certain security positions to protect other security positions, for example, was clear evidence of liquidity panic. As Barrie Wigmore wrote, market activity spread during Black Thursday, so that "[c]haos reigned in the commodities exchanges as prices broke there, partly

1 Barrie Wigmore, *The Crash and Its Aftermath*, Greenwood Press, 1985, p. 103.

2 Fisher (1932), p. 195.

in sympathy with stock prices and partly because stock speculators sold out commodity positions to protect their capital for stocks."[3] Clearly the week of the Crash produced the deflationary effect of falling prices of both stocks and commodities.

In *The World in Depression 1929-1930,* Professor Charles Kindleberger offered further evidence of a liquidity panic and its broadening impact, especially falling prices:

> Firms that had counted on ready access to the New York stock and bond markets joined in the race for liquidity and cut their spending. Production fell sharply, and inventories were run off. The liquidity panic extended to mortgages.... The price of housing and new building dropped sharply.... The crash led to a scramble for liquidity on the part of both lenders to the call market and owners of stocks. In the process, orders were canceled and loans called. [4]

The fall in the stock market continued until mid-November, and Wigmore wrote of the unavoidable and stark implications to anyone buying stock on margin when prices drop:

> There appears to have been little sympathy or hesitation in selling out undermargined accounts. Friends and old customers suffered along with new customers.... [A]ccounts were sold out ...if no satisfactory response was given.[5]

---

3 Wigmore (1985), p. 10.

4 Charles Kindleberger, *The World in Depression, 1929-1939,* University of California Press, 1986), p. 112, 116.

5 Wigmore (1985), p. 99.

Late 1929: General Deflation Begins

Wigmore's account expanded to include falling wholesale prices throughout the post-Crash economy:

> Prices began to decline in the last quarter of 1929 in many industries where prices had been stable or up because of the boom. Prices of sensitive commodities such as cotton, lead, zinc, wool, oil, and lumber, declined 5%-8% immediately as the active financial markets in most of these commodities were *immediately* affected by the Crash. Price declines in steel scrap and rubber of over 15% during the fourth quarter were more disconcerting and closely related to the rapid decline in automobile production. The wholesale price index dropped from over 96 before the Crash to 93.3 in December. This was the lowest wholesale price level since World War I, and it clearly put business on notice that a more serious than usual business decline was in prospect.[6] (emphasis ours)

Kindleberger's look at commodity prices in *The World in Depression 1929-1930* concurred with Wigmore's assessment as we see in Tables 3.1(opposite) and 3.2. (page 72) Table 3.1 shows Kindleberger's statistics on commodity prices. Table 3.2, based on statistics in Table 3.1, shows the drops—some considerable— in the prices of fourteen market-traded commodities over the four-month period September-December 1929. Of the commodities listed in Table 3.2, wheat dropped 3.6%. Four others (cotton, sugar, copper and lead) dropped between 5% and 10% and seven dropped between 10% and 18.4% (cocoa, coffee, hides, silk, tin, zinc and corn). Rubber dropped a material 25.7%. Each decline had its own significant story to tell about the ramifications in industry of the Crash. Whether it was rubber, tin, copper or hides, the price drops indicated softening

6 Ibid., p. 103. Wigmore cited *Statistical Abstract of the United States,* 1939, p. 321.

Table 3.1

Prices Of Specified Commoditites

(selected months, 1929-30)

	Cocoa	Coffee	Copper	Corn	Cotton	Hides	Lead	Rubber	Silk	Sugar	Tin	Wheat	Wool	Zinc
	¢ per pound	¢ per pound	£ per long ton	¢ per bushel	¢ per pound	¢ per pound	¢ per pound	¢ per pound	¢ per pound	¢ per pound	¢ per pound	¢ per bushel	¢ per pound	¢ per pound
1929														
June	10.5	23.5	74.3		18.0	16.8	6.8	20.6	5.0	3.5	44.3	1.5	—	6.6
September	10.8	22.5	75.3	91.9	17.6	19.6	6.7	20.2	5.2	4.0	45.4	1.4	—	6.8
December	9.1	15.5	68.3	78.0	16.6	16.0	6.1	16.1	4.7	3.7	39.8	1.3	—	5.7
1930														
March	8.7	14.0	69.2	74.5	14.7	14.2	5.6	15.3	4.7	3.4	36.8	1.2	98	4.9
June	8.3	13.4	50.0	79.0	13.2	15.2	5.3	12.4	3.6	3.3	30.3	1.1	92	4.5
September	6.3	12.0	46.3	91.7	10.2	14.6	5.4	8.2	2.9	3.1	29.6	0.9	91	4.3
December	6.2	10.5	46.8	64.9	9.2	10.7	5.0	8.9	2.7	3.3	25.3	0.8	86	4.1
Percent change (%)	-41	-55	-37	-29	-49	-36	-27	-57	-46	-7	-43	-49	-12	-38

Source: Charles Kindleberger, *The World in Depression*. p. 137.

demand for the end products using those commodities, with automobiles and new home construction being standout bellwethers.

Focusing on this uncertain period immediately following the Crash, Kindleberger elaborated on his description as to how effects of an imploding market quickly spread out:

> [T]he economy does not always behave symmetrically, and a difference may be made if the stock market decline takes place in a shorter compass than the rise. There may

Table 3.2			
Changes In U.S. Prices of Selected Commodities (September - December, 1929) (% Percent)			
Imported commodities	(%) change	Exported commodities	(%) change
Cocoa	-15.4	Corn	-14.1
Coffee	-13.1	Cotton	-5.6
Copper	-9.3	Wheat	-3.6
Hides	-18.4		
Lead	-8.8		
Rubber	-25.7		
Silk	-10.0		
Sugar	-6.9		
Tin	-10.1		
Zinc	-16.7		

Source: Charles Kindleberger, *The World in Depression*, p. 137.

well be no aid for business in lower interest rates overtaken by faster and more powerful forces of deflation.

U.S. out-of-town banks and corporations who withdrew call money from the New York market caused large losses to individual investors, who cut their spending ....

The speed of the drop [in economic activity] was impressive. Industrial production fell from 110 in October (on a seasonally adjusted basis) to 105 in November and 100 in December—the fastest drop in the index since 1920.... More impressive than industrial production was the decline in commodity prices and in imports....

[A] crucial part of the rapid decline turned on finance. Most imports at that time were shipped to New York and

> other ports on consignment and sold on arrival in commodities markets. Buyers financed their purchases at banks. However, New York banks, [given] the necessity to take on brokers' loans abandoned precipitously by out-of-town banks and "all others," cut credit lines to commodity buyers.[7]

Kindleberger's observations are potent examples of what Fisher called distress sales, whether of houses, commodities or imports.

The pain of deflation in the housing market in the mid-to-late 2000s lives on in recent memory among many Americans who assumed mortgages on prices inflated by the housing-bubble then watched in anguish as the value of their houses plunged. Buyers became scarce and interest rates on adjustable-rate mortgages rose as the teaser-rate period ran out. About 30% of homeowners were upside down with mortgages exceeding the home value. In the case of mortgaged houses in 1929-30, the path of deflation transmission was clear. Many mortgages at the time were short, five years maximum, with interest-only paid in the early years and the entire principal due at the end of the last year. If the mortgage came due during a deflationary period, and the mortgage holder—say, a commercial bank—demanded repayment because the value of the property had declined or because the borrower's income had declined, the homeowner (instead of Kindleberger's less familiar term house owner) had to pay off the mortgage or secure a new loan elsewhere. If neither was possible, a foreclosure took place. This distress sale (possibly at auction) likely yielded a considerably lower price than the homeowner desired. The proceeds of the sale (presumably conveyed in a check drawn on a deposit account) then paid off the mortgage holder's loan (or, if insufficient, brought on the homeowner's bankruptcy). The outcome of these transactions, aside from the stress experienced by the potentially displaced homeowner and family, was a further contraction in what Fisher called the "Volume of Currency" (or what we call the money supply) due to the bank's decision not to relend to the homeowner, prompting repayment of the loan from a distressed

7 Kindleberger (1986), pp. 112-3.

sale. Chapter 8 discusses mortgages at the time in greater detail.

How does — and did — this deflationary transmission path work in the case of the commodities as prices dropped? Kindleberger wrote:

> Deflation, then, moved from the decline in stock markets to production cuts and inventory runoffs in one sequence, and from stock prices to commodity prices to the reduced value of imports in another. *Both were fast.* The connection between the stock market and commodity markets was partly psychological and undoubtedly at the outset partly through the credit machinery as banks and firms struggled to become liquid.[8] (emphasis ours)

From the Debt Disease to the Dollar Disease

Fisher's 1932 *Booms and Depressions* introduced the three main factors in the deflationary process that we have discussed as well as six additional factors. He summarized all nine main factors with brief, easily understood commentary:

> We have now mentioned, on their depression side, the cycle tendencies...of our [nine main] factors.
>
> 1. Debts (their liquidation)
>
> 2. Volume of Currency (its contraction)
>
> 3. The Dollar (it's swelling — usually considered in terms of a shrinking scale of prices).
>
> 4. Net Worth Reduction (turned sometimes to failure)

8 Ibid., p. 115.

5. Profit Reduction (turned sometimes to losses)

6. Reduced Production (especially of equipment) along with reduced Trade, and reduced Employment.

7. Increased Pessimism and loss of confidence

8. Hoarding and a general slackening in velocity of circulation, both of deposits and of physical money.

9. Lowered Money Interest—but raised real interest. [9]

Fisher proceeded to offer a careful explanation of how the nine factors operate in the real world, and, with his own painful losses much on his mind, he did not shy away from ways the undeniable factor of "mood" impacted how the factors operated. Fisher used words and phrases familiar to behavioral economists now, such as cautious, pessimism, depressing effect, psychological discouragement and disappointment to emphasize the individual suffering inherent in each factor:

> But, while the order of the nine major events as above set forth is a good pedagogical order, it is not a strictly chronological order. Its principal departures from chronology lie in the items of interest and pessimism, both of which, if treated chronologically, should come earlier. Pessimism was purposely delayed in the exposition until all the chief reasons for it had been cataloged. It was then inserted once for all. Perhaps, more than any of the other factors, it really comes in progressively all along the line. The first touch of liquidation has a depressing effect on *moods;* and this first approach of the pessimistic *mood* retards circulation. (emphasis ours)
>
> Even the very start of the liquidation may be the psychological discouragement—either of the debtor or the

9 Ibid., pp. 26-39.

> creditor—from a realization that the debts they owe, or the debts owing to them, are too high and should be reduced. This realization may be borne home by many causes; but the chief cause may well be that *earnings, current or expected, have begun to disappoint the excessive expectations which originally led to the debts.* It is often said that the "turn of the cycle" may be due to a very trivial precipitating cause. Anything which causes a slight revulsion of *mood* may be *the last straw.* Then, with liquidation and distress selling, the depression spiral begins its tail spin. (emphasis ours)

As these passages proceed, we begin to see comments on "tangles and crosscurrents" referring to actions that could lead to unforeseen consequences. For example, speculators (mostly investors, as we will see) in the so-called Little Bull Market, disappointed in earnings reported in the second quarter of 1930, might decide to sell. If their actions caused per share prices to drop, other speculators might decide also to sell, and these collective actions might have brought about the collapse of the Little Bull Market in the second quarter of 1930. Actions in one area could entangle with another factor to cause unanticipated damage elsewhere. Irving Fisher continued:

> So the slowing of circulation may show itself statistically in advance of the credit contraction, though the contraction was listed first for convenience of exposition and the retardation of velocity was not mentioned until the full reasons for it had come into view.
>
> Not only may the retardation of currency begin before its contraction, but there may be at first an actual expansion of currency, if enough cautious people set about accumulating cash studiously.
>
> Nor are these the only chronological complications. Our Nine Factors are only a part of the whole complex picture in any actual depression, and their many effects on each

> other have not been exhaustively stated. If we may mix our metaphors, a depression may be said to be *full of tangles and crosscurrents*. Moreover, dislocations may occur through *a great variety of interferences*.[10] (emphasis ours)

Such entanglements, interferences or crosscurrents certainly included bad management practices and even criminality resulting in convictions and prison incarceration.

Implications of Hoarding

We return to the deflationary impact of hoarding post-Crash on the slowdown in the velocity of money. Nothing reduces the velocity of money like the phenomenon of currency holding—hoarding. Economists at the Fed and elsewhere closely watch the velocity of money to see how quickly and easily businesses and individuals can exchange money for their needs, whether through earnings or borrowings. A healthy economy has a robust velocity of money. Fisher brought up the economic influence of hoarding as something done by many of the cautious people he mentioned. Statistics show, as is well recognized, that as the Depression advanced, with its many overlapping factors, and, especially as banking crises occurred, depositors, afraid of losing everything if their bank failed, withdrew circulating currency from their banks and hoarded it. Indeed, some people probably did hide their money for safekeeping under a proverbial mattress. However, as we noted earlier, Fisher recognized that a great deal of hoarding occurs in plain sight in the form of idle time deposit accounts.

Clearly, from Fisher's point of view, money could be stockpiled in time deposits and, we add, in the compensating-balances component of demand deposits. But the effect of hoarding, while it conjures up graphic visions of lumpy mattresses and loose floorboards under a rug, was crucial to post-Crash deflation. Looking at statistics on

10 Ibid., pp. 40-1.

the velocity of money in circulation following the Crash will soon show how much hoarding existed and how it affected the economy.

The Velocity of Money and the Equation of Exchange

How did Irving Fisher think about and measure the velocity of money?

The equation of exchange was developed and presented by Irving Fisher in his much earlier work, *The Purchasing Power of Money: Its Determination and Relation to Credit, Interest and Crises,* published in 1911. In this volume, Fisher developed the concepts underlying the equation of exchange and presented them in an algebraic equation familiar to generations of economists and students of economics:

$$MV = PT \qquad (1)$$

> Where M represents "the average amount of money in circulation in the community during [a period of time]." V represents "the velocity of the circulation of money" in the period. And "MV, therefore, expresses the money side of the equation."[11] On the right side of equation (1), "P... represents...the level of prices ... and T... represents the volume of trade."[12] In other words, PT, is "the goods side of the equation, ... the prices of goods exchanged and the quantities of goods exchanged."[13] Equation (1) expresses what is well known as the quantity theory of money.

Significantly, however, Fisher further elaborated on the algebraic form of equation (1) to include another component of the circulation of money, the circulation of checks drawn on demand

11 Irving Fisher, *The Purchasing Power of Money: Its Determination and Relation to Credit[,] Interest and Crises,* Augustus M. Kelley, Publishers; 1911, pp. 24-25.

12 Ibid., p. 27.

13 Ibid., p. 25.

deposits (M'V'):

$$MV + M'V' = PT \tag{2}$$

In equation (2), *MV*, as in equation (1) represents the amount of coins and paper money in circulation (M) and the velocity of

Fisher's View of the Velocity of Bank Deposits

Chart 3.2

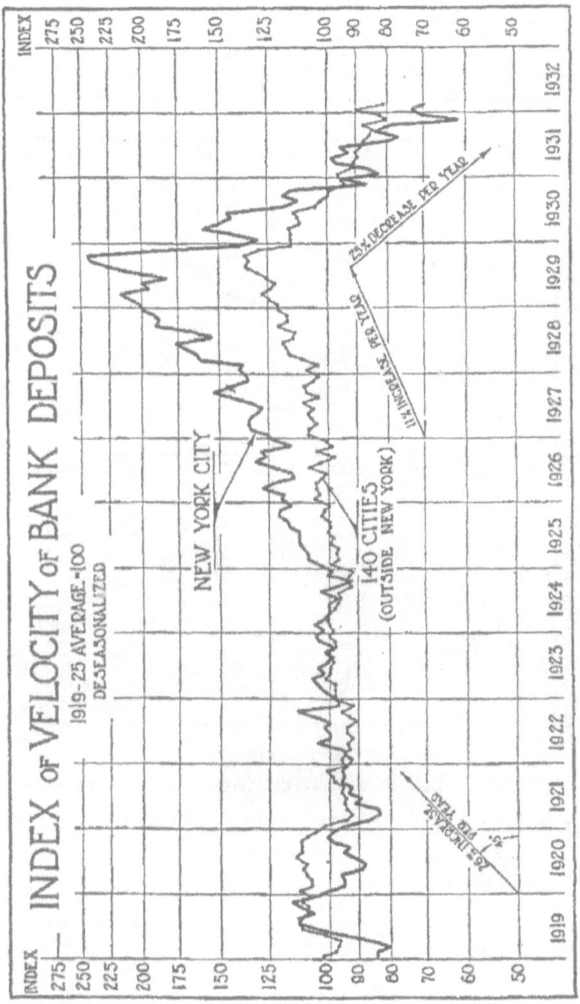

circulation of those coins and paper money (V). The additional pair of variables, *M'V'*, represents 1) the aggregate amount of deposits upon which checks are written—in other words, demand deposits—and 2) the velocity at which such checks circulate.Using this second pair of variables, *M'V'*, Fisher measured and graphed the velocity of bank deposits, our Chart 3.2, (previous page) reproduced from Chart 3 in *Booms and Depressions.* The table below shows two series of bank deposit velocity, one for New York City and the other for 140 cities outside New York.[14] We pair the chart with our Table 3.3 (Fisher's Table 13), which presents the data upon which the chart is plotted.[15]

Table 3.3

Indexes of Velocity of Bank Deposits

Daily basis. Normal equals 1919-25 average. Seasonal allowed for Velocity based on relation of debits to individual account to demand deposits in weekly reporting member banks

I

New York City

Years	Jan.	Feb.	Mar.	Apr.	May	June	July	Aug.	Sept.	Oct.	Nov.	Dec.	Aver.
1919	84	84	80	85	94	104	111	112	106	110	115	105	99
1920	101	95	95	96	89	88	91	95	93	99	101	99	95
1921	95	87	83	84	91	89	93	92	96	95	96	94	91
1922	92	95	95	105	100	100	102	100	106	113	97	97	100
1923	99	103	105	107	102	105	101	99	102	98	104	105	103
1924	102	106	102	100	100	100	97	103	97	92	101	99	100
1925	104	108	108	100	112	112	112	116	117	121	120	115	112
1926	120	118	128	124	114	115	123	132	127	129	115	124	122
1927	127	134	135	134	131	128	135	145	153	144	135	136	136
1928	140	138	162	164	169	177	154	166	190	188	191	201	170
1929	202	210	216	195	201	182	208	228	242	244	189	139	
1930	129	143	159	150	143	146	118	112	118	115	87	95	
1931	83	87	97	99	93	96	80	77	84	80	62	71	
1932	73	70	68										

II

140 Cities (Outside New York City)

Years	Jan.	Feb.	Mar.	Apr.	May	June	July	Aug.	Sept.	Oct.	Nov.	Dec.	Aver.
1919	103	98	97	96	102	111	112	111	108	108	111	107	105
1920	112	107	107	109	110	109	113	111	111	111	109	105	110
1921	102	94	92	94	95	94	96	95	98	99	101	94	96
1922	96	95	93	94	92	94	94	91	93	96	92	97	94
1923	98	98	98	102	100	100	99	99	102	98	98	100	99
1924	99	100	101	100	98	97	96	97	92	94	93	92	97
1925	100	97	98	97	100	99	101	100	100	103	102	100	100
1926	106	104	105	105	103	101	108	103	98	105	99	101	103
1927	108	108	105	107	108	106	110	104	109	110	106	104	107
1928	109	104	111	116	117	119	114	113	121	117	117	121	115
1929	121	125	128	124	123	126	131	136	135	137	130	115	128
1930	115	115	116	111	112	114	105	103	100	100	94	95	107
1931	97	91	91	90	91	89	88	86	85	88	81	83	
1932	90	81	77										

Source: Federal Reserve Bank of New York, Reports Department.

Fed member banks reported their daily statistics on a weekly basis to the Fed who used those statistics to measure the daily ve-

14 Fisher (1932), p. 94.

15 Ibid., p. 192.

locity based on the relation of 1) *debits to* individual demand deposit accounts to 2) *deposits to* demand deposit accounts.[16] Each bank reported the speed at which its total demand deposit accounts were turning over day-by-day, an important measure of deposit velocity for use, among other things, in risk management by the banks. In using these statistics, Fisher counted *all payments made by check*, taking no account of who the payees were or why the payments were made. Economist Joseph Schumpeter pronounced Fisher's technique an "ingenious method of estimating the velocity of money."[17]

On the basis of these velocity statistics, *V'*, and their related demand deposit statistics, *M'*, Fisher reported on the significance on deflation of the sharp decline in velocity:

> From October, 1929, to February, 1932, the deposit currency of the member banks of the country (in 141 cities including New York City) fell from $18,726,000,000 to $14,789,000,000.[18] This was a full 21 per cent, leaving only 79 per cent of the earlier amount; and the velocity in the same period fell 61 per cent—that is, to 39 per cent of the earlier rate, so that the efficiency of deposit money for sustaining the price level in the levels of production, trade and employment became, in 1932, only 31 per cent of what it had been in 1929.[19]

Fisher's broadly defined transactions equation, it turns out, provided a substantially accurate take on what was happening with regards to velocity and deflation.

---

16 For the Daily statistics, Normal equaled the 1919-25 average allowing for seasonality.

17 Schumpeter (1948), p. 227.

18 We are unable to validate the accuracy of these numbers because we have found ourselves unable to locate any statistics focused on deposits of Fed member banks in, quite specifically, 141 cities in the U.S. including New York City.

19 Fisher (1932), p. 96.

Friedman's View on the Equation of Exchange

We now turn back to Friedman and Schwartz to discuss their views on velocity. In *Monetary History*, they defined "velocity of money" as "the ratio of money income to the stock of money."[20] In other words, they replaced Fisher's use of *all* transactions with an incomed-based notion virtually impossible for laymen to measure or perhaps even relate to. In Appendix A of *Monetary History*, Friedman and Schwartz provided two pages of statistics which they gave for 1920-1941, for which their sources included "worksheets underlying Simon Kuznets, *Capital in the American Economy.*"[21] Table 3.4 shows the product of Friedman's ruminations on income velocity as presented in *Monetary History.*[22]

Table 3.4

Two Measures of Friedman's Income Velocity

	Income velocity of money		Income velocity of currency and demand deposits	
Year	Statistic	% Change from prior year	Statistic	% Change from prior year
1928	1.84	-1.6%	3.25	+1.2%
1929	1.95	+6.0%	3.42	+5.2%
1930	1.70	-12.8%	3.02	-11.7%
1931	1.47	-13.5%	2.60	-13.9%
1932	1.28	-12.9%	2.16	-16.9%
1933	1.38	+7.8%	2.19	+1.4%
1934	1.52	+10.1%	2.36	+7.8%

Source: *Monetary History* pp. 774-5.

In *Theoretical Framework for Monetary Analysis,* Friedman explained his transition from Fisher's transactions version to Fried-

20 Milton Friedman and Anna J. Schwartz *A Monetary History of the United States 1867-1960*, Princeton University Press, 1963a, p. 34.

21 Ibid., pp. 774-5.

man's own version that he termed (as italicized by him) his *"Income Form of the Quantity Equation"*:

> In [Fisher's] transactions version of the quantity equation, each intermediate transaction—that is, purchase by one enterprise from another—is included in the total value of the transaction.... In the income version, only the *net value added* by each of these transactions is included.... [I]n the transactions version the elementary event is ...an actual, clearly observable event.... In the income version, the elementary event is a *hypothetical event* that can be inferred from observation *that is not directly observable.*[23] (emphasis ours)

In our view, one drawback to Friedman's income version is that assessing its performance "that can be inferred" requires a high degree of human expertise, which is why, we contend, that Friedman and Schwartz cited the authority of "worksheets underlying Simon Kuznets, *Capital in the American Economy"* as a source, as opposed to citing widely available government databases we've relied on to tell a (somewhat) different story.

Who Explained the Real World Better — Fisher or Friedman and Schwartz?

Basically, in considering transactions velocity and income velocity, Fisher, on the one hand, and Friedman and Schwartz, on the other, were discussing different things.

In *Monetary History,* Friedman and Schwartz often discussed "velocity" within their meaning of the term. For example:

---

23 Milton Friedman, A Theoretical Framework for Monetaty Analysis, *The Journal of Political Economy,* Vol 78, No. 2, March-April 1970, pp. 198-199.

> In general, the magnitude of the movement in velocity varies directly with the magnitude of corresponding movement in income and in money.... [T]he sharp decline in velocity from 1929 to 1933 was roughly matched in the opposite direction by the sharp rise during World War I, which accompanied the rapid rise in the stock of money and in money income.... On the other hand, in mild cycles, the movement of velocity is also mild.[24]

In our Transitional Introduction, we presented what we regard as the basic argument made by Friedman and Schwartz in Chapter 7 of *Monetary History*, which is that "nonmonetary forces" started "The Great Contraction, 1929-33." But their argument as to those forces was insufficiently specific, and their fundamental conclusion was that the "monetary character of the contraction changed dramatically" in the fourth quarter of 1930 when a series of banking crises began. Some readers, such as Professor Temin, interpreted this to mean that the banking crises caused the banking system to collapse. Others, such as Professor Wicker interpreted the bank crises to result in deposits at suspended banks being removed from the money supply for an indefinite period of time as the suspended banks were examined and put right. (We believe both conclusions have merit.)

Decades earlier than Friedman and Schwartz's analysis from the 1960s and early 1970s, Irving Fisher had argued along different lines, ones that conform more closely with our own Chapter 12 in *How the Crash Caused*, which clearly lays out and identifies the Crash as a springboard to, and cause of, the Great Depression. Irving Fisher also viewed the downturn as having begun in earnest with the Crash:

> Between the loans on the stock market and the stock market price level there could not be a better example of a vicious spiral. With every distress liquidation the price

24 Friedman and Schwartz (1963a), pp. 302-3.

> level fell; and every fall of the price level drove a new set of people into further liquidation, which still further lowered the price level which compelled still further liquidation, and so on and on....
>
> What seems sure is that the crash of the stock market helped to force the rest of our debt structure into liquidation, and then it was the *hopeless magnitude of the debt burden* which made it so difficult for the economic organism to right itself. [25] (emphasis ours).

While Fisher, as we have pointed out, failed to find the IRS balance sheet data that could have forcefully supported his ideas, we respect his powerful assessment in this second paragraph—even without supporting data—of what made the length and severity of the Great Depression so stubborn. We can't help but wish we were able to discuss matters with him now, considering our findings.

Fisher continued his analysis describing the impact on decreased commodities prices and on increased time deposits at banks right after the Crash:

> In the first place, many who were involved in both the stock and commodities markets sold commodities in order to avoid selling stocks. In the second place, consumers took fright and reduced their purchases—in other words, reduced the turnover or velocity of their money. Deposit currency, as we have seen, grows out of the demand deposits in commercial banks. The demand deposits do not exactly correspond with the commercial bank loans, but the great majority of demand deposits are based on commercial bank loans; and, except for short periods, the movements of the two tend to run parallel....
>
> In the first half of 1930 the demand deposits and the loans joined each other in the downturn, but there appeared an

25 Fisher (1932), pp. 91-92.

increase in *time* deposits which was little short of hoarding.[26]

We suggest that so far as the period leading through 1929 and up to the fourth quarter of 1930 is concerned, in focusing on income and income velocity Friedman and Schwartz gave a more limited explanation than Fisher did.

Kindleberger's Informative Account of the Paths of Falling Prices

In our ongoing quest to understand deflation and its contribution to the Great Depression, we turn to Charles Kindleberger, who, in the mid-1980s, offered a useful explanation of the transmission paths that brought about the fall of prices:

> Deflation, then, moved from the decline in stock markets to production cuts and inventory runoffs in one sequence, and from stock prices to commodity prices to the reduced value of imports in another. *Both were fast.* The connection between the stock market and commodity markets was partly psychological and undoubtedly at the outset partly through the credit machinery as banks and firms struggled to become liquid. By the end of the year, credit markets were easing rapidly and this source of pressure was over. It was too late. The positive-feedback mechanism—cutting imports from less developed countries, which cut imports from the developed—was well under way and gathering force. On the rise, the stock market cut off capital movements to the developing countries; in decline it produced a liquidity crisis that led to rapid reduction in these countries' exports. The process fed back to the United States. By the turn of the year, US exports had turned sharply downward.[27] (emphasis ours)

---

26 Ibid., p. 93.

27 Charles Kindleberger *The World in Depression 1929-1939,* University of California Press, 1986, p. 114-16.

The other connections between the stock market and business conditions through credit availability for business and through wealth and income effect on owners of securities doubtless came into operation in 1930. None of them can have had time to work in 1929, except perhaps in the anticipations of businessman. Such of them that were expansive were overwhelmed by the cumulative forces of deflation already underway.[28]

Passenger Car Production and Sales Figures Reveal Deflation

A clear and detailed example of these forces showed up in our research. Because of its uniquely influential position in U.S.

Figure 3.1

Passenger Car Output Adjusted to Domestic and Foreign Sales

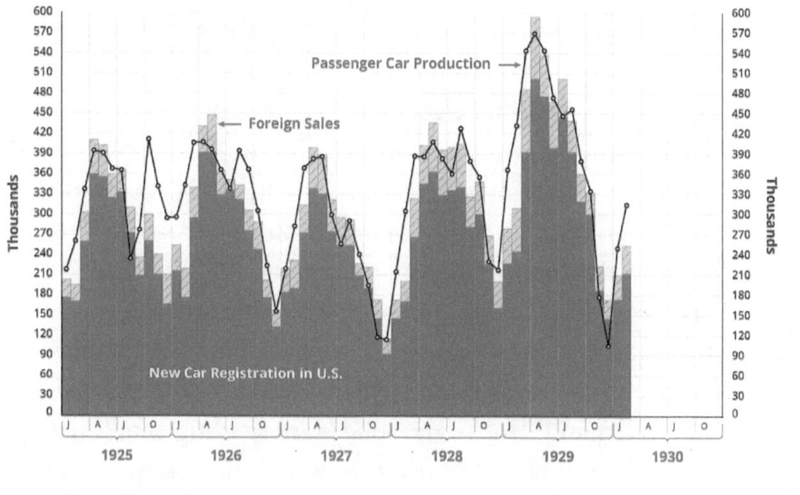

The passenger car production curve includes output in United States and Canada. The monthly vertical bars represent new car registrations in United Sates and foreign sales (cross-hatched top portion). Export sales include United States exports, foreign assemblies and Canadian production. New car registration based on R. L. Polk figures.

28 Ibid., p. 116.

manufacturing, employment and Americans' lifestyle priorities, we must return to the automotive industry in order to introduce into our record for 1929 key information for passenger car production and sales for 1929 and early 1930 that came to our attention in *Facts and Figures of the Automobile Industry* for both 1930 and 1931 publications of the National Automobile Chamber of Commerce.

We begin from a top-down point of view, with the automobile industry standing unique among American manufacturing. Figure 3.1 (previous page) appeared in the 1931 edition of *Facts and Figures of the Automobile Industry* and shows how important the automobile industry was within the U. S. economy based on the 1929 Census of Manufactures. Not only does it show Motor vehicles as the largest of the first ten industries in the U.S. in size. but in the lower part of the figure it adds aspects of other industries, such as Motor vehicle bodies and parts, to the numbers listed for Motor vehicles themselves to reveal the extent of the overall economic importance to the U.S. economy of automobiles. As the figure clearly shows, automobiles impacted at least one-eighth of overall manufactures. However, our estimate of the actual economic impact of automobiles is broader still. For example, we would add to the numbers in Figure 3.1 statistics such as 1) construction of paved roads and highways and 2) property/casualty insurance coverage of automobiles.

We continue our discussion with Figure 3.2 (opposite page) from the same source of publication which shows the number of automobiles produced and delivered to customers both domestic and for export through the first quarter of 1930.[29] Passenger car production is represented by a dark line moving, quarter-by-quarter along the x-axis, cycling—consistent with seasonal sales trends—upwards as each year begins and demand builds and downwards as it ends and demand drops. The solid-dark shading shows new car registrations in the U.S.[30] Above the solid-dark section are hashed

29 Figure 3.2 says nothing about revenues or the prices at which the automobiles were sold.

30 Registration statistics are much easier to find than sales statistics,

Figure 3.2

Passenger Car Output Adjusted to Domestic and Foreign Sales

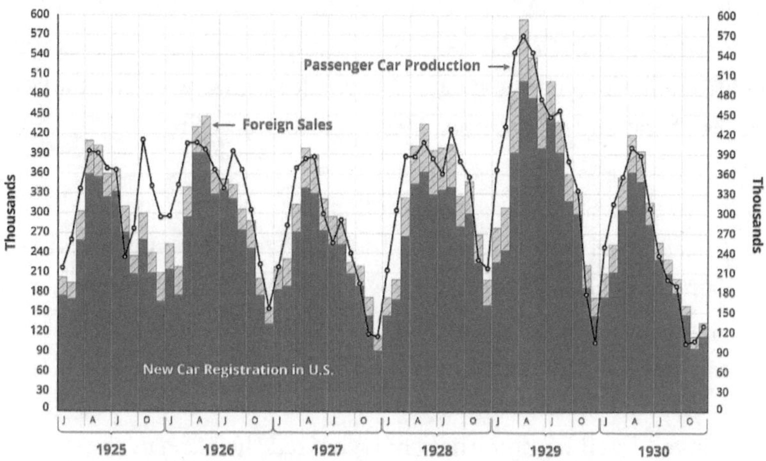

Production curve includes United States and Canada output. Monthly vertical bars represent new car registration in United Sates and foreign sales (cross-hatched top portion). Foreign sales include exports from United Sates, foreign assemblies and Canadian production.

entries showing foreign sales.

Two important observations stand out. First is the precipitous drop in production in 1929 from a high of 571,956 automobiles produced in April 1929 to a low of 96,920 produced in December. Clearly this indicates that many automobile workers must have been laid off in the last eight months of 1929. Then we also see rising production and sales numbers in the first two months of 1930.[31] While unemployment in the automobile industry in early 1930 must have been high, the outlook for 1930 appeared to look promising. Unfortunately, that outlook changed.[32]

---

which are often considered trade secrets.

31 The 1930 edition of *Facts and Figures of the Automobile Industry* presented information for all of 1929, p. 2 and was distributed early in 1930 with some information on the first months of 1930.

32 National Automobile Chamber of Commerce entitled *Facts and Figures of the Automobile Industry, 1931 Edition,* p. 5.

A Final Word

In summation and for context, we return to Charles Kindleberger in his Chapter 5, "The 1929 Stock Market Crash," of *The World in Depression 1929-1939.* Succinctly describing the inexorable path to deflation that he posited, as we do, began with the shocking events of the end of October 1929, Kindleberger reflected:

> In the light of the sudden collapse of business, commodity prices, and imports at the end of 1929, it is difficult to maintain that the stock market was a superficial phenomenon, a signal, or a triggering, rather than a part of the deflationary mechanism. One should not be dogmatic about it, but it is hard to avoid the conclusion that there is something to the conventional wisdom that characterized the crash as the start of the process. The crash led to a scramble for liquidity on the part of both lenders to the call market and owners of stocks. In the process, orders were canceled and loans called. The action of the Federal Reserve in buying securities in the open market and lowering the rediscount rate in New York brought credit markets quickly into good order. By this time, however, the deflation had been communicated to fragile commodity markets and durable goods industries. The stock market crash is less interesting for the irony it permits the historian, bemused by the foibles of greedy men, than for starting a process that took on a dynamic of its own.[33]

It is heartening to us to see that the causal linkage shown above in the automotive industry and in other retail segments as discussed in Chapter 12 of *How the Crash Caused* appears to have validated what Kindleberger described as "the conventional wisdom that characterized the crash as the start of the process." But, given that the Federal Reserve had proved unable to bring stock speculation under control back in the spring of 1929, our own view is that the

---

33 Kindleberger (1986), p. 116.

runaway speculation is really what started the process by making the Crash of 1929 virtually inevitable.

In the following chapter, we explore some of the results of these "foibles of greedy men" as exemplified in the behaviors of both speculators and even many investors as 1929 comes to its dramatic close.

Table 3.5

Statistics of U.S. Economic Activity

($ billion)

	Aug. '29	Sep. '29	Oct. '29	Nov. '29	Dec. '29
Annualized personal income	$86.9	$86.4	$86.3	$83.6	$82.8
Index of factory employment	108.4	107.3	106.6	104.4	101.9
Index of industrial production	114	112	110	105	100
Index of wholesale prices	96.3	96.1	95.1	93.5	93.3
Friedman & Schwartz demand deposits	$22.6	$22.6	$24.4	$21.7	$22.6
Fed member bank loans		$26.2			$26.2

Sources: *HSUS* 1789-1945, pp. 328-330, 344; *Monetary History*, p.712; *BMS*, p.72.

Of Note

All above-the-line statistics were significantly down in December from November and from the August peak:

- Annualized personal income:
  - -down $0.8 billion from November
  - -down $4.1 billion from August (-4.7%)
- Index of factory employment:

-down 2.4% from November
-down 6.0% from August

- Industrial production:
  -down 4.8% from November
  -down 12/3% from August
- Wholesale prices:
  -down 0.02% in November
  -down 3.1% from August (annualized rate of -9.1%)

CHAPTER 4

Year-End Reckoning for 1929: Meet the Speculators and Investors

WITH THE END OF 1929 we reach a point where the IRS data source—our evidentiary Rembrandt — takes center stage in terms of revealing the story of who the major financial players were and what they were doing.

Most of us probably have a mixed-to-negative view of the IRS because of its very mandate, despite the reality that paying income taxes has been a part of American life for over one hundred years. In fact, we tend to joke, uncomfortably, about the inevitability of death and taxes. Whether from the vantage point of the political right or the political left, few of us would express much enthusiasm for performing our annual tax preparation duties. Even those who have paid tax preparers still have to assemble the documentation. Furthermore, tax policy has only grown in complexity. Yet for most Americans, aiming for accuracy in tax reporting is a high priority due to the repercussions of the alternatives, whether an audit or worse.

For our purposes, however, the IRS took on a new and indispensable value—as a treasure trove of contemporaneous statistics about America in 1929-33. Starting in 1916, the IRS has published an annual statistical report, *Statistics of Income* (referred to herein as *SOI)*—for example, *SOI for 1929*, a particular year of focus in this book. We might think of these volumes as our nation's Prosperity Report Card.

Each report offers extensive data on both corporate and individual taxfilers, thus giving a look at their economic performance and well-being for that year.[1] Of particular interest in this chapter, *SOI for 1929* provided considerable detailed information about individual taxpayers who were, at that time, the upwardly mobile, the affluent, the wealthy and the rich—likely the very individuals participating in the stock market.

The IRS Statistical Unit went to great lengths to present annual taxpayer data in detail within each *SOI*. Comprehending, all these years later, why they did so, who they imagined would find that data useful and what they thought analyzing the data would reveal is, of course, unknowable. For example, with regards to U.S. business, we have found no explanation as to how and why the IRS unit came to publish such increasingly fine-grained data by sector—and even further by sub-sector—on corporate balance sheets for 1930-33. Of particular interest to us would be to know why the readily available and abundant IRS data failed to draw the attention of other researchers into the cause and duration of the Great Depression. Despite these unanswered questions, we find ourselves extremely grateful to those intrepid government statisticians whose decisions so long ago as to what information to collect enabled us—due to our particular skill sets—to follow clues, dive deeply into the archives and arrive at some worthwhile, perhaps even startling, observations and conclusions that add greatly to our nation's longstanding conversation and debate about the Great Depression.

In this chapter, we delve into data from individual tax returns for 1928 and 1929 as published in *SOI for 1928* and *SOI for 1929*. Our objective is to portray and then distinguish between speculators and investors during those eventful years by focusing in particular on the amounts reported on tax returns as capital gains and losses.

---

1 Beginning in 1934, the IRS separated the annual report into two parts, one for individuals and one for businesses. In the 1950s, the IRS switched to annual and special reports, and in 1981 the IRS introduced the *SOI* Bulletin.

This revealing data helped us consider the demographic profiles of both of these highly engaged stock market participants, explore what motivated them and examine how they behaved.

Individual Americans as Seen by the IRS

For perspective, as we have noted, only a small fraction of the adult U.S. population even filed tax returns in 1929. With a total U.S. population of 121.8 million in 1929 and a labor force (white collar, blue collar, etc.) of just under 48.1 million, only eight percent of the labor force earned enough to file. *SOI for 1929* elaborated on the much smaller number of taxfilers, of whom only 60.8% paid taxes:

> The number of returns for 1929, filed by individuals, was 4,044,327, of which 2,458,049 were taxable and 1,586,278 nontaxable. The aggregate net income was $24,800,735,564; the net income on taxable returns was $20,493,491,443, on which the tax liability was $1,001,938,147.[2]

Perhaps our first reaction to the specificity of the numbers in that paragraph was to wonder at the exactitude of these ten- and eleven-digit numbers. We began to arrive at an understanding by describing how the IRS data collection, evaluation and publication process worked. From our point of view, IRS statisticians truly cared about detailed accuracy. Integrity and attention to detail were job requirements. Chapter 6 of *How the Crash Caused* explained how the data began as "draft evidence" that, should a taxfiler be audited, needed to be able to stand up in court. After all, filers, then as now, signed their returns, meaning they submitted their data under oath. To mitigate their risk and to ensure the accuracy of those filings, many taxfilers of means had come to engage professional accoun-

2 *SOI for 1929*, p.4.

tants to prepare their tax returns, contributing to the growth in that profession. As the IRS received tax filings, the filings went first to internal examiners and auditors whose job it was to ensure that filed data was correct and complete (and that the Treasury Department got correct payments or made correct refunds).

Once the examiners and auditors completed their task, they turned the filings over to the IRS Statistical Unit to tabulate the data. As we shall see shortly in Table 4.2 (page 98), for tax year 1929, slightly more than three million of the roughly four million who filed tax returns reported less than $5,000 of *net* income (i.e., <5) and produced a negligible 0.45% of the Federal government's income tax revenue. The Statistical Unit conducted samples of all filed returns of <5 net income in order to arrive at estimates reported in *SOI for 1929*. (It is reasonable to assume that sampling—which served as the basis for the IRS estimates of the lowest four income classes—included all returns that resulted in tax revenue.)

The Statistical Unit then delved into the data from the nine higher income categories—aggregated as "Returns Filed" in Table 4.2 (page 98). This was a group of particular interest to us because they paid 99.55% of the Federal government's income tax revenue from individuals and covered all earners of $5,000 and above (5>over). The results were fully tabulated rather than estimated from sample returns. The Unit carefully examined this significant group of returns, then tabulated, published and archived their results *to the dollar* for posterity. Furthermore, unlike some other governmental data, IRS data has never been revised. It is safe to say the results constitute solid and incontrovertible evidence. Because of our confidence in this information, we present tables and data directly from *SOI 1928* and *SOI for 1929* as well as from later years in order to support our arguments with respect to the underlying economics of the period.

Table 4.1 (opposite) offers summary statistics for 1928 and 1929, which provide useful perspective on that era's very different taxation realities from ours today. We rely on averaging to do this. In 1929, the average net income was $6,132.22 for all filed returns

Table 4.1			
Summary Statistics			
Individual Filers			
	1928	1929	% Change
Returns filed	4,070,851	4,044,327	-0.65%
Taxable returns	2,523,063	2,458,049	-2.58%
Aggregate net income	$25,226M	$24,801M	-1.68%
Net income on taxable returns	not reported	$20,493M	n/a
Tax liability	$1,164M	$1,002M	-13.92%

Source: IRS *Statistics of Income 1928* and *1929*.

and $8,337.30 for all taxable returns. Taxpayers had an average tax liability of $407.62. The average tax rate was 4.89% for all 1929 taxable returns, down from 5.54% in 1928, because Congress authorized a significant tax cut that President Hoover signed into law on December 16, 1929.[3] As we can see in Table 4.1, aggregate 1929 statistics were down slightly from 1928. No category declined as dramatically as the Crash might presage, but the Crash occurred late in the year, so its major impact took more time to manifest in IRS statistics. Nonetheless, as we shall see, *SOI for 1929* still revealed significant ramifications for taxfilers.

We place Tables 4.2 and 4.3 on the following same page to invite and facilitate comparisons between 1929 and 1928 in terms of filed returns, net income and tax liability as broken down into the thirteen IRS net income classes. Of note immediately is how little the first four classes paid in taxes. The first net income class—filers reporting net incomes "Under 1" or <1—totaled 126,173 individuals who reported net income of slightly more than $73.4 million. However, given the 1929 tax structure, the total tax liability for this group in aggregate was a trifling $17,308. In fact, the average filer in this first net income class had a tax liability of 13.7 cents, an

3 *SOI for 1929,* p.4. The rate of "normal tax" on individuals for the calendar year 1929 was reduced from 5, 3, and 1½ per cent to 4, 2, and ½%. (Certain tax credits and progressively rising rates on income remained in effect.) The corporate income tax rate was reduced from 12% to 11%.

Table 4.2

Simple distribution of individual returns for 1929, by net income classes, showing number of returns, net income, tax, and percentages

Net income classes (Thousands of dollars)	Returns		Net income ($ million)		Tax ($ million)	
	Number	Percent	Amount	Percent	Amount	Percent
Under 1 (estimated)	126,172	3.12	$73.7	0.30	$0.02	0.01
1 under 2 (estimated)	903,082	22.33	1,499.9	6.05	0.6	0.06
2 under 3 (estimated)	810,347	20.04	1,958.6	7.90	1.4	0.14
3 under 5 (estimated)	1,172,655	29.00	4,572.6	18.44	2.4	0.24
Subtotal	3,012,256	74.49	8,104.8	32.69	4.4	0.45
5 under 10	658,039	16.27	4,481.6	18.07	9.6	0.95
10 under 25	271,454	6.71	4,025.2	16.23	59.9	5.98
25 under 50	63,689	1.57	2,174.5	8.77	113.9	11.37
50 under 100	24,073	0.60	1,646.5	6.64	160.8	16.05
100 under 150	6,376	0.16	770.5	3.11	99.6	9.94
150 under 300	5,310	0.13	1,087.4	4.38	159.2	15.89
300 under 500	1,641	0.04	628.2	2.53	97.3	9.71
500 under 1,000	976	0.02	669.9	2.70	106.2	10.60
1,000 and over	513	0.01	1,212.1	4.88	191.1	19.06
Total	4,044,327	100.00	24,800.7	100.00	1,002.0	100.00

Source: IRS *Statistics of Income 1929*.

Table 4.3

Simple distribution of individual returns for 1928, by net income classes, showing number of returns, net income, tax, and percentages

Net income classes (Thousands of dollars)	Returns		Net income ($ million)		Tax ($ million)	
	Number	Percent	Amount	Percent	Amount	Percent
Under 1 (estimated)	111,123	2.73	$64.5	0.26	$0.06	0.01
1 under 2 (estimated)	918,447	22.56	1,526.8	6.05	1.5	0.13
2 under 3 (estimated)	837,781	20.58	2,030.9	8.05	4.3	0.37
3 under 5 (estimated)	1,192,613	29.30	4,648.1	18.43	7.5	0.64
Subtotal	3,059,964	75.17	8,270.3	32.79	13.4	1.15
5 under 10	628,766	15.44	4,282.5	16.98	22.9	1.97
10 under 25	270,889	6.66	4,037.9	16.00	82.8	7.11
25 under 50	68,048	1.67	2,326.5	9.22	136.6	11.73
50 under 100	27,207	0.67	1,857.9	7.36	194.4	16.70
100 under 150	7,049	0.17	850.5	3.37	116.9	10.04
150 under 300	5,678	0.14	1,157.1	4.59	182.5	15.68
300 under 500	1,756	0.043	663.9	2.63	113.2	9.72
500 under 1,000	983	0.024	670.9	2.66	116.4	10.00
1,000 and over	511	0.013	1,108.9	4.40	185.1	15.90
Total	4,070,851	100.00	25,226.4	100.00	1,164.2	100.00

Source: IRS *Statistics of Income 1928*.

unimaginably low number today.

In contrast, the highest net income class in 1929 comprised the 513 filers reporting net incomes of $1,000,000 and higher (1 million>over). Their reported net income totaled slightly more than $1.2 billion, and, given the progressive tax structure applying in 1929, the grand total of their tax liability was $191.1 million. Though these high earners made up only 0.01% of the 4,044,327 filers, their reported net incomes made up 4.88% of the $24.8 billion aggregate net income reported, and they provided 19.06% of the more than $1 billion in U.S. income tax revenue from individuals in 1929. In fact, the average tax liability for these highest earners exceeded $372,000.

Between the lowest net income class and the highest net income class of filers shown in the tables were eleven intermediate classes, each with its own characteristics that added to the story about speculation, a main topic of this chapter. Of particular note, for 1929, the 25<50 category was made up of the 63,689 filers reporting net incomes of $25,000 to $49,999 (roughly $450,000 to $900,000 today). Their total tax liability was $113.9 million on total net income of slightly less than $2.2 billion. Although they comprised only 1.57% of the total number of returns filed, their reported net income was 8.77% of the aggregate net income reported, and they paid 11.37% of the income tax paid by individuals. The tax liability of the average individual in this net income class exceeded $1,750 (the equivalent of over $30,000 in 2023.) We will be revisiting this significant category.

Sources of Income Throw Light on Speculation in 1928 and 1929

Table 4.4 (page 102) shows the IRS breakdown into ten categories of all individual taxfilers' gross aggregate sources of income, as well as allowable deductions, to arrive at net, or taxable, income. We discuss three important income sources as examples. "Wages and salaries," the largest source of income for taxfilers in aggregate, constituted pay for blue-collar or white-collar work. "Business" constituted sole proprietors' profits from unincorporated business enterprises. "Partnership" constituted the profits from a wide range of professional activities that operated as partnerships at that time such as many law, accounting and medical practices, advertising agencies, investment banking firms and asset brokerage firms and even certain private banks. In partnerships, the individual partners reported their share of the income and paid taxes on that amount.

To help us in exploring stock speculation in particular, we zero in on a fourth income source—gains from investments. Within this income source, the key distinction was how long a taxfiler had owned an asset before selling it. Short-term gains, described wordily by the IRS as "Profit from real estate, stocks, bonds, etc., *other than* capital net gain from sale of assets held more than 2 years" (emphasis ours), today we call "Profit from sale of assets held 2 years or less" or, succinctly, "Short-term capital gains." On the long-term side, "Capital net gain from sale of assets held more than 2 years" we now call "Capital net gain from assets held more than 2 years" or "Long-term capital gains." Tax rates, then as now, differed between short-term gains and long-term gains.

The last four income source names remain the same now and are self-explanatory: "Rents and royalties," "Dividends on the stock of domestic corporations," "Fiduciary" (fees paid for the management of trusts and estates) and "Interest and other income."

As for the treatment of deductions from income, of particular interest is the category with another unwieldy label, "Net loss from real estate, stocks, bonds, etc., other than reported for *tax credit* on capital net loss from sale of assets held more than 2 years" (emphasis ours). Losses we now call "Long-term capital losses" (or "Losses on sale of assets held 2 years or more") were then fully deductible. In addition, there was a 12.5% tax credit on capital losses on assets held more than 2 years. The remaining categories of deductions: "Contributions" (charitable contributions), "Net loss from business and partnership" and "All/other" are familiar to this day.

Comparing 1928 with 1929, statistics on asset sales highlight the immediate impact of the Crash on speculation. As we have said, how long a taxfiler had owned the asset prior to selling it was key. On the short side, and not surprisingly, "Profit from sale of assets held 2 years or less" dropped 20% from $2,928.1 million in 1928 to $2,337.9 million in 1929. In contrast, on the long side, "Capital net gain from assets held more than 2 years" rose 24.8% from $1,879.8 million in 1928 to $2,346.7 million in 1929, an increase that suggests many long-term investors found 1929 to be a good year in which to take long-term profits, as we will discuss later. A look at short-term *losses* proves even more revealing. "Losses on sale of assets held 2 years or less" more than quintupled from $171.7 million in 1928 to $995.9 million in 1929. This enormous Crash-induced increase in short-term asset sale losses—one category where speculation activity clearly belonged—had a measurable impact on the taxable income statistics of 1929.

Taxpayer Demographics by Net Income Class: Percentage-data Revelations

Percentages show relative weight among two or more variables rendering comparisons easier than having to assess and compare multi-digit dollar statistics. We converted the statistics in Tables 4.4 (next page) to percentages in Tables 4.5 (page 103) and 4.6 (page 104) in order to show the relative weight by income class among the various sources of income. Before we draw valuable conclusions from the data in Tables 4.5 and 4.6, we first need to navigate these tables.

Each column presents statistics regarding a particular source of income, e.g., "Wages and salaries" or "Business" (meaning sole-proprietorships), etc. The different income classes inhabit the rows, measure the percent of total income earned by taxfilers in that particular income category (e.g., <5 earned 61.2% of income from wages and salaries.) and sum to 100%, thus accounting for all income sources in any income class. The total row breaks total taxfilers into what percentage each income source (say, "Wages and salaries" or "Business") provided. For instance, Wages and salaries comprised 37.47% of total taxfiler income. Each row, then, totals to 100%.

Table 4.4

Sources of income and deductions in individual returns, amounts and percentages

Sources of income and deductions	1928 Amount ($ million)	1928 Percent (%)	1929 Amount ($ million)	1929 Percent (%)
Wages and salaries	10,862.3	37.47	11,199.0	37.40
Business	3,244.0	11.19	3,379.0	11.28
Partnership	1,929.5	6.66	1,853.1	6.19
Profit from sale of assets held 2 years or less [1]	2,928.1	10.10	2,337.9	7.81
Capital net gain from assets held more than 2 years [2]	1,879.8	6.49	2,346.7	7.84
Rents and royalties	1,164.5	4.02	1,286.1	4.29
Interest on government obligations not wholly exempt from tax	2,143.9	7.39	40.2	0.13
Dividends on stock of domestic corporations	40.6	0.14	4,786.0	15.98
Fiduciary	4,351.0	15.01	508.5	1.70
Interest and other income	444.0	1.53	2,210.5	7.38
Total income	28,987.6	100.00	29,947.0	100.00
General deductions:				
Net loss from sale of assets other than reported for tax credit [3]	171.7	0.59	995.9	3.33
Contributions	532.9	1.84	528.9	1.76
Miscellaneous	3,056.7	10.54	3,621.4	12.09
Total deductions	3,761.3	12.97	5,146.2	17.18
Net income	25,226.3	87.03	24,800.7	82.82

[1] Labeled "Profit from sale of real estate, stocks, bonds, etc., other than taxed as capital net gain from sale of assets held more than 2 years" in IRS tables.

[2] Labeled "Capital net gain from sale of assets held more than 2 years" in IRS tables.

[3] Labeled "Net Loss from sale of real estate, stocks, bonds, etc., other than reported for tax credit on capital net loss from sale of assets held more than 2 years" in IRS tables.

Source: IRS *Statistics of Income 1929*.

What Do These Demographic Statistics Show Us about 1928 and 1929?

Unlike today when most working Americans file tax returns, IRS demographic statistics in the 1920s reflected the tax structure of the time, which impacted the upper middle class, the well-to-do and the rich. Less well-off Americans, while in the majority, simply didn't have to file. The IRS wasn't concerned with their financial footprint, so to speak, and didn't collect data on non-filers. However, our research focus on taxfilers and payers, rather than on working Americans as a whole, has yielded ample insights into which Americans had taken financial center stage in the late 1920s.

We look first at 1928, a full year of significant prosperity matched by aggressively growing stock speculation. As the percentages in Table 4.5 clearly show, the higher a filer's net income, the more

Table 4.5						
Percentage distribution of total income in individual returns, by income classes, showing sources of income in detail, calendar year 1928						
Income classes	Wages and salaries	Business	Partnership	Profit from sale of assets held 2-years or less [1]	Capital net gain from sale of assets held more than 2-years	
Under $5,000 [2]	61.20	15.39	3.62	2.38	------------	
$5,000 under $10,000	45.05	17.27	7.22	7.35	------------	
$10,000 under $25,000	32.17	11.55	7.58	15.21	------------	
$25,000 under $50,000	22.50	6.96	7.37	20.46	1.74	
$50,000 under $100,000	15.95	4.49	7.87	16.74	11.70	
$100,000 under $150,000	11.97	3.06	8.91	16.14	19.07	
$150,000 under $300,000	8.85	2.51	11.46	15.24	25.34	
$300,000 under $500,000	6.16	2.01	12.54	14.54	29.63	
$500,000 under $1,000,000	4.05	2.06	11.59	14.65	35.76	
$1,000,000 and over	2.01	0.21	7.39	12.11	47.31	
Total	37.47	11.19	6.66	10.10	6.49	
Income classes	Rents and royalties	Interest and other income	Interest on Government obligations not wholly exempt from tax	Dividends on stock of domestic corporations	Fiduciary	Total income
Under $5,000 [2]	5.51	7.50	------------	3.57	0.83	100.00
$5,000 under $10,000	5.06	7.68	------------	8.86	1.15	100.00
$10,000 under $25,000	4.22	8.74	0.32	17.87	2.34	100.00
$25,000 under $50,000	3.20	8.63	0.36	25.95	2.83	100.00
$50,000 under $100,000	2.43	7.71	0.31	30.20	2.60	100.00
$100,000 under $150,000	1.63	6.21	0.24	31.23	1.54	100.00
$150,000 under $300,000	1.21	5.22	0.18	28.73	1.26	100.00
$300,000 under $500,000	0.95	4.78	0.15	27.96	1.28	100.00
$500,000 under $1,000,000	0.78	3.99	0.12	26.39	0.61	100.00
$1,000,000 and over	0.63	3.97	0.25	25.78	0.34	100.00
Total	4.02	7.39	0.14	15.01	1.53	100.00

[1] Labeled "Profit from sale of real estate, stocks, bonds, etc., other than taxed as capital net gain from sale of assets held more than 2-years" in IRS tables.

[2] Data for returns of net income under $5,000 partly tabulated, partly estimated on basis of sample. (See pp. 1, 19-24).

Note: Slight formatting differences between tables 15.5 & 15.6 due to changes in SOI format configuration.

Source: IRS *Statistics of Income 1928*.

important *unearned* income, such as income on stock speculation, was. As benchmarks of that 1928 prosperity, the Dow industrials opened the year at 198, according to the St. Louis Federal Reserve's data research arm FRED, and closed at 278.65.[4] Stock bellwether Radio Corporation of America—widely familiar to Americans because the price of "Radio," as brokerage offices knew it, was discussed frequently on the radio—opened 1928 at 90½ and closed the year at 374½, a dizzying rise of over 400%.[5]

---

4 Source for the 198 Dow opening was FRED.

5 RCA fell to $10 by 1931.

Table 4.6

Percentage distribution of total income in individual returns for 1929, by net income classes, showing sources of income in detail

Net income classes (Thousands of dollars)	Wages and salaries	Business	Partnership	Profit from sale of assets held 2-years or less [1]	Capital net gain from sale of assets held more than 2-years	Rents and royalties
Under 5	58.81	15.07	3.47	2.87	----------	6.22
5 under 10	45.86	17.55	6.92	6.22	----------	4.93
10 under 25	32.64	11.96	7.52	12.84	----------	4.21
25 under 50	22.61	6.84	7.22	17.75	1.10	3.30
50 under 100	15.46	4.17	7.44	12.66	13.15	2.47
100 under 150	11.36	3.25	8.41	8.83	24.34	1.81
150 under 300	8.48	2.25	9.82	8.63	33.05	1.27
300 under 500	5.87	1.69	9.43	6.59	41.21	0.76
500 under 1,000	3.75	0.94	9.46	6.71	45.71	0.80
1,000 and over	1.83	0.13	6.82	7.14	54.76	0.66
Total	37.40	11.28	6.19	7.81	7.84	4.29

Net income classes (Thousands of dollars)	Interest on Government obligations not wholly exempt from tax	Dividends on stock of domestic corporations	Fiduciary	Interest and other income	Total income
Under 5	----------	5.27	0.84	7.45	100.00
5 under 10	----------	9.65	1.55	7.32	100.00
10 under 25	0.31	19.30	2.55	8.67	100.00
25 under 50	0.35	28.36	3.59	8.88	100.00
50 under 100	0.33	32.92	3.20	8.20	100.00
100 under 150	0.27	33.23	2.09	6.41	100.00
150 under 300	0.20	29.53	1.45	5.32	100.00
300 under 500	0.18	27.50	1.60	5.17	100.00
500 under 1,000	0.15	27.66	0.53	4.29	100.00
1,000 and over	0.15	23.85	0.57	4.09	100.00
Total	0.13	15.98	1.70	7.38	100.00

[1] Labeled "Profit from sale of real estate, stocks, bonds, etc., other than taxed as capital net gain from sale of assets held more than 2-years" in IRS tables.

Note: Slight formatting differences between tables 15.5 & 15.6 due to changes in SOI format configuration.

Source: IRS *Statistics of Income 1929*.

A broader look at how the various IRS income classes earned their income yields additional understanding. We offer a breakdown of those income sources in order of predominance, along with our comments as to who was earning and from what source.

1928 Sources of Total Income for Taxfilers

1. Wages and salaries: The largest source of reported total income: 37.5%. *Comment*: Of note is the fact that as individuals' incomes rose from the <5 class to the 1 million>over class, wages and salaries as a percentage of total income consistently fell, and sources of unearned income increased in importance.

2. Dividends on stock of domestic corporations: 15.01% of all income. *Comment*: The importance of dividend income as a percent of income rose until the 100<150 net income class, below which it then gradually fell.

3. Business income: 11.19% of all income. *Comment*: Business income covered enterprises operated by sole proprietors. While all net income classes earned business income, it was concentrated at the lower end.

4. Profit from sale of assets held 2 years or less: 10.1% of all income. *Comment*: This is the category we would now call "short-term capital gains." Stock speculators reported their speculative gains in this category. The impact of this category as an income source was low in the first net income class, rose to 20.46% of net income in the 25<50 class, then fell gradually to 12.11% in the 1 million>over class.

5. Interest and other income: 7.39% of all income. *Comment*: This category of earnings from interest-bearing accounts and government and corporate bonds comprised 7.50% of all income in the <5 net income class, rose to 8.74% of net income in the 10<25 class, then fell gradually to 3.97% in the 1 million>over class.

6. Partnership: 6.66% of all income.*Comment*: Partnership income comprised 3.62% of net income in the <5 class, rose to 8.74% of net income in the 10<25 class (partners in law, accounting, engineering firms, etc.), then gradually fell to 3.97% in the 1 million>over class. As most of Wall

Street operated as partnerships at this time, the twenty-nine partners of J. P. Morgan & Co., for instance, earned their income from the firm's operations based on their partnership interests.

7. Capital net gain from assets held more than 2 years: 6.49% of all income. *Comment*: This is the income category where stock investors who held stocks long-term reported their investment gains. Today, we call this category "long-term capital gains." It is noteworthy that *no* filers in the first three net income classes had any capital net long asset gains in 1928, most likely because these filers were not wealthy enough in 1928 to have owned a stock for two years. The first income class entry was 1.74% of net income in the 25<50 class and, not surprisingly, rose steadily to 47.31% in the 1 million>over class. Reliance on long-term investments as an income source verifies their dominance among investors, as distinct from speculators.

8. Rents and royalties: 4.02% of all income. *Comment*: All net income classes received rent and royalty income from such holdings as investment properties, mineral, oil or gas rights, patent licensing or creative endeavors like books and music composition. However, the prominence of this category dropped steadily from 5.51% of net income in the <5 class to 0.63% of income in the 1 million>over class. From this, we might say that the higher the income, the more likely it was that these high earners were making their money from investments (capital gains), some of which may have been attributable to innovation or invention, and a much smaller group for their creativity in the arts, such as likely filers George Gershwin, Irving Berlin or Cole Porter.

9. Fiduciary: 1.53% of all income.*Comment*: This income source comes from the management of trusts and estates, and the greatest share of income from this source was in the 10<100 net income classes where it is likely most attorneys fell.

10. Interest on Government obligations not wholly exempt from tax: 0.14% of all income.*Comment*: This was not a material income source for any income class.

Separating the Speculators from the Investors in 1928

We focus first on 1928 because it was a full year of enthusiastic and growing speculation unchecked by a Crash. Table 4.5 (page 103)—reproduced from *SOI for 1928* and using our shortened versions of the IRS column heading descriptions—identifies who in the upper income classes was doing what with their money—specifically as it came to speculation and investing. The gains of stock *speculators* appear in the fourth source of income from our list above, "Profit from sale of assets held 2 years or less." Table 4.5 shows that speculative gains accounted for 10.1% of overall 1928 income and occurred in *all net income classes*. However, short gains were heaviest proportionally in the 25<50 class, where they accounted for a material 20.46% of net income. (Hereafter we designate the 25<50 class as the "most speculating income class.")

SOI for 1928 revealed that 68,048 taxfilers in 1928 were in the 25<50 income class, 111,232 returns were in all 25>over income classes and 1,010,887 returns in all classes 5>over. How does knowing that data help us identify speculators?[6]

Slightly more than 4 million tax returns were filed both in 1928 and 1929 as Table 4.1 (page 97) shows, but despite claims that "everyone" was speculating, estimates as to a realistic number of speculators in the late 1920s was considerably smaller. The best estimation of the number of speculators in any year from 1928-1933

6 *SOI for 1928*, p. 4.

is found in *Stock Exchange Practices* (hereafter *SEP*), which was the formal report of the Senate Committee on Banking and Currency on hearings conducted in 1932-4 into speculation, the Crash and its aftermath. History knows these hearings informally as the Pecora Hearings acknowledging Ferdinand Pecora, the Committee's effective main counsel. According to *SEP*, the U.S. had a total of 29 stock exchanges with 1,548,707 customers. *SEP* also offered that 61.31% of the customers' transactions were of a cash character, and just under 600,000 were of a margin character. The NYSE "had 1,371,920 customers out of the total" and "the transactions of 559,984, or 40.81 percent, of their customers were of a margin character."[7] It is clear (at least to us) that speculation could, and did, occur on both a cash basis and a margin basis, though it was margin buyers who got into the most trouble in the week of the Crash.

As a point of interest, we chose to base our estimations on the number of accounts, even though a single account could be in more than one name. Fathers and children or husbands and wives did not necessarily have separate accounts, meaning that speculation by one member of a family might well include others in the family. Ramifications from trading might impact any number of members in a family unit associated with an account that was actively traded.

Using these assumptions and our research, we can make several conclusions about speculation demographics. One is that in our view the "most speculating income class" was the 25<50 class. Our second conclusion is that speculators numbered fewer than one million and, most likely, in the 500,000 range.

In contrast to speculators, the gains of investors—those who bought and held stocks for the long-term (two years or more at the time)—appear in the fifth income source category, "Capital net gain from assets held more than 2 years." In 1928, long-term investment gains accounted for 6.49% of all income. But in this regard income class mattered. The lowest three net income classes had *no* long-term investment gains. As net income rose, however, long-term gains also

---

7 *SEP*, p. 9.

rose. For the 100<150 net income class, both long-term investment gains *and* short-term speculative gains actually exceeded wage and salary income. For net income classes of 150>over, the value of long investment gains plus dividends on stock of domestic corporations exceeded the value of all other sources of income put together. Within the rarified net income class of 1 million>over, long investment gains alone approached all other sources of income combined. The statistics are clear: the higher the net income, the more likely the taxpayer was to have long-term gains to report.

Differentiating Long-Term Gains and Losses from Short-Term Gains and Losses

The tax codes and tax treatment at the time highlight the focus of the IRS on long-term *net* gains as a source of income—i.e., long-term gains minus long-term losses. This treatment of long-term gains contrasted with the reporting of short-term gains. Short-term gains appeared "above the line" as a gross figure, and short-term losses appeared "below the line" as a deduction. In the late 1920s and early 1930s, losses on capital investments held for at least 2 years were eligible for a 12.5% tax *credit.* In contrast, short-term losses could be written off, but there was no tax credit for those losses. This distinction raised its head significantly in 1929.

As a result of the different treatments, we rendered the 1928 and 1929 statistics on capital gains—long-term and short-term—into comparable forms. As observed above, Table 4.4 (page 102) treats long-term capital gains and losses differently from short-term capital gains and losses. because those with long-term capital gains were allowed to reduce that amount by any long-term capital losses. In contrast, short-term losses appear as a "below the line" deduction rather than as a reduction in an "above the line" source of income. The reality is, of course, that losses have real impact whether they are long-term or short-term, and treating short-term capital losses separately from any short-term gains obscures the impact of those losses on the people whose income the losses pertained to. A new table comes to our aid to rectify this distinct and misleading treatment.

We recast the IRS data from earlier tables into Table 4.7 (opposite) by treating short-term losses in the same way the IRS treated long-term losses—as an above-the-line deduction from gross long-term gains. This makes it easier—in a decidedly more dramatic way—to see exactly how negatively short-term losses, likely from speculation, impacted earners in 1929 in contrast with 1928. First, we simplified the thirteen income classes by dividing them into under or over $100,000 (<100 and >100). The upper portion of the table presents statistics on short-term gains or profits for these two broader income categories for 1928 and 1929.

The contrast in numbers between the two years tells a big story about material declines in wealth. Looking at 1929 in particular, from the $2,338 million total profit from short-term asset sales, we subtracted the $996 million in net short-term losses shown in Table 4.4 (page 102) under General deductions—"below the line" as the IRS would have placed them—to arrive at a greatly reduced Revised Total under Short-Term Profits of $1,342 million. Right away we see the huge change from 1928 to 1929, with short-term gains down 20% at the same time short-term losses increased from $172 million to almost one billion dollars. For 1928, the Revised Total of Short-Term Profits of $2,756 million was almost twice as much as in 1929.

What do these statistics say about the impact of the Crash? Even with the Crash not occurring until the last quarter of the year, the combination of the much larger short-term losses with 20% lower short-term gains in 1929 indicates the true impact of the Crash on taxfilers' income and their sense of well-being. Again, income class mattered in terms of the particular impact of lower short-term gains and larger short-term losses.

Table 4.7 (opposite) makes two other trends clear. First was the growth in the participation of net income classes <100 in generating Short-Term Profits—the speculators' category—from 75.3% in 1928

Table 4.7				
Gains 1928-1929				
Short-term net gains ($ million)				
Net income class	1928	% of Total	1929	% of Total
Under $100,000	2,205.8	75.3	1,947.4	83.3
$100,000 and over	722.3	24.7	390.2	16.7
Total	2,928.1		2,337.6	
Short-term losses	-171.7		-995.9	
Revised total	2,756.4		1,341.7	
Long-term net gains ($ million)				
Net income class	1928	% of Total	1929	% of Total
Under $100,000	295.0	15.7	286.4	12.2
$100,000 and over	1,584.8	84.3	2,060.3	87.8
Grand total	1,879.8		2,346.7	

Source: IRS *Statistics of Income 1928* and *1929*, and authors' calculations.

to 83.3% in 1929. The other trend was that for those making >100, participation in speculative trading shrank from 24.7% in 1928 to 16.7% in 1929. *These two trends make it obvious that while lower net income classes became more involved in speculation, the higher net income classes became less involved.* There is more to say on this observation.

Comparing Income Sources in 1929 with 1928

In Table 4.8, (page 113) we make use of our Table 4.7 analysis as to the true impact of Short-term losses in 1929 and return to the ten aggregate sources of income we examined in Table 4.4 (page 102). Arrows show how two particular sources of income—Short-term profits and Long-term gains—swapped places in terms of ranking between 1928 and 1929. [8] Short-term profits fell from 4th to 7th and Long-term gains—the 7th source of income 1928—moved

8 The Short profits figure for each year is taken from the Revised Total in Table 4.8.

up to 4th. Before we turn to short profits and long gains, however, a brief review of the other sources of income conveys the prosperity of the time.

Table 4.8 (opposite) shows us that, indeed, 1928 was very prosperous and suggests that 1929, at least until the Crash, was even more so.

• The growth of income from the largest income source, Wages and salaries, was a respectable 3.1% and would almost certainly have been higher had the Crash not occurred, but most tax-paying Americans, at least, were still employed at the end of 1929. (The growth of Wages and salaries in 1928 over 1927 was 6.3%.).

• Dividends, the 2nd largest income source in both years, rose a healthy 9.9% in 1929 over 1928.

• Business income, the 3rd largest source, was up 4.2% in 1929 over 1928 (after declining 1.3% from 1927.)

• The 5th source of income in both years was Interest income, which rose 3.2% over 1928. Short-term interest rates were high in the first three quarters of 1929, though they fell significantly following the Crash, sharply reducing the attractiveness of the call loan market as we shall see in the next chapter. In contrast, longer-term interest rates remained relatively steady.

• In 1928, Partnership income (an important income source for the partners of investment firms that mainly operated as partnerships at the time) was the 6th source and rose 10.0% over 1927 reflecting the buoyancy of that exuberant year of speculation before falling 4.0% in 1929 due to the impact of the Crash.

• Income from Rents, the 8th source, was up 10.4%.

• Even the minor 9th category of Fiduciary income grew 14.4% perhaps indicating an increase in legal fees for trusts and estates as clients reassessed their financial health.

• Finally, the tiny quantity of "Interest on Government obligations not wholly exempt from tax," the smallest source of income, fell a modest 2.4%.

• As to Long-term gains, 1929 as noted was a strong year for

Table 4.8

Comparison of Sources of Income for 1928 and 1929

($ million)

	1928			1929		Percent Change
1	Wages and salaries	$10,862		Same	$11,199	+3.1%
2	Dividends	4,351		Same	4,780	+9.9%
3	Business	3,244		Same	3,379	+4.2%
4	Short profits	2,756		Long gains	2,347	+24.8%
5	Interest	2,143		Same	2,211	+3.2%
6	Partnership	1,930		Same	1,853	-4.0%
7	Long gains	1,680		Short profits	1,341	-51.3%
8	Rents	1,165		Same	1,286	+10.4
9	Fiduciary	444		Same	508	+14.4%
10	Interest on Gov. securities	41		Same	40	-2.4%

Source: IRS *Statistics of Income 1928* and *1929*, and author's calculations.

long-term profit-taking through capital asset sales, with Long gains up 24.8% over 1928. Between 1928 and 1929, *investors increased their profit-taking 39.7%* from $1,680 million to $2,347 million. These transactions as reported to the IRS were sufficiently large in aggregate to account for the rise in the ranking of Long gains from 7th to 4th in 1929. Had the Crash not occurred, Long gains might well have gone even higher. It is certainly reasonable to posit that investors realized a major portion of these long gains in the months before the Crash, even as many wearing their speculator hats were also realizing short profits. However, given that many stock prices did not fall back quite to 1927 levels either during or after the Crash, investors, though much diminished, were still—at least selectively—able to realize long gains late in 1929.

• However, while Long gains were up in 1929, Short profits, as already discussed, went down significantly, particularly in late 1929, indicating how differently speculators experienced 1929 from investors. Short profits, which had risen 61.5% in 1928 (over 1927), fell 51.3% in 1929. A fall of this magnitude had to impact speculators in terms of their financial well-being.

Considering Speculator and Investor Activity—A New Lens

Table 4.9					
Average 1928 Income Per Filer					
Category ($ thousand)	Filers in category	Wages & salaries	Profit from short-term sales	Capital net long gains	Dividend income
< 5	3,059,964	$ 1913	$ 74	------	$ 111
5 < 10	628,766	3,547	579	------	697
10 < 25	270,889	5,554	2,626	------	3,084
25 < 50	68,048	8,848	9,051	684	10,201
50 < 100	27,207	12,453	13,064	9,133	23,572
100 < 150	7,049	16,467	22,211	26,242	42,976
150 < 300	5,678	20,444	35,211	58,558	66,399
300 < 500	1,756	26,035	61,460	125,225	118,180
500 < 1,000	983	30,737	111,324	271,734	200,537
1,000 & over	511	48,298	290,585	1,135,595	618,651
Total	4,070,851				

Source: *SOI for 1928*, pp. 4 & 8 and author's calculations.

Table 4.10					
Average 1929 Income Per Filer					
Category ($ thousand)	Filers in category	Wages & salaries	Profit from short-term sales	Capital net long gains	Dividend income
< 5	3,012,256	$ 1998	$ 98	------	$ 179
5 < 10	658,039	3,655	495	------	769
10 < 25	271,454	5,797	2,280	------	4,280
25 < 50	63,689	9,215	7,234	447	11,558
50 < 100	24,073	12,604	10,316	10,714	26,827
100 < 150	6,376	16,351	12,712	36,616	47,854
150 < 300	5,310	20,430	20,776	79,576	71,104,08
300 < 500	1,641	26,143	29,375	183,678	122,574
500 < 1,000	976	29,658	52,985	361,180	218,586
1,000 & over	513	49,633	193,056	1,482,159	645,509
Total	4,044,327				

Source: *SOI for 1929*, pp. 5 & 9 and author's calculations.

When making use of demographic data, it is helpful to look from different points of view at what occurred in any particular period of time. One of those different points of view utilizes averaging—creating data of the "average" or typical individual in a sample in order to gain a better understanding of what data show in human terms. Tables 4.9 and 4.10 (opposite) reconfigure the income-class data to show how the statistics would look for the average person in each of the ten net income-class categories. Our objective in creating these tables was to see if we could discern how activities in the stock market in 1928 and 1929 looked to the hypothetical average speculator and investor by income class, while keeping in mind that some individual members of any income class earned far more or far less than that class's average and thus could have had far different experiences.

Averaging showed that *every net income class included people who speculated at least to some extent* simply because filers in each class reported "Profit from sale of assets held 2 years or less." Further, these tables show that every net income class also reported dividend income, presumably indicating they owned equities. But for the three lowest net income classes, the equity positions that paid dividends appeared to be of a kind that were utterly illiquid (such as equity in family-owned enterprises or interests in mutual savings banks, mutual insurance companies or small country banks) and thus not available to sell in order to speculate.

A Word About Mob Psychology

As we attempted to distinguish speculators from investors, we found descriptive reflections by several prominent writers of the time. Turning to an unquantifiable though unfortunately recognizable aspect of human nature, Gilbert Seldes, in his 1933 history *The Years of the Locust (America, 1929-1932)*, described a collective environment feeding on the momentum of the soaring stock market in 1928 and early 1929:

> America in 1928, and the first months of 1929, was a mob, a little maddened by the sight of sudden wealth, its hysteria concealed because it was making money, which is the normal thing to do in America....There was a chance

> that if the warnings of the Federal Reserve, and the more specific warnings of the industrial records, were accepted by the Government and a check put to speculation, the break in Wall Street could have been averted; yet if the warning were issued, it might bring on the very calamity it intended to avoid. That is the argument. Behind it lies the awful symptom of panic—indecision. The individual lacked courage to withdraw from the market, because the financial mob might hoot; the Government lacked courage to tell the truth and continued to inflate public optimism like a small boy who is afraid to stop blowing up a balloon. The America of eccentrics, of individuals with strength of character enough not to want to make too much money, disappeared in these years engulfed in a mob.[9]

In his 1957 autobiography *My Own Story* written when he was 87, eminent financier and advisor to many presidents Bernard Baruch pondered about how the Crash could possibly have happened. He attributed it simply to both crowd and market madness. Baruch had gained wisdom from Englishman Charles MacKay's 1841 opus, *Extraordinary Popular Delusions and the Madness of Crowds.* Long out of print, the book was re-issued in October 1932 with an enthusiastic Foreword by Baruch. According to the book's Publisher's Note, Baruch's library contained a "battered calf-bound volume, the perusal of which he said had saved him millions of dollars." [10] In *My Own Story*, Baruch mused:

> Just why do we fall victim to such madnesses as the frenzy of stock market gambling that preceded the 1929 crash? I believe it is largely a reflection of the curious psychology of crowds which has been demonstrated again and again

9 Seldes (1933), p. 41.

10 Charles MacKay, *Extraordinary Popular Delusions and the Madness of Crowds*, L.C. Page & Company, 1932, p. xi, xiii.

> in human history....No nation has been immune to these frenzies....Perhaps it is the same kind of force that motivates the migrations of birds or the mass performances of whole species of ocean eels....Education and high rank is no immunization against the virus....[T]he stock market madness of 1927 to 1929 swept through every level of society.
>
> Repeatedly in my market operations I have sold a stock while it still was rising—and that has been one reason why I have held on to my fortune. Many a time I might have made a good deal more by holding a stock, but then I would also have been caught in the fall when the price of the stock collapsed. If I have missed some opportunities for money making because of this practice, I have also avoided "going broke," as I have seen many other man do....I have bought when things seemed low enough and sold when they seemed high enough. In that way I have managed to avoid being swept along to those wild extremes of market fluctuations which prove so disastrous.[11]

It is also instructive to recall the words of Alexander Dana Noyes from 1938 and cited in Chapter 8 of *How the Crash Caused*, about the strength of prevailing attitudes. Here, in a more extended version, Noyes writes of the warning against speculation given by Paul Warburg, whom Noyes described as being "alone of all eminent New York bankers":

> Unless what [Warburg] bluntly called "the orgy of unrestrained speculation" could be stopped, not only would ultimate collapse cause personal disaster to the speculators, "but it would also bring about a general depression involving the entire country." This was plain language; it came from

11 Bernard M. Baruch, *My Own Story,* Holt, Rinehart and Winston, 1957, pp. 241-3.

> a high source, and the longer sequel proved it to be perhaps the most accurate prediction made in that strange era. But, except for a brief reaction on the Stock Exchange, the sober warning had no visible effect. Professional Wall Street's usual comment on the speech ranged from characterization of Warburg's arguments as "obsolete" to description of his public warnings as "sandbagging American prosperity," or to the suggestion that anyone who talked like that must have some ulterior purpose of his own. To the speculating public Warburg's warnings first caused alarm, then indignation, and presently, when the stock market resumed its upward rush, expressions of supercilious contempt. For when, as happened in December of 1928 and in March 1929, a sudden break in stocks was quickly followed by a tempestuous recovery to heights previously unattained, belief in an indefinitely continued rise seemed to be irresistible.[12]

Clearly, our data and statistics on 1928-29 must be situated in context of the vagaries of the human personality, especially when confronted with the irresistible prospect of making easy money.

The "Game of Speculation"—Who Played It and How Was It Played?

As discussed earlier, statistics on the precise number of speculators vary hugely and have been, by our reckoning, impossible to substantiate conclusively. We reported that the Pecora Hearings in 1933 revealed that U.S. stockbrokers collectively had nearly 1,800,000 brokerage accounts held by their 1,548,707 customers, of which about one third, or 600,000, were margin accounts. We previously quoted John T. Flynn, Pecora Hearings' investigator, as reporting, "The game of speculation is one played by some three or four thousand insiders and some half a million outsiders on terms of

12 Noyes (1938), p. 324.

complete inequality."[13] We stand by our estimate of about 500,000.

But how was the game of speculation actually played by the few insiders and the many outsiders? One way revealed by direct questioning of begrudging Wall Street witnesses during the contentious Pecora Hearings was that those rarified insiders—who were professionals on Wall Street—formed investment "pools," the express purpose of which was quickly to drive up the prices of individual stocks, RCA being only one example. That rapid rise alerted the less informed outsiders that the stock was "in play." Seizing what they saw as an opportunity of the moment, the outsiders dove in, acquiring shares like fish to fish food. When the stock price reached a higher level that represented an acceptable gain or when insider information made selling advisable, the insiders sold their stock and exited the game, booking their quickly-made profits. The buying spree of the larger group of outsiders drove the price higher still until demand tapered off. Lucky outsiders—or perhaps practiced ones—sold and booked profits. So long as the market generally rose, the outsiders, in fact, usually made profits, but their gains were neither as certain nor as large as those of the insiders, and timing, as always, was key.

Speculation was a game of chance, akin to gambling, especially for the information-disadvantaged outsiders, where timing determined outcome. Knowing when to take those quick profits mattered—whether on a hunch, advice from a reliable source or a stock reaching some pre-established profit goal firmly adhered to.

Referring back to the data in Tables 4.5 and 4.6 (page 103-104), we see that while all taxfiler classes participated in "Profit from short-term asset sales" in 1928 and 1929, one particular class, as we said, caught our eye: 25<50, the income class we designated the "most speculating income class." In this class, undeniably affluent for the times, the highest percentage of net income from Profit from

---

13 John Brooks, *Once in Golconda: A True Drama of Wall Street 1920-38* Allwood Press, 1969, p. 68. How, when and where Flynn, who later became an ultra-conservative who supported repeal of the income tax amendment and opposed U.S. entry into World War II, arrived at his estimates is unknown. Brooks did not identify the source of Flynn's estimates.

short-term asset sales occurred in both years: 20.46% in 1928 and 17.75% in 1929. It was also in this net income class that "Capital net long asset gains" first appeared in both tables, though it was only 1.74% of net income in 1928 and 1.10% in 1929, indicating that a few in that income class had been investing over two years. Regardless, for many people in this income class, speculation had stopped being a game; it was the road to riches.

We also did some combining in order to corroborate Flynn's estimates of the number of speculators, particularly his figure of half a million disadvantaged outsiders. There were 270,889 1928 filers and 271,454 1929 filers in the 10<25 net income class who reported short gains in both 1928 and 1929, but *no* capital net gain from sale of long-term assets. Adding these filers to all net income classes above them we arrive at totals of 382,121 in 1928 and 374,032 in 1929, providing yet another supportable estimate of the number of stock market speculators. [14]

What Were the Benefits of Speculation?

As to identifying who was speculating, we came to see from the data on who reported earning short gains that the net income classes earning 10>over were the ones involved in that risky activity, and those in the 25<50 class dominated.[15] The prospect of *getting* rich motivated speculators in these affluent but less than wealthy net income classes. They enjoyed their gains, at least for a time, though they had become aggressive risk-takers, blind to the approaching debacle.

Using the statistics in Tables 4.4 (page 102) and 4.5 (page 103), we readily calculated the benefits of speculation in 1928. For example, Table 4.4 shows that while all 1928 taxfilers received 37.47% of their total income in the form of Wages and salaries, they received 10.10% of their total income from "Profit from sale of assets held 2 years or less."

---

14 *SOI for 1928*, p. 4, and *SOI for 1929*, p. 5.

15 $10,000 in 1929 = $179,384 in 2025.

Even taxfilers who filed but met only the barest minimum requirement for filing evidently participated in the bonanza. In 1929, a married couple who lived together was required to file if they had a net income of $3,500. A couple with that income, for example, composed of wages of $2,757 and short-term speculative profits (not common for their income class) of $743 would complete IRS Form 1040 A. On it they would report a total income of $3,500, subtract the personal exemption of $3,500 they were entitled to and end up with no taxable income or tax liability.[16] Yet, they saw a material 27% increase in their disposable income that year due to speculative profits.

Life for the Most Speculating Income Class

In both Table 4.5 (page 103) and 4.6 (page 104), as we have said, the highest percentage of "Profit from sale of assets held two years or less" occurred in the 25<50 net income class: 20.48% in 1928 and 17.75% in 1929. To picture life for this "most speculating income class" we give an overview of the brokerage industry at the time, then shift to a description of a typical branch office, informally called a "wirehouse," to depict their actual trading environment. Firms were called "wirehouses" because they traditionally received stock prices and transaction information via glass dome-topped "ticker" equipment that used telegraph lines. Their in-house stockbrokers, called then "customers' men," placed orders and communicated with headquarters in New York by telephone.

A macro view of the brokerage industry as stock trading gained in popularity confirms tremendous growth in the number of branch offices around the country. According to the *New York Stock Exchange YEAR BOOK 1929-1930*, in 1923 there were 741 branch offices of NYSE member brokerage firms, with 129 in New York and 612 located "Out-of-Town." By the beginning of 1928, there were 1,059 branch offices; 203 were in New York and 856 were Out-of-Town. The beginning of 1929 saw 1,392 branch offices, 280 of which were

16 *SOI for 1930,* p. 335.

in New York and 1,112 were Out-of-Town. And by the beginning of 1930, of 1,658 branch offices, 294 were in New York and 1,364 were Out-of-Town.[17] In and of itself, this more than doubling of the number of wirehouses from 1923-1930 signaled the growing frenzy across the country, as well as the eagerness with which the brokerage industry expanded in order to meet and encourage that explosion in demand.

In our era of trading stocks on laptops and smartphones, it is instructive to describe, from long-ago first-hand experience, a typical wirehouse in New York or any "out-of-town" city and convey the environment for eager stock market participants in the late 1920s.[18] The office was situated at street level for easy access by customers, who, well familiar with the company stock symbols, wanted to follow trades and prices. In terms of look, the space was probably smaller than a tennis court, had high ceilings and was broken down into a large customers' room, a back office and several small conference rooms. (New York wirehouses could be much larger and busier.)

The key locus for action was the customers' room. Dimly lit, it was furnished simply with rows of 10 to 20 chairs divided by one or two aisles where customers sat or stood and watched a large blackboard hung on a wall and lit by spotlights and a large rear-projection Trans-Lux screen at the top of the blackboard (state of the art at the time and soon to be introduced in movie theaters). Behind the blackboard was the stock ticker, which printed its data on translucent "paper" tape fed automatically over a projector and projected its on-going feed of stock quotes onto the Trans-Lux screen. Meanwhile, several "boardmarkers" used chalk to mark the current prices of perhaps a thousand stocks shown on the ribbon of ticker tape next to the stock's symbol on the blackboard. Every

---

17 NYSE, *New York Stock Exchange YEAR BOOK 1929-1930.*

18 Our description of the "look and feel" within a wirehouse comes from experience by one author who once, very early in his career, filled in for three vacationing longtime "boardmarkers," men who had worked writing stock prices on a big chalk board for a Chicago firm during and well after this period.

day, a record of prices for each stock grew in length and was not erased until after the wirehouse closed in the evening for cleaning. Customers interested in the price of a particular stock could shout out an identifier such as "Radio" for RCA or "Steel" for U.S. Steel and a boardmarker shouted back with the most current price of the stock. Along the long wall opposite the blackboard was a raised dais bordered by a brass railing where stockbrokers sat behind desks. To execute trades, customers approached their stockbroker and placed a buy or sell order. As the order was executed, customers learned the price at which they had traded.

As for 1,392 NYSE brokerage firm branch offices that existed at the end of 1928 and the beginning of 1929, how many speculating customers could these offices reasonably accommodate? Unable to find statistics on wirehouse customer capacity, we made some guesstimates based on the varying sizes of the nation's wirehouses in order to arrive at a rough total daily capacity of 190,000 customers, far short of the half a million speculators who, in the crisis of the October Crash period, would have overwhelmed the capacity of every wirehouse in the country. Perhaps this is why photographs of Wall Street during the Crash showed such large crowds outside; the space in brokerage offices was limited (given the fire codes).

Indeed, we can also only imagine the noise level in those crowded and smoke-filled customers' rooms as nervous speculators and brokers exchanged hot tips and updates and shouted out orders, interspersed with various epithets. An unusual commingling of diverse speculators, from our "most speculating income class" of the well-to-do (25<50) to taxi cab drivers and elevator operators who didn't earn enough to file tax returns, united in this fraught environment in the singular hope-filled desire to make money and improve their circumstances.

Again, looking at the numbers, we suspect it is likely that many in the 25<50 income class were, to some degree, speculators. The average taxfiler received 10.10% of his or her income from short-term capital gains, but the 68,048 members of the 25<50 class received more than twice that, or 20.46% of their incomes from short-term capital gains. This reliance suggests that the members of the 25<50 class probably spent time, even an unusually high proportion of their time, in their local wirehouse, with some even employed by the firm.

Tables 4.4, 4.5, and 4.6 (pages 102-104) enable us to see readily what sources of income predominated in what income classes. Taking the 25<50 income class, an affluent income class at the time, and, as we have said, a class in which it is likely nearly everyone speculated, the short-term gains statistics for 1928 confirm that these gains contributed a material 20.46% of their total income. As this was an aggregate figure, for some in this class the percentage was much higher, especially if they had shifted income sources from earning a salary to trading for gains. Table 4.5 shows that in 1928 "Wages and salaries" contributed 22.5% of income, and "Dividends on stock of domestic corporations" contributed 25.95%, for a total of almost 69% of income coming from those three sources to the 25<50 class. For 1929—and keeping in mind that the number of taxfilers in the 25<50 income class dropped 6.4% from 68,048 in 1928 to 63,689 in 1929, a measurable and indicative decline—we can also see in Table 4.4 that while Wages and salaries went up from 1928 to 1929 overall (despite the slight decline in the category's weight), Table 4.6 shows that "Wages and salaries" for 25<50 were basically stable (22.6%). However, income from "Dividends on stock of domestic corporations" increased to 28.36% of total income, and, more significantly on the downside, short-term gains dropped from 20.46% to 12.66% of income, indicating less success speculating for income. Those same three income sources for 1929 contributed 63.62% of total income, down almost 10% from the prior year.

Table 4.4 also shows that while income grew from 1928 to 1929, the dollar size of "Profits from sale of assets held 2 years or less" or short-term gains—the measure of speculation—fell, not just as a percentage of income earned from that source, but in dollar amounts: from $2,928.1 million in 1928 to $2,337.9 million in 1929, a drop of 20.2%. Comparison of Tables 4.5 and 4.6 shows that speculation income dropped in *every net income class but one* (the class labeled <5). What's more, the drop in short-term gains was especially significant in the five 100>over income classes; for each of these, those gains declined from double-digit growth in 1928 to single-digit growth in 1929. *SOI for 1928* reported that the highest-income classes contributed $722.3 million in tax revenue in 1928. A year later, *SOI for 1929* reported that these five high-income classes contributed 46% less, or $390.2 million, in 1929, making it clear that the investor classes had turned significantly away from speculation in 1929, though they continued influencing the situation nonetheless, as we shall see.

From Investors' Point of View

Up until now, the story of the late 1920s through the Crash has been told from the point of view of speculators. Central to the overall story are narratives about brokerages and their financing of speculation—margin accounts, margin calls, the call money market and the commensurate ballooning of brokers' loans— and half-hearted attempts by the Fed, as it functioned at that time, to rein in speculation. We now turn to another group of Wall Street participants, investors.

In Table 4.11, (page 127) a second net income class catches the eye: 100<150 (the equivalent of $1.7 to $2.6 million today). In this rarefied income class of the wealthy—numbering only 7,049 in 1928 and dropping 10% to 6,376 in 1929—the percentage of net income they earned from "Capital net gain from assets held more than 2 years" for the first time clearly exceeded that from "Profit from sale of assets held 2 years or less." This upper income class was where the interests of investors and investing predominated over the interests of short-term speculators and speculating. This shift became only more pronounced from a statistical point of view as income rose.

Generally speaking, what was in the interest of investors? It was simply to preserve and grow their wealth, i.e., to *stay* rich. Then, as now, experienced investors like Bernard Baruch tried to rehearse and practice prudent, risk-sensitive behavior as they made their investment decisions privately or in consultation with trusted advisors. Fortunately, we have tax returns and the aggregated IRS data to reveal exactly how the various upper-income tax classes changed their behavior and how they and/or their advisors managed their money, both short and longer term.

Of particular note, the data in Tables 4.9 and 4.10 (page 114) reveal that, while the average investor in every net income class 100>over speculated to some extent, none of them needed margin accounts for that purpose. Unless they were profligate or trying too hard to keep up with the Joneses whom they perceived as being wealthier, they had substantial dividend income and didn't need margin accounts to acquire or hold stocks. In keeping with professional investment practices, they sold stocks when they decided to take a profit (or realize a loss). Furthermore, if they sold, they probably didn't sell out all at once. Nor did they "plunge," buying entirely new positions aggressively as was common among speculators. Instead, they were likely widely invested and adjusted the weightings of their investment portfolio holdings—for example, the proportions of their stocks in industrials, railroads, and utilities—only gradually.

How might these upper-income investors have felt about the speculation they knew was taking place and about engaging in speculation themselves? Some may have told themselves that speculating kept them in touch with the market. Some of them were doubtless among John T. Flynn's "insiders" who used investment pools or trusts to game the system. Given that they were likely fully paid-up owners of stocks, some may well have quietly supported speculation, at least up to the point where things began to look dicey, since speculator activity drove up share prices, thus increasing the value of their portfolios.

But dicey periods did appear in December of 1928 and in March 1929 when the sudden breaks in stocks that Paul Warburg referred to took place. What might investors with stock market

Table 4.11

Short and Long-term Profit for 1928-1929, by Net Income Class

	1928	1929
Net income classes ($ million)	Profit from sale of assets held 2 years or less [1] ($ million)	Profit from sale of assets held 2 years or less [1] ($ million)
Under 5 (estimated)	227.6	293.8
5 under 10	364.0	325.8
10 under 25	711.4	618.8
25 under 50	547.4	460.7
50 under 100	355.4	248.3
100 under 150	156.6	81.0
150 under 300	199.9	110.3
300 under 500	107.9	48.2
500 under 1,000	109.4	52.7
1,000 and over	148.5	99.0
Total	2,928.1	2,338.9
Net income classes ($ million)	Capital net gain from sale of assets held more than 2 years ($ million)	Capital net gain from sale of assets held more than 2 years ($ million)
Under 5 (estimated)	----------	----------
5 under 10	----------	----------
10 under 25	----------	----------
25 under 50	46.5	28.5
50 under 100	248.5	257.9
100 under 150	185.0	223.5
150 under 300	332.5	422.6
300 under 500	219.9	301.4
500 under 1,000	267.1	352.5
1,000 and over	580.3	760.3
Total	1,879.8	2,346.7

[1] Labeled "Profit from sale of real estate, stocks, bonds, etc., other than taxed as capital net gain from sale of assets held more than 2 years" in IRS tables.

Source: IRS *Statistics of Income 1928* and *1929*.

gains have done in response? The data make it apparent that over the course of 1929, vigilant investors increasingly adopted and acted on Paul Warburg's point of view, regardless of what the publicized pundits said. As the data show, many of them, as a precaution, were taking long-term profits and sitting on the sidelines, at least of the stock market.

Sage and experienced investors clearly wavered during the 1928-29 stock market frenzy. As Bernard Baruch recalled in his 1960 memoir *The Public Years*:

> I shared my apprehension about the state of the market with others.....My opinion was asked. My advice was to pull out of speculative situations, get out of debt, and put one's funds into sound bonds. I don't think my advice was well-regarded.
>
> I, myself, was doing as I advised. By 1928, I had begun to liquidate my stock holdings and to put my money into bonds and into a cash reserve. I am very old-fashioned in this respect. I always like to have some hard cash around, especially in times of trouble.[19]

Baruch went on to describe a request to participate in a trust:

> In the summer of 1929, I went abroad...to Scotland.
>
> In August, I received an invitation to participate in the formation of two new investment trusts. Investment trusts were then the rage.... The Shenandoah and Blue Ridge

19 Baruch (1960), p. 222. In his 1997 biography, *Bernard Baruch: The Adventures of a Wall Street Legend*, James Grant writes of having scoured Baruch's Princeton University archive to review voluminous accounts of his actual stock trade records. It appears that in his memoirs Baruch was not so accurate about his results. He didn't cease trading altogether, but he did reduce the volume considerably.

corporations, whose stock I was being offered, were among the largest and, as events were to prove, the least solid.

I went for a walk with General Pershing, who was my guest. We talked at length about the state of affairs in America, and I expressed my growing concern over the danger signs in the market. As we strolled along, I went over all the factors involved in the Shenandoah and Blue Ridge issues; even at a distance of three thousand miles, I could see that these and many other enterprises were foolhardy. My intuition, which after all is the accumulated force of experience, was sending out warning signals.

I decided to shorten my stay in Scotland and depart for home.

Immediately after arriving in New York, I decided to sell everything I could, in anticipation of the break I now felt to be imminent. This was near the end of September. The condition of the market could be measured by its wild fluctuations, followed by assurances from every direction that all was well. But I had heard of this lullaby before. I knew that the continuity of confidence was beginning to break.[20]

Profit-Taking by Investors: Fuel for Speculation?

Of course, taking profits, as Baruch did, created the problem of what to do with the cash proceeds. One particular outlet that at least some availed themselves of (ultimately not including Baruch) turned out to fuel speculation further. At least for a time, some of these newly cash-flush investors became call loan lenders thus add-

20 Baruch (1960), pp. 224-5.

ing to the supply of call loan funds that brokers could then lend to margin clients. The attractive rates of return and call loans' liquidity appealed. Investors could keep rolling the loans over while searching for longer term investment opportunities. The statistics bear out that, indeed, call loan lending took place in this group. Participation in the call loan money market "By others [than banks]", the category that included individuals, rose $2,755 million, between December 31, 1928, and October 4, 1929, making it reasonable to conclude that at least some of the proceeds of the Capital net long asset gains were, indeed, invested in overnight call loans. While there is no way to know exactly how much was so invested, that some investor/lenders did so seems clear in the data. This, of course, was a short-term investment strategy that ended (or at least paused) with the Crash when these lenders withdrew from the call loan market as the perceived risk increased and the rates on call loans declined.

Overall, however, people of means tended to focus on making investments for the longer term and not in the overnight market, and the *SOI for 1929* verifies this emphasis. The "Long-term net gains" section in Table 4.7 (page 111) confirms that investors in the "$100,000 and above" net income classes made $2,060.3 million in Long-term net gains in the full year 1929. While the data don't show exactly when over the course of 1929 the long assets sales occurred or what was sold, investors may have sold long-term holdings due to the Crash and their awareness of the margin calls speculators were receiving. Like Baruch, they sought to lock in gains before some or all of those gains could evaporate.

In addition, accustomed to taking profits when stock prices were rising before the Crash, investors were unlikely to use long-term proceeds to buy in the furor of the Crash when stock prices were plummeting, especially following the failure of "organized support" to appear on Monday, October 28 or the next day, which history knows as "Black Tuesday."

The Last Four Months Leading Up to The Crash

Table 4.12								
Call Loan Statistics & Rates in 1929 ($ million)								
NYSE		Non-bank others				Call loan rates (%)	
Brokers' loans		Qtrly		Weekly		Date	New/Renewal
7/1	7,071	6/29	5,045	7/3	2,934	7/6	11.05/11.00
8/1	7,474			7/31	3,058	8/3	10.26/9.80
9/1	7,882			8/28	3,468	8/31	8.54/8.20
10/1	8,549	10/4	6,640	10/2	3,907	10/5	8.08/8.20
				10/16	3,875	10/19	6.29/6.40

Source: *NYSE* p.11, *BMS* pp.456, 484 & 488.

Table 4.12 provides another view of the data, this time using both Federal Reserve and NYSE statistics to look at call loan volumes lent by member banks on behalf of non-bank others, the category that included individual investors as well as corporations. In these statistics, which are based on the quarterly and weekly statistics of the Federal Reserve System as well as the NYSE weekly average call loan rates for new loans and renewals, two things are quite apparent.

In the three months from the beginning of July to the beginning of October 1929, the overall volume of call loans grew a remarkable 20.9%, an annualized rate of almost 84%. Significantly, in the same period, the overall volume of call loans lent by Fed Member Banks for the accounts of non-bank others grew at an even higher rate—31.6% on a quarterly basis, and the volume lent by weekly-reporting NYC banks for the accounts of non-bank others grew 33.2%.

A counter-intuitive trend is interesting to note, however: call loan rates were falling rapidly during this pre-Crash period, while the volumes lent in the call money market were exploding. Why would call loans explode in volume even as rates fell?[21] The answer

21 Later, by the week ending November 2, call loan rates had fallen sufficiently for individuals or companies with idle cash but also bank loans would have saved more by repaying their bank loans than by lending the cash in the call money market or investing in some other form of short-term instrument.

lies in the additional supply of investible cash that found its way into the call money market. Investors who had sold positions, as we've seen, entered the call loan market in the third quarter of 1929. But other entities entered as well. Newly established investment trusts, such as Shenandoah and Blue Ridge that pitched a skeptical Bernard Baruch, were likely among them. Lending by them of funds not immediately invested in stocks would be understandable in an environment of *rising* call money rates, but it is also obvious that a flood of new lending from new investment trusts could *cause* call money market rates to fall due to the law of supply and demand. Barrie Wigmore appeared to support this position when he wrote that investment trusts were widely active prior to the Crash:

> September witnessed a record volume of new issues… of which $1 billion was common stocks.…Virtually every significant common stock offering that month was for an investment company.[22]

Wigmore did not say who these entities were, nor did he estimate what proportion of stock issuers were investment trusts, how much money they actually raised, what amount they might have lent in the call money market or how fast these trusts might have withdrawn that lent money in order to invest in stocks. He merely stated that in the period of the Crash, "The investment trusts bought heavily…and were rumored to have exhausted their cash reserves."[23]

With no easy answers presenting themselves, we are left asking who else would have had cause to lend significant sums in the call money market as call money rates dropped significantly? To answer this, we return to investors who were making strategic moves at that time and suggest that a significant portion of the rise in the volume of call loans in the period leading up to the Crash

22 Wigmore (1985), p. 5. On p. 489, *BMS* reports the volume of new common stock issues in September 1929, as $858 million.

23 Ibid., p. 22.

was a reflection of the degree to which some investors, like Baruch, were increasingly uncomfortable holding appreciated long-owned securities and elected to take profits rather than risk holding them any longer. Table 4.7 (page 111) confirms that investors realized $2,347 million in long gains over the course of 1929. Baruch put his profits into bonds and a cash reserve (which could, of course, be held in call loans, though he didn't say). But the statistics in Table 4.12 suggest that other investors were not only aggressively getting out of the stock market in the months leading up to the Crash, but also putting the proceeds of their profit-taking into the call money market to get the best return available rather than simply holding idle cash. We propose that the drop in call money rates was importantly the result of investors' profit-taking in the months leading up to the Crash and of their search for return with the proceeds in a liquid short-term market that allowed for quick adjustment during these uncertain days.

The question has long been asked why the Crash occurred in October 1929. We suggest that the most likely answer is that, sensing a sea change, a great many uncomfortable investors like Bernard Baruch—autonomously and concurrently— had effectively ceased buying stocks. Instead of looking for opportunities to put money *into* the market, they were aggressively taking money *out* and had been doing so for months as they made autonomous (and usually private) decisions, first to reduce significantly their purchase of stocks, second to liquidate long-held positions and third—seeking both return and liquidity at least in the short-term—to lend the proceeds from their stock sales to the already bloated call money market. In doing so, however, they drove call money rates down and helped to push the stock market over the edge.

CHAPTER 5

Over-indebtedness Recognized: From Consumption to Repayment (1930)

Our focus thus far—primarily on the late 1920s and particularly 1929—shifts now to 1930, a year that began with what turned out to be false optimism. Before turning to our exploration of the facts that emerged from the IRS archives about this pivotal time, we briefly return to Charles Kindleberger to review the end of 1929 and the strong motivations of some of our Cast of Characters as 1930 began.

As quoted previously, Kindleberger in his 1973 book, *The World in Depression 1929-1939,* offered perspective on the precarious situation in the stock market and business in general at year-end 1929:

> Deflation, then, moved from the decline in stock markets to production cuts and inventory runoffs in one sequence, and from stock prices to commodity prices to the reduced value of imports in another. Both were fast....By the end of the year of 1929, credit markets were easing rapidly....[Though none of the] connections between the stock market and business conditions...can have had time to work in 1929....[s]uch of them that were expansive were overwhelmed by the cumulative forces of deflation already underway.[1]

With this backdrop of Kindleberger's gloomy take on the environment post-Crash, particularly the specter of deflation, we revisit

---

1 Kindleberger (1986), pp. 114-6.

the three most affected members of our Cast of Characters in terms of their new financial realities, moods and motivations:

Repentant Ex-Speculators (post-Crash). In the words of Bernard Baruch, "Many people I had known for years, professionals on Wall Street as well as amateurs, were wiped out."[2] In early October 1929, many participants had considered themselves financially secure, even comfortably rich. But by the end of 1929, their cushion of stocks had vanished, often replaced by major debt obligations incurred in a futile and self-injurious attempt to keep responding to margin calls. For Repentant Ex-Speculators (post-Crash), their future must have looked like one of involuntary servitude to their debtors. This bleak outlook motivated them to get out of debt as fast as possible and by whatever means it took. Borne out by statistics of the time, for a desperate, perhaps not-so-few, even suicide became an option.[3]

Debtors (in general). Individuals carrying debts such as mortgages, installment debts or credit accounts with merchants were accustomed to receiving monthly statements of the amounts due and then making those monthly payments. Following the Crash, these regular reminders caused debtors to contemplate how having to repay those debts would impact their standard of living. Those who were wage earners feared the implications if they were to have their pay cut, their hours reduced and certainly if they were laid off or lost their jobs altogether. The indignity, distress and upheaval of foreclosures or even repossessions loomed large. Many business owners, remembering the severe deflation of 1920-21 less than a decade earlier, feared having to service debts at fixed dollar amounts despite falling incomes and prices.

Corporate Financial Executives. Corporations, of course, also had debts. In depression times corporate financial executives focused especially on minimizing risks of insolvency (that is, running out of cash) and bankruptcy. As Irving Fisher observed, how much debt was owed and when it was due measured over-indebtedness.

2 Baruch (1960), p. 213.

3 One estimate is that there were between 18,000-20,000 suicides in the U.S. in 1930: https://www.acpjournals.org/doi/pdf/10.7326/0003-4819-5-2-232

The bottom line for corporate financial executives was to determine how much debt the corporation needed to pay off soon and how to replace that short-term debt with longer-term debt obligations, kicking the can, so to speak, further down the road when conditions would—optimistically speaking—improve.

Financial Management Tools Light the Way

In this chapter we focus on factual economic information about 1930 that, while well familiar to financial managers, is outside the normal scrutiny of both the Income-Expenditure Approach, as discussed in *How the Crash Caused* in Chapter 3, and the Monetary Approach considered in Chapter 4. For our purposes, the tools of financial analysis have been critical, enabling us to conduct what is, in essence, forensic financial analysis to look at the data for clues and suspects. The Income-Expenditure Approach focuses on facts normally found in income statements—revenues, expenses, profits, personal income, taxes, etc. The Monetary Approach focuses on facts about money stocks held by banks and the general public—demand deposits, time deposits, currency in circulation, etc.—as reported on bank balance sheets. Financial managers use those same critical tools to conduct analyses that utilize the data in income statements and balance sheets—and also go further, as we shall see shortly in our consideration of another tool, Sources and Uses of Funds statements.

Our emphasis here is on the data-backed realities of how corporations, including banks, evolved in the financing of their operations and their investment activities as the economy tottered. We have relied, for instance, on using balance sheets covering different time periods to make comparisons that show changes, trends and effects. The deeper analysis technique we bring in here, a Sources and Uses of Funds Analysis, well familiar to experienced financial executives and analysts, identifies where a firm's monetary assets come from—their sources and amounts—and the uses to which a business entity puts the funds. The entity being analyzed couldt be a single business or corporation, such as U.S. Steel; a group of businesses, such as the steel industry; or *all* businesses in a country, as the IRS *Statistics of Income for 1929* has provided for us. The IRS annual aggregate data for roughly a half million corporations in the United States is the particular entity we look at here.

As described in Chapter 6 in *How the Crash Caused*, the Internal Revenue Service submits public annual reports providing comprehensive data about both U.S. tax-filing individuals and U.S. corporations. These reports—*Statistics of Income* ("*SOI*")—contain what for us has been critical information—an Aggregate Balance Sheet for U.S. Corporations for a given year, e.g., *SOI for 1930*. Since all U.S. corporations were required to file tax returns, this compilation provided a thorough aggregate look at a particular point in time of all U.S. corporate activity, in every industry.

Within each year's Aggregate Balance Sheet is the asset category "Notes and accounts receivable," which, by definition, accounts for the short-term (near-term) debts due for payment to all corporations within one year of the date of the balance sheet. These debt payments for goods and services bought on credit are due, now as then, both from other corporations and, most critically, from individuals.

Also within each year's Aggregate Balance Sheet is the liability category "Notes and accounts payable," accounting for all the short-term (near-term) debt obligations due for payment by corporations within one year of the date of the balance sheet. Focusing specifically on the Crash and post-Crash period, the indebted corporations owed these liability payments primarily to other corporations, but also to individuals and other parties, as they came due for goods and services corporations purchased on credit. Other parties included, for example, the Federal Government and all manner of state and local government entities, such as water and sewage districts providing services to factories.

Of particular importance here is that our scrutiny of Notes and accounts receivable within these Aggregate Balance Sheets for 1930-33 revealed the large quantity of short-term debts that were owed to U.S. corporations at the end of 1929—*and repaid*. In accounting terms, creditor corporations, including banks, reported these short-term debts on their books as assets called "notes receivable."

Merchants offering installment plans who filed as corporations or sole proprietors booked them as assets called "accounts receivable."

As seen in Table 6.1 (*How the Crash Caused,*), Notes and accounts receivable reported in *SOI for 1929* for all U.S. corporations (including banks) were $66.8 billion. Four years later, Notes and accounts receivable reported in *SOI for 1933* had almost halved to $35.8 billion. Quite simply, $31.0 billion in short-term debt obligations, those due and payable within one year, were repaid to U.S. corporations, including banks, between December 31, 1929, and December 31, 1933, an average repayment of over $7.74 billion per year. This significant debt repayment amount had dire consequences.

As to who played a role in this repayment process in 1930 in the wake of the Crash and how much they repaid, answers emerge first by considering how much U.S. corporations repaid to other U.S. corporations, banks included. Secondly in this chapter, we focus on the enormous impact U.S. individuals, as consumers, had on this repayment process and explore to what degree these repayments were, in fact, a precipitating factor in the onset of the Great Depression. We bring in Peter Temin's *Did Monetary Forces* to offer our insights into his thinking about the economic influence of consumer behavior. Lastly, we also examine how monetarists Milton Friedman and Anna Schwartz dealt with this important reality in their *Monetary History.*

U.S. Corporate Sources and Uses of Funds in 1930

Table 5.1 (opposite) presents a Sources and Uses of Funds Analysis for 1930 based on the Aggregate Corporate Balance Sheets reported in the IRS data for 1929 and 1930. [4] This table identifies in which direction each asset and liability class changed over the course of 1930 and by how much. As a notable example, the data shows us that the amount of cash held by U.S. corporations (including banks) declined by $1,359 million during 1930 from $22,371 million to

4 *SOI for 1929,* p. 25; *SOI for 1930,* p. 27.

Table 5.1			
1930 Aggregate U.S. Corporate Sources & Uses of Funds ($ million)			
Assets	1929	1930	Difference
Cash	22,371	21,012	-1,359
Notes & accounts receivable	66,810	59,675	-7,135
Inventory	21,911	18,771	-3,140
Tax exempts	10,338	10,228	-110
Investments other	55,844	83,809	27,965
Capital assets	116,446	120,994	4,548
Misc.	42,057	19,511	-22,546
Total assets	335,778	334,002	-1,776
Liabilities			
Notes & accounts payable	29,453	26,870	-2,583
Bonded debt & mortgages	46,643	50,282	3,639
Misc.	94,714	95,768	1,055
Capital stock -			
Preferred	19,738	19,117	-621
Common	90,119	87,067	-3,052
Total capital stock	109,858	106,184	-3,674
Surplus	60,699	61,632	933
Less deficit	5,588	6,734	1,146
Net surplus	55,111	54,898	-213
Total liabilities	335,778	334,002	-1,776

Source: *SOI for 1929 & 30*: 1929, p.25, 1930, p.27.

$21,012 million, likely indicating an aggregate decline in revenue. The following 1929-30 year-over-year changes are noteworthy: [5]

5 The IRS also made changes in various classifications that had nothing to do with what was happening in the country. In particular, the increase of $27,965 million in "Investments other than tax exempt—Stocks, bonds, mortgages, loans, real estate, etc." and the decrease of $32,546 million in "Miscellaneous assets not distributed." These accounting changes arose out of a reassessment by IRS statistical accounting personnel of the nature of certain assets. They reevaluated and determined that a quantity of assets that had been held as "Miscellaneous assets not distributed" more properly constituted "Investments other than tax exempt—Stocks, bonds, mortgages, loans, real estate, etc." This reclassification, however, did not affect the total quantity of assets nor did it affect working capital. For the curious, these accounting changes were explained in *Statistics of Income for 1930*, pp 26-7.

- Decrease of $7,135 million in Notes and accounts receivable
- Decrease of $2,583 million in Notes and accounts payable
- Increase of $3,639 million in Bonded debt and mortgages
- Decrease of $3,674 million in Total capital stock

The first of these changes stands out because the decrease clearly indicates that borrowers who owed U.S. corporations (including banks) short-term or nearest-term funds—what notes and accounts receivable on a balance sheet measure—*repaid the large sum of $7,135 million* over the course of 1930. Notes and accounts receivable on the books of U.S. corporations shrank from $66,810 million owed on December 31, 1929 to $59,675 million owed on December 31, 1930. With the U.S. Gross National Product (in then-current dollars) declining from $103.4 billion in 1929 to $90.700 billion in 1930, those aggregate repayments comprised an impactful 7.87% of GNP for 1930.[6]

Over Half of the $7,135 Million Was Repaid to Banks

The next task of our analysis was to determine what portion of aggregate repayments was made to banks and what portion was made to non-bank corporations, such as manufacturers of consumer goods and department and other retail stores. We utilized Federal Reserve

6 For scale, 2023 U.S. GDP was $27.36 trillion. If reduced by 7.87%, GDP would drop by $2.15 trillion.

records to determine that outstanding loans by all commercial banks stood at $35,966 million on December 31, 1929, and had declined $3,932 million to $32,034 million by December 31, 1930.[7] Since in 1930 the great majority of U.S. banks were corporations (with a small number operating as private banks owned by partnerships or sole proprietors), we considered it to be reasonable to treat all commercial banks as corporations. Under this assumption, bank loan repayments accounted for about 55% of the $7,135 million in Notes and accounts receivable repaid to corporations (including banks) over the course of 1930.

While banks and non-bank corporations experienced similar declines, the impact on each segment reflected their distinct businesses. As we explored those distinctions and compared and analyzed different economic variables and corporate sectors, the IRS statistics on repayment of Notes and accounts payable to corporations (including banks) in 1930 revealed that in 1930 many non-bank corporations repaid loans (or notes) outstanding that they carried on their books as Notes and accounts payable to other non-bank corporations. The most likely reason for these payments was for costs of goods sold. These payments had been booked by non-bank corporations, generally speaking, for four types of sales made in the ordinary course of business:[8]

- Sales of raw materials to industrial corporations (e.g., commodities like copper, iron, etc.)

- Sales to industrial corporations of semi-finished manufactured goods (e.g., steel, automobile parts such as upholstery and glass)

- Sales of finished goods and services to all corporations (e.g.

7 *BMS,* p. 19.

8 These payments by non-bank corporations to other non-bank corporations are also distinct from bank repayments because these payments do not impact the money supply.

factory machinery, office equipment, store cleaning supplies, etc.)

- Sales of all kinds of finished goods and services to consumers.[9]

Since Notes and accounts receivable include both notes (i.e. loans due within one year) and accounts receivable (i.e., sums owed as payments for sales of goods and services), this aggregated category presented a data roadblock, for as rich as the IRS archives are, they did not break down what portion of the $7,135 million repaid constituted repayments of notes as distinct from accounts receivable

Table 5.2

Spreading the Repayments of $7,135 Million Over 1930 on the Basis of Bank Loan Repayments

($ million)

All commercial banks				
	Total loans	Change in loans	Period %	Change in notes & accounts receivable
12/31/29	35,966			
6/30/30	34,539	-1,427	36.3%	-2,590
12/31/30	32,034	-2,505	63.7%	-4,545
Total change	-3,932	-3,932	100.0%	-7,135
All member banks				
	Total loans	Change in loans	Period %	Change in notes & accounts receivable
12/31/29	26,150			
3/27/30	25,119	-1,031	-45.2%	-3,225
6/30/30	25,214	+95	+4.2%	+300
9/24/30	24,738	-476	-20.9%	-1,491
12/31/30	23,870	-868	-38.1%	-2,718
Total change	-2,280	-2,280	100.0%	-7,134

Source: *BMS*, pp.19, 72, 74.

9 Because the IRS only began to publish its tabulation of the balance sheet information on an industry group and sub-group basis in 1931, we were unable to determine what portions of the decrease of $7,135 million in notes and accounts receivable in 1930 were paid to industry groups other than commercial banks. Accordingly, development of a narrative regarding what amounts American industrial groups and sub-groups received from and paid to each other must await further research.

Moreover, because *SOI* covers only annual data, we were not able to estimate how the repayments were spread over 1930, a year that proved, after a promising start, to be difficult (covered ahead in Chapter 6). Needing intra-year breakdowns in order to draw more accurate conclusions, we sought additional data elsewhere.

To determine the breakdown and spread of repayments over the course of 1930, we turned from the IRS to the Federal Reserve Board who reported semiannual and quarterly data for all commercial banks in their *Banking and Monetary Statistics (BMS)*. This allowed us to get a somewhat better idea of how the volume of loans changed as 1930 progressed. Table 5.2 (opposite) shows that of the total decline in Notes and accounts receivable of banks in 1930 of $3,932 million, 36.3% occurred in the first half and 63.7% occurred in the second half. Spreading the $7,135 million repayment in Notes and accounts receivable of all U.S. corporations (including banks) in these same proportions yields $2,590 million in the first half of 1930 and a much greater $4,545 million in the second half of the year.

Other entries in *BMS* enabled us to break the statistics down further into quarterly data, at least for Fed member banks, as the lower half of Table 5.2 shows. For perspective, it is a useful reminder that on June 30, 1930, of the 23,251 commercial banks in the U.S., 8,315 were members of the Federal Reserve System.[10] Absolute numbers, however, are misleading as to the relative size of member versus nonmember banks. Of the $34,539 million in total loans outstanding on June 30, 1930, Fed member banks held 73% or $25,214 million.[11] By December 31, 1930, total loans at all member banks declined $2,280 million from $26,150 million on December 31, 1929, to $23,870 million, with 45.2% of the year's total decline occurring in the first quarter alone. While bank loans increased slightly by 4.2% in the second quarter, the third quarter showed

10 *BMS*, pp. 19 and 23.

11 *BMS*, pp. 72-4. The average member bank had slightly over $3.0 million in loans, or twice the all-banks average of approximately $1.5 million in loans, *BMS*, p. 19.

a 20.9% decline, and the fourth quarter was down 38.1%. Using those percentages to spread the repayments of the $7,135 million in Notes and accounts receivable of all U.S. corporations, we find a repayment of $3,225 million in the first quarter, a small increase in Notes and accounts receivable of $300 million in the second period, followed by net repayments of $1,491 million in the third quarter and $2,718 million in the final quarter of 1930.

Since statistics comparing all commercial banks with member banks show the same downward trend in outstanding loans, we came to the obvious conclusion that the second half of 1930 saw all commercial banks, member and nonmember alike, experiencing substantial loan repayments as reflected in the change in their Notes and accounts receivable.

Bank Borrowing in Context: 1918-1930

Bank borrowing fell an unusually large amount in the first quarter of 1930. To consider properly the magnitude of this decline, we offer this time series of quarterly member bank loan statistics from *BMS*. In the period from late 1918 up through the end of 1930, bank loans declined at Fed member banks in fourteen quarters. The following table shows us by how much.

One thing this series clearly shows is that in the early 20th century, periods during which bank loans were repaid were not uncommon and generally reflected business slowdowns.[12] For instance, the last quarter of 1918, during which the Germans and their allies surrendered, and the first quarter

12 Before the last quarter of 1914, we need to rely on annual HSUS volumes for statistics that reveal repayment of bank loans. *HSUS 1789-1945* showed only one year in the period 1900-1915 when bank loans were lower than the year before. That year was 1908 when bank loans totaled $10,438 million, down $330 million from $10,769 in 1907. *HSUS 1789-1945*, p. 262.

Table 5.SB.1

Quarters of Member Bank Borrowing Decline

($ million)

Date	Bank loans	Change from prior peroid	% Change
Nov. 1, 1918	$14,550	+$1,317	+10.0%
Dec. 31, 1918	14,224	-326	-2.2
Mar. 4, 1919	13,877	-347	-2.4
June 30, 1919	15,414	+1,537	+11.1
Nov. 15, 1920	19,852	+319	+1.6
Dec. 29, 1920	19,555	-297	-1.5
Apr. 28, 1921	18,487	-1,068	-5.5
June 30, 1921	18,119	-368	-2.0
Dec. 29, 1921	17,394	-725	-4.0
Mar. 10, 1922	17,080	-314	-1.8
June 30, 1922	17,165	+85	+0.5
June 30, 1923	18,750	+331	+1.8
Sep. 14, 1923	18,719	-31	-0.2
Dec. 31, 1923	18,842	+123	+0.7
Dec. 31, 1925	21,996	+711	+3.3
Apr. 12, 1926	21,785	-211	-1.0
June 30, 1926	22,060	+274	+1.3
Dec. 31, 1926	22,652	+592	+2.7
Mar. 23, 1927	22,327	-325	-1.4
June 30, 1927	22,938	+611	+2.7
Oct. 4, 1929	26,165	+507	+2.0
Dec. 31, 1929	26,150	-15	-0.1
Mar. 27, 1930	25,119	-1,031	-3.9
June 30, 1930	25,214	+95	+0.4
Sep. 24, 1930	24,738	-476	-1.9
Dec. 31, 1930	23,870	-868	-3.5

Source: *BMS*, pp.72 & 74.

of 1919 were such periods of slowdowns and repayments. Other downturns were the Depression of 1921-22 and two recessions in the mid-1920s. Then, the period following the Crash resulted in repayments that were comparatively significant, beginning with the $2,781 million repayment to banks in November 1929 (see Chapter 10 in *How the Crash Caused*), which marked the beginning of the prolonged period of major business downturn in 1929-33.

These quarterly loan volume statistics, combined with the broader economic conditions, indicate the growing economic distress in 1930. No source we have found so far suggests to us that these loan volume statistics had gained the attention of economic theorists in the period of the Hoover Administration, much less had any impact on policy. In fact, the insights offered by this data as they relate to business conditions may well be underappreciated even up to the present day.

How Did Corporate Financial Executives Respond in 1930?

We return now to important members of our Cast of Characters, Corporate Financial Executives, whose outlook at the time might well have been: "It's vital to repay debt obligations before or, if necessary, when they come due, even if doing so requires replacing them with longer term debt obligations."[13] They definitely did both—repaid *and* extended debt maturities in 1930. Table 5.3 presents supporting evidence.

Table 5.3

Rebalancing of Debt Maturities by Corporations

($ million)

	1929	1930	Differences
Notes & accounts payable	29,453	26,870	-2,583
Bonded debt & mortgages	46,643	50,282	3,639

Source: *BMS*, pp.19, 72, 74.

Over the course of 1930, corporations, in aggregate, *paid down* short-term Notes and accounts payable by $2,583 million and *increased* their long-term borrowings of bonded debt and mortgages by $3,639 million. These numbers and their direction clearly indi-

13 This is a hypothetical statement made in the spirit of Irving Fisher.

cate that at least some portion of the $3,639 million sourced from long-term lenders of bonded debt and mortgages repaid short-term debt obligations, that is, Notes and accounts payable that were due and payable in 1930.

Who Repaid $7,135 Million in Notes and Accounts Receivable in 1930?

While the data in Table 5.3 (opposite) show the financial actions taken by corporations to repay, often delay, their debt obligations, who else was repaying their debts? Given the size of the large, still-undesignated repayment amounts, answering this crucial question motivated us to embark on an extended exercise in estimation. In this and the following section we summarize these estimations.

As described in Chapter 6 in *How the Crash Caused*, we considered two alternative estimations regarding who was responsible for the repayment of U.S. corporations' aggregate Notes and accounts receivable by other U.S. corporations. One estimation, covered in Table 6.3 (*How the Crash Caused,*), assumed that 100% of aggregate U.S. Corporate payables were owed and paid to other U.S. corporations (including banks). Table 5.3 shows that $2,583 million of the total amount of Notes and accounts payable in 1930 was paid down. The second estimation from Table 6.4 (*How the Crash Caused,*), offered an alternative assumption—that only 90% of aggregate U.S. Corporate payables were owed and paid to other U.S. corporations. Under this second assumption, U.S. corporations paid $2,325 million to other U.S. corporations (including banks). Realistically, however, we know that our 100% assumption *included* transactions that didn't involve payments by U.S. corporations to U.S. corporations (including banks). The most obvious of these payments involved purchases from foreign entities that, while corporations, were not U.S. corporations. Such purchases would entail accounts payable to "others" that were neither U.S. corporations nor U.S. individuals. Accordingly, we determined that presenting a middle ground case of 95% made sense, as seen in Table 5.4 below.

Table 5.4 **Repayment of Notes & Accounts Receivable in 1930 by** U.S. Corporations, U.S. Individuals & Others ($ million)			
	1929	1930	Difference
Notes & accounts receivable	$66,810	$59,675	-$7,135
100% of payables of corporations	-29,453	-26,870	-2,583
Payables of individuals & others	37,357	32,805	-9,718
Notes & accounts receivable	$66,810	$59,675	-$7,135
95% of payables of corporations	-27,980	-25,527	-2,453
Payables of individuals & others	38,830	34,148	-9,588
Notes & accounts receivable	$66,810	$59,675	-$7,135
90% of payables of corporations	-26,508	-24,183	-2,325
Payables of individuals & others	40,302	35,492	-9,460

Source: *SOI for 1929 & 30*: 1929, p.25, 1930, p.27.

Using the three estimations, Table 5.4 presents how each scenario impacted the 1929 and 1930 statistics with regard to aggregate corporate Notes and accounts receivable.

• The top section assumes U.S. corporations paid 100% of their Notes and accounts payable due in 1930 to other U.S. corporations. Subtracting that amount, $2,583 million, from total corporate Notes and accounts receivable due in 1930, we derived that Individuals and others must have owed and paid $4,552 million to U.S. corporations in 1930, as the top section of Table 5.4 shows.

• The second alternative assumption is that U.S. corporations paid 95% of their Notes and accounts payable due in 1930 to other U.S. corporations. Under this assumption, we subtracted $2,453 million (95% of $2,583 million) from total Notes and accounts receivable of $7,135 million, arriving at $4,682 million as the sum Individuals and others repaid to U.S. corporations. (As we noted in *How the Crash Caused* (see page 148), Goldsmith, Brady and Mendershausen provided statistics in *A Study of Saving in The United States* that indicated that 95.9% of corporate payables were owed in 1929 to other corporations.)

• The third alternative assumption shown is that U.S. corporations paid 90% of their Notes and accounts payable due in 1930 to other U.S. corporations. Under this assumption, we subtracted $2,325 million (90% of $2,583 million) from Notes and accounts receivable of $7,135 million, arriving at $4,810 million as the sum Individuals and others repaid to U.S. corporations.

Of course, adjusting the U.S. corporate statistics downwards necessarily raised the amount Individuals and others paid to U.S. corporations (including banks). We estimated that our assumed 5% decline from 100% to 95% in U.S. corporate accounts payable caused payables by Individuals and others to rise $130 million from $4,552 million to $4,682 million. The further decline from 95% to 90% of corporate Notes and accounts payable paid in 1930 to other U.S. corporations (including banks) meant that U.S. corporations paid $2,325 million to other corporations and caused payables by Individuals and others to rise $258 million, from $4,552 million to $4,810 million.

Once again, after careful consideration of the alternatives presented in Table 5.4, we chose the second alternative, that U.S. corporations paid 95% of their Notes and accounts payable due in 1930 to other U.S. corporations, thereby arriving at $4,682 million as the sum Individuals and others paid to U.S. corporations (hereafter called "the 95% assumption").

Individuals' Financial Decisions in 1930: Reaching Our Conclusions

Assessing the debt repayments made in 1930 by U.S. individuals—autonomously and in aggregate—has, from the beginning, stood front and center in terms of our research objectives. We knew there were definitely important questions we needed to find answers

Table 5A.Results

Estimated Assignment of "Others" On December 31, 1930 to U.S. Corporations and Individuals
($ million)

"Others"	Amount	U.S. corporations	U.S. individuals
Federal gov't			
Notes payable	-$411		-$411
Accounts payable	+21		+21
State & Local gov't			
Notes payable	+154		+154
Accounts payable	+58		+58
Foreigners	-135[1]		-135
Bankruptcies			
Personal	-29.0[2]		-29.0
Private banks	-4.3[3]		-4.3
Business failure	-189.2[4]	-169.3	-19.9
Total	-535.5	-169.3	-366.2

Source: Authors' estimates.

Note: "Others" include federal, state and local governments which are removed from the individual column by subtraction, but, if positive, are interpreted as causing individuals to maintain additional sums on deposit to offset their added effect.

[1] Assigned entirely to individuals on the grounds that foreigners are not U.S. corporations.

[2] Personal bankruptcies are all assigned to individuals.

[3] Private banks are all unincorporated institutions..

[4] Individuals get (39,759/378,760) per cent based on statistics in Table 5A.5. Corporations receive the remainder of the amount in the first column.

to in order to prove our case, but we sometimes encountered impediments to finding those answers easily or accurately. One ongoing stumbling block was when available statistics were not broken down in a way that provided direct answers. In such cases, we had to find alternative, understandable and credible ways to back into those answers.

Table 5A.Results (opposite) shows the conclusions we drew in our extended estimation process. Under the 95% assumption, U.S. individuals and other entities repaid $4,682 millions to U.S. corporations (including banks). However, since our main focus is on U.S. individuals, first we went through the precursor step of estimating payments by "others"—specifically the Federal Government, state and local governments and foreigners, plus the bankruptcies attributable to individuals in the U.S.—so that we could arrive at figures for U.S. individuals only. As Table 5A.Results shows, U.S. individuals' repayments aggregated to -$366.2 million, thus reducing the $4,682 million from Table 5.4 (page 148) based on the 95% assumption to $4,316 million repaid by U.S. individuals alone.

Because we strongly prefer to exercise caution in estimation, we will refer to our estimate for 1930 henceforth as a "$4+ billion" debt repayment by individuals, including mainly and importantly, consumers.[14][15]

---

14 As discussed in Chapter 12 of *How the Crash Caused*, some individuals went into debt, not as individual consumers, but for their businesses, as sole proprietors or partners in partnerships. In general, throughout this book use of "individuals" covers both. However, when appropriate, particularly as it relates to indebtedness, we specifically include "and consumers" to make it clear that there can be a difference. Not all individuals were indebted due to individual consumption, whereas all indebted consumers went into debt due to consumption.

15 In addition, we note that included in this repayment estimate is the reduction of -$495.6 million in outstanding debt obligation owed to the Five Retail Establishments Combined in 1930 as presented in Table 2.2 on page 54. The sum constituted more than 12% of the $4+ billion repayment.

Where Did U.S. Individuals Get the $4+ Billion They Repaid in 1930?

While individuals who earn wages or operate businesses as sole proprietors or as partners in partnerships, pay taxes depending on earnings, their principal contribution to the U.S. economy has come to be as consumers of the wide variety of goods and services Americans have available. Today, we don't question this designation of ourselves as "consumers." As we described in our Prologue to *How the Crash Caused*, the 1920s comprised the period when that shift from citizen to consumer took place. We cannot overstate the implications of this permanent change in identity and, *en masse*, in power and economic impact, as each individual consumer autonomously made his or her own consumption choices.

In *Did Monetary Forces Cause the Great Depression?*, Peter Temin's ruminations on consumers and consumption still left him unable to answer fully the question he posed in his title. In Professor Temin's Chapter III, "Precipitating Factors," he properly called attention to "sharply falling consumption...in 1930."[16] Later in his book, he clearly struggled with the inadequacy of proof for his conclusion, calling the fall in consumption both "truly autonomous" and "unexplained." As we cited in *How the Crash Caused's* Chapter 5 Temin wrote:

> The fall in consumption must be regarded as truly autonomous, which in this case means also unexplained. The unexplained component of consumption, therefore, was approximately $3 billion in 1929 prices (out of a total fall of $4.3 billion. When added to the smaller falls in exports and in consumption due to the fall in asset prices, this implies a fall in autonomous spending of about $4 billion in 1929 prices. Compared to a total Gross National Product

16 Temin (1976), p. 65.

> of approximately $100 billion, this fall—if it was indeed an autonomous fall—could have had multiplier effects large enough to explain the continued downward path of national income.
>
> It is somewhat unsatisfactory to say that the Depression was caused by an unexplained event, but this alternative is preferable to statements that are inconsistent with the data. The income- expenditure approach is consistent with the data if we accept the autonomous nature of a large part of the fall in consumption in 1930. It is not, however, a complete story.[17]

Just as we had resonated with Temin's hesitancies when we first read his book early on in our research, we also resonated with Temin's use of "autonomous." Among our Cast of Characters, we identified a broad class of indebted individuals, including Repentant Ex-Speculators and Debtors (in general) who, while acting autonomously, urgently repaid their debts, thus creating, in aggregate, a very serious country-wide situation. As we said earlier, we have reached the conclusion that these autonomous individuals repaid, in aggregate, the enormous sum of $4+ billion in debt in 1930.[18] Based on our research, as we discussed in detail in Chapter 12 of *How the Crash Caused*, we reached the conclusion that individuals accomplished this Herculean repayment by reducing their expenditures on consumption—belt tightening—in 1930 by that same $4+ billion. With fear as a huge motivating factor, many individuals ceased consuming beyond essentials and instead prudently reduced their debt burden.[19]

From our perspective, it looks like our $4+ billion debt repayment estimation in 1930 offers Professor Temin a reasonable explanation for that "unexplained component of consumption [which]

17 Ibid., p. 83.

18 $71 billion in 2022.

19 See Martha Olney quote in Chapter 8 (p. 227).

was approximately $3 billion in 1929 prices (out of a total fall of $4.3 billion)" or "a fall in autonomous spending of about $4 billion."

Would Professor Temin have characterized $4+ billion in debt repayment in 1930 as "a precipitating factor" of the Great Depression? We certainly think so. He wrote in his Conclusions:

> [S]omething...happened to depress consumption in 1930. At the current stage of our knowledge, the unexplained fall in consumption is larger than the part we can explain, but the magnitude of the total fall is incontrovertible. The large decline in consumption expenditures for both durable and non-durable goods had a profoundly depressing effect for the economy.[20]

Furthermore, we also know Temin's unambiguous view on the other much-pointed-to, possible precipitating factor—the precipitous drop in investment by businesses:

> It is worth emphasizing that the fall in consumption was unusually large in 1930, because the conventional literature assumes that it was investment that experienced the unusual fall. But although the composition of the fall in investment differed in 1930 from the composition in other shorter depressions, the magnitude of the fall was not larger. Investment fell in 1930, as it falls in all recessions, but it did not fall more than usual. The Depression was not caused by a dramatic collapse of investment.[21]

We turn next to Friedman and Schwartz to see how they participated in this precipitating-factor discourse.

---

20 Temin (1976), p. 172.

21 Ibid.

Consumer Debt Repayment and the Theories of Friedman and Schwartz

While the IRS statistics we present may be old—having been compiled and archived during the Great Depression—they are also new as they appear to have received little scrutiny to speak of up to now.[22] That said, our deep dive into the IRS archives has led us to form the view that the debt repayment statistics in 1930 showed a broad spectrum of Americans across almost all wealth levels strongly motivated—certainly partly due to a sense of obligation and responsibility, even of personal pride—to get out of debt. We see this impetus as a powerful monetary force, and the IRS data was not the only data source to support this conclusion. *BMS* data cited earlier in this chapter showed a -$3,932 million decrease in total loans of all commercial banks in 1930. As both individuals and corporations repaid portions of this sum, these data bolstered the effect of this monetary force. However, we have as yet seen no evidence that Milton Friedman or Anna Schwartz, either alone or together, took into consideration the importance of this reduction in outstanding bank loans, much less the drop in overall corporate receivables.

In *How the Crash Caused* (Chapter 10), we discussed Friedman and Schwartz's focus on "the sharp wiggle in the money series, *entirely a result of a corresponding wiggle in demand deposits*" (our emphasis) that is clearly visible in Chart 10.1. They placed their attention particularly on the upside of the wiggle, explaining that early in the week of the Crash, New York City banks had replaced funds withdrawn by nervous call market lenders by making loans themselves to call loan borrowers (brokers and dealers) and crediting those funds to the borrowers' demand deposits by the end of October. We then scrutinized the *downside of the wiggle* when, during November, the demand deposit money supply fell $2,781 million,

22 Raymond Goldsmith used *Statistics of Income* in his project of estimating U.S. saving and the national balance sheet. It is listed in multiple locations in his index. See Goldsmith (1955, Vol. 2), p. 622 and (1956, Vol. 3), p. 471.

from $24,432 million at the end of October to $21,651 million at the end of November. Why did the $2,781 million vanish? The answer is straightforward—when checks are drawn on demand deposits and paid to banks as repayment of bank loans, the total amount of the loans, of course, declines by the total amount of the checks, and, all else being equal, the supply of demand deposits is also reduced by the same amount.

Though Friedman and Schwarz could have discussed this process, they did not. We found in their exegesis neither any suspicion that the downside of the wiggle represented a *repayment* to banks of bank loans, certainly not $2,781 million worth, nor any attempt to assimilate this idea into their thinking as to the causes of what they called "The Great Contraction."

Early in *Did Monetary Forces*, Professor Temin pointed us to a summary Friedman and Schwarz wrote for the *Review of Economics and Statistics* that came out shortly after the publication of *Monetary History*. In that article, they clearly gave their cause for the decline in the money stock, at first small then growing, as due to the number of bank failures beginning in 1930. However, they also made an assertion early in their Chapter 7 of *Monetary History*, "The Great Contraction 1929-1933," that introduced nonmonetary forces into the causes of the events that took place up to the end of 1930. "True, as events unfolded," they wrote, "the decline in the stock of money and the near-collapse of the banking system can be regarded as a consequence of *nonmonetary forces* in the United States...." (emphasis ours).[23] While their position apparently shifted blame from the "wave of bank failures" in late 1930 to "nonmonetary forces in the United States...as events unfolded," they offered no further analysis of what those forces might have been.

Later in their Chapter 7, in a section called "Onset of the First Banking Crisis, October 1930," they held firm to their view about the crucial role of bank failures and suspensions. They wrote, "In October 1930, the *monetary character of the contraction changed* dramatically—a change reflected...by the extraordinary rise in the

23 Friedman and Schwartz (1963), p. 300.

deposits of suspended banks" (emphasis ours), starting with a "crop of bank failures," particularly in agricultural areas where banks had been impacted throughout the 1920s, that spread a "contagion of fear" outward.[24]

Our considered view, however, is that none of the four banking crises nor all four in aggregate changed the monetary character of the contraction and what was happening in 1929-33. Instead, we found that the monetary character of the contraction began considerably earlier than the Fall 1930 bank failures. It began with the torrent of margin calls in the course of the Crash and the start of what the Fed called the "drastic liquidation of security loans."[25] The effects of these intertwined actions were statistically visible in the repayment of $2,781 million in bank loans over November 1929 shown in Table A1 in *Monetary History.*[26]

At the end of December 1929, many corporations, individuals and public officials—some autonomously and some in response to encouragement by President Hoover and other government officials—took steps to make things appear more normal for year-end reporting, but reality broke through as the monetary forces reappeared and gathered momentum in January 1930. Pointless jawboning aside, these potent Crash-induced forces eroded the foundations of America's financial institutions—in banking and especially for brokers and dealers—and continued to intensify, leading piecemeal thereafter to the banking crises that were the main focus of Friedman and Schwartz's research regarding 1929-1933.

Before we return to our historical narrative and the scene as financial markets briefly rebounded in the first quarter of 1930, we extend this chapter with an explanatory Endnote that introduces our methodology in arriving at Monthly Loan Repayment Estimates for the "Statistics of U.S. Economic Activity" tables that appear at the end of upcoming Chapters 7 to 10.

---

24 Ibid, p. 308.

25 *ARBG for 1929,* p. 1.

26 Friedman and Schwarz (1963a), p. 712. We gratefully acknowledge the careful work by Milton Friedman and Anna Schwartz in coming up with statistics we have found most valuable.

Chapter 5 Endnote

Monthly Loan Repayment Estimates for Our "Statistics of U.S. Economic Activity" Tables

As already presented in Chapter 10 of *How the Crash Caused* and in Chapter 2 in this volume, Statistics of U. S. Economic Activity tables will now appear at the end of the next five chapters. These tables offer key monthly data showing trends and directionality at work for the quarter covered within the chapter and the two months prior. Following certain chapters is one additional category—debt repayment data. The subsequent discussion describes our methodology for arriving at those estimates.

Having established $4+ billion as our estimate of the debt repayment by individuals and consumers in 1930, we then developed monthly estimates of debt repayment over the course of that eventful year using four sets of statistics covered in Table 5.2 (page 142), configured in Table 5.5 (page 160) to show the development of those monthly statistics of repayment.

• Set 1: Quarterly loans volumes outstanding at All member banks of the Federal Reserve System as shown in our Statistics of U.S. Economic Activity tables. For example, Table 6.1 (page 166) shows the volume of Fed Member Bank Loans as $26.2 billion at the end of December 1929 and as $25.1 billion at the end of March 1930.) *BMS* showed these loan volumes as $26,150 million and $25,119 million respectively, which means that $1,031 million was repaid in this three-month period. With minus signs indicating a decrease in loans, the average monthly rate of repayment January, February and March was -$344 million which appears in our Statistical tables containing those months. Similarly, Table 6.1 (page 166) shows the volume of Fed Member Bank Loans as $25.1 billion at the end of March 1929 and as $25.2 billion at the end of June 1930. *BMS* showed them as $25,119 million and $25,214 million respectively, a $95 million *increase* in bank borrowing in this three-month period. With an average monthly rate of repayment in these three months up $32 million, that amount appears in our tables for each month of the second quarter of 1930. This procedure carries on quarterly from there.[27]

• Set 2: The semiannual volume of loans outstanding at All commercial banks in the U.S. *BMS* showed loan volumes of $35,966 million, $34,539 million, and $32,034 million for December 1929, June 1930 and December 1930 respectively, indicating repayments of $1,427 million between December 1929 and June 1930 and $2,505 million between June and December 1930. The average monthly rate of repayment was -$238 million in each of the first six months and -$418 million in each month of the second six months. These averages appear in our tables that cover the first and second halves of 1930.

• Set 3: The annual change in the Aggregate Corporate Notes and Accounts Receivable quantity on the Aggregate Corporate Balance Sheets for 1929 and 1930 as shown in Table 5.1 (page 139). Short-term debt repayment over 1930 was -$7,135 million—a substantial 7.87% of Gross National Product. The average monthly sums of -$595 million appear in our tables for all twelve months of 1930.

• Set 4: Of the -$7,135 million repayment in Aggregate corporate notes and accounts receivable in 1930, the individuals' share as stated in this chapter was -$4+ million, an estimated monthly decline of -$333.4 million.

Just as the first and second sets of bank loan repayment figures started with lower monthly figures that increased over 1930, within the third and fourth sets we applied a similar rate of increase of the fixed monthly average estimates over the year. Applying that system,

27 *BMS*, pp. 72 and 74.

Table 5.5			
Derivation of Monthly Debt Repayment Averages ($ million)			
All Fed member bank loans			
Date	Amount	Change	Monthly average
12/31/29	26,150		
3/27/30	25,214	-936	-312.0
6/30/30	25,124	+95	+31.7
9/24/30	24,738	-386	-158.7
12/31/30	23,870	-868	-289.3
	Total	-2,280	-760.0
All commercial bank loans			
Date	Amount	Change	Monthly average
12/31/29	35,966		
6/30/30	34,539	-1,427	-237.8
12/31/30	32,034	-2,505	-417.5
	Total	-3,932	-327.7
Aggregate corp. notes & accounts receivable (ACNAR)			
Date	Amount	Change	Monthly average
12/31/29	66,810		
12/31/30	59,675	-7,135	-594.6
Estimated individual/consumer share of ACNAR			
Date	Amount	Change	Monthly average
In 1930	-4,000		-333.4

we provide statistical estimates of repayment rates (and one small set of borrowing rates) for our "Statistics of U.S. Economic Activity" tables at the end the next five chapters.

CHAPTER 6

Speculation Renewed and Hoover's Stabilization Plan Launched (Late 1929 through First Quarter 1930)

As 1929 ENDED and the decade of the 1930s commenced, many perceived various, seemingly quite positive notes in the economic situation. Financial historian Barrie A. Wigmore, who spent a long career as a corporate finance partner at Goldman, Sachs & Co., described the tone on Wall Street:

> Old hands in the securities business remember vividly the optimism that prevailed in the early months of 1930.[1]

The view from Washington was also decidedly optimistic. During his eight years as Secretary of Commerce for Presidents Harding and Coolidge and as Chairman of the 1921 President's Conference on Unemployment, Herbert Hoover had overseen the development of an extensive and widely approved economic stabilization strategy that focused on the principal of countercyclical phasing of public works. Even following the Crash, now President Hoover was firmly convinced of the strength of American business and of his administration's ability to maintain into the 1930s the prosperity America enjoyed in the 1920s. Financial editor of the *New York Times* Alexander Dana Noyes recalled:

1 Wigmore (1985), p. 128.

> Conferences of businessmen, called hastily to the White House… by President Hoover, agreed in principle not to cut wages or reduce sweepingly their working staffs. Henry Ford, in a public interview, declared that the situation called for higher, not lower, wages.[2]

Even the Federal Reserve Board viewed the financial situation at the start of 1930 with optimism. At the end of 1929, banks appeared in good health, with their deposit, loan and investment statistics looking much as they had at the end of September 1929, less than a month before the Crash. The Board optimistically concluded its commentary in the 1929 *Annual Report* in a section entitled, "Improvement in Credit Conditions" with the following:

> Liquidation of bank credit in the last two months of 1929 and the easing policy of the reserve system were reflected in a decline of money rates in the United States, and particularly of the open market rates on call and short-term money…. Open-market rates abroad also became easier. It was apparent at the close of 1929, therefore, that the liquidation of security loans, which took place in the last two months of the year and resulted in an improvement in the credit situation in the United States, had also exerted an important favorable influence on the world-credit conditions.[3]

Appearances, however, deceived a lot of people. This chapter focuses on what was going on behind the scenes, below the surface, and on how people were reacting to what *looked* like optimistic forces. Hidden ones, however, were propelling events in ways that became ineluctable. Those ineluctable forces are the subject of Chapter 6. But, first, as we will begin to learn in this chapter, Hoover's previously touted stabilization policy was inadequate for post-Crash

2 Alexander Noyes, *The Market Place: Reminiscences of a Financial Editor*, Little, Brown and Company, 1938, p. 342.

3 *ARBG for 1929*, p. 12.

realities because, among other things, Hoover declined to use the presidential Bully Pulpit. This meant that Hoover sought to deal with greedy, self-centered, powerful and highly competitive people by using friendly persuasion rather than command.

Growing Optimism Experienced in the First Quarter of 1930

Along with the optimistic memories of old hands in the securities business, Wigmore recounted more examples of positive assessments in a variety of different sectors as 1930 began and progressed:

> At the time, the optimism appeared justified. A business recession similar to those following stock market panics in 1907, 1914, and 1920 was expected but it was expected to be limited to trade in luxury items. All the Federal Reserve districts predicted an upturn in the economy in the second half of 1930. The commercial banks also forecast an upturn. The Guaranty Trust Company, a perennial optimist, predicted a quick recovery in building construction because of the easy money. The Hoover administration vociferously expressed its confidence in a business recovery, and industry supported the projections. Sophisticated journalists questioned whether there was any connection between securities prices and the business of the United States, and they persuaded themselves that if some vague connection existed Hoover's quick actions had been sufficient to restrain it, and the leading nations had united in goodwill several years earlier to sign the Kellogg-Briand Pact, which forswore the use of arms.
>
> There was good cause for optimism at the beginning of the year. In Washington, a businesslike administration ran a balanced budget and had acted quickly and decisively

> to shore up confidence and promote expansion.... [E]ven the international scene appeared peaceful. The Young Plan promised to restore Germany's credit.
>
> Stock prices boomed in the first quarter 1930 amid the confidence, many stocks doubling and tripling from their 1929 lows. Trading volumes on the New York Stock Exchange recovered to the level of 5-6 million shares a day. Banks and brokers scrambled to rehire the experienced staffs laid off in December 1929. Albert Wiggin, and other speculators like him, got back into the stock market.
>
> Wall Street continued to expand as if nothing had happened. There was an office-building boom in the first half of 1930.
>
> Outside Wall Street, industry looked strong. Most companies reported record 1929 earnings during the first quarter 1930, and February dividend payments were $436 million versus $387 million in February 1929.... The rate of completed and proposed mergers in the first months of 1930 showed little reduction from 1929.[4]

In his biography *Bernard Baruch: The Adventures of a Wall Street Legend,* James Grant, financial writer and founder of *Grant's Interest Rate Observer,* wrote of the cautiously optimistic viewpoints floating around Wall Street:

> In [Baruch's] previous Wall Street experience, panic had been foreshadowed by monetary troubles or conspicuous bankruptcies. So far there were no such portents. Indeed, as Richard Whitney, then vice president of the Stock Exchange and later president, would observe, an oddity of the Crash

4 Wigmore (1985), pp. 128-130.

was the virtual absence of distress in the money market; and as for nonagricultural bankruptcies the National City Bank letter, as late as December 1929, could say with all apparent confidence, "There are no great failures, nor are there likely to be."[5]

The Little Bull Market, Begun by Investors

Commenting in 1938 on the way things looked to Wall Street at the end of 1929, Alexander Dana Noyes offered further observations:

> To [the markets after the panic shock of October 1929], the salient fact of the moment was only that an overdone speculation for the rise in stocks had broken down. There was no expectation of the 40 per cent fall in commodity prices which was destined to occur in the next three years, or of that period's nation-wide bank suspensions and the ruinous crumbling away of production, consumption, earnings, private incomes, and employment. Speculative Wall Street drew a different inference from the excessive violence of the decline. Later experience proved that the all but unprecedented fall of stocks foreshadowed, as it had usually done in other panics, proportionately violent reaction in general trade. But at the end of 1929, Wall Street did not appear to recognize any such probability.
>
> On the contrary, one began to hear that the fall was only a consequence of an exceptionally overexploited stock market; that it did not foreshadow equivalent trade reaction; that the decline in stocks had itself been too great, and that, as soon as outright panic should subside and forced selling of stocks by unlucky margin speculators should have run its course, recovery on the Stock Exchange would be proportionately

5 James Grant, *Bernard Baruch: The Adventures of a Wall Street Legend*, Axios Press, 1983, p. 281.

great. It was true that a part of the Stock Exchange's usual clientage, even of the professional sort, had been badly crippled; but there were still professional speculators who had withdrawn from the market when, in the middle of 1929, it began to look dangerous to them, and who now at the year end reentered it, buying stocks with borrowed money on a very substantial scale.[6]

We already know from Wigmore's words above that many stocks doubled and tripled in price from their 1929 lows during what was

Table 6.1

Percent of New York Stock Exchange Loans to Total Market Values of Listed Shares

The appended table shows the ratio of total Stock Exchange member borrowings on security collateral to total listed share values ($ million)

1929	Call market loans	Market value all listed stocks	Ratio %
1-Jan	6,440	67,472	9.54
1-Feb	6,735	71,060	9.48
1-Mar	6,679	71,872	9.29
1-Apr	6,805	69,770	9.75
1-May	6,775	73,719	9.19
1-Jun	6,665	70,921	9.39
1-Jul	7,071	77,264	9.15
*1-Aug	7,474	81,569	9.16
1-Sep	7,882	89,668	8.79
1-Oct	8,549	87,074	9.82
1-Nov	6,109	71,753	8.51
1-Dec	4,017	63,589	6.32
1930			
1-Jan	3,990	64,708	6.16
1-Feb	3,985	69,009	5.77
1-Mar	4,168	70,807	5.89
1-Apr	4,656	76,075	6.12

*Corrected total

Source: NYSE: *New York Stock Exchange Year Book 1929-30*, p.111.

6 Noyes (1938), pp. 340-1.

called the "Little Bull Market," a phenomenon of the first quarter of 1930. However, questions abound. When did it begin? Why? Who led the charge? What brought it to its quick and sorry end?

Table 6.1 (opposite) presents statistics showing that the Little Bull Market actually began in the fourth quarter of 1929. A brief review of what the statistics show, month-by-month, gives us the answers as to when the Little Bull Market began and who precipitated it. On January 1, 1930, the market value of all stocks listed on the New York Stock Exchange was $64.7 billion, up $1.1 billion from the market value of all listed stocks on December 1, 1929. A month later, February 1, 1930, the market value had risen $4.3 billion to $69.0 billion. Given that call money market loans had fallen $2.1 billion in December 1929 and a further $5 million in January, we can conclude that the beginning of the Little Bull Market, up to the end of January 1930, was due to investors, not speculators who to participate depended on brokers loans, and thus the availing by brokers of call loans. This is not to call Noyes's recollections into question. Brokers used call money market loans to underwrite their own portfolios, and they very possibly reduced their own portfolio financings enough to have brokers loan funds available to lend to newly entering, or reentering, speculators in January.

Moving forward one month, on March 1, 1930, the market value of all stocks listed on the NYSE was $70.8 billion, up $1.8 billion from February 1 (and up $7.2 billion from December 1, 1929). February was the month that marked clear renewal of speculation as call market loans rose $183 million thus funding 10.2% of the rising value of all listed stocks, and again pointing to investors accounting for the remaining 89.8% as the predominant participants.

Then on April 1, 1930, the market value of all stocks listed on the NYSE rose again $76.1 billion, up $5.3 billion from March 1 (up $12.5 billion from December 1, 1929). Table 6.1 shows that the Little Bull Market had risen almost to the total value that was achieved by the Big Bull Market at the end of June 1929, though still $13.6 billion below the early September 1929 high value. In March 1930, call market loans were up $488 million, with only 9.2% of the $5.3 billion rise due to speculation. For the third month in a row, investors led the way.

Though some emboldened speculators re-entered the market, their small numbers reflected how burned most speculators had been by the Crash. Investors, however, old hands that they were, knew they could profit, and handily, by their participation.

Hoover's Stabilization Plan Launched

As observed at the beginning of this chapter, President Hoover's confidence in the inherent strength of American business and in his administration's ability to sustain prosperity into the 1930s remained firmly—one might even say stubbornly—undiminished. His convictions, however, lacked the teeth, and perhaps the guile, that were needed to identify and rein in strong countervailing forces. In short, though engaging and energetic, Hoover sorely lacked command presence when it counted, as it did in March 1930, as we will see. With good fortune, nations find the right leaders at the right time. Tragically, despite all of his demonstrated competence and integrity, we fear Hoover was not one of them.

In *From New Era to New Deal: Herbert Hoover, the Economists, and American Economic Policy, 1921-1933,* economic historian William J. Barber described Hoover's activities during the post-Crash period, eight months after taking office, as "Demand management, Hoover-style":

> On November 15, 1929 Hoover broke his public silence. In press conference remarks made available for quotation, he observed: "In market booms we developed overoptimism with a corresponding reverse into overpessimism. They are equally unjustified but the sad thing is that many unfortunate people are drawn into the vortex of these movements with the tragic loss of savings and reserves. Any lack of confidence in the economic future or the basic strength of the business in the United States is foolish." And he added:

> "My own experience has been, however, that words are not of any great importance in times of economic disturbance. It is action that counts."
>
> Hoover was now indeed ready to act. The time seemed to have arrived to pull the trigger on the plans for stabilizing downturns in spending which had been worked out in the discussions begun in the early 1920s. As a first step, he asked the heads of all cabinet departments to investigate the possibilities of accelerating their spending on construction projects already authorized and to assess the feasibility of new construction programs for which appropriations had not yet been obtained.
>
> This step was followed up with the telegrams dispatched to governors in each of the nation's states, pointing out that it would "be helpful if road, street, public building, and other construction of this type could be speeded up and adjusted in such fashion to further employment." The governors also were asked to initiate a canvas of state, municipal, and county spending programs and to report to Washington on "the volume expenditure that can be prudently arranged for the next 12 months and for the next six months."
>
> Meanwhile, Hoover organized conferences at the White House....[7]

Beginning in the closing weeks of 1929, the East Wing of the White House, which at the time served as the entrance for formal and informal visitors, welcomed a seemingly endless succession of the principal businessmen, labor leaders and government officials of the day to meet with President Hoover and each other. In his book,

7 William Barber, *From New Era to New Deal: Herbert Hoover, the Economists, and American Economic Policy 1921-1933*, Cambridge University Press, 1985, pp. 80-1.

1929: The Year of the Great Crash, William Klingaman summarized the resulting enthusiasm:

> After every meeting, the business leaders announced that they had pledged their cooperation to the President's program to ensure that the crash did not lead to a full-fledged depression. Employers agreed to maintain wage levels and refrain from laying off workers; workers promised not to disrupt the orderly flow of production with strikes or demands for higher wages.[8]

Hoover later acknowledged that the Federal government had only $420 million appropriated for public works in late 1929.[9] He indicated that the spending by the Federal government on what Hoover called "nonproductive public works" or "indirect aid to employment" rose to $2,358 million in fiscal years 1930-33.[10] He also insisted that his efforts to "organize indirect relief" from the private sector described above were consequential, writing, "As a result, we were assured that many billions of dollars would be spent and many thousands employed on capital improvement during the first phase of the depression."[11] Assurances, however, were hollow. He went on to attribute many positive results to his broad conferencing efforts in the nation's capital:

> Those conferences in Washington established four understandings vital to the recovery program: (a) no strikes lockouts that leaders could prevent; (b) wage rates not to be reduced except as the cost of living fell; (c) within their resources, employers to look after the relief of their own employees; (d) where possible, a sharing of work. The last

8 Klingaman (1989), p. 305.

9 Herbert Hoover, *The Memoirs of Herbert Hoover 1920-33: The Cabinet and the Presidency, Volume 2,* The Macmillan Company, 1952, p. 42.

10 Ibid., p. 143.

11 Ibid., p. 42.

three provisions were currently referred to in our discussions as "employers' direct relief." As all of this was voluntary, we did not expect a 100 per cent compliance; but we did receive an astonishing support.[12]

President Hoover Urges Confidence, Cushioning and Cooperation.

Long after leaving office, Hoover expressed his view that the Depression had successive phases, the first five of which occurred during his administration. In his *Memoirs*, he wrote:

> Each phase began with new destructive force; each had its own acute crisis. As each developed we undertook new measures to ward it off, to cushion its effect and restore the constructive forces in our economic life. Except for the last [which occurred after Hoover left office], each ended in an upturn and a brief hope that the worst was over.
>
> The first phase spanned the seventeen months from the stock market crash in October, 1929, to April, 1931. This was a period of comparatively mild domestic readjustment, such as the country had experienced before. Unemployment of the family breadwinners rose to about 2,000,000, or probably not more than 1,000,000 over the normal. By January, 1931, we had paid the price for our economic misdeeds and were convalescing. We made steady upward progress from January until April, 1931, when the earthquake of financial panic reached us from Central Europe.[13]

12 Ibid., p. 45.

13 Ibid., p. 38.

Hoover, as we know, expended great effort communicating in person or in writing with many leaders to urge behaviors that could alleviate the quickly worsening situation. But, philosophically, when "unemployment reached such threatening dimensions that relief of distress was imperative," he operated within a narrow band of options as to the parameters of his approach:

> At the outset I must clarify the distinction between "direct relief" and "indirect relief." "Direct relief," as used here, means relief given directly to individuals or families through charitable, local, county, or state action. "Indirect relief" comprises Federal and state public works, together with stimulation of private construction, "spreading of work," restrictions of immigration, government financial measures to support private employment, and action in the foreign field. [14]

We will consider the unemployment picture further in Chapter 11.

Hoover Issues Warnings

Acting within his personal belief system, Hoover reflected the times, especially following in the footsteps of his presidential predecessors when *laisser-faire* attitudes prevailed and the U.S. was primarily an agricultural nation. In Chapter 4 of his *Memoirs,* Hoover addressed "Federal Government Responsibilities and Functions in Economic Crises." There he insisted:

> No President before had ever believed there was a governmental responsibility in such cases [as the stock-market crash].... [S]uch eruptions ... had always been left to blow themselves out. [15]

---

14 Ibid., pp. 42-45.

15 Ibid., p. 29.

Hoover certainly recognized how the rapid changes that took place following the outbreak of "the Great War"—World War I—had changed the nation in profound ways. Before 1914 the U.S. had been the world's biggest debtor nation; after the war we had become the world's biggest creditor nation. Before 1914 the U.S. was largely an agricultural nation; after the war we were well on the way to becoming a mighty industrial power that would become recognized in World War II as the "arsenal of democracy." To these considerations we add all the innovation described in our Prologue of *How the Crashed Caused,* including electrification, product development and manufacturing processes, not to mention marketing techniques. Altogether, the U.S. had evolved into a nation that none of our previously elected leaders could possibly have had experience in governing, and in Hoover's view:

> Because of this lack of governmental experience, ... we had to pioneer a new field. As a matter of fact there was little economic knowledge to guide us.[16]

Hoover also warned of the suddenness at which economic problems could arise:

> Economic storms do not develop all at once, and they can change without notice. In my three years of the slump and depression they changed repeatedly for the worse—and with the speed of lightning.[17]

Although hardly Hoover scholars, we see Hoover—with sympathy—as not being up to the task of taking the needed assertive, effective action to rein in speculation early in 1929 so as to prevent the much more serious Crash and ensuing economic depression. Failing to do that in early 1929 put Hoover in what, for him, was the impossible position of taking even greater assertive and effective actions to turn things around after the Crash. Raised in the Quaker

16 Ibid.

17 Ibid.

tradition, he had integrity, was honest and approached leadership through consensus-building rather than outright command authority. Up to the point where that consensus-building no longer succeeded, he had been both extremely capable, and, as well, just plain lucky, something we discuss below.

A Contrary View from a Distinguished Former Fed Executive

While hopeful enthusiasm emanated from Washington and financial markets seemed to recover their footing after the Crash, optimism was not universal. The February 1930 edition of *The North American Review* included an erudite and impassioned article entitled "Who Caused the Panic of 1929?" written by H. Parker Willis, a man of broad financial experience and authority, who had served as the first secretary of the Federal Reserve Board from 1914 to 1918, as well as its director of research from 1918-1922. A prolific writer about banking, Willis became a respected economics professor, editor-in-chief of *The New York Journal of Commerce* and an American financial correspondent for many of the leading financial newspapers of Europe. According to his obituary, "His part in drafting the Federal Reserve Act was probably greater than any other one man; and this, no doubt, will remain as his finest achievement."[18]

Willis' article included this pointed, if lengthy, subtitle, "A distinguished economist sees the Wall Street crash as a disaster for which responsibility can be definitely fixed and from which the public should learn lasting lessons."[19] In his well-organized and unflinching account—which proved to be prescient—Willis offered a stern list of those he found to be the parties responsible for the Crash:

---

18 *New York Times,* July 20, 1937, p. 22.

19 H. Parker Willis, "Who Caused the Panic of 1929?", *The North American Review,* February 1930, p. 174.

• The Federal Reserve system

• The Treasury Department

• Contributary operations at Federal Reserve banks

• Banks and investment houses

• Financing companies affiliated with banks

• According to Willis' overarching indictment, *practically every maxim of sound banking formerly known has been disregarded,* the whole effort being to build up an immense structure of paper profit, which might be cashed, as opportunity offered in some tangible form, while the community was left to "hold the bag." [20] (emphasis ours)

As to who was to pay the cost of this tremendous breakdown of credit, Willis knew the fundamental answer:

> There can be no doubt that someone must do so....[T]he real costs involved in this crash are great though they are not to be measured in money. The panic has been tremendously expensive....(T)he real costs spread from U.S. financial markets to general confidence at home and abroad: [21]

Mindful of how soon after the Crash the publication of Willis' article took place, we were impressed by his cogent arguments and moved by his underlying anguish over the Crash. He wrote eloquently of the impact still to come and to a crucial missed opportunity to correct things that tragically was, of course, not acted on:

> All this says nothing of the effect of the collapse upon individuals; the sweeping away of savings, the crippling of

20 Ibid, pp. 174-181. Each category is discussed in turn.

21 Ibid., p. 181.

> many commercial undertakings and a great modification of the financial plans of others. As yet there is but little conception on the part of anyone of the vast extent and of the deeply rooted character of the speculation which has been eating into American life since 1925, fostered and encouraged as it was by our banking leaders, our politicians and our financiers. It was a disastrous influence upon the individual existence of a large fraction of American citizens and its elimination is in some ways an offset for the tremendous material losses and costs involved by the collapse. *But this elimination has been made unnecessarily expensive and has meant ruin in a good many cases where it might have meant only inconvenience and suffering on a limited scale, had correctives been applied at some time during the past year or so....* Many of those who have been "wiped out" in the disaster will never recover the position as property owners which they had before they attempted to enter the market. Many others will recover only partly and incompletely. This situation suggests the cost of the panic to the individual. [22] (emphasis ours)
>
> The breakdown of 1929 was as nearly the result of willful mismanagement and violation of every principle of sound finance as such an occurrence ever has been. It was the outcome of vulgar grasping for gain at the cost of the community. It has been a national disgrace and a source of untold national and individual loss. In paying the bill entailed by it, the American people should think seriously about how they can best avoid running up another. [23]

Willis' article provides valuable insights into the speculation of the 1920s and early 1930, the Crash, the Great Depression, and their aftermath, individually and in sequence, with echoes even

22 Ibid., p. 183.

23 Ibid.

into the present. Certainly Willis' comment about the possible correctives that might have worked if applied "at some time during the past year or so" caught our attention, as coming from a highly respected source but hinted at nowhere else that we were able to find. We turned to the data in Table 6.1 (page 166) that provide clear support for Willis' point of view.

First of all, the statistics shown in Table 6.1 reveal that it would have been far less costly to rein in speculation at the end of March 1929 than it was to experience the collapse of the market in the panic at the end of October. The facts are undeniable. Between April 1 and October 1 of 1929 the market value of all listed shares on the NYSE grew 28.5% from $69,770 million the week after the March 26 crisis to $89,668 million several weeks before the first day of the Crash. Furthermore, call market loans had grown 25.7% or $1,744 million in the same six-month period.

At the end of March 1929, data shows that the U.S. economy was growing robustly. By contrast, the data also shows that in October 1929 the economy was contracting. As a key example, Figure 3.1 on page 87 reveals that automobile production rose and peaked in April 1929. After that, production fell. By October, it had fallen for six months. The market was *far less vulnerable to downside reaction* in March 1929 than it was in October.

Although Galbraith, in his book on the Great Crash did not hold a high opinion of Federal Reserve authorities, he did express the opinion that "someone in high authority" could have successfully influenced events:

> [T]he Federal Reserve was helpless only because it wanted to be. Had it been determined to do something, it could for example have asked Congress for authority to halt trading on margin by granting the Board power to set margin requirements....

Actually, not even new legislation, or the threat of it, was needed. In 1929, a robust denunciation of speculators and

> speculation by *someone in high authority* and a warning that the market was too high would almost certainly have broken the spell.[24] (emphasis ours)

Who was that someone in high authority? We believe it was the 31st President of the United States, the Hon. Herbert Hoover who had a bully pulpit from which to issue warnings.

The Crisis Confronting Hoover on Day One as President

Hoover became the 31st President of the United States on March 4, 1929. This widely-celebrated event occurred in the midst of a two-month period in which a crisis had nonetheless developed over the acceleration of stock speculation, fueled not just by borrowed funds from banks but, increasingly, by the participation by "others" such as individuals and corporations into the call money market. A month before Inauguration Day, the Federal Reserve Board had sent a letter to all member banks that they then released to the public, with supplemental information, on February 7. The published statement read in part:

> The Federal reserve act does not, in the opinion of the Federal Reserve Board, contemplate the use of the resources of the Federal reserve banks for the creation or extension of speculative credit. A member bank is not within its reasonable claims for rediscount facilities at its Federal reserve bank when it borrows either for the purpose of making speculative loans or for the purpose of maintaining speculative loans.[25]

Tensions were mounting throughout the financial community.

---

24 Galbraith (1954), p. 32.

25 Ibid., p. 3. See pp. 192-202 of *How the Crash Caused the Great Depression* for our account of this crisis.

It was during this period that Paul M. Warburg's prediction was reported in the press that "unless the orgies of unrestrained speculation" were brought under control "the ultimate collapse is certain ... to bring a general depression involving the entire country."[26]

Three weeks after Hoover was sworn in, with the Federal Reserve Board maintaining its silence as an expression of its resolve to rein in speculation, the financial crisis peaked on March 26, 1929, as the rate on call market loans reached 20% and Charles E. Mitchell, the President of National City Bank of New York and a director of the New York Federal Reserve Bank, stepped into the breach to declare that his bank would lend money as necessary to prevent liquidation of call loans. With that bold move, the resolve of the Board of the Fed evaporated, and the crisis ended. The market proceeded to rally. In his *Memoirs*, Hoover commented, "[P]eople who dreamed of 100 per cent profit in a week were not deterred by an interest rate of 20 per cent per annum."[27]

Herbert Hoover's Attitude Toward Speculation

Hoover also wrote in detail about the "great guns" environment on Wall Street and his reaction to it as he began his term, and his actions tell us much about his leadership approach:

> The stock boom was blowing great guns when I came into the White House. Being fully alive to the danger inherent in this South Sea Bubble and its inevitable reaction, my first interest was to get it under restraint. It was obvious that there had to be vast liquidation of paper values, and especially a liquidation of the mental attitude of people mesmerized by the idea of speculation as a basis of living and of national progress.
>
> The initial difficulty was a lack of government authority,

26 *Commercial & Financial Chronicle*, March 9, 1929, p. 1444.

27 Hoover (1952), p. 18.

except such as could be exerted by the Federal Reserve System. To ask Congress for powers to interfere in the stock market was futile and, in any event, for the President to dictate the price of stocks was an expansion of Presidential power without any established constitutional basis.

I, therefore, resolved to attack the problem from several directions in addition to securing cooperation from the Federal Reserve System.

To create a spirit of caution in the public, I sent individually for the editors and publishers of major newspapers and magazines and requested them systematically to warn the country against speculation and the unusually high price of stocks. Most of them responded with strong editorials. This had no appreciable effect....

My second line of attack, six weeks after my inauguration, was to request Henry M. Robinson, President of the First Security National Bank of Los Angeles, to go to New York and to talk in my name to the promoters and bankers behind the market. He fully agreed with me as to the dangers of the situation. But the New York bankers all scoffed at the idea that the market was not "sound." They were certain this was a "New Era," to which old economic experience did not apply. To prove it, Thomas Lamont of Morgan's wrote me a long memorandum which makes curious reading today.

My third effort was to send for Richard Whitney, the President (sic) of the New York Stock Exchange, and urge that the Exchange itself curb the manipulation of stocks.... Mr. Whitney made profuse promises, but did nothing....

All our efforts to secure an orderly readjustment covered

six months and perhaps served somewhat to slow up the orgy. The real trouble was that the bell boys, the waiters, and the host of unknowing people, as well as the financial community, had become so obsessed with the constant press reports of great winnings that the movement was uncontrollable.

The stock-market slump on October 29, 1929, came seven months after I entered the White House.

When the inevitable black morning of their dreams dawned, the exponents of the "New Era" were surprised. Promptly we had a flood of reassuring statements....

I am not a pessimistic soul, but I was not impressed by any of this optimism. The press insistently urged that I make a statement. Obviously, as President, I had no business to make things worse in the middle of a crash. Loath to speak of the stock market, I offered as encouragement a short statement on our progress in the productive system and the long-view strength of our country.

The normal business cycle periodically must readjust disequilibriums which are part of the rhythm of any growing free economy. But this was more than rhythms. Our overpriced stocks and real estate were bound to come down; and the degree of down is influenced by the degree of up—which means a descent from overvalue to undervalue. The boom had lifted securities and real estate far up and, to this degree, was to deepen further the slump by the downward swing.

Within a few weeks the slump began seriously to affect industrial employment and farm prices, confronting us with problems of the first order.[28]

28 Ibid.,, pp. 16-20.

Reexamining Facts Surrounding March 26, 1929

March 26, 1929, in the midst of a tumultuous week, was actually quite a crucial date in economic history. As background, Hoover began the second chapter of his *Memoirs* entitled, "We Attempt to Stop the Orgy of Speculation" with the following:

> By the last months of 1928, Benjamin Strong of the Federal Reserve Bank of New York had died and ...Roy Young had been appointed by President Coolidge to the Governorship of the Federal Reserve Board. Young was an able, courageous, and cooperative man. Prior to my inauguration as President I conferred several times with him and found him fully alive to the situation. He agreed to use the full powers of the Board to strangle the speculative movement.
>
> On February 7, 1929, the Board issued public notice of "direct action" to the banks to restrain indirect use of federal reserve credits for speculative loans. But the stimulant [post-Crash] had been too successful. The fever was beyond control.
>
> Moreover, the effect of the Board's action was greatly minimized by an unfortunate press statement by President Coolidge, a few days before he left office, in which he assured the country that its prosperity was "absolutely sound," and that stocks were "cheap at current prices." [29]

We searched the archives of the *New York Times* for reaction to Coolidge's press statement but found nothing. However, according to economic historian and Coolidge scholar Amity Shlaes, it appears that while Coolidge indeed made those statements, he did so in the midst of the prosperity of 1928, a year earlier than Hoover's account, an unfortunate memory lapse on Hoover's part.[30]

---

29 Ibid., p. 16.
30 Amity Shlaes, "Calvin Coolidge Revisited: New Find on 1929 Crash," *Forbes* Magazine, July 14, 2013.

Curious about Hoover's involvement with the members of the Board of the Fed while still Secretary of Commerce, we found the following in Hoover's *Memoirs*:

> [A]gain I urged President Coolidge, as I had done eighteen months before, to send for [the Governor of the Fed] and express alarm at the situation. Mr. Coolidge, a strict legalist, again insisted that the Reserve Board had been created by the Congress entirely independent of the Executive and that he would not interfere. The Secretary of the Treasury, Mr. Mellon, [who was the Chairman *ex-officio* of the Board of the Fed, which apparently meant not entirely independent of the Executive] also declined and seemed to think my anxiety was alarmist and my interference unwarranted.[31]

Whatever Hoover considered to be the positions on the speculation "situation" by those he regarded as experts, Hoover as newly inaugurated President (only a month after the Fed's February 2 letter to member banks urging restraint) could have spoken authoritatively for himself as he considered necessary. He could have, but did he? Did anyone else?

More Facts Surrounding March 26, 1929

We scoured contemporaneous issues of the respected and heavily relied-on weekly *Commercial and Financial Chronicle* (*henceforth referred to as the Chronicle*) to learn more about what had happened on March 26 and how the financial world had responded. In its March 30 issue, we found the following:

> This statement by Mr. Mitchell appeared in the "Herald-Tribune" of March 27 as follows:
>
> "So far as this institution is concerned," declared Charles

31 Hoover (1952), p. 10.

> E. Mitchell, president of the National City Bank, yesterday, "we feel that we have an obligation which is paramount to any Federal Reserve warning, or anything else, to avert, so far as lies within our power, any dangerous crisis in the money market.
>
> "While we are averse to resorting to rediscounting for the purpose of making a profit in the call market, we certainly would not stand by and see a situation arise where money became impossible to secure at any price."[32]

In using the term, "rediscounting," Mitchell indicated his bank's contingent antipathy to borrowing at the Federal Reserve's discount window to make call loans to brokers. The March 30 *Chronicle* continued:

> Disclaiming any attempt to speak for New York bankers as a whole, Mr. Mitchell made it plain, nevertheless, that he doubted whether any of the great banks of the city would deliberately stand aside and see a crisis precipitated rather than extend credit to the stock market. As far as the National City was concerned Mr. Mitchell said, no sooner did the word come of the straightened credit conditions which had caused the rates on demand loans to leap successively from the renewal rate of 12% to 15%, 17 and finally 20% then the bank supplied a substantial sum of money to the market.
>
> Another prominent bank president, who refused to be quoted, asserted that his institution was prepared to do everything in his power to relieve the situation. "Our statement will show," he said, "that we have gone to the Reserve heavily in order to meet the present credit crisis."[33]

In using the phrase, "gone to the Reserve," this anonymous

32 *Commercial and Financial Chronicle,* March 30 1929, p. 2014.

33 Ibid.

banker acknowledged that his bank did precisely what the Federal Reserve Board decried. It borrowed heavily at the Reserve's discount window in order to make call loans to brokers. The *Chronicle* continued:

> There has been widespread credence given to the belief that, in response to Federal Reserve pressure, local member banks had agreed to refrain from "easing the situation" over the end of the quarter as they did over the year's end, at which time the rise in call money was halted at 12%.
>
> This belief was vigorously denied by prominent bankers yesterday, who asserted that it is ridiculous to suppose that the great New York Banks would deliberately co-operate to bring about a state of demoralization in the stock market. Money, they emphasized, was tight. But, they declared, the banks would not see the situation grow to panic proportions, and they were well able to lend assistance before such a state was reached.[34]

This was a moment that called for decisive action by Hoover. Having establishing his agreement with Young as described in his *Memoirs*, new President Hoover had a prospective tentpole and a location in which to place it. What he needed to accomplish was the raising of the tent with the Federal Reserve Board inside it and its members firmly in agreement on the "closed-window" policy it would pursue. But Hoover failed to get that tent raised with the critical players inside. As Hoover wrote later in his *Memoirs*:

> We did at one time almost secure a stranglehold on the stock market when the Reserve Banks had so tightened the call-loan situation that a moment arrived when there was no money available to the market. A break seemed inevitable. But Charles E. Mitchell, President of the National City Bank

34 Ibid.

of New York, announced that in this emergency his bank would furnish the deficient credit.[35]

> Senator [Carter] Glass [Federal Reserve legislative founder] expressed *my feelings* when he said of Mr. Mitchell:
>
> > He vows his superior obligation to a frantic stock market over against the obligations of his oath as a Director of the New York Federal Reserve Bank....
> >
> > Mr. Mitchell's proclamation is a challenge to the authority and the announced policy of the Federal Reserve Board. The challenge ought to be promptly met and courageously dealt with.
> >
> > The Board should ask for the immediate resignation of Mr. Mitchell as a Class A director of the New York Federal Reserve Bank.[36] (emphasis ours)

What should happen doesn't necessarily happen. *Almost* securing a stranglehold on the stock market missed the mark that Willis called for in his February 1930 article. Willis wanted Hoover to take decisive action, to *seize the moment, stiffen the spines of the Federal Reserve Board members and carry the day.* The message of Willis' lament— "*had correctives been applied at some time during the past year or so*"— was that by achieving such a stranglehold, Hoover would have put the nation in a position where the cost and difficulty associated with the necessary contraction would have been *far less* than that brought about by the Crash of 1929 and the Great Depression.

Sadly, taking the kind of decisive action mentioned above, including forcing wayward Fed directors to resign, may have been

---

35 Hoover (1952), p. 18.

36 Ibid.

skills in others' wheelhouse— including those of Carter Glass or H. Parker Willis. They did not seem to be among Hoover's strengths. Hoover's basic techniques were extensive planning, widespread efforts at consensus-building and zealous attempts to persuade *others* to take the necessary, authoritative actions—in other words, friendly persuasion, consistent with the tenets of the Quaker faith in which he'd been raised. Instead of messengers like Senator Glass giving voice to Hoover's views, Willis wanted Hoover to speak decisively for himself. [37] But Hoover did not, and the data has much to say about this failure.

Friedman and Schwartz's Comment on "Direct Pressure" by the Fed

As Hoover noted, the subject that came to a head on March 26 had to do with the attempt by the Board of the Fed to impose "direct action," thereby causing banks to restrain indirect use of federal reserve credits for speculative loans. Rather than including this subject in their chapter in *Monetary History* on "The Great Contraction, 1929-33" (Chapter 7), they considered it earlier in

---

37 On Friday, March 29, 1929. an article quoting Glass, whom Hoover referred to later in his *Memoirs* as "[expressing] my feelings," appeared prominently on page 1 of the *New York Times*. (Lamentably, Hoover himself did not take a public position at the time.) A second *Times* article, appearing on page 4 conspicuously alongside the continuation of the article about Senator Glass, quoted Sunshine Charley Mitchell as saying, in response to the Senator's exhortation that he resign, "That's very interesting, but I have no comment to make." Sunshine Charley evidently didn't see the need to comment; he had won. His victory was clearly much to H. Parker Willis' regret in his article in February 1930, eleven tumultuous months later. As to Willis, his *Times* obituary in 1937 stated of the prolific writer and economics professor, "He liked a good fight, and…usually was in one," further pointing out that, "He was for years the advisor and close friend of Carter Glass, and the two shared many characteristics."

Chapter 6, "The High Tide of the Reserve System, 1921-29." There, in a section that ran 12 pages following the headline, "THE DISPUTE OVER CONTROL OF SPECULATION BY 'DIRECT PRESSURE,'" we learned that:

> Governor Strong disagreed [with a report that seemed to recommend direct pressure], pointing out that direct pressure could not succeed in New York unless the Federal Reserve Bank refused to discount for banks carrying speculative loans, and that it would mean rationing of credit, "which would be disastrous."[38]

As support for this statement, Friedman and Schwartz cited several entries in the Diaries of Charles S. Hamlin from the year 1925. Hamlin was appointed by President Wilson in 1914 as the first Governor of the Federal Reserve Board and by reappointment he remained a member of the Board until 1936 when he retired.[39]

Of Benjamin Strong, the long-time head of the Federal Reserve Bank of New York who died in October 1928, Friedman and Schwartz stated:

> Strong, more than any other individual, had the confidence and backing of other financial leaders inside and outside system, the personal force to make his own views prevail, and also the courage to act upon them.[40]

By May of 1928, it appeared to Friedman and Schwartz that:

> [T]he view attributed to the board was that direct pressure was a feasible means of restricting the availability of credit for speculative purposes without unduly restricting

38 Friedman and Schwartz (1963a), p. 254.

39 Ibid., pp. 251-2 and 254. For the cited diary entries, see their footnote 22 on page 254.

40 Ibid., p. 412.

its availability for productive purposes."[41]

In the account they give of the period from early February 1929 to March 26, they make clear that Charles Mitchell's discomfort with the evolving decision-making regarding "direct pressure" must have become known to both Harrison and Governor Young by March 25. Finally, Friedman and Schwartz concluded:

> In retrospect, it seems exceedingly doubtful that "direct pressure" had any significant effect on the amount of security loans, though it may have produced some minor changes in their source.[42]

1st Quarter of 1930: Linking the Crash to the Great Depression

In Chapter 12 of *How the Crash Caused,* we established the causal linkage connecting the Crash of 1929 to the start of the Great Depression seven months later in May 1930. Tables 12.3, 12.4 and 12.5 presented statistics for automobile dealers and four other retail sectors. For our analysis, we relied on *net credit change* statistics that reflect not only the purchases made each month but also the repayments of debt obligations entered into—and "fixed" in amount—over ten or twelve earlier months. We now perform an analogous analysis using *credit granted* statistics. Table 6.2 (following page) presents the results.

The pertinence of credit granted statistics is their clear focus on the most important parties in the purchasing decisions: the actual customers who bought on credit month-by-month. The bottom line is that both the analysis in Chapter 12 of *How the Crash Caused* and the analysis performed here reached the same conclusion—the

41 Ibid., pp. 254-5.

42 Ibid., p. 265.

Table 6.2

Instalment Credit Granted and Rate of Change for Automobiles[1] and Five Types of Reatail Establishments[2] Selected Months, 1928-30

($ million)

Month	Credit granted		Rate of change[3]	Credit granted		Rate of change[3]
	1928	1929				
Sep	163.9	185.7	13%			
Oct	168.1	190.7	13%			
Nov	138.1	142.2	3%			
Dec	118.6	121.2	2%			
	1929	1930		1929	1930	
Jan	110.7	103.5	-7%	$200.8	190.4	-5%
Feb	132.5	120.0	-9%	234.9	214.9	-9%
Mar	205.9	175.0	-15%	331.2	282.8	-15%

[1]New and used passenger cars only.

[2]Includes dealers in new and used (passenger) automobiles, department stores, furniture stores, household appliance stores and jewelry stores.

[3]Minus sign indicates decrease in net credit; otherwise increase is to be understood.

Source: "The Volume of Consumer Instalment Credit, 1929-1938," NBER, Feb 1940, pp. 2, & 9, Appendix A.

Crash of 1929 *caused* the commencement of the Great Depression seven months later.

Table 6.2 presents credit granted statistics comparing credit granted in later months of 1929 and in the first quarter of 1930 with amounts granted twelve months earlier, both for automobiles alone and for automobiles plus four other retail segments. As regards automobiles, the table shows that the volume of credit granted was 13% higher in September and October 1929 than it was twelve months earlier. With the Crash occurring at the end of October, as we argued in Chapter 12 of *How the Crash Caused*, the shock and magnitude of the Crash caused net credit change to go negative and then decline at an accelerating rate. Here too we show that consumers' reaction to the Crash caused the demand for automobile purchases on credit to decline significantly from September and October to November and December and to accelerate in the rate of decline thereafter into 1930. Credit granted declined from being up 13%

in October to up only 3% in November 1929, likely indicating that fewer prospective for-credit buyers entered automobile showrooms in that dismal month. It was certainly the case that those who did enter a showroom financed lower amounts, a sign that they purchased less expensive cars. It was also certainly the case that the rate of decline of automobile financings was accelerating. The rate of decline went from +3% in December 1929 to -7% in January 1930 and reached -15% in March 1930.

We show the pattern of decline for the five retail establishments (which included automobile dealers) on the right side of Table 6.2. While NBER's publication, "The Volume of Consumer Instalment Credit, 1929-38," which formed the backbone of our previous volumes's Chapter 12 analysis, included automobile statistics for years prior to 1929, it did not do so for all five retail establishments. As a result, we were not able to calculate rate of change statistics for months earlier than January 1930, but, nonetheless, the statistics for January through March 1930 parallel closely the automobile statistics shown on the left side of Table 6.2.[43] Once again, bellwether statistics indisputably show a decline in demand for credit to purchase important goods after the Crash that was immediate and rapid as depression conditions accelerated.

A Closing Word About Luck

Until the first year of his presidency most Americans would have viewed Herbert Hoover as a hard-working and remarkably lucky man. Born in Iowa in 1874, he survived a potentially often-fatal childhood illness (croup), and though orphaned at age ten, he was taken in by an uncle who was a cultured Quaker physician and businessman in a Quaker frontier town in Oregon. Young Hoover preferred working in his uncle's Oregon Land Office to school and excelled at bookkeeping and math studied at night. Luck (and pluck) firmly

43 We will present more extensive statistics on automobile installment sales and on automobile sales in general in Chapter 7.

on his side, in 1891, he became the youngest of nine members of the first freshman class of Stanford University where he studied geology and engineering (and met his future wife, the estimable Lil Henry). Still shy of twenty-one, Hoover graduated and was soon employed by a well-connected San Francisco mining engineer, then, in 1897, by a London firm whose objective was to technologize backward mining industries in resource-rich places outside the U.S. As further luck would have it, history credits Hoover with discovering a rich vein of gold at the Sons of Gwalia mine in the Australian Outback. According to Hoover biographer Richard Norton Smith, his employer "snapped up the place for a million dollars, and earned back $65 million in ore and interest." [44] Soon Hoover was overseeing the firm's huge new engineering enterprise in Imperial China, then set up his own consulting firm with offices around the globe. Smith relates a story to underscore how Hoover's significance had grown on the world stage. When asked by Lord Kitchener to become Britain's minister of munitions during the Great War, Hoover rejected out of hand this offer to join the British Cabinet. "I'll be damned if I'll give up my American citizenship," he replied.[45]

Again in the right place at the right time, Hoover was living in London at the outset of the First World War. Liaising with the United States ambassador Walter Hines Page, Hoover began immediately applying his "time, talent and treasure" (Smith) to relief work on behalf of Belgian civilians trapped and rapidly approaching starvation between the lines of German invaders and defending Allied forces and with massive amounts of consensus building and friendly persuasion, ultimately more widely to more Europeans. Hoover's biographer quotes Ambassador Page as saying, "[This] simple, modest, energetic little man ... began his career in California and

44 Richard Norton Smith, *An Uncommon Man; The Triumph of Herbert Hoover,* Simon and Shuster, 1984, p. 74.

45 Ibid., p. 77.

will end it in Heaven."[46] Of Hoover's encounter with an important American journalist, Smith writes, "William Allen White … came away from meeting Hoover for the first time 'mesmerized by the strange low-voltage of his magnetism.'"[47]

Hoover's timely and remunerative mining expertise, his relief work in World War I and his energetic leadership as Secretary of Commerce were enormously fortunate and valuable in every respect. While lucky that Coolidge decided not to run for another term, resulting in a landslide win, Hoover's presidency is another story. It was extremely *un*fortunate, starting with his third week in office when his team "*almost* secure[d] a stranglehold on the stock market." From that point on, despite his preternatural confidence, Hoover's luck ran out as things simply worsened until March 4, 1933, when he was succeeded as President by Franklin Roosevelt. Hoover's well-established skills did not lend themselves to a forceful ending of speculation or curing a burgeoning depression. His friendly-persuasion leadership style and the blind spots in his personal and political philosophies prevented him from taking control of events and turning things around. Instead, they enabled things to get worse, much worse.

We now proceed to Chapter 7 and pivotal events of the "unlucky" second quarter of 1930.

46 Ibid., p. 87.

47 Ibid., pp. 86-7.

Table 6.3 **Statistics of U.S. Economic Activity** ($ billion)					
	Nov. '29	Dec. '29	Jan. '30	Feb. '30	Mar. '30
Annualized personal income	$83.6	$82.8	$81.7	$80.9	$79.6
Index of factory employment	104.4	101.9	100.6	99.0	97.7
Index of industrial production	105	100	100	100	98
Index of wholesale prices	93.5	93.3	92.5	91.4	90.2
Friedman & Schwartz demand deposits	$21.7	$22.6	$21.9	$22.2	$22.6
Fed member bank loans		$26.2			$25.1

Sources: *HSUS* 1789-1945, pp. 328-330, 344; *Monetary History*, pp.712-3; *BMS*, pp.72,74.

1st Quarter 1930 Statistics of Debt Repayment:

All Fed Member Banks: The volume of borrowing at All Fed Member Banks declined $1,031 million in the 1st quarter of 1930—an average monthly debt repayment of -$344 million.

All U.S. Commercial Banks: Repayments to All U.S. Commercial Banks totaled -$1,427 million in the 1st half of 1930—an average monthly debt repayment of -$238 million. All Fed Member Banks are included in All U.S. Commercial Banks.

Aggregate Corporate Notes and Accounts Receivable (ACNAR) — All Payers: Total ACNAR repaid in full year 1930 equaled -$7,135 million—an average monthly debt repayment of -$595 million by businesses, individuals and "others".

Individuals only: We estimate that individuals and consumers repaid more than $4+ billion to U.S. corporations in 1930—an average monthly debt repayment of more than -$333 million.

Except for the 2nd quarter, debt repayments grew throughout the year.

CHAPTER 7

Prospects Dim Then Darken (Second Quarter of 1930)

NOW WE ARRIVE at the "baffling second quarter of 1930," Professor Kindleberger's description in the closing of his Introduction to *The World in Depression 1929-1939*. He offered perspective on April through June and various other key periods in those years:

> In this chronological treatment a number of turning points deserve emphasis: 1929, 1930, 1931, and 1933— the stock market crash, the financial crisis, the failure of revival in the spring of 1930. Most analysis concentrates on October 1929 and May–June 1931. The baffling second quarter of 1930 and June–July 1933, covering the World Economic Conference, are, however, important in explaining why the depression went so deep and lasted so long and why recovery was so incomplete.[1]

Since the "failure of revival in the spring of 1930" and the "baffling second quarter of 1930" clearly describe the same period, these expressions raise the question as to exactly what happened. Answering that question is the intent of this Chapter 7.

As we posit in Chapter 12 of *How the Crash Caused*, the shock and magnitude of the Crash led to determination of a cause-and-effect linkage between the Crash of 1929 as cause and the Great Depression as effect. We based this determination on comprehensive statistics

1 Kindleberger (1986), pp. 12-3.

contained in NBER's 1940 study *The Volume of Consumer Instalment Credit, 1929-38*, that show the linkage process that took shape over the course of seven months beginning at the end of October 1929 and culminating with the Great Depression, reaching full effect in the second quarter of 1930. Specifically, the month in which the effect became most obviously fully operative was May. The component facts of this linkage were not, however, known or understood by participants in the events of the spring of 1930. Economists and historians, too, were unaware of the connection. In fact, data on consumer installment credit were not published by NBER until 1940, well after the official end of the Great Depression, and we have seen no evidence that anyone viewed the information in that study as a focal part of such a cause-and-effect linkage until our research yielded facts that then enabled us to connect them with the timing of the Crash and its aftermath.[2,3]

The Transition from the First Quarter of 1930 to the Second Quarter

In the first three months of 1930, as the so-called Little Bull Market heated up, stock prices rose once more, gratifyingly for at least for two of our Cast of Characters: Successful Speculators (post-Crash) and Insider Speculator Instigators who were still willing—and able — to play the game. For the Repentant Ex-Speculators

2 Of course, if we missed a key reference that has viewed the consumer installment credit statistics (or some other statistics) as a basis for such a cause-and-effect linkage, please let us know.

3 Inasmuch as Chapter 12 in *How the Crash Caused* focused on the pivot that borrowers made from borrowing growing sums month-by-month prior to the Crash to repaying debt month-by-month after the Crash, we gave particular scrutiny to the statistics in Tables 12.3A and B and 12.4A and B that revealed especially the net cash flow component of the linkage. In the autumn of 1929, the volume of borrowing, which until then had grown aggressively, pivoted to repayment of borrowed funds which went on with only a few breaks until March 1933.

(post-Crash) who had suffered losses, however, the first quarter was a painful time to assess the damage. How deep was the hole they had fallen into and how were they going to climb out of it? Except for the hopeful few who managed to jump back into the market, they were definitely sidelined from their prior frantic activity. From their much lower perches, they could only watch in dismay as stock prices rose past the point at which they had been margined out only a few months earlier. Their personal reality clashed with the news out of Washington. In March, as the first quarter neared its end, President Hoover issued a statement that projected hope, yet proved to be glaringly wrong: "The worst effects of the crash upon employment will have been passed during the next sixty days."[4]

As recounted in the prior chapter, Hoover's resolutely optimistic mood was not wholly unjustified. As Table 6.1 shows (page 166), Market Value of All Listed Stocks on the NYSE rose 17.6% in the first quarter of 1930. This occurred despite the fact that since the Crash things had consistently been turning down. (As the term "the economy" had not yet been coined and become the standard-bearing term it is today, in 1930, "things" was a realistic descriptor.) Given that the Market Value of All Listed Stocks rose 6.6% in January, a further 2.6% in February, and still further by 7.5% in March, "hopium"—from today's urban dictionary, but certainly appropriate for then—was, at least briefly, in ample supply. [5] Concurrently, the Dow Industrials rose 15.1% in the first quarter of 1930.

Financial historian Barrie Wigmore described the second quarter of 1930 as opening promisingly on Wall Street:

> April trading volume on the New York Stock Exchange leapt to steady 5-million-share days, and the buying became

4 Noyes (1938), p. 342.

5 The NYSE "Market Value All Listed Stocks" statistics are shown in Table 6.1 (p. 166) and Table 7.1 (p. 201). Unlike most financial statistics which use month-end statistics for closings—e.g., Dec. 31, 1929—as their basis—the NYSE uses month opening statistics—e.g., "1-Jan"—e.g., for the beginning of 1930.

excited for the first time since the Crash. In the third week of April, the Dow Jones Industrial and Utility indices hit their recovery highs of 297 and 108 respectively. There was talk of a summer bull market. Foreign bond issues jumped to $175 million for the month, which was above most months in the 1920s, a sure sign of optimism. A number of domestic bond issues using warrants or conversion features to attract buyers were issued after a hiatus since the Crash. Even the leading investment trust shares were above their breakup values, after trading well below them since the Crash.

There were dramatic recoveries in the stocks of particular industries by this point, which illustrates the quick fortunes made. The most prominent recoveries were among the speculative favorites of 1929. Film company stocks, such as Paramount, Warner Bros., Loew's, and RKO, were up over 100% from their 1929 lows, making fortunes for Joseph Kennedy and other speculators.[6]

The Prospect of Unemployment Statistics

As the second quarter began, a source of nearly real-time information about a badly needed indicator of reality—actual employment figures—was about to appear. April 1930 saw the decennial Census of the United States required by the Constitution that, according to Wesleyan University economist William J. Barber, was newly designed in part to provide the Hoover administration with timely information about levels of employment. This kind of up-to-date research and reporting had been almost nonexistent. Barber wrote:

> Information on the precise dimensions of the problem was cloudy at best. Accurate current data on trends in the

6 Wigmore (1985), p. 139.

labor force were simply not available. The Committee on Recent Economic Changes had lamented this shortcoming in its report in 1929 and the administration had sought to do something about it by gathering information on employment status in the census of April 1930. In official circles, this exercise was hailed as a courageous attempt to gather, for the first time, systematic and accurate information on the volume of unemployment and its incidence.[7]

Stock Market Retreat Begins

As to the stock market, until mid-April the market continued making headway, but the picture as painted by Wigmore showed worrisome signs:

> New common stock issues were $161 million in April, which did not compare with the monthly average of $367 million in 1929 but still exceeded the monthly average for any prior year....
>
> Amid the excitement of recovery, however, notes of concern became sharper. There were numerous comments that the rise was too fast. Both the trend of commodities prices and the international financial scene were becoming matters of serious concern.... Optimism began to vanish. Between April 17th and May 3rd the Dow Jones Industrial Index dropped from 294 to 258—over 12%.[8]

7 Barber (1985), p. 94.
8 Wigmore (1985), p.140.

Table 7.1

Percent of New York Stock Exchange Loans to Total Market Values of Listed Shares

The appended table shows the ratio of total Stock Exchange member borrowings on security collateral to total listed share values

($ million)

1930	Call market loans	Market value all listed stocks	Ratio %
1-Jan	3,990	64,708	6.16
1-Feb	3,985	69,009	5.77
1-Mar	4,168	70,807	5.89
1-Apr	4,656	76,075	6.12
1-May	5,063	75,305	6.72
1-Jun	4,748	75,019	6.33
1-Jul	3,728	63,892	5.83
1-Aug	3,690	67,221	5.49
1-Sep	3,599	67,721	5.31
1-Oct	3,482	60,143	5.79
1-Nov	2,556	55,026	4.65
1-Dec	2,162	53,312	4.06

Source: NYSE: *New York Stock Exchange Year Book 1929-30*, p.111.

Table 7.1 shows that April, the start of a new quarter, marked a noteworthy turning point, with an actual 1% decline in the Market Value of All Listed Stocks on the NYSE. While the market had risen 17.6% in the first quarter, one month later (at the start of May), April's declines brought down the rise to 16.4% from the start of the year, an unsettling reversal of the first quarter's encouraging trend.

The Census of 1930: A (Partial) Picture of Unemployment Emerges

Meanwhile, as April proceeded, Census Bureau personnel began to review returns from their canvassers which included their anticipated employment figures, an increasing national concern.

Regrettably, some questions appeared as to the accuracy of the definitions the Bureau had used for measuring unemployment. According to economist William J. Barber:

> The ambiguity arose from the procedure used by the Census Bureau in classifying the unemployed. The jobless were divided into two categories. The first (schedule A) enumerated those who were not working, but able and willing to do so and also actively seeking employment. These definitions excluded many who were also jobless, but did not describe themselves as looking for work because they regarded themselves as on temporary "lay-off" and expected to return to their regular activities when economic conditions improved. Persons in this category were classified in schedule B.[9]

The unemployed as enumerated from the Census Bureau's schedule A was 2.5 million, 5% of the labor force, but therein lay a controversy. According to Barber, Census Bureau employment expert Charles E. Persons, whom we introduce in *How the Crash Caused*, was caught in a crossfire:

> Charles [E.] Persons, the official in charge of the preparation of the census tabulations, resigned in protest over the exclusion of the jobless in schedule B from the unemployment figures and charged the administration with suppressing information that would reveal the gravity of the problem.

> Agreement on the facts remained hard to come by. Hoover tried to make some headway on this matter when he appointed an Advisory Committee on Employment Statistics in August 1930. When the committee submitted its report in the following February, the Census Bureau had still not completed a comprehensive tabulation of the returns. On the basis of the data available, the committee's best judgment on the unemployment situation as of April, 1930 was that "the

9 Barber (1985), pp. 94-5.

> combined total of classes A and B run from 3,000,000 to 3,350,000 depending on whether deductions are made from Class B of persons estimated to be employed on part time.[10]

Unable to influence policy, Persons departed from the Census Bureau in May 1930. But, determined to make known his assessments based on his experience there, he quickly wrote several forceful journal articles which appear to have remained obscure and seldom referenced. (Our Chapters 7, 8 and 12 in *How the Crash Caused* discuss those articles in detail.)

The Economic Situation Deteriorates

As May progressed, the financial picture grew gloomier. (See the Statistics of U.S. Economic Activity shown in Table 7.5 (page 226) According to Barrie Wigmore:

> In May the characteristics of the end of a strong market emerged, such as high volume with little change in prices, a peak in new issues, a sharp rise in dealer call loans to finance unsold inventories, and then a sudden drop in trading volume as people realize the game is over.[11]

The Table 7.1 data for the Market Value of All Listed Stocks on the NYSE show that all did not yet appear totally lost, though the trend was definitely down. April's 1% decline was followed by a small 0.4% decline in May. The market still showed a rise from the end of 1929, but two months of declines chipped away at the rise. The first quarter had risen 17.6%. Adding in April, lowered the rise to 16.4%, and including May to 15.9%.[12] Comparatively, the

10 Ibid.

11 Wigmore (1985), pp. 139-140.

12 In defense of Wigmore, he was probably paying closer attention to the various stock market averages such as the Dow Industrials which did drop more seriously in May than the Market Value of All Listed Stocks on the NYSE.

Dow Industrials were up 15.1% in the first quarter, still up 12.4% through April, and, again, up 10.7% through May.[13]

The Great Depression Reaches Full Operational Effectiveness

Table 7.2

Instalment Credit Granted and Rate of Change for Automobiles[1] and Five Types of Reatail Establishments[2] Selected Months, 1928-30

($ million)

Month	Automobiles credit granted		Rate of change[3]	Five retailers combined credit granted		Rate of change[3]
	1928	1929				
Sep	$163.9	$185.7	13%			
Oct	168.1	190.7	13%			
Nov	138.1	142.2	3%			
Dec	118.6	121.2	2%			
	1929	1930		1929	1930	
Jan	$110.7	$103.5	-7%	$200.8	$190.4	-5%
Feb	132.5	120.0	-9%	234.9	214.9	-9%
Mar	205.9	175.0	-15%	331.2	282.8	-15%
Apr	251.7	207.3	-18%	402.0	339.5	-16%
May	270.3	164.2	-39%	426.2	296.0	-31%
Jun	264.6	193.6	-27%	410.9	313.3	-24%
Jul	265.9	170.2	-36%	387.5	268.7	-31%
Aug	240.9	146.8	-39%	374.4	255.2	-32%
Sep	185.7	130.7	-30%	319.5	240.1	-25%
Oct	190.7	118.7	-38%	331.3	233.0	-30%
Nov	142.2	88.8	-38%	274.3	196.7	-28%
Dec	121.2	96.8	-20%	308.8	247.3	-20%

[1]New and used passenger cars only.

[2]Includes dealers in new and used (passenger) automobiles, department stores, furniture stores, household appliance stores and jewelry stores.

[3]Minus sign indicates decrease in net credit; otherwise increase is to be understood.

Source: "The Volume of Consumer Instalment Credit, 1929-1938," NBER, Feb 1940, pp. 2, & 9, Appendix A.

While Table 6.2 (page 190) showed the steps that took place in the first quarter of 1930 in the causal linkage connecting the Crash

13 Pierce, Phyllis S., Editor, *The Dow Jones Averages 1885-1995, 4th Edition*, Irwin Professional Publishing, 1996.

of 1929 to the full-scale commencement of the Great Depression in the second quarter of 1930, Table 7.2 (opposite) extends the statistics to the end of 1930. The influence of the automotive industry on the nation's overall economic health is hard to overstate, and data from the sector feature prominently in the three lefthand columns. Covering monthly installment credit granted by automobile dealers to automobile purchasers, they show how credit granted compared from year-to-year. That comparison is eye-opening. In January 1930 the amount of credit granted was 7% lower than in January 1929, and that was just the beginning. Thereafter the comparative rate of credit granted fell month-by-month progressively faster each month until May 1930 when credit granted for purchasing automobiles declined a shocking 39% compared to 1929. From then on credit granted continued to decline at roughly the same general rate for the remainder of 1930.

The three righthand columns extend the nationwide installment credit picture to include credit granted for automobile dealers plus four retail establishments as delineated in the table. In January 1930 the amount of credit granted for this aggregate group was 5% lower than in January 1929. Thereafter the total credit granted fell progressively faster until May 1930 when total credit granted was down 31% in comparison to 1929. From then on, as with automotive dealer credit, aggregate credit in five major retail segments continued to decline at roughly the same general rate for the remainder of 1930.

A Short-Fall in Installment-Financed Consumer Sales in Spring 1930

Table 7.3 (following page) presents retail installment credit sales statistics for the Spring of 1930, compared with 1929 and 1928, based on the frequently cited 1940 NBER study. The data shows the down-then-up-then-down nature of installment credit over that period of the late twenties into 1930. Taking the month of

Table 7.3

Instalment Credit Granted in 2nd Quarter

($ million)

Automobile dealers[1]			
Month	1928	1929	1930
Apr	$180.9	$251.7	$207.3
May	211.6	270.3	164.2
Jun	206.1	264.6	193.6
Total	$598.6	$786.6	$565.1
5-retail establishments combined[2]			
		1929	1930
Apr		$402.0	$339.5
May		426.2	296.0
Jun		410.9	313.3
Total		$1,239.1	$948.8
Total Credit Outstanding on Two Dates			
	Automobile dealers	5-retail establishments	
31-Oct-1929	$1,446.5	$2,510.8	
30-Jun-1930	1,129.9	2,161.6	
Decline of	-$316.6	-$349.2	

[1]New and used passenger cars only.

[2]Includes dealers in new and used (passenger) automobiles, department stores, furniture stores, household appliance stores and jewelry stores.

Source: "The Volume of Consumer Instalment Credit, 1929-1938," NBER, Feb 1940, pp. 2, & 9, Appendix A.

April for automobile credit alone, for instance, while 12.7% above the April 1928 amount, it was 17.6% below the April 1929 figure. The full second quarter 1930 data confirms the downward trend. Total automobile installment sales statistics for the second quarter of 1930 were $565.1 million 28.2% below Spring 1929 and 5.6% below Spring 1928.

The shortfall in new credit granted by automobile dealers as reported in the NBER statistical study took effect nationwide during the Spring of 1930. In our view, its impact resulted in the full-scale commencement of the Great Depression at that time. However, given that the study was not published until 1940, it is unlikely that anyone on Wall Street or Washington in 1930 could have seen what those later-published statistics showed. Furthermore, we do not believe any others have determined a cause-and-effect linkage between the Crash of 1929 as cause and the Great Depression as effect, let alone done so by using the statistics in NBER's 1940 study.

Table 7.3 also presents third and fourth quarter 1930 data that show the ongoing shortfalls that sustained the Great Depression.

In any case, business owners across the country who used installment credit to sell merchandise on our nation's Main Streets likely recognized, based on their own experience as well as that of nearby establishments, what was going on. Even Calvin Coolidge, from his post-Presidential perch as a newspaper columnist, hinted that he knew a problem was developing with for-credit sales. As Kindleberger later wrote:

> [I]t is hard to avoid the conclusion that there is something to the conventional wisdom that characterized the crash as the start of the process.... The stock market crash is less interesting for the irony it permits the historian, bemused by the foibles of greedy men, than for starting a process that took on a dynamic of its own.[14]

Rough Seas on Wall Street Cut a Holiday Voyage Short

Versions of history written contemporaneously, especially eyewitness reports, hold special resonance. Aboard a ship that left New York Harbor in late Spring 1930 was our oft-reference source, *New York Times* financial editor Noyes. In his memoir he recalled the optimism that was on his fellow voyagers' minds, yet how

---

14 Kindleberger (1986), p. 116.

short-lived it turned out to be as along with them he experienced first-hand what he called the "harsh realities of the whole situation." We offer Noyes's dramatic account of that stressful descent—taking place mid-Atlantic—of once-affluent ocean voyagers moving from Successful Speculators (post-Crash) towards becoming Repentant Ex-Speculators (post-Crash):

> Early in June of 1930 I happened to have taken passage on an east-bound trans-Atlantic steamer. Its passenger-list included numerous Wall Street men, who had sailed in a mood of happiness over the market's substantial and apparently sustained recovery. The radio and the steamer's daily "news sheet" (which will not nowadays allow vacationists to enjoy their rest) reported every morning, as a matter of course, the preceding day's New York stock-market prices. Not even a broker's downtown office blackboard, with the crumbling prices marked on it as they were established on the Stock Exchange, could produce the stunning effect of these successive mid-ocean bulletins. Everyone realized at once that the market's previous recovery had been fallacious; that reaction and depression, instead of being ended, had in reality only begun. The hurried canceling of expensive motor car tours, preparation for the earliest possible return to America, the desperate and usually unsuccessful effort to straighten out by wireless such personal speculative accounts as had been left outstanding on the New York market—all this was only one of a thousand incidents in that month's crushing disappointment. On land as at sea, illusion disappeared. The harsh realities of the whole situation began to present themselves.[15]

Thereafter, we will see, especially with Hoover's signing of the controversial Smoot-Hawley Tariff Act in late June, the addition of more and more storm clouds to the increasingly woeful atmosphere.

15 Noyes (1938), p. 343.

There was deepening pessimism and even a sense of hopelessness as bad news became more widespread. In due course, what austerity advocate Ogden Livingston Mills, who became Hoover's Treasury Secretary in 1932, described as the "psychology of fear" seized the entire national community.[16]

Indeed, economic conditions were heading directly into stormy seas.

Economic Decline Accelerates

June brought much more rapid deterioration notably with the fall in commodity prices. In his memoir, Noyes called attention to the ongoing fall of commodity prices in 1930 as an especially ominous sign of weakness on the demand side, particularly in farming, but in many business sectors as well. Noyes reported that the government's average of commodity prices, which even in September 1929 was about the same as in 1927, had fallen 11 per cent by June 1930. In June alone, the price of wheat declined 25 per cent, making a total fall of 50% since the end of 1929, the lowest figure in sixteen years.[17]

June also brought a rapidly collapsing stock market that spelled the end of the Little Bull Market. While all listed NYSE stocks declined in market value only -0.4% from May 1 to June 1 as Table 7.1 (page 201) shows, the decline from June 1 to July 1 was -14.8%. Then, following the market rise of 15.9% between January 1 and June 1, June's decline caused a -1.3% drop from January 1 to July 1. Furthermore, the Dow Industrials provided, of the two measures, the more pessimistic assessment of stock performance in that, having been up 10.7% from December 31, 1929 to May 31, 1930, it then declined -17.7% in June 1930. For the entire first half of 1930, the Dow Industrials were down –8.9%.

---

16 Ibid. Under Secretary of the Treasury until early 1932 when he replaced Secretary Mellon, Ogden Livingston Mills (1884-1937), a pedigreed member of America's upper class, was a Harvard-educated lawyer, politician and businessman with interests in mining, railroads and banking.

17 Noyes (1938), pp. 342-3.

The Search for A Second Opinion

We turn now to the financial sphere other than the stock markets, specifically on the demand for and supply of money at banks and in money markets. Was money readily available or was it scarce? Did banks have a ready supply available for borrowers? Or were they rationing credit? As we shall see, these questions tie in with an assertion made by Charles Persons (and scrutinized in Chapter 12 in *How the Crash Caused*) that retailers, long accustomed to using installment credit to sell merchandise, and their customers who were accustomed to using installment credit to make purchases, had somehow exceeded articulated credit limits in the fourth quarter of 1929. Our research led us to question there being credit limits.

Early in his *Only Yesterday's* Chapter XIII, entitled "Crash!," Frederick Lewis Allen awarded "1929 gold medals for foresight" to six parties who he felt had called the situation correctly. His first three awardees gave investment advice, specifically Roger W. Babson, the Standard Trade and Securities Service of the Standard Statistics Company and Poor's *Weekly Business and Investment Letter.* Next Allen named a senior banker (and former Fed Vice Chairman) Paul M. Warburg, whom we have devoted attention to. Finally, he included two journalists: the (unnamed) editors of the weekly *The Commercial & Financial Chronicle* and the financial editor of the *New York Times* (who, as we know, was our oft-quoted Alexander Dana Noyes.)[18]

It turns out that *The Commercial & Financial Chronicle* had been around since 1865. Published every Saturday, it could only be described as a miracle of conscientious statistical and business reporting at a remarkably in-depth level of, at times, excruciating detail considering the manual data collection and printing methods of the time.[19] Each edition, just shy of two hundred pages, report-

18 Allen (1931), p. 280.

19 The subscription price was $10 for 12 months (equivalent to $180 in 2024). The issues contained advertising as well. We were unable to determine its weekly circulation. The C&FC also offered periodic industry-specific reports for an additional amount.

ed on and analyzed "The Financial Situation" in New York, the U.S. and the world. Given its reputation and diligence, we chose to scrutinize its issues for May and June of 1930 to get a sense of contemporaneous reporting and in search of further insights about the baffling quarter. What follows is a series of observations made by the prolific editorial voice of *The Chronicle* from various editions beginning May 3:

May 3:

> Outside the United States trade depression was already a widely prevalent condition before the stock market collapse in this country, and the cheapening of money rates which followed so quickly thereafter has not served to relieve the state of trade depression in the least, demonstrating that cheap money is no panacea for such a state of things.... [H]ere, likewise, growing ease in money has failed to furnish relief, trade prostration having steadily grown in intensity.[20]

On the *highly unusual rate structure* offered by the Reserve Banks:

> [O]ur Federal Reserve Banks, contrary to the custom abroad, make it a practice to keep their rediscount rates *below market rates* for money, thereby inviting and encouraging borrowing at the Federal Reserve institutions.[21] (our emphasis)

In other words, by charging rediscount rates that were below money market rates, the Reserve Banks offered to member banks rates that made it possible for them to lend the money in money markets profitably.

---

20 *The Commercial & Financial Chronicle,* May 3, 1930, Vol. 130, No. 3384, p. 3043.

21 Ibid., p. 3044.

At present there is a super abundance of loanable funds, and trade is in no need of extra funds.... [T]he member banks find no means of placing additional funds, and hence have no occasion to avail of the facilities of the Reserve institutions, even after putting out greatly increased amounts in brokers' loans. This being so, they refrain from going into debt, even with the Federal Reserve Bank rate so attractive at present. On that point it is worth noting that the Federal Reserve Bank of New York shows [at] the present week discount holdings (which reflect member bank borrowing) of only [$41.3 million].... [22]

May 31:

It is safe to say that there is not the least likelihood of starting a new speculation on the Stock Exchange, inasmuch as the professional traders on the Exchange after this second crash in less than six months have become wary, while the growing depression in trade, with the poor income statements made by the railroads month after month, and by the industrial corporations in their returns for the first quarter of the year, render such an undertaking altogether out of the question.[23]

June 21:

The week has been marked by a number of important events, among the chief of which have been (1) the signing by the President of the Smoot-Hawley tariff bill.... (2) a renewed violent collapse in the stock market, carrying a long list of stocks not only to the lowest figures of 1930, but in not a few instances lower even than at the time of

---

22 Ibid., p. 3044.

23 *The Commercial & Financial Chronicle,* May 31, 1930, Vol. 130, No. 3388, p. 3767.

the great smash in the stock market last fall; (3) the action of the Federal Reserve Bank of New York in announcing … another reduction of ½ of 1% in its rediscount rate, carrying the rate down to 2½%, this cut being made at a time when there is a plenitude of banking credit and banking funds everywhere at extremely low interest rates, indicating that there is no need … for putting out additional Reserve credit or adding to the inducements existing for borrowing at the Reserve institutions or for availing of Reserve credit; (4) further breaks in large number of cases in the commodities market to the lowest figures of the year, and, in some cases, … all time, and (5) growing intensity of trade depression, with apparently no prospect of early relief.

The whole presents a very gloomy picture.… It seems to us that all these unfavorable features can be traced to a common cause, and that is mistaken attempts to maintain an artificial state of things instead of letting a needed adjustment take place in a natural, normal way.…

Member banks have stopped borrowing, but the Federal Reserve Banks have kept pouring out reserve credit through their open market operations … even though there was not the slightest need for any extra "high powered" credit of this kind.… [24]

Is it not about time that the plan of producing abnormal ease in the money market were abandoned?[25]

The stock market suffered another severe breakdown this week. Selling proceeded at a furious pace, and the declines in prices reached prodigious proportions, finding

24 *The Commercial & Financial Chronicle,* June 21, 1930, Vol. 130, No. 3391, p. 4289.

25 Ibid., p. 4290.

its only counterpart in that other and major collapse which occurred last October–November. The losses were especially heavy on Monday and Wednesday, when the market had a very panicky appearance, and it seemed as if there were no bottom to it. The collapse on Monday was referred to in several newspapers as being a response to the announcement made by President Hoover on Sunday night that he would immediately sign the new tariff bill as agreed upon in conference and adopted by the two houses of Congress. The bill is certainly not looked upon with favor by the mercantile and financial community.[26]

June 28:

The trade and industrial outlook has not changed any for the better during the present week. The developments have all been along the lines noted last week and have tended to accentuate the prevailing feeling of gloom and depression. There have been further violent declines on the Stock Exchange; the agricultural markets have suffered a new collapse[;] … returns of railroad earnings for the month of May, now coming to hand show losses of appalling magnitude[;] … banking funds are almost unlendable….

The country is suffering from business depression as severe as any in the country's history….

The action now taken is like that taken on all similar occasions in the past, and is the usual attendant of periods of business depression. On this occasion, however, the glut of loanable funds and the inability to obtain remunerative employment for them has been greatly aggravated by the

26 Ibid., p. 4292.

> policy pursued by the Federal Reserve Banks in keeping reserve credit out unnecessarily and by reducing rediscount rates to abnormally low figures.[27]

These various quotations from over the two months of May and June, confirm the "real time" seriousness of the downward trend and the attempt by the *The Chronicle* to explain why.

Available Statistics Showed Demand for Cars and Trucks Declining Fast

We return to the automotive sector because of its wide-ranging influence on Wall Street and Main Street. While investors, speculators and those on Wall Street in 1930 were unaware of the shortfall in installment credit sales reported above and shown in Tables 7.2 and 7.3, (pages 204 and 206) they certainly had available to them monthly car and truck production statistics. Manufacturers reported their vehicle production output monthly to the U.S. Commerce Department and to trade publications such as *Automobile Trade Journal and Motor Age* following their monthly closes, and the statistics were available in the financial press toward the end of the following month. For example, *The Chronicle* reported the April production of automobiles in its Saturday, May 24, 1930 issue, but the question arises as to how Wall Street interpreted what was going on in Detroi

Table 7.4 (following page) (which corresponds to Table 8.2 in *How the Crash Caused*) shows the dramatic month-to-month drop in the factory output of motor vehicles in 1929 and 1930, statistics that would, of course, have been known on Wall Street. The average drop from January through May of 1930 of - 31.3%, was only exceeded by a -49.2% fall from June through October, with the average for November and December down a further -4.5%.

27 *The Commercial & Financial Chronicle,* June 28, 1930, Vol. 130, No. 3392, p. 4471.

Table 7.4			
Cars and Trucks Produced (In Thousands)			
Month	1929	1930	Percent gain or loss
Jan.	422.5	283.6	-32.9%
Feb.	497.7	346.0	-30.5%
Mar.	626.1	417.1	-33.4%
Apr.	663.8	468.3	-29.5%
May	636.3	444.7	-30.1%
June	567.4	349.6	-38.4%
July	518.3	275.7	-46.8%
Aug.	512.8	234.2	-54.3%
Sept.	429.7	228.6	-46.8%
Oct.	394.5	158.9	-59.7%
Nov.	227.0	142.2	-37.4%
Dec.	125.5	161.3	28.5%
Totals	5,621.6	3,510.2	-37.6%

(Data differs from Vol. 1, Table 8.2 due to source difference)

Source: *Facts and Figures of the Automobile Industry,* 1931 Edition, National Automobile Chamber of Commerce, p. 6.

Passenger Car Production Figures for 1930

Having looked at figures for the production of both cars and trucks, we now break out statistics for the production of passenger cars alone. Figure 7.1, (opposite) extends Figure 3.1 (page 87) through a sixth year to the end of 1930. The line labeled "Passenger Car Production" connects monthly production levels through December 1930. The solid area, which was blue in the image originally

Figure 7.1

Passenger Car Output Adjusted to Domestic and Foreign Sales

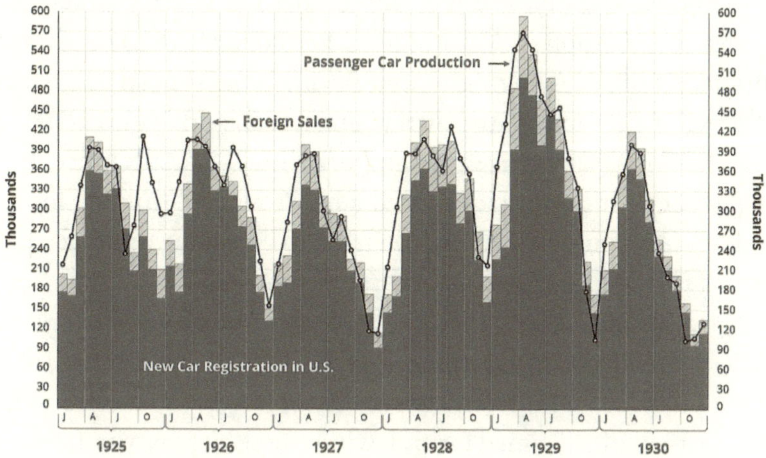

Production curve includes United States and Canada output. Monthly vertical bars represent new car registration in United Sates and foreign sales (cross-hatched top portion). Foreign sales include exports from United Sates, foreign assemblies and Canadian production.

published, shows columns of "New Car Registrations in the U.S. The shaded area at the top of each column shows "Foreign Sales." Reflecting President Hoover's entreaty to U.S. manufacturers that they not lay off workers, production, which had fallen sharply in the final months of 1929, rebounded briefly for the first two months of 1930, exceeding U.S. registrations plus foreign sales. After the peak in production in April, however, Hoover's exhortations all but forgotten, production fell steeply, interrupted only once with an uptick. In 1929, that uptick had taken place in August; in 1930, the uptick was in December.

Curiously, the drop in production that occurred in the automobile industry in 1930 was actually 60.9% of the drop in 1929. Nevertheless, it created many layoffs, and those workers who were laid off in late 1930 had much less hope that they would be called back to manufacturing automobiles in 1931.

June's Smoot-Hawley Tariff Bill

In mid-1930, adding to the various signs of weakness in the automotive industry, the job market and the stock market, was disputed legislation in Washington. For context, the U.S. Constitution authorized Congress to impose duties on imports as a means of providing revenue to the then young nation and to give domestic production an advantage over imports. But especially since 1913 when federal income taxes created a new source of funding for the Federal Government, the use of tariffs had become a tool for politicians favoring isolationism and protectionism.

In his 2011 book, *Peddling Protectionism: Smoot-Hawley and the Great Depression*, Dartmouth economics professor Douglas A. Irwin provided an in-depth look at the controversy that surrounded this particularly ill-timed tariff. Irwin himself determined from his research that Smoot-Hawley was "an unnecessary piece of legislation, indeed a futile one."[28] Professor Irwin summed up:

> In the end, we conclude that the stigma of Smoot-Hawley is well deserved. It failed to achieve its domestic goal of helping farmers and it backfired against the United States around the world. It should always be remembered as a warning about the adverse consequences of poorly considered trade policies.[29]

Introduced well before the Crash ostensibly to help financially-strapped farmers, the Smoot-Hawley tariff worked its way through the Republican-dominated House where it was passed in late May 1929. The Senate then began tedious modifications of the House-passed version (making an absurd 1,253 amendments) and, on March 24, 1930, after acceding to Hoover's demands for flexible

---

28 Douglas Irwin, *Peddling Protectionism: Smoot-Hawley and the Grest Depression,* Princeton University Press, 2011, p. 218.

29 Ibid., p. 221.

tariff authority for the executive branch, the Senate passed the Act by a mostly partisan vote of 53-31. Logrolling—trading votes for favors—dominated the Senate debates. The bill then went to the White House to for President Hoover's signature.

Strong opposition to the Act included a May 1930 letter to President Hoover signed by over one thousand American economists, Irving Fisher among them, urging Hoover to veto the bill. Their voices were joined by other leading citizens including Henry Ford, Secretary of State Henry Stimson and Thomas Lamont of J.P. Morgan. [30] On June 15, the New York Stock Exchange dropped 1.16 % upon the news that Hoover intended to sign the bill, which he did on June 17. It went into effect as the post-Crash economy teetered on the edge. Timing is everything. Smoot-Hawley may have been the final straw.

The following, taken from Irwin's book, is a sampling of quotes, both contemporaneous and written later, addressing the role of the Smoot-Hawley Tariff Act as a tipping point:

> *Reporter and political commentator Walter Lippmann:* The Act was "a wretched and mischievous product of stupidity and greed."[31]

> *Economist and author Joseph M. Jones:* The Smoot-Hawley tariff "has doubtless occasioned more comment, more controversy, more vituperation in the national as well as in the international sphere than any other tariff measure in history."[32]

> *Harvard professor, policy advisor and chairman of the Boston Federal Reserve Richard N. Cooper:* "The most disastrous

30 Ibid., p. 86.

31 Ibid.

32 Ibid., p. 33.

> single mistake any U.S. president has made in international relations was Herbert Hoover's signing of the Smoot–Hawley Tariff Act into law in June 1930."[33]

About this inopportune piece of legislation Irwin concluded:

> The final outcome satisfied very few of the interested parties and drew widespread criticism from the public. Even worse, the two major premises behind the tariff revision were flawed: that it could bring relief to farmers and that the flexible tariff provision could smooth out the iniquities of tariff."[34]

Retaliation by other nations, including close trade partner Canada, followed, worsening the economic environment worldwide. In the Democratic wave that hit the 1932 U.S. elections, neither Senator Reed Smoot of Utah nor Congressman Willis Hawley of Oregon was re-elected. Their dubious legacy has been indelible.

The Market Situation in June and Some Revealing Bank Loan Statistics

As we come to the end of the second quarter of 1930, we return to Wigmore's account of the stock market in which he elaborated further on the dark prospects in the market that June:

> June was the worst month for the stock market in 1930. The Dow Jones Industrial Index dropped almost 23% in response to commodities prices smashed to their lowest levels since 1914 and the enactment of the Smoot-Hawley tariff. Only 3 of 240 stocks followed by the New York Times rose

33 Ibid., p. 4.

34 Ibid., p. 95.

> in the month.... There was an air of inevitability in the June stock market as it declined.[35]

Beyond the stock market, bank loan statistics—both outstanding loans and loan repayments—reveal important clues as to what was going on. The Fed's *Banking and Monetary Statistics 1914-1941* shows that the volume of Bank Loans at All Member Banks declined in every quarter from October 4, 1929, to June 30, 1933, except for the second quarter of 1930, when loans show a slight increase of $95 million from $25,119 million on March 27 to $25,214 million on June 30.[36] While we have not been able to verify when within the second quarter this increase took place, we found it telling how urgently Noyes's fellow passengers ended European jaunts and returned to the States to try and put their affairs in order concurrent with the precipitous fall in June's stock market. The $95 million increase in loans outstanding likely came about at the end of June as speculators sought cover.

The Market Value of All Listed Stocks on the NYSE shown in Table 7.1 (page 201) declined 14.8% from the opening of June to July 1, more than wiping out the albeit declining gains from January to May. June's decline brought the market down 1.26% from the optimistic start of the year.

Picturing the Market Decline

Data can reveal considerable drama, especially over eventful short-term periods such as those first six months of 1930 and certainly over each of the three momentous years of 1928, 1929 and 1930. But the data also offer a broader historical perspective.

---

35 Wigmore (1985), pp. 140-142.

36 *BMS, 1914-1941,* Table 18, p. 72.

Chart 7.1

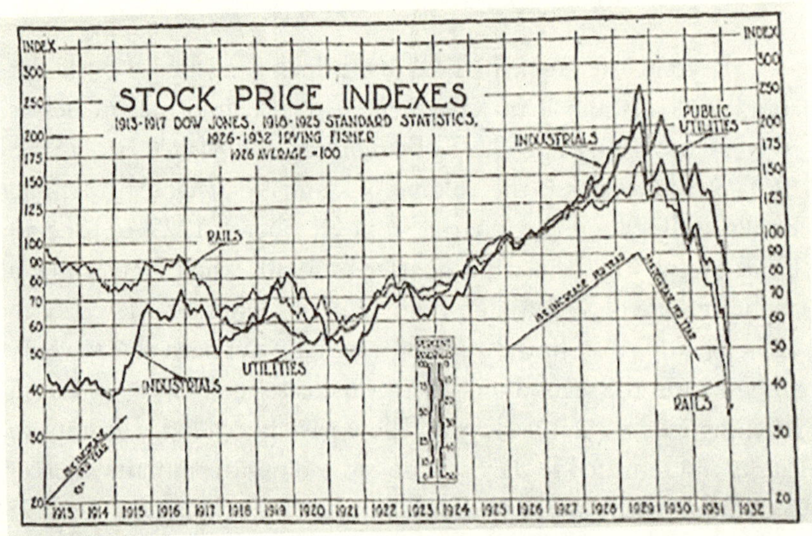

Chart 7.1, (above) reproduced from Irving Fisher's 1932 book *Booms and Depressions*, is a prime example of the power of data to tell a story of the times. The chart presents a sweeping, if vintage, look at the monthly performance of three early indices—the Industrials Index, the Rails Index and the Utilities Index—from January 1913 to December 1931.[37]

Of particular interest, the chart shows the evolution of the three indices both independently and relative to each other, and that story serves as a telling indicator of industrialization and the electrification of the country.[38] In 1913, the Rails average was roughly twice that of the Industrial average, but by the start of 1918, the Rails had dropped considerably, the Industrials had risen somewhat, and the Utilities Index commenced between the two. Not surprisingly, by

37 The Industrials and Rails Indices began being tracked, so to speak, at the start of 1913 based on Dow Jones data, and the Utilities Index began at the start of 1918. Figures from the period 1918-25 were based on Standard Statistics' data, and Fisher himself compiled the data for the period 1926-32. All three indexes were normalized by Fisher such that the 1926 figures were each averaged to equal 100.

38 Irving Fisher (1932), p. 194.

the end of 1928, the Industrials Index was highest, the Rails Index was lowest and the Utilities Index was still between the other two.

The chart also tells an eloquent story about the growing contraction in demand during the Crash period. From the Crash through November, all three indices plummeted, rose through March 1930, then, with a brief rise in early 1931, they fell precipitously until the end of 1931.

How Successful Speculators Became Repentant Ex-Speculators in 1930

Noyes described what was happening to two particular members of our Cast of Characters—Successful Speculators (post-Crash) and Repentant Ex-Speculators (post-Crash):

> [T]here were...professional speculators who had withdrawn from the market when, in the middle of 1929, it began to look dangerous to them, and who...at the year end [of 1929] reentered [the market], buying stocks with borrowed money on a very substantial scale. This turned out to be a most unfortunate experiment.
>
> The stock market did regain part of the lost ground but, instead of maintaining the recovery, it presently resumed its precipitous decline.... The singular result of the recovery in stocks at the end of 1929 was that a long list of Wall Street men, who by their prudence had escaped being wrecked in the October storm, went on the rocks through buying stocks for the anticipated upturn. In numerous instances, speculators confronted with ruin at the year end [1929] applied later for help to acquaintances who were known to have acted wisely early in 1929, only to find that these men also had incurred paralyzing losses through their ventures of 1930.[39]

39 Noyes (1938), pp. 341-2.

In other words, by renewing their speculative activities at the end of 1929 and into 1930, "a long list of Wall Street men," as Noyes called them, or "old hands" in Wigmore's words, whom we would include as Successful Speculators (post-Crash), fell from that normally prudent group to join, most unhappily, the Repentant Ex-Speculators in 1930. As Wigmore put it:

> Old hands in the securities business remember vividly the optimism that prevailed in the early months of 1930, because many investors were enticed back into the stock market only to be wiped out in the drawn-out market decline which followed. The smart money was lost in this aftermath.[40]

In point of fact, as a consequence of the market's behavior in 1930—plummeting stock prices and massive financial losses—there effectively ceased to be any members left within the Successful Speculators (post-Crash) group. It was a role that had virtually disappeared, as had for the time being the whole phenomenon of speculation.

January Through June 1930 — Ups Then Downs

From the vantage point of 1939, Professor Joseph Schumpeter of Harvard described the tumultuous first half of 1930 as producing a "meaningless flurry" of financial activity, while business overall limped along:

> The businessmen and forecasters, who in the fall of 1929 had made up their minds that nothing worse was ahead than a "recession" not much more serious than that of, say, 1924, cannot have been very disappointed by the general look of things during the first half of 1930. At the beginning, stock prices rallied strongly, security issues were large, signs of

40 Wigmore (1985), p. 128.

> the improvement showed in many spots, money was easy. All that, except the easy money—prime commercial paper rate fell from about 4.89 per cent in January to 2 per cent in August, and was 2.88 in December; for June it was 3.54 per cent—passed quickly, it is true, and proved to have been a meaningless flurry, due perhaps to the confidence that was so widely felt or to the organized effort [by Hoover in Washington and corporate heads] to make a stand that prompted some additional spending. But until about the end of June business moved along on a but slowly falling level not much below the figures of 1929 in practically all lines.[41]

At some point markets react to trends. We consider June 1930 to be one such inflection point. In comparison with October 1929 (see Table 9.1 of *How the Crash Caused,*), by April 1930, as soon shown in Table 7.5, just ahead, annualized personal income was down 7.3%, the index of factory employment was down 9.0, and the index of industrial production was down 10.9%. In May, these three statistics were down 8.6%, 10.2% and 12.7% respectively from October 1929. We suggest that the dramatic drop of the stock market in June 1930 constituted a growing recognition that economic activity was on a distinctly downward trendline that was not likely to experience a reversal as 1930 went on. As we continue to show tables of these statistics quarterly through 1930, it will be clear that this is what occurred. We suggest that in June 1930 the stock market was finally registering reality.

41 Schumpeter (1939), p. 911.

Table 7.5					
Statistics of U.S. Economic Activity ($ billion)					
	Feb. '30	Mar. '30	Apr. '30	May '30	Jun. '30
Annualized personal income	$80.9	$79.6	$80.0	$78.9	$77.5
Index of factory employment	99.0	97.7	97.0	95.7	93.9
Index of industrial production	100	98	98	96	93
Index of wholesale prices	91.4	90.2	90.0	88.8	86.8
Friedman & Schwartz demand deposits	$22.2	$22.6	$22.3	$21.6	$21.6
Fed member bank loans		$25.1			$25.2

Sources: *HSUS* 1789-1945, pp. 328-330, 344; *Monetary History*, p.713; *BMS*, p.74.

2nd QTR 1930 Statistics of Debt Repayment

All Fed Member Banks: The volume of borrowing at All Fed Member Banks increased +$95 million in the 2nd quarter of 1930 with an average monthly debt repayment of -$344 million in the 1st quarter and a monthly average of +$32 million in increased borrowing in the 2nd quarter.

All U.S. Commercial Banks: Repayments to All U.S. Commercial Banks totaled -$1,427 million in the 1st half of 1930—an average monthly debt repayment by businesses, individuals and "others" of -$238 million. All Fed Member Banks are included in All U.S. Commercial Banks.

Aggregate Corporate Notes and Accounts Receivable (ACNAR) — All Payers: Total ACNAR repaid by businesses, individuals and "others" in full year 1930 equaled -$7,135 million—an average monthly repayment of -$595 million.

Individuals only: We estimate that individuals and consumers repaid more than $4+ billion to U.S. corporations in 1930—an average monthly repayment of more than -$333 million.

Following the 2nd quarter, debt repayments resumed and grew.

CHAPTER 8

Thoughts of a Quick Recovery Vanish (Third Quarter of 1930)

> By the middle of 1930, the country knew it was in an industrial depression; it knew little of the causes; it was beginning to suspect that its leaders, in industry and politics, had been stupid. By the end of June it knew, also, that the President would neither lead nor be led. There was nothing to be done and the country sat back and waited. The summer months are a lull in the excitement of the crisis.[1]

We take advantage of this lull described by cultural commentator Gilbert Seldes for some reflections of our own. In July 1930, as the economy was shuddering, former President Coolidge, whose decision not to run for a second term had opened the way for his popular Commerce Secretary, Herbert Hoover, to win a landslide victory in the 1928 election, began a brief career as a syndicated newspaper columnist. Coolidge's inaugural column was "a survey of conditions" on the new decade that had begun, especially about the increasingly serious national economic downturn. Seldes found Coolidge's attitude in that article "quite hard-headed and realistic" and added that Coolidge "seemed to be aware of the new economics of capitalism which created demand and in which a steady and steadily growing demand, even to the point of extravagance, was essential to prosperity."[2] In the Prologue

1 Seldes (1933), p. 56.

2 Ibid., p. 60.

of *How the Crash Caused*, we described the confluence of factors powering demand in the 1920s that manifested, at its extreme, in stock speculation. Prosperity had, in fact, become the American Dream for many Americans, who willingly went into debt, either consuming or speculating on margin —and, for some, both —in efforts to make their version of that dream come true.

The painful outcome of those two forms of indebtedness quickly materialized during the Crash period. First, stock-price freefalls occured during the week of the Crash as the volume of sell orders greatly exceeded the volume of buy orders. The first occured during the morning of Black Thursday, October 24. In the course of these freefalls, the authors determined that many speculators lost considerably more than they thought they had at risk, and we defined such losses as as "unexpected residual losses." Our estimate was that more than $5 billion was lost in the Crash by speculators with margin accounts. Of this quantity our guesstimates were that more than $1.7 billions probably constituted unexpected residual losses while a low of $1.3 billion and a high of $3.2 billion were within reason. (See pages 223-25 and pages 238-9 in *How the Crash Caused.*) Seacond, on top of that, consumer indebtedness, which had reached far more broadly into society and touched far more people than stock speculation, moved front and center for many more Americans. True, both forms of debt had expanded purchasing power in the prosperous 1920s, to the benefit of U.S. corporations and their shareholders, just as that expanded purchasing power improved people's standard of living. But, at what ultimate cost?

Seldes quoted Coolidge further about the downside to these developments. "We need more faith in ourselves," Coolidge insisted, advising his readers that,

> [T]he principal consuming power is in the people who have work. Unless they buy [from] the other fellow, he cannot buy [from] them. If those who have the means would pay all their retail merchandise bills and in addition purchase what they need and can afford, a healthy commerce would

quickly be created.[3]

Seldes pointed out, however, that by the time of Coolidge's column, "[t]he newspapers with their campaigns, Buy Now, and the department stores who echoed it…were not so scrupulous." Such bald encouragement to take on even further indebtedness as the depression was deepening contrasted with Coolidge's concept of the "healthy commerce" he felt the nation needed.[4]

By mid-1930, the faith Coolidge urged was inadequate to the task of calming the mounting anxiety enough to maintain the status quo. Recognizing the size of the hole they had dug, Americans quickly became risk averse. Consumption activity, even stimulated by advertising (buy now) and easy credit terms (pay later), stalled as individuals refocused from speculating and consuming toward repaying debts. Seldes, writing in the depths of 1933, continued philosophically:

> The Administration and the governors of thought were saying that except we become as little children we should not enter the heaven of prosperity; prosperity, in short, was something which would *happen* to us again, not something we had to create ourselves….They could hardly have known that they were paralyzing the will of the American people and, by compelling us to avert our faces from actuality, were draining off our moral power.
>
> The effects were noticeable….For a people given to action, and not to contemplation….[t]hey had passed through two periods of excited action in a generation—the war and the great boom—and both had been more or less common enterprises of the nation. The third—recovery from the evils engendered by the other two—found them without a call to action.[5]

3 Ibid., pp. 58-9.
4 Ibid., pp. 59-60.
5 Ibid., pp. 61-2.

For the benefit of 21st Century readers, we point out that Gilbert Seldes was expressing the common notion at the time that, once peacetime adjustments came to a rocky end in 1920 and 1921 with its own deep depression and a smooth recovery in 1922-3, these earlier "two periods of excited action"—the Great War and the great boom of prosperity—both occurred in response to strong influence expressed volubly by opinion leaders, both presidential and in the private sector. But as of the summer of 1930, President Hoover had not formulated a federal government approach that he believed would achieve as smooth a recovery as had taken place a decade earlier. Reluctant as he was to interfere in "natural" and private-sector economic processes, Hoover offered no motivating call to united action and certainly no specific remedies. Individuals were thus left to create their own calls to action, and they did just that by individually and autonomously focusing on paying their debts instead of buying.

The Economic Process Shifts and Changes.

As Harvard political economist Joseph Schumpeter summarized in his 1939 book, *Business Cycles*, for the first half of 1930, business moved along "on a but slowly falling level." He added:

> The second half of the year presents a wholly different picture. What was generally recognized as a liquidation all round was the outstanding feature. Rates of contraction quickened and comparison with 1929 figures became increasingly melancholy. .... [P]eople felt that the ground under their feet was giving way.[6]

Professor Schumpeter's choice of the word "melancholy" accurately described the mood as the ground underfoot indeed shook for both individuals and corporations. For a growing number of individuals, the shaking involved unemployment or its threat, on top of whatever indebtedness they had.

---

6 Schumpeter, p. 911.

Table 8.1

Consumer Price Index: All Urban Consumers 1930

Monthly Percentage Change, Annualized

(% percent)

Jan	Feb	Mar	Apr	May	Jun	Jul	Aug	Sep	Oct	Nov	Dec
0.0	-0.6	-0.6	0.6	-0.6	-1.8	-4.0	-4.6	-4.0	-4.6	-5.2	-6.4

Wholesale Prices for the United States 1930

Monthly Percentage Change, Annualized

(% percent)

Jan	Feb	Mar	Apr	May	Jun	Jul	Aug	Sep	Oct	Nov	Dec
-3.6	-4.2	-6.3	-5.7	-6.2	-8.8	-12.7	-12.5	-12.2	-12.7	-12.9	-14.7

Source: (CPI): Bureau of Labor Statistics (BLS), all items in U.S city average, 1913-2017. (WPI): Index of Wholesale Prices for the United States, Federal Reserve Bank of St. Louis, Economic Research Division, 1913-1968.

We now turn to monthly (annualized) data for 1930 for the consumer price index (CPI) and the wholesale price index (WPI) for a quick look at what was taking place over the course of the year. In January, the CPI annualized number was zero which means that no aggregate price changes occurred. April's positive number showed very slight inflation, but over the first five months of 1930, prices changed collectively at a deflationary rate of less than -1.0% per annum. Then, in June, deflation accelerated to -1.8%, again annualized. In the second half of the year, consumer prices overall fell much faster. From July 1930 to October deflation occurred at annualized rates of -4.0% or greater. Then in November the rate of deflation rose to -5.2% and in December to -6.4%.

As to the WPI, deflation occurred in every month, by a generally rising amount, and faster than CPI deflation grew. In the first half of 1930, wholesale prices fell in the U.S. at generally accelerating single digit rates from an annualized rate of -3.6% in January to -8.8% in June. But, from July to November deflation worsened at annualized rates between -12.0% and -13.0% before reaching -14.7% in December.

We continue by addressing a number of other deflationary concerns as 1930 wore on, starting with a rapidly developing problem with mortgage loans in the U.S.

A Labyrinth of Borrowers and Lenders

While we have covered the installment debt situation and the slippery slope of speculation, we now focus on a critical component of the indebtedness trap so many Americans found themselves in—mortgages. More often than one might think, American family histories include stories of foreclosure or other mortgage difficulties during the Depression period with their often-traumatic effects.

Mortgages, then as now, were the means by which millions of wage-earning and salaried Americans moved from rural areas or crowded cities and bought homes in the rapidly expanding suburbs around major cities. Ready credit offered by various types of mortgage lenders brought an explosion in homeownership and its accompanying indebtedness: mortgages for new houses and installment debt for the necessities of suburban living, including for automobiles and furnishings for new homes. In prosperity and a period stable employment, such debts were deemed manageable. However, they became a powder keg in the aftermath of the Crash, which Irving Fisher accurately labeled over-indebtedness.

Statistics on loan repayments showed how quickly debtors felt that over-indebtedness and shifted on balance to repaying their debts, usually by cutting back on consumption spending. Yet when we sought facts and figures about mortgages in the late 1920s and 1930s—both for mortgage lenders (mortgagees) and mortgage holders (mortgagors)—we encountered a labyrinth of financial structures that created obstacles to finding helpful data. These data challenges, of concern as they were to us, were doubtless considerably more disturbing at the time to government, banking and business leaders who were trying to respond to the increasing financial distress of mortgagors and the deflation that was rapidly and alarmingly affecting the values of mortgaged properties and thus mortgages.

We encountered issues with mortgages in Chapter 3 (p. 65) in the context of the "distress selling" that was happening after the Crash. We quoted Professor Kindleberger regarding what mortgage holders were contending with as cash-strapped homeowners, many with unamortized three-year obligations they could not pay off, then failed to secure loans elsewhere and faced foreclosures, thus causing a sharp drop in home prices. Clearly, compared to today, the mortgage of the time was structured precariously. Mortgages then fell into three categories: interest payments only with a balloon payment of principle upon maturity; partially self-amortizing; or fully self-amortizing over longer maturities. Most commercially-financed mortgages were relatively short-term in nature. It wasn't until 1927 with passage of the McFadden Act that national banks were entitled legally to enter into mortgage agreements for up to five years.

Deflation Leads to Falling Real Estate Prices and Problems with Mortgages

The overarching problem in terms of researching the mortgage sector transcended just the complexity of terms regarding the repayment of principal. There was, in fact, a total absence of reliable contemporary statistics, which was a big obstacle to addressing meaningful corrective actions much less taking them. One factor was the diversity of the enterprises that offered mortgages. Mortgage lending practices, real estate sales, even foreclosures were activities, sometimes regulated by states, but certainly undertaken at *local* mostly unregulated levels except for specific activities like title registrations, zoning oversight and sheriff's sales. When the economy sputtered, government policymakers at all levels—federal, state and local—quickly recognized that they had almost no information on the practices followed by the diverse mortgage lenders or about the types of mortgages made. As problems arose within the residential real estate sector in 1930 and beyond, the lack of reliable information and data on property sales and financing led slowly to more coordinated efforts to gather relevant statistics, but not until well after the crises of those years had passed. Meanwhile, officials and others for whom that information might have proven useful at the time were pretty much in the dark as prices fell, foreclosures increased, and families lost their homes.

In order for us to fill in certain details about how this large sector influenced the trajectory of the Great Depression, we drew on research conducted in the late 1930s, 1940s and 1950s that specifically looked at what had occurred especially within residential mortgages from 1930-33. One valuable research discovery was a meticulously researched report written by economist David L. Wickens for the Social Science Research Association that was published in 1941 by NBER.[7] (See Sidebar for a description.) Wickens' report confirmed

7 David L. Wickens, *Residential Real Estate, it's Economic Position as shown by Values, Rents, Family Incomes, Financing and Construction, together with Estimates for all Real Estate,* National Bureau of Economic Research, 1941.

the relatively short term of many mortgages of the period, depending upon type of lender:

> The prevailing practice of the chief classes of lenders is illustrated by the terms of outstanding loans reported in 1934 in the 52 Financial Survey cities. Three-year loans were held largely by commercial banks, 5-year loans by life insurance companies, 10- and 12-year loans by building and loan associations; loans for 15 years or more were usually held by individual investors, the Home Owners Loan Corporation, and a few life insurance companies.[8]

An Inquiry into Local Mortgage Problems

One early post-period publication with the cumbersome title *Residential Real Estate, it's Economic Position as shown by Values, Rents, Family Incomes, Financing and Construction, together with Estimates for all Real Estate* (for short, *"RRE"*) was by farmer, economist and politician David L. Wickens. The Foreword to this 1941 book began:

> The Division of Industry and Trade of the Committee on Credit and Banking of the Social Science Research Council outlined in December 1932 a program of studies in banking policy and credit control in relation to economic stability.... The initial project, a study of durable goods and capital formation in the United States, 1919–1933, was started in January 1933 by the National Bureau of Economic Research under the direction of Simon Kuznetz.

> The only project undertaken [in the second stage of the program was] the investigation by David L. Wickens of real

8 Ibid., p. 9.

estate financing and economic stability. Some of the results … are published in *[Residential Real Estate].*

As a result of [Wickens'] efforts, the fullest and most reliable data on values of urban residential properties, the relation of these values to mortgage debts, current rentals, construction, incomes of occupants, rates of obsolescence of properties, terms of financing, and sources of funds are now available in one book. In it one finds that urban real estate had a total value in 1930 of [$266.3 billion], of which [$122.6 billion] represented urban residential properties; at about 49 per cent of residential properties were held free of mortgages and 51 per cent were mortgaged; that in 1934 indebtedness on owner-occupied residential properties amounted to 55.6 per cent of their value; and that the total mortgage debt against urban residential properties amounted to [$26.1 billion].

The facts made available in the tables, which constitute the greater part of this volume, remove real estate and mortgage financing from the list of economic and financial factors *about which we know least.*[9] (emphasis ours)

In the first paragraph of his Preface in *RRE,* David Wickens elaborated on the lack of information:

[K]nowledge did not exist upon which to base sound public policy and sound private judgments.... Even the aggregate value of non-farm residential real estate in the United States was unknown. No estimate was available for any more recent year than 1922.[10]

---

9 Ibid., pp. vii-viii.

10 Ibid., p. xxi.

Beginning at the macro level, Wickens's *RRE* estimated that the total value of all real estate in the U.S. was $314.2 billion on April 1, 1930. By January 1, 1934, 45 months later, the total value had fallen 35.3% to $203.6 billion. In that same period, the total value of the residential portion fell almost an identical 35.4% from $122.6 billion to $79.2 billion. We interpret both declines as almost entirely due to deflation.[11]

For Wickens, the laborious process of estimating the value of U.S. residential real estate and of the mortgages on these properties involved conducting surveys of real estate and mortgages in U.S. cities for the key years of 1930 and 1934. The 1930 survey sought to estimate values on April 1, 1930. The 1934 survey focused on owner-occupied and rented properties in 52 U.S. cities on January 1, 1934. Wickens determined that:

> [U]npaid balances vary from small percentages to the full value of the property and on some properties exceed it. New properties, or those recently bought, are likely to have larger proportions of the value remaining unpaid. A high debt ratio is produced also by a decline in the value of the property after a mortgage has been placed on it.[12]

Based on the 1934 survey, Wickens gathered data from the institutions or agencies that provided the $26.1 billion in business-to-individual mortgage credit and categorized them into ten groups, including life insurance companies, building and loan associations, commercial banks, savings banks and mortgage companies shown in Figure 8.1 (opposite). Also included was the Home Owners' Loan Corporation (HOLC), a product of Roosevelt's legendary first hundred days in office, signed into law just one day after that hundred-day period ended.[13] Interestingly, however, as it

11 Ibid., pp. 1, 82, and 93.

12 Ibid., p. 9.

13 We have not determined if any aspect of the Home Owners' Loan Corporation (HOLC) was suggested in the Hoover Administration.

turns out, the largest single group of mortgages was comprised of individuals making mortgage loans to other individuals. Since the terms of these transactions between individuals were private, they were impossible to find. Thus, there is, in reality, a big hole in any

Figure 8.1

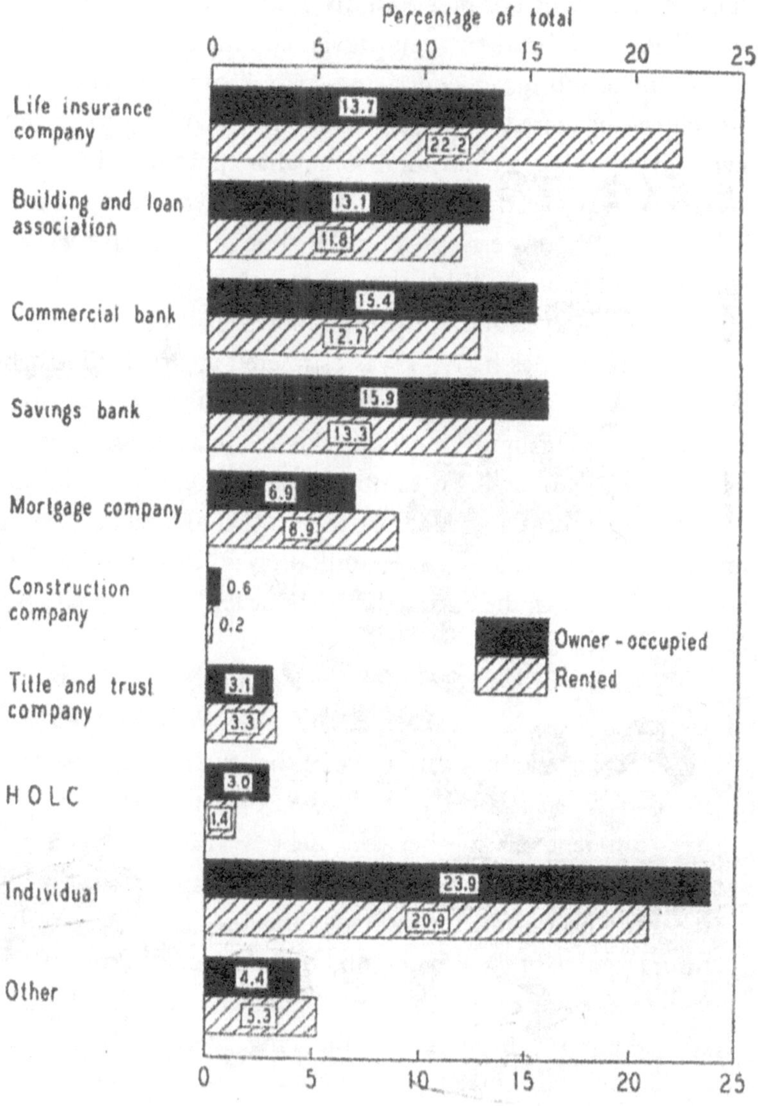

attempts to aggregate mortgage indebtedness, and we acknowledge this significant unknown. It is important to keep in mind individual-to-individual mortgages, due to the sheer number of them, since it might have been valuable to learn what the circumstances and outcomes of those loans were, in aggregate, in terms of any insights the missing category might have added to or contrasted with the clues offered by the business-to-individual sector.

Figure 8.1 breaks the mortgage commitments of Wickens' ten groups of mortgage lenders into two occupancy classes: owner-occupied or rented by owners to others. According to Wickens, "owner-occupied properties total somewhat more in value for the country as a whole than rented." One consideration in terms of valuation is that owners are generally thought to keep their own dwellings in better condition than renters do.

As we observed above, the total mortgage debt against urban residential properties in 1934 was estimated at $26.1 billion, but, always interested in comparable data from other years, we found the corresponding figure for 1930 elusive. In fact, we were only able to find the following carefully-worded statement by Wickens acknowledging that the absence of data for 1930 necessitated, even for him his assessment that the $26.1 million was "an amount *probably considerably less* than the outstanding debt in 1930."[14] (emphasis ours)

> When a property is covered by a loan or a *purchase money mortgage*, the *problems associated with the fulfillment of the credit part* of the transaction are to that extent *postponed to the time payment comes due.* By then or before, there may be a different relation between debt service and [interest payments] and even a major change as compared to the time the credit arrangement was made. *This uncertainty* as to the future relation of these factors and the effect on the economic system as compared with that originally contemplated is a central problem in real estate financing.[15] (emphasis ours)

14 Ibid., p. 8.

15 Ibid.

One likely explanation for the lack of outstanding mortgage indebtedness statistics in 1930 had to do, at least in part, with the prevalence of this lending vehicle called a "purchase money mortgage." To learn more, we consulted urban land use experts Leo Grebler, et al., writing in the 1950s, who stated:

> A purchase money mortgage is a lien taken back by the seller from the buyer of a parcel of real estate. Unfortunately, few data are available on this type of financing. A large but unknown share of purchase money mortgage transactions result from the resale by mortgagees of foreclosed property. Nearly all purchase money mortgages in institutional portfolios arise in this manner....
>
> The experience of Massachusetts savings banks indicates that purchase money mortgages made during the period 1932-1945 offset more than 75 per cent of the mortgage reductions through foreclosures.[16]

If we return to Figure 8.1, we can see that of the listed Holding Agencies, only Individuals and perhaps Others and Construction Companies were not "institutional" as Grebler meant the term. Clearly Grebler implied that a significant volume of purchase money mortgages could exist in institutional portfolios as a result of foreclosures. It seems likely that a high proportion of the mortgages also existed in the portfolios of non-institutions such as individuals, that is, seller/mortgagees who sold their homes to other individuals who became their mortgagors. The purpose of a purchase money mortgage was, and is, to enable a seller to encourage a buyer to acquire a home or other real estate by offering to finance its acquisition, especially when buyers were not qualifying for regular mortgages from banks

16 Leo Grebler, David M. Blank & Louis Winnick, *Capital Formation in Residential Real Estate: Trends and Prospects,* Princeton University Press, 1956, p. 162.

and elsewhere. At a time of foreclosures, what easier way could there be for one individual to get another individual to close on a purchase? The terms of these owner-financed mortgages varied, of course, inherent in any situation that involves a heightened volume of foreclosures.

Since we were unable to find the corresponding 1930 data on the size of the mortgage market, we wondered how mortgage contract terms on April 1, 1930 might have differed from those prevailing on January 1, 1934. Buyers (and their lawyers) would likely have felt quite optimistic that economic conditions were improving on April 1, 1930, and would continue to improve thereafter. After all, on April 1, 1930, the stock market was rising (to a level close to its value early in the summer of 1929), and Table 8.1 (page 232) shows that consumer prices looked relatively stable. Under such conditions purchase money mortgage terms could easily be written by which seller/lenders would choose to share in the upside potential with buyer/borrowers (as well as sharing in the downside). However, by January 1, 1934, following several years of severe deflation, conditions certainly looked very different.

As we contend, this kind of mortgage likely comprised a meaningful, if silent, portion of total mortgage debt of the early 1930s. But, its very structure made it impossible to determine the practical terms of the principal repayment portion of debt service on this large volume of mortgages until the debt became "due and payable," say in 1933, 1934 or even beyond. In addition, since most of these would have remained private, there would have been no data to gather. This may explain why Wickens, who estimated the total mortgage debt of urban residential properties on January 1, 1934, as a concrete number—$26.1 billion—found himself unable to give a corresponding concrete number for April 1, 1930, because much of it had not become "due and payable" and fell into the ether.

A Note on the Meaning of "Due and Payable"

As a result, we find that what seems to have a concrete meaning, "due and payable," can suggest issues that seem evanescent and ephemeral. That is to say, seemingly fleeting and immaterial or transient and, quite likely, unquantifiable.

In the late 1930s, the Twentieth Century Fund, a respected American philanthropy and "think tank," funded a broad-gauged study on how the nature of America's debt structure impacted, and was impacted by, the Great Depression. Based on the study, a book entitled *Debts and Recovery; A Study of Changes in the Internal Debt Structure from 1929 To 1937 and a Program for the Future* was published. The book included seven chapters of Factual Findings authored by Albert Gailord Hart, a professor of economics at Columbia University, together with ninety Appendix pages. The book also included Findings and Recommendations contributed by the Committee on Debt Adjustment of the Twentieth Century Fund. In Chapter 1, "The Debt Problem and the Depression," of this commendable work about debt at the time. Hart wrote:

> Every debt—excepting only a few perpetual bonds—is payable either on demand or on some definite time schedule.... In most fields it is the exception rather than the rule for the debtor to plan to get out of debt by the time the payment is called for. Typically the debt is either allowed to run along "open" (payable on demand) from time to time—*as happens with an astonishingly large proportion of past-due mortgages,* for example—or else is renewed or refinanced on maturity.... (emphasis ours)

Not only do few debtors intend to get out of debt when their obligations mature, but the economic system is so made up that *any sudden and general attempt to get out of debt would*

> *be a great calamity.* If the banks tried successfully to pay off their debts, for instance, they would deprive us of most of what serves as money in this country, and we should have a catastrophic fall of prices.[17] (emphasis ours)

Our first volume in *The Great Deleverage* series, *How the Crashof 1929 Caused the Great Depression,* described how debtors—and consumers, in particular—were incentivized by the shock and magnitude of the Crash of 1929 "in aggregate" to take steps as fast as they could to get out of the great quantity of debt they had become committed to in the prosperity of the 1920s. This second volume in our series is devoted to the how this action led to a rapid fall in prices—the deflation that began at the time of the Crash and developed with growing impact into and through 1930. According to Hart:

> If there is a *mass demand for repayment,* accordingly, the fictitious character of the maturity structure is exposed. "Liquidity" is essentially a matter of the parts of a financial system, and cannot exist for the whole. That is to say, debt repayment cannot turn the whole structure into nonexistent currency.[18] (emphasis ours)

In other words, if everyone strives to repay their debts, there is simply not enough cash to pay off debts *and* to circulate and use for other purposes. But while Hart's statement might apply to the financial system *as a whole,* it does not apply to a major part or parts of the system. For example, were some or all banks to call *some* loans, demanding that bank borrowers use deposited funds to repay their

---

17 Albert Gailord Hart and The Committee on Debt Adjustment, *Debts and Recovery; A Study of Changes in the Internal Debt Structure from 1929 to 1937 and A Program for the Future,* The Twentieth Century Fund, New York, 1938, pp. 14-15.

18 Ibid., p. 16.

loans, their borrower/depositors *could have done so* (although their remaining deposits would have been zero, with no compensating balances). We observe that while we have demonstrated that bank borrowers sought widely to repay bank loans in the year or two after the Crash, we have found no indication that banks were calling bank loans in this period, nor would we expect them to have done so as interest rates—and bank revenues—fell. As is usually the case, some debt obligations can be repaid to banks at any given time.

Hart's instructive Factual Findings on debt during the Depression continued:

> But if many of the public come to doubt the "liquidity" of their banks, etc., a cash hoarding movement can develop, *has happened in late 1931, and again in early 1933.* The emergency which results is beyond the power of the credit system to meet from its own resources. Governments must intervene *or allow the credit institutions, and much of the rest of the debt structure to collapse....*
>
> If the mortgage debtor is forced out by foreclosure of his mortgage, he not only suffers during the business decline, but is cut off from his hope of recovery when revival comes. The same applies to stockholders whose ownership of corporations is wiped out by reorganization. It was largely to prevent debtor groups from losing their economic foothold in this way that the government intervened in the debt situation in 1932 and later years. Mortgage debtors were kept in possession first by moratoriums and later by government refinancing; and changes in the bankruptcy laws eased the position of business debtors and of stockholders of corporations in reorganization.[19]

---

19 Ibid., p. 8, pp. 17-18.

Foreclosures

Table 8.2

Home Foreclosures 1925-1934

Year	Annual number	Change from prior year
1925	n/a	——
1926	68,100	——
1927	91,000	22,900
1928	116,000	25,000
1929	134,900	18,900
1930	150,100	15,200
1931	193,800	43,700
1932	248,700	54,900
1933	252,400	3,700
1934	230,350	-22,050

Source: *HSUS* 1789-1945, H-127, p. 174 & authors' calculations.

Although statistics on mortgage indebtedness overall were elusive, foreclosure data were more accessible because foreclosures required legal filings, making that information available to the public. Table 8.2 (above) shows annual foreclosures from 1926 to 1934, followed by the change from the prior year. For example, 134,900 foreclosures took place in 1929, and 150,100 foreclosures took place in 1930. While foreclosures were definitely taking place in the late 1920s, their numbers rose from the 1920s into the 1930s even as the rate of increase fell in both 1929 and 1930. Owing to a recession in 1927, the number of foreclosures rose from the prior year at what must have been an unusually high rate. From 1926 to 1927, foreclosures increased by 33.6% and from 1927 to 1928 by

27.5%, before the boom of 1928-9 lowered that rate of increase in foreclosures to 16.3%.

What strikes us as noteworthy about this data is that the rate of rise in foreclosures fell in 1930. Despite the appearance of impending mortgage defaults in the autumn of 1930 as deflation grew rapidly, the rate of rise in foreclosures in 1930 fell to only 11.3%. Why did this happen? One logical answer is that many people, bankers doubtless included, thought that the economy would "snap back" and resume buoyant growth quickly as had happened in the earlier depression of 1920-21.

Thereafter, we note that foreclosures grew significantly in 1931-32 before Franklin Roosevelt's 1933 "bank holiday" held the high rate.

Back to Summer and Autumn of 1930 as Economic Troubles Worsen

According to Barrie Wigmore, Hoover's overall leadership strategies of establishing committees, holding gatherings of financial and business leaders, collecting statistics, making public pronouncements touting widespread optimism (and belatedly the passage in July 1932 of the Federal Home Loan Bank Act) might indeed have sustained a business recovery, but only if the decline had been milder. Wigmore offered the following view and statistics to support that view:

> It became clear by mid-year, however, allowing for the time lag in substantiating economic conditions, that the economy was in trouble and its problems were deepening.
>
> Increasing unemployment was the most visible sign of the trend of the economic conditions....The Federal Reserve index of employment dropped to 93.9 in June from

> a peak of 108.4 in August 1929 and fell further to 83.8 in December 1930....
>
> The most visible declines...were in larger industries, such as iron and steel, in which employment dropped by 125,000 jobs; or automobiles, in which employment dropped by 130,000 jobs from less than half the base employment of the iron and steel industry. Railroad employment dropped by almost 200,000 jobs.
>
> There were also job losses in widely diffused small enterprises beyond the more prominent industries. Farms dropped 135,000 workers, textile mills dropped 165,000 workers, and private households dropped 150,000 servants....In aggregate there was the equivalent of over 2,250,000 fewer employees at work in the United States at the end of 1930 than at the end of 1929.[20]

Correcting Charles Persons' Misconceptions

Meanwhile, someone who had been in the thick of the government's conversation about how to measure unemployment, especially the extent of involuntary joblessness, found himself on the wrong side of the definitional argument. Sometime in the spring or summer of 1930, economist Charles E. Persons, whom we introduced in *How the Crash Caused* and featured in Chapter 7, abruptly left the Census Bureau over that disagreement as he prepared final revisions to his singular paper on the growth in credit use that appeared in the November 1930 issue of *The Quarterly Journal of Economic, an invaluable historic discovery and source that we have cited and referred to extensively.*

Concluding his paper, Persons offered what he considered the

20 Wigmore (1985), pp. 130-131.

"lessons of credit expansion." To reassure his readers, Persons wrote:

> This discussion should not be construed as an attack on, nor yet a criticism of, the new methods of credit sales. Mortgage bonds, building and loan financing of home ownership and installment selling will doubtless all prove useful and sound methods of financing. Their increasing use and their extension to income levels hitherto denied their advantages may well be justified by ... the rising intelligence and responsibility of the general public.

Persons then presented the analytical core of his argument, to which almost a century later we add important and pertinent insights:

> The essential point here is that during the period of introduction of these new financial devices and while the newly opened reservoirs of credit are filling, we have a *temporary increase* in the nation's purchasing power. A combination of circumstances has rendered this expansion of large dimensions in the decade just closed. While the new credit is expanding to *its justified limits,* more than the normal amount of commodities may be sold. The industries affected are stimulated to expand their productive capacity and to build up their labor force to the level set by this temporary bulge in consumption. In the working out of competitive forces their great prosperity leads to expansion even beyond this limit as over-eager producers seek an enlarged share of the market and profits. Once the newly developed credit resources reach maturity, new debt created *is balanced by* installments due on previously assumed obligations.[21] (emphasis ours)

---

21 Charles E. Persons, "Credit Expansion, 1920 to 1929, and Its Lessons," *The Quarterly Journal of Economics,* Vol. 45, No. 1, Nov. 1930, p. 129.

It was Persons' assumption that there was, in fact, a *limited* reservoir of credit that could or would be offered which we can today find ourselves questioning. In Persons's view:

> When every potential debtor and installment buyer has assumed the *full burden of indebtedness* which the new credit policies allow ...there is, of necessity an end of the process. While credit expansion continues we can produce, sell, and enjoy as much more than the annual money income as is covered by the increased debt burden. When expansion stops we *snap back* to the volume of goods covered by the national income.[22] (emphasis ours)

Persons regarded there being a definitive extent of a "full burden of indebtedness" as determined by some authoritative credit policy source, and we can see how, under conditions he observed in 1930, Persons might have believed the correct equilibrium would then reestablish itself. But as to installment sales in 1929-33, this is manifestly not what happened. As we saw in Table 12.4 in *How the Crash Caused*, while each month there was an equilibrium established of credit sought by buyers of goods at five retail establishments and credit granted by the retailers from September 1929 to March 1933, Total credit outstanding declined from $2,504.9 million at the end of August 1929 to $829.1 million at end of March 1933. The economy did not "snap back." Instead Net credit change, month by month, went negative. Americans repaid debt consistently in 38 of 46 months between August 31, 1929, and March 31, 1933. And we experienced the Great Depression.

Persons had reached, at least in 1930, what proved to be incorrect assumptions about who held the lever of prosperity: the lender or the borrower. The lever was held by borrowers who sought to take on less and less debt and repay more and more.

22 Ibid, p. 120.

Insights from a Present-Day Consumer Finance Historian

Martha L. Olney, an economist at UC Berkeley, explored some surprising aspects of the full 1930 picture regarding consumption and debt, especially the counterintuitive absence of high default levels. As introduced in Chapter 10 of *How the Crash Caused*, Olney's 1999 article in T*he Quarterly Journal of Economics* (the same journal that published the Persons paper) asserted:

> The collapse of consumption in 1930 came on the heels of a decade of virtual explosion in household use of installment credit. Authorities believed that "easy credit" was creating a generation of "deadbeats" who would default at the first sign of financial stress....Yet when financial stress hit in the 1930s, households did not default. The default rate on consumer credit was so low that the Census Bureau [1943, p.798] later claimed ".... Consumer credit was a safer investment in 1933 than cash in banks....[C]onsumers did not repudiate their debts en masse...[b]ut merely tightened their belts until they could pay what they owed and then buy more."[23]

In other words, debt repayment after the Crash was not only a statistically verifiable fact, most American consumers dependably paid their debts, with a level of responsibility well worth noting.[24]

As with Persons decades before, Professor Olney did not connect the Crash-induced decline in installment credit use and the simultaneous drop in stock market speculation as being two sides of

---

23 Martha Olney "Avoiding Default: The Role of Credit in the Consumption Collapse of 1930." *The Quarterly Journal of Economics*, Vol. 114, No 1, February 1999, p. 320.

24 As the Depression ground on and more workers joined the ranks of the unemployed, default rates inevitably rose despite the strong incentives to keep up with payments or lose the house, the car or the living room furniture and all the money that had been repaid already.

the same borrowed coin. But in any case, prioritizing debt repayment and belt-tightening ruled the day, regardless of whether the origin of the indebtedness was stock speculation and/or the purchase of a new house, automobile or radio.

Federal Budget Considerations Loom as the Finance Industry Declines in Strength.

As 1930 wore on, along with the worsening employment picture, the widespread shift from consumption to debt repayment, financial markets behaving timidly and companies omitting dividends, there was a rare federal budget deficit. Duties and tax revenue were down, and farm aid was up due to a drought and low commodities prices. A balanced federal budget became a main focus—and mental stumbling block— for both Hoover and his staunchly "liquidationist" Treasury Secretary Andrew Mellon. According to Barry Wigmore, "the budget focus was extreme and debilitating. It prevented effective action which, although it would have required deficit financing, would have caused deficits far short of problematical levels."[25]

As the summer of 1930 peaked and headed towards autumn, there was also shaky ground for those in the banking and brokerage communities, causing them to "squeeze" their customers, even famous speculators, like automotive pioneer William Durant. As Wigmore recounted:

> Benjamin Block & Co. sold out William C. Durant for the last time beginning October 10, 1930, after two weeks of efforts to get more margin from him, and this famous plunger, who had founded General Motors, lost it, and re-

25 Wigmore (1985), p. 116.

> gained it only to lose it again, was retired from the market involuntarily....
>
> During the fall of 1930 there was a rash of difficulties in the brokerage community which depressed stock prices.... Sidney Weinberg, who became famous as a corporate director and adviser to Presidents, stayed on only because the Sachs family absorbed his share of the losses.[26]
>
> The banks, too, showed signs of financial trouble in the last four months of 1930, which had an unfavorable impact on stock prices.... The list of corporations cutting or eliminating dividends grew considerably during the last quarter [of 1930].... The stock market groped downward through the last four months of 1930 with an air of invariability.... The economic and financial structures were being debilitated without any countervailing forces. The stock market, the bond market, the banks, the international markets, the economy—all were locked in downward drift.[27]

Participation in the stock market in 1930 clearly required nerves of steel. Table 7.1 on page 201 shows market value of all stocks listed on the NYSE at the beginning of each month in 1930. The year opened with a total market value of $64,708 million. By about the middle of April, the market value exceeded $76 billion, its high for the year and for the Little Bull Market. June opened with a total market value of $75,019 million before falling 14.8% to $63,892 million at the opening of July, making it the worst month of 1930. The market then rose to $67,721 million at the opening of September, before dropping to $49,020 million by the January 1, 1931, opening, more than a 35% drop from mid-April.

26 Ibid., pp. 142-143.

27 Ibid., pp. 144-145.

Table 8.3 **Yield Curves** **Jan. 1930 - Mar. 1931** (% Percent)						
	Call market loan renewals	Commercial paper	Corporate bonds (Moody's) by ratings			
			Aaa	Aa	A	Baa
1930						
Jan	4.90	4.94	4.66	4.86	5.23	5.92
Feb	4.30	4.76	4.69	4.89	5.25	5.89
Mar	3.82	4.33	4.62	4.80	5.15	5.73
Apr	4.00	3.88	4.60	4.78	5.12	5.70
May	3.22	3.80	4.60	4.77	5.07	5.72
June	2.65	3.57	4.57	4.76	5.08	5.78
Jul	2.25	3.22	4.52	4.74	5.06	5.77
Aug	2.18	3.03	4.47	4.68	5.00	5.73
Sep	2.24	3.00	4.42	4.65	4.94	5.65
Oct	1.98	3.00	4.42	4.67	5.06	5.94
Nov	2.00	2.93	4.47	4.75	5.21	6.25
Dec	2.08	2.88	4.52	4.85	5.43	6.71
1931						
Jan	1.83	2.85	4.42	4.70	5.26	6.41
Feb	1.50	2.60	4.43	4.70	5.29	6.38
Mar	1.55	2.50	4.39	4.67	5.30	6.44

Source: *BMS*, pp. 456 & 470.

Even a casual examination of Table 8.3 (above) tells us where things were going on the debt side of the investment world through monthly yield curves from January 1930 to March 1931. Short and long-term yields—and the growing spread between them—reflected a shift by increasingly risk-averse investors from short to longer-term instruments, as well as to the highest rated bonds. January began with the short-term rates for call loan renewals and commercial paper higher than the rates of Aaa and Aa bonds. In February, the call loan rate fell 60 basis points but the commercial paper rate was still above the Aaa bond rate as corporations tried to lure in investors. Thereafter, as the demand for call loan renewals fell, the commercial paper rate, regarded as high-grade marketable corporate debt, became the true short-term rate applying to these yield curves, but fewer corporations were selling commercial paper because of its short-term nature as they, too, wanted to lock in longer-term financing. The commercial paper rate then fell consistently from month to month with a single, brief pause in September and October when it remained 3.00% before dropping again at year end 1930 and into 1931.

The Aaa bond rate also fell fairly consistently through this period, but, as evidence of investors' preference for longer-term debt, the yield spread between the shorter-term commercial paper rate and the Aaa bond rate generally rose reaching 189 in March 1931, confirmation of investor preference for quality. Aa bond rates also generally fell, and the yield spreads between Aaa and Aa bond rates, which were 20 basis points or less until July 1930, entered 1931 at 30. Risk-aversion was further in evidence in the Baa bond rate, and flight to quality was pronounced in the substantial and growing yield spread between Baa and Aaa bond rates.

As we reported in Chapter 3, the persistently optimistic brokerage industry, as the business sector that managed marketing those instruments along with stocks, opened 1930 with the highest number of branch offices in its history. By late September, however, it was contracting.[28] *The New York Stock Exchange YEAR BOOK 1929-1930* reported the industry had 294 branch offices in New York and 1,364 branches "out-of-town" on January 1, 1930. By September 27, the industry had closed fifteen branch offices in New York and ninety offices out-of-town. We will see in Chapter 12 that the brokerage business, as a whole, lost money in 1930.

Wigmore's "downward drift" and Noyes's "crushing severity of the business reaction" described almost all sectors of the American economy in 1930, including the financial sector. President Hoover continued to give speeches while conditions in some of the nation's banks were leading them to the brink of failure and some into insolvency. Bank failures—including Tennessee's Caldwell and Company in November and New York's Bank of United States in

28 In Chapter 12 we will learn that the brokerage industry, as a whole, lost money in 1930.

December—would come to loom large as early warning signs of what became the explanation of the Great Depression in the views of later monetarists, most obviously, Milton Friedman and Anna Schwartz. We will see if their analysis stands the tests of both time and—more significantly to us—the data.

Concluding Thoughts About 1930 — an Entre'acte

Given the multiple forces at play as the economy contracted 1930, we turned to one of our most valued contemporary references. As financial editor of the *New York Times*, Alexander Dana Noyes wrote weekly columns called "Financial Markets," as well as a column early every January reviewing the year just ended and offering thoughts about the year to come. He was the perfect pundit for us to consult.

In one of his weekly Financial Markets columns, we found Noyes reflecting on the state of things historically. As a great believer in looking to history for perspective and guidance in the present, in this case history about prior periods of economic hardship and depression, Noyes observed that the course of their stories had essentially not varied. Befitting the wisdom he had gained during his long career as a financial writer, he provided this well-considered assessment of the stages following a panic:

> In each [preceding period], the crash of financial panic has been followed by uncertain and always underestimated trade reaction; then by a season of acute and bewildering distress, in which timid souls abandoned all hope of the financial future; next by a pause of seeming exhaustion bringing little sign of positive recovery but no renewal of spectacular collapse and, finally by return of hope and confidence.[29]

---

29 Alexander Dana Noyes, "Financial Markets: New Year Prophecies, New Year Uncertainties, and Underlying Economic Facts," *New York Times,* January 4, 1932, p. 28.

By the beginning of the fourth quarter of 1930, America was beyond the first phase of financial panic and into the uncertain phase of trying to understand the shockwaves of the "always underestimated trade reaction." The future appeared to hold little solace as distress became evident and spread throughout the U. S. economy. A "return of hope and confidence" seemed almost unimaginable.

In the next chapter, we will consider the view from President Hoover's White House.

Table 8.4 Statistics of U.S. Economic Activity ($ billion)					
	May '30	Jun. '30	Jul. '30	Aug. '30	Sep. '30
Annualized personal income	$78.9	$77.5	$75.3	$74.3	$73.7
Index of factory employment	95.7	93.9	91.2	89.0	87.7
Index of industrial production	96.0	93.0	89.0	86.0	85.0
Index of wholesale prices	88.8	86.8	84.4	84.3	84.4
Friedman & Schwartz demand deposits	$21.6	$21.6	$21.7	$21.4	$21.4
Fed member bank loans		$25.2			$24.7

Sources: *HSUS* 1789-1945, pp. 328-330, 344; *Monetary History*, p.713; *BMS*, p.74.

2nd and 3rd QTR 1930 Statistics of Debt Repayment

All Fed Member Banks: The volume of borrowing at All Fed Member Banks increased +$95 million in the 2nd quarter of 1930 with an average monthly debt repayment of -$344 million in the 1st quarter and a monthly average of +$32 million in increased borrowing in the 2nd quarter.

All U.S. Commercial Banks: Repayments to All U.S. Commercial Banks totaled -$1,427 million in the 1st half of 1930—an average monthly debt repayment by businesses, individuals and "others" of -$238 million. All Fed Member Banks are included in All U.S. Commercial Banks.

Aggregate Corporate Notes and Accounts Receivable (ACNAR) — All Payers: Total ACNAR repaid by businesses, individuals and "others" in full year 1930 equaled -$7,135 million—an average monthly repayment of -$595 million.

Individuals only: We estimate that individuals and consumers repaid more than $4+ billion to U.S. corporations in 1930—an average monthly repayment of more than -$333 million.

Following the 2nd quarter, debt repayments resumed and grew.

CHAPTER 9

Pausing in October 1930

IN THE REALM OF REASON [Hoover was] an unusually bold man; in the realm of unreason he [was], for a statesman, an exceptionally thin-skinned and easily bewildered man.

—Walter Lippmann[1]

On October 7, 1930, with the first anniversary of the Crash fast approaching, President Hoover gave the speech many had been waiting for. To a reported crowd of tens of thousands in Kings Mountain, North Carolina, and joined remotely by a nationwide radio audience of eager listeners, Hoover commemorated a Revolutionary War victory fought there that had helped turn the tide of America's war of independence 150 years earlier. Hoover, likely hoping the location would rouse that spirit of patriotic heroism with regards to the nation's ongoing economic battles, reiterated his "American Policy" full of determined optimism about the "mighty march of the United States" with its "driving force of equal opportunity" for individual initiative. He supported his optimism with data from his vaunted statistical research. His spirited speech included the following excerpt intended to bolster confidence among his fellow citizens, many of whose situations had deteriorated

1 Walter Lippmann, "The Peculiar Weakness of Mr. Hoover," *Harpers Magazine*, Vol. 161, (June,1930), p. 5. Also in Ronald Steel, *Walter Lippmann and the American Century,* Little Brown and Company, 1980, p. 288.

well beyond the reach of such lofty words:

> Compared with even the most advanced other country in Europe, we shall find an incomparably greater diffusion of material well-being. We have twice the number of homes owned among every thousand people that they have; we consume four times as much electricity and we have seven times as many automobiles; for each thousand people we have more than four times as many telephones and radio sets; our use of food and clothing is far greater; we have proportionately only one-twentieth as many people in the poorhouse or upon public charity.... There is a profound proof, moreover, that the doors of opportunity have indeed been kept open....Despite the misrepresentations of demagoguery, there are today more chances for young men to rise, and for young women too, than there were 30 years ago.[2]

The speech badly missed the mark. Rather than offering specific government programs to aid the suffering nation—his public works legislation and Reconstruction Finance Corporation to come were too little, too late — Hoover held fast in his speech to his deep-seated beliefs that prevented such direct action:

> Government in business, except in emergency, is also a destruction of equal opportunity and the incarnation of tyranny through bureaucracy. Tendencies of communities and States to shirk their own responsibilities or to unload them upon the Federal Government, or of the Federal Government to encroach upon the responsibilities of the States, are destructive of our whole pattern of self-government. But these evils cannot shatter our ideals or subvert our institutions if we hold the faith....The world about us is tormented with the spiritual and economic struggles that attend changing

2 Herbert Hoover, Public Papers of the Presidents, "Address on the 150th Anniversary of the Battle of Kings Mountain," October 7, 1930, p. 319,

> ideals and systems. Old faiths are being shaken. But we must follow our own destiny....
>
> Our problems are the problems of growth. They are not the problems of decay. They are less difficult than those which confronted generations before us. The forces of righteousness and wisdom work as powerfully in our generation as in theirs.[3]

To the American who since the Crash had lost his job, perhaps his home, and who saw his community under stress around him, Hoover's words rang hollow, even seemed shockingly insensitive and out of touch with what so many were going through around the country.

Gilbert Seldes in *The Years of the Locust,* which was published in February 1933, right before Hoover left office, offered further context and background for Hoover's lofty, outdated words:

> It should be remembered in favor of Mr. Hoover that he began his assertion of principles in October, 1930, before his party, and by implication his program, were defeated in the midterm elections, and neither defeat, nor the clamor of his adversaries, nor the miseries of his people caused him for a moment to abandoned his ideals. What the President said at Kings Mountain in October was what every President in modern time is bound to say, what Emerson said, better, for all of them: "America means opportunity"; but Mr. Hoover had to convert his principles into definite standards by which actions could be measured. It would have been by far the easier way to abandon popular phrases and accomplish popular deeds; at the end of two years it is clear that the President deeply believed in the common words of flattery always given to America and was evolving out of them a philosophy of American life. He risked his popularity and his reelection to stand by his beliefs. It was unfortunate that

3 Ibid.

> the actualities to which his beliefs correspond had vanished from America a generation before.[4]

Seldes continued with words that raise arguments well familiar today about the proper role of government and what essential fiscal actions were appropriate in order to deal with what he called in the quote below, the "disagreeable facts" about increasingly widespread economic hardship:

> "The door of opportunity and the ladder to leadership should be free for every new generation," [Hoover] said, and called this "the American system," rejecting the name of Capitalism because "under its ideals capital is but an instrument, not a master." The Government is conceived as an umpire between men engaged in a race for which they have been trained and in which "we strive to give them an equal start." And he ended with an echo of his campaign in 1928. At that time he said, "The present issue is the well-being and comfort and security of the American family and the American home. On that issue my party presents…the record of the growing comfort and security of the past seven years." With no such glowing record for the past two years to fall back on, the President still had impressive figures: "twice the number of homes owned…four times as much electricity…seven times as many automobiles…four times as many telephones and radio sets…." The comparison was with less favored nations, not with ourselves under Coolidge, but it was not bad for hard times….
>
> [I]n the coming months the President had to face disagreeable facts, chief among them the slashing of wages and the outcry for relief of starving men and women and children. His principles forbade him to help and, jealous of the spiritual strength and purity of the American people, he fought for months against a hostile Congress….

4 Seldes (1933), p. 82.

> But the principles laid down by Mr. Hoover carried on beyond the middle of June, 1931; they dictated the form and spirit of the entire program for reconstruction which was elaborated and, haltingly, set in motion a year later. The whole course of the depression in its central years was determined by Mr. Hoover's principles, acting upon those of his supporters and enemies, and at the end, compromising with them. The delays, the inadequacies, and the successes all come from the same source, a specific philosophy, or ideal, of what America's destiny should be, held, at a moment of crisis, by its chief executive.
>
> What strikes us at once is that a scientifically trained mind was substituting a memory of the past for the facts of the present.[5]

We could question Seldes for regarding it as merely disagreeable that American families were starving, but, in fairness, he was actually using a word that might have applied to how Hoover regarded what was going on. America's chief executive, despite or because of his "scientifically trained mind," found the realities so disagreeable that he actually lived in an out-of-step alternative reality woefully inadequate to the complex tragedy that was unfolding in the country on both micro and macro levels.

Problems Caused by Debt and Deflation

Early in Chapter 7, entitled "The Great Contraction" in *Monetary History,* Friedman and Schwartz stated:

> The monetary collapse was not the inescapable consequence of other forces, but rather a largely independent factor which exerted a powerful influence on the course of

5 Ibid., pp. 82-3.

> events. The failure of the Federal Reserve System to prevent the collapse reflected not the impotence of monetary policy but rather the particular policies followed by the monetary authorities and, in smaller degree the particular monetary arrangements in existence.[6]

We must recognize, however, that the repayment of debts whenever required was (and is) an inescapable force if the debtor wants to avoid repossession, foreclosure or bankruptcy. Broadly speaking, that makes it pretty compelling. But it is not necessarily the only such force contributing to 1930's monetary distress.

Another very powerful force in 1930 was aggressively rising unemployment. We focus on unemployment in Chapter 11, especially in "The Unemployment Picture" on pages 313-14. Table 11.2 (page 316) presents unemployment rising from 3.1% in 1929 to 8.8% in 1930 and 16.1% in 1931, and Table 11.3 (page 317) presents illuminating unemployment statistics from a host of non-governmental sources. Clearly, rapidly rising unemployment introduced to debtors and consumers a further source of great anxiety and uncertainty.

We will put forward as yet another powerful force: deflation. However, at this point, we defer our discussion until we give fuller attention to Friedman and Schwartz's observations on economic influences operating in 1930.

Trouble in the Nation's Banks

While many families, at a micro level, faced economic uncertainty, banking was a critical sector that was bound to feel deflation's impact, and did, sparing neither individual depositors nor the entirety of finance, including the Federal Reserve.

In the fall of 1930, what Friedman and Schwartz characterized as "a wave of bank failures" began. In the previous chapter, we mentioned the two early headliners of that fall, Tennessee's Cald-

6 Friedman and Schwartz (1963a), p. 300.

well and Company—an investment banking firm that controlled numerous small banks and insurance companies in several small southern states—that failed in November and New York's Bank of United States that closed in December. According to Friedman and Schwartz, these and other failures deepened the Depression or "The Great Contraction" as they called it, looking through their lens focused as it was on the size of the money supply. As Friedman and Schwartz wrote in a paper published in the same year as their *Monetary History*:

> An initial mild decline in the money stock from 1929 to 1930, accompanying a decline in Federal Reserve credit outstanding, was converted into a sharp decline by a wave of bank failures beginning in late 1930.[7]

While we will soon introduce some caveats as to certain assumptions Friedman and Schwartz made in order to draw their conclusions, there is no question that demand for bank loans, an all-important indicator of economic enterprise and confidence, had declined at an accelerating rate since 1929. A review of the rates of decline in U.S. bank loans as reported by the Federal Reserve in *Banking and Monetary Statistics, 1914-1941* shows how significantly and rapidly demand for borrowings fell:

> Through mid-year 1930:
>
> • Loans at *All Member Banks* declined -1.7% from $25,658 million on June 29, 1929, to $25,214 million on June 30, 1930.
>
> • Loans at *All Commercial Banks* declined -3.4% from $35,738 million on June 29, 1929, to $34,539 million on June 30, 1930.

7 Milton Friedman and Anna Schwartz "Money and Business Cycles." *The Review of Economics and Statistics,* Vol. 45, No. 1, Part 2, Supplement, February 1963b, p. 52.

Through the third quarter 1930:

- Loans at *All Member Banks* declined -5.5% from $26,165 million on October 4, 1929, to $24,738 million on September 24, 1930. (Loans at *All Commercial Banks* were only reported twice a year.)

Through year-end 1930:

- Loans at *All Member Banks* declined -8.7% from $26,150 million on December 31, 1929, to $23,870 million on Dec. 31, 1930.

- Loans at *All Commercial Banks* declined -10.9% from $35,966 million on December 31, 1929, to $32,034 million on December 31, 1930.

In 1930, loan demand at U.S. banks clearly fell broadly and quickly. The fact that rates of decline were higher among all commercial banks than among all member banks indicates that declines affected smaller (nonmember) banks in more rural areas disproportionately, especially those where lending to one commercial activity, such as farming, predominated. With bank loan portfolios shrinking, interest rates on bank lending falling materially and depositors withdrawing savings to cover living costs or repay debt, bank loan revenues and bank profitability were rapidly diminishing. The financial strength of the nation's banks overall was ebbing fast, with smaller, rural banks hit hardest.

Fourth Quarter Data Show Loan Demand Falling Faster

We now shift our focus from year-to-year comparisons in loan volumes to Fed data for the second half of 1930 and the fourth quarter of 1930 alone, a full year following the Crash, as October passed into November.

> 4th Quarter 1930: Loans outstanding at *All Member Banks* declined almost -1.2% per month—an annualized decline of -14.4%—or $868 million over the three-month period, from $24,738 million on September 24, 1930, to $23,870 on December 31.

> July 1 to December 31, 1930: Loans at *All Commercial Banks* also declined -1.2% per month—an annualized decline of -14.5%—or $2,505 million over the six-month period from $34,539 million on June 30 to $32,034 on December 31.

Altogether, these statistics told a clear story that regardless of bank size or Fed membership status, bank loans fell, in aggregate, at an alarming and accelerating rate throughout 1930.

To look deeper into the behavior of bank loan demand, we offer statistics from mid-1928 to the end of 1934 that confirm fourth quarter 1930 was only an early point along the way of the steep decline. Table 9.1 (opposite) is a reproduction of data in *Banking and Monetary Statistics (BMS)* for All Commercial Banks from 1928 to 1934, including statistics well beyond loan demand.[8] From June 30, 1928, to December 29, 1934, loan demand fell -55.9% and, Deposits at All Commercial Banks fell -18.7%. Meanwhile, investments held by All Commercial Banks in interest-bearing securities, especially of the U.S. Government, rose 29.4%, spotlighting *the lack of loan demand*. Finally, the number of banks in operation in the U.S. fell -38.7% over the same period from 25,330 to 15,519.

Again, we mention an important and perhaps unexpected aspect of this debt repayment phenomenon, the dependability in 1930 on the part of debtors, as Martha L. Olney discussed:

8 *BMS*, p. 19.

Table 9.1

All Commercial Banks: Number, Loans, Investments, and Deposits, 1928 - 1934[1]

($ million)

Call Date		Number of banks	Loans and Investments					Deposits		
			Total	Loans	Investments					
					Total	United States government obligations[2]	Other securities[2]	Total	Interbank	Other
1928	Jun. 30[3]	25,330	48,522	34,035	14,487	5,162	9,325	49,215	4,304	44,911
	Dec. 31	24,968	49,339	35,123	14,216	—	—	52,710	4,658	48,052
1929	Jun. 29	24,504	49,424	35,738	13,686	4,941	8,745	49,036	3,978	45,058
	Dec. 31	24,026	49,467	35,966	13,501	—	—	50,994	4,686	46,308
1930	Jun. 30	23,251	48,892	34,539	14,353	4,977	9,376	50,711	5,125	45,586
	Dec. 31	22,172	46,700	32,034	14,666	—	—	48,668	5,155	43,513
1931	Jun. 30	21,309	44,853	29,166	15,687	6,014	9,673	46,974	5,133	41,841
	Dec. 31	19,375	39,653	25,226	14,427	—	—	39,497	3,584	35,913
1932	Jun. 30	18,449	36,091	21,806	14,285	6,217	8,068	35,484	3,318	32,166
	Dec. 29	17,802	35,083	20,081	15,002	—	—	35,957	4,134	31,823
1933	Jun. 30	13,949	30,357	16,349	14,008	7,476	6,532	31,911	3,443	28,468
	Dec. 31	14,440	30,789	16,246	14,543	—	—	32,637	3,537	29,100
1934	Jun. 30	15,353	32,742	15,700	17,042	10,307	6,735	36,744	4,560	32,184
	Dec. 29	15,519	33,735	14,988	18,747	—	—	39,970	5,109	34,861

[1]Figures exclude those unincorporated or "private" banks not reporting to State banking authorities, except as noted in footnote 3 of this table. Banks in United States possessions are excluded except one national bank in Alaska; which was a member of the Federal Reserve System from the time it opened for business in April 1915 until it ws placed in voluntary liquidation in April 1921 and which in June 1919 had total deposits of $351,000.

[2]Prior to 1936, December figures are not available The figures for some of the earlier years are rough approximations.

[3]Beginning with June 1928, the figures previously published have been revised to include certain large private banks which did not report to State banking authorities until 1934.

[W]hen financial stress hit in the 1930s, households did *not* default. The default rate on consumer credit was so low that the Census Bureau [1943, p. 798] later claimed '… consumer credit was a safer investment in 1933 than cash in banks… Consumers did not repudiate their debts en masse…

> but merely tightened their belts until they could pay what they owed and then buy more.'[9]

Only, for the time being, they did not buy more

The Situation in October 1930 from the Monetarist Point of View

Since the publication of *Monetary History* in 1963 and especially since the 1980s, the views of Milton Friedman and Anna Schwartz have strongly influenced economic thinking and especially government policymakers about the importance of monitoring the money supply and having the Federal Reserve engage aggressively in using its various growth management tools such as open market operations and, since the 2008 financial crisis, provide liquidity to certain challenged business sectors by opening various loan windows. Our research into the economic behavior of Americans in response to the Crash, however, has shed new light on, and raised questions about, the sufficiency of Friedman and Schwartz's approach.

In *Monetary History*, Friedman and Schwartz commented on the decline of the money stock as follows:

> Compared to the collapse in the next two years, the decline in the stock of money up to October 1930 seems mild. Viewed in a longer perspective, it was sizable indeed. From the cyclical peak in August 1929...the money stock declined 2.6 per cent to October 1930, a larger decline than during the whole of all but four proceeding reference cycle contractions— 1873-79, 1893-94, 1907-08, and 1920-21 —and all the exceptions are contractions that were extraordinarily severe by other indications as well. The decline was also larger than in all succeeding reference cycle contractions,

9 Olney, Martha L., "Avoiding Default: The Role of Credit in the Consumption Collapse of 1930," *Quarterly Journal of Economics,* February 1999, Vol. 114, p. 320.

> though only slightly larger than in 1937-38, the only later contraction comparable in severity to the earlier ones listed.[10]

This account requires commentary on our part, first with regards to the critical definition of the money stock they used in their calculations. The measure used by Friedman and Schwartz included 1) currency held by the public plus 2) demand deposits at commercial banks plus 3) time deposits at commercial banks.[11] Based on this definition, their estimate of the drop in the money stock was -2.645% over the fourteen-month period from August 1929, when it was $46,278 million, to October 1930, when it was $45,054 million.[12]

However, we contend that M-1, defined as 1) currency held by the public plus 2) demand deposits at commercial banks, is today the generally accepted definition of the money supply that most economists apply to 1929 to 1933 because, at that time, only demand deposits served as the basis for making payments.[13] In the 1920s and 1930s, checks were drawn on demand deposits. Depositors held their savings in various places (like in savings and loan associations), and when they used savings, including, most obviously, to repay loans, they had to move those funds to a demand deposit account and draw a check. As Irving Fisher observed, hoarding can occur in "plain sight" by holding funds in time deposits. In periods of liquidity panic such as late 1929 and 1930. the volume of time deposits reflected a need to preserve buying power while earning interest. Time deposits, in effect, are actually "near money" rather than "money." As regards the distinction between M-1 and M-2, what is important is to identify and measure where the basic action (in this case bank loan repayment) occurred directly and immediately (out of demand deposits). We contend that this is the reason for holding M-1 as the essential element of the money supply and

10 Friedman and Schwartz (1963a), pp. 307-8.

11 Ibid., pp. 712-13. See amounts in column 8.

12 Ibid.

13 Today, even many money market fund accounts come with pre-printed checks.

not including M-2.

Using the M-1 definition of the money supply led to *an even faster rate of decline in the money supply* over the same period than the -2.6% Friedman and Schwartz calculated using M-2 which includes time deposits. Excluding time deposits, the August 1929 money stock estimate of $26,471 million fell -5.610% to $24,986 million in October 1930, more than double the M-2 rate of decline.[14]

This faster rate of decline of M-1 is not, however, the most important reason for keeping the decline in bank loan statistics cited above at the forefront of our thinking.

As we have frequently observed, net bank loan repayments can result in reduction of the money supply. When a borrower repays some or all of a bank loan with a check written on the borrower's demand deposit account, unless overridden by the acts of other borrowers who *increase* the amounts of their own bank loans, the money supply shrinks because the repayment reduces both the amount of the loan outstanding and the amount of funds the borrower has on deposit. In this post-Crash period, other borrowers were not overriding the actions of those repaying bank loans.

Thus, in aggregate, bank borrowers were paying down (or off) their bank loans, and this cumulative action in and of itself over time caused the money supply, M-1, to shrink and deflation to occur. Thus, as sustained reductions of bank borrowing of the kind described in this chapter occurred, declines in the money supply and deflation were inevitable. Friedman and Schwartz neglected to address this important economic influence.

Were Friedman and Schwartz Being Realistic?

Over time through our thorough, deliberate and conscientious research, our bottom line is that we have found ourselves doubting the very road map Friedman and Schwartz laid out for us to traverse. Did their road map chart the actual territory of 1929-33?

It is our carefully considered opinion, supported by Professor Olney and many other observers, that from the earliest days of the

---

14 Ibid.

Depression consumers were acting reliably 1) to repay bank loans and other indebtedness such as installment debt owed to retailers and 2) to cease taking out other forms of indebtedness such as new bank loans. Both processes involved disciplined belt tightening. This increasingly massive effort at debt repayment was a critical part of the actual economic territory in America from 1929-33 that Friedman and Schwartz failed to address.

Instead, they focused on different factors— time deposits in M-2—to explain the plunge of the money stock and thus the deflationary conditions that were its pernicious consequences. In *Monetary History* they stated:

> In October 1930, the monetary character of the contraction changed dramatically.... Before October 1930, deposits of suspended banks had been somewhat higher during most of 1929 but not out of line with experience during the preceding decade. In November 1930 they were more than double the highest value recorded since the start of monthly data in 1929.[15]

Thus, the first factor they pointed to was the suspension of banks by bank examiners, the attendant suspension of deposits in those banks and the removal of those deposits from M-1. We consider the first "banking crises" in Chapter 10 and merely observe, for now, that a significantly elevated number of bank suspensions began in November 1930, not in October

The second factor they relied on was mathematics. In their Appendix B they derived an equation, in Figure 9.2, (next page) that included several variables representing influences which they considered altogether to define mathematically the *maximum amount* that banks, in aggregate, were *allowed by regulatory authorities to lend* their borrowers. Of the equation, Friedman and Schwartz stated,

15 Friedman and Schwartz (1963a), p. 308.

Figure 9.2

$$M = H * \frac{\frac{D}{R}\left(1 + \frac{D}{C}\right)}{\frac{D}{R} + \frac{D}{C}}$$

"Equation 12 is the basic equation that we have used in most of our analysis of the factors affecting the money stock.[16]

In *Monetary History* Friedman and Schwartz expressed their stated position for 1929-33:

> 2. Factors Accounting for Changes in the Stock of Money.
>
> The factors accounting for changes in the stock of money during the four years from 1929 to 1933 are strikingly different from those in other periods we have examined. Generally, the pattern for high powered money has impressed itself most strongly on the total stock of money, the behavior of the two ratios serving mainly to alter the tilt of the money stock relative to the tilt of high-powered money. That relation holds in Chart [our Chart 9.1 (opposite) which is discussed below] only for the period up to October 1930, the onset of the first banking crisis. Thereafter, the two deposit ratios take command. High powered money moves in a direction opposite to that of the total stock of money, and not even most of its short-term movements leave an impress on the stock of money.[17]

Chart 9.1 (opposite) is our reproduction of Friedman and Schwartz's Chart 31 that appears on page 333 of *Monetary History.*

16 Ibid., p. 791.

17 Ibid., p. 332.

Chart 9.1

The Stock of Money and Its Proximate Determinates, Monthly, 1929-March 1933

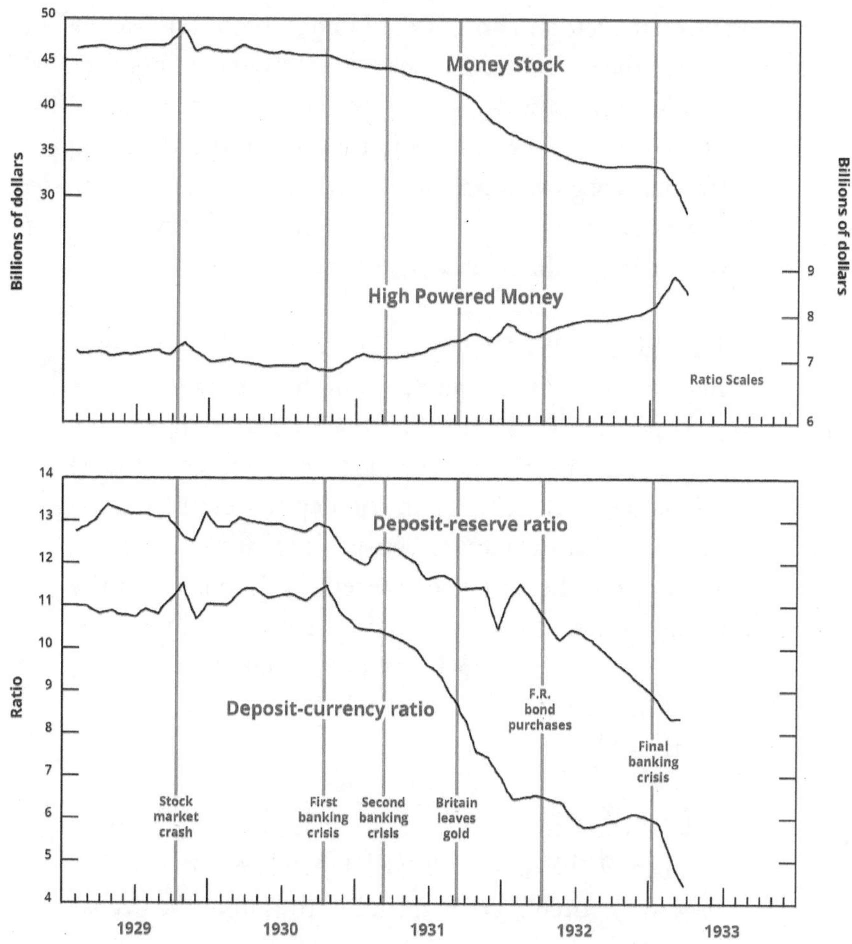

Most important, this chart shows that the rate of high-powered money grew and even accelerated, even as the rate of decline in the money stock fell and also accelerated. Our reaction upon looking at this is that they are engaging in denial. Our contention is that the money supply—or the money stock as they have labeled it—fell because bank borrowers, especially consumers, repaid their bank loans which the statistics we have cited repeatedly have shown.

Friedman and Schwartz considered the volume of the money stock so vitally important to the period 1929-1933 that they aspired to change the name of the period from "The Great Depression" to "The Great Contraction." They developed Equation 12 to explain the "Proximate Determinants of the Nominal Stock of Money" in periods when the money stock—elsewhere more commonly called "the money supply"—was growing, which was from almost 1867 until 1960. In other words, its objective was to specify the upper limits of monetary growth permitted *at times when* the Fed's reserve requirements determined the maximum amount of growth *allowed.* Yet according to Friedman and Schwartz:

> From August 1929 to March 1933 as a whole, the change in high-powered money alone would have produced a *rise* of 17½ per cent in the stock of money. The change in the deposit-currency ratio alone would have produced a decline of 37 per cent; the change in the deposit-reserve ratio, a decline of 20%; interaction between the two ratios, a rise of 10 per cent; these three converted the 17½ per cent rise that high-powered money would have produced into a 35 per cent *decline* in the stock of money.[18] (emphasis ours)

Further, they added:

> [A]fter the first banking crisis [which extended from November 1930 to January 1931], the decline in the stock of money was entirely a consequence of the fall in the deposit ratios. (emphasis ours)

It is our position that Equation 12 was not developed by Friedman and Schwartz to explain a period—nearly four years in length—of *sustained money stock* (or *supply*) *shrinkage.* To use Equation 12 to "explain" 1929-33 leads to confusion and error.

18 Ibid., pp. 332-333.

A Warning We've Heard Before

In *How the Crash Caused* (pages 81-82), we cited a warning by Harvard professor Gottfried Haberler:

> Such a complex phenomenon as the business cycle, which embraces almost all parts of the economic system, does not easily lend itself to explanation by any one factor.... [E]xplanations which run in terms of one single cause have been more and more discredited and should be regarded with suspicion. The majority of modern writers on the subject are careful to point out that a whole set of factors, and perhaps not always the same combination of factors, contribute toward producing an alternation of prosperity and depression.[19]

We have found ourselves asking how we can consider *one equation* to explain something as important as "changes in the money stock." We also must ask how we can consider a vital aspect of such change, that is "the decline in the stock of money," to occur "*entirely [as] a consequence of the fall in*"—what are normally minor parts of that equation— *"the deposit ratios"*?

The Situation According to Herbert Hoover

In his *Memoirs,* Hoover observed that, during the period of the Depression, there were two points of view:

> Two schools of thought quickly developed within our administration discussions.
>
> First was the "leave it alone liquidationists" headed by Secretary of the Treasury Mellon, who felt that government must keep its hands off and let the slump liquidate itself. Mr.

19 Gottfried Haberler, *Prosperity and Depression,* The League of Nations, 1937, pp. 5-6.

> Mellon had only one formula: "Liquidate labor, liquidate stocks, liquidate farmers, liquidate real estate." He insisted that when people get *an inflation brainstorm,* the only way to get it out of their blood is to let it collapse. He held that even a panic was not all together a bad thing. He said: "It will *purge the rottenness out of the system.* High costs of living and high living will come down. People will work harder, live a more moral life. Values will be adjusted, and enterprising people will pick up the wrecks from less competent people." He often used the expression, "There is a mighty lot of real estate lying around the United States which does not know who owns it," referring to excessive mortgages. (emphasis ours)
>
> At great length, Mr. Mellon recounted to me his recollection of the great depression of the seventies which followed the Civil War....
>
> I, of course, reminded the Secretary that back in the seventies an untold amount of suffering did take place which might have been prevented; that our economy had been far simpler 60 years ago, when we were 75 per cent an agricultural people contrasted with 30 per cent now; that unemployment during the earlier crisis had been mitigated by the return of large numbers of the unemployed to relatives on the farms; and that farm economy itself had been largely self- contained. But he shook his head with the observation that human nature had not changed in sixty years.
>
> Secretary Mellon was not hard-hearted. In fact he was generous and sympathetic with all suffering. He felt there would be less suffering if his course were pursued....
>
> But the other members of the Administration, also having economic responsibilities—Under Secretary of the Treasury Mills, Governor Young of the Reserve Board, Secretary of

> Commerce Lamont and Secretary of Agriculture Hyde—believed with me that we should use the powers of the government to cushion the situation. To our minds, the prime needs were to prevent bank panics such as had marked the earlier slumps, to mitigate the privation among the unemployed and the farmers which would certainly ensue.[20]

Unfortunately, we believe that President Hoover and the members of his Administration, including, we suspect, Secretary of the Treasury Mellon, did not understand the *full* powers of the federal government, including, most particularly, the federal debt-management powers of the Treasury Department that were set as precedents during the presidency of Theodore Roosevelt. We will have more to say on this topic in the final chapter of this book, in which we present our "Incipient Conclusions."

In the next chapter, we take a hard look at Friedman and Schwartz's assertions regarding what they labeled as the "first banking crisis" that occurred in November 1930 through January 1930, and we will consider if it deserved to be considered a *national* banking "crisis." Friedman and Schwartz's argument tied the increasing decline in the money supply over 1930 to the "wave of bank failures" that, they argue, caused the collapse of the banking system. We regard this to be an as-yet-unproven explanation. Instead, as we have described, use of bank deposits to repay bank loans shrank the money stock. In fact, we assert that what converted the not-so-mild decline in the money supply into a sharp decline was a rapidly accelerating drop in bank loan demand as debtors paid down loans, even preceding and certainly continuing through the fourth quarter of 1930. We carry this argument forward into Chapter 10.

The Impact of Deflation

Finally, having considered the point of view of Friedman and Schwartz, let us make several observations about deflation.

---

20 Hoover (1952), pp. 30-31.

On page 300 of *Moneteary Forces*, Friedman and Schwartz stated, "The monetary collapse was not the inescaable consequence of other forces...."

Table 8.1 on page 232 shows the Monthly Percentage Change, Annualized, of the Consumer Price Index as 0.00% in January 1930. For the next four months through May 1930, it changed only slightly. In June, deflation of the CPI annualized became -1.8%. By October, deflation of the CPI annualized had reached -4.6%. Table 8.1 also shows deflation as measured by wholesale prices spiraling downwards from -3.6% in January of 1930 to -12.7% in July.

It is our position that deflation as measured by the WPI had become an inexorable force by July 1930 and as measured by the CPI was well along by October 1930 to becoming a consequential inexorable force in itself.

We now turn to Chapter 10 to learn more.

Table 9.2

Statistics of U.S. Economic Activity

($ billion)

	Jun. '30	Jul. '30	Aug. '30	Sep. '30	Oct. '30
Annualized personal income	$77.5	$75.3	$74.3	$73.7	$72.4
Index of factory employment	93.9	91.2	89.0	87.7	86.7
Index of industrial production	93	89	86	85	83
Index of wholesale prices	86.8	84.4	84.3	84.4	83.0
Friedman & Schwartz demand deposits	$21.6	$21.7	$21.4	$21.4	$21.4
Fed member bank loans	$25.2			$24.7	

Sources: *HSUS* 1789-1945, pp. 328-330, 344; *Monetary History*, p.713; *BMS*, p.74.

CHAPTER 10

Friedman & Schwartz's First "Banking Crisis" (November and December 1930)

> [W]ITH THE LAST QUARTER of 1930 we come into full economic depression, during which an "American policy" was elaborated to take the place of the discredited explanation of the crash. That period, extending roughly from Mr. Hoover's Kings Mountain Speech to his declaration of a Moratorium [of war debt repayments in June 1931], is marked by a vast increase in unemployment and—a new and important factor—an acute and widespread consciousness of unemployment; by wage cutting (signifying that the fundamentals of the first plans for recovery were insufficiently understood); by the threat of a dole; and by the general attitude which is called "deflation."[1]

Making these dark recollections in 1933, wise cultural observer of the day Gilbert Seldes looked back on conditions of only two years

1 Seldes (1933), p. 63. We believe that the "discredited explanation" that this "American Policy" was meant to replace was, in Seldes words, "The early theory, that the Wall Street crash came because of speculation (in which we were all engaged) and that industry was carried down in the debacle, ... was easy to believe because a vast, complicated machinery of credit existed about which most people knew nothing." (p. 36) We, of course, contend that the Great Depression was fully operative in May 1930, the second, not the fourth quarter.

earlier. By November 1930, stocks had declined in value rapidly following the demise of the Little Bull Market, bank suspensions in rural areas appeared suddenly to explode in number and unemployment rose, all portending an ongoing downward trend virtually everywhere one looked, despite increasingly hollow statements from Hoover Administration officials about the elusive corner we were about to turn. Revisiting key members of our Cast of Characters as 1930 was coming to a close, we see the issue of outstanding debt remained center stage, even as growing numbers of the unemployed were anxiously trying to make ends meet for themselves and their families, many additionally burdened by the pressure of making payments on mortgages or installment loans or other debt obligations committed to during better days when the future looked rosy and before deflation developed. Among the upper income brackets but sharing in the pain, many of the half million or more Repentant Ex-Speculators, grievously hurt in the panic, were working desperately to keep up appearances, as behind the scenes their savings were much diminished or gone altogether. Also pursued by paralyzing debt, formerly eager speculators reduced their consumption expenditures as fast as possible to pay off their obligations. Business owners and managers tried to reduce their spending anywhere they could, and they, too, paid off every loan possible. The "general attitude" of deflation took hold.

Adding to the stressors that crossed income lines, bankers in towns and cities across America examined their books in dismay, as regulators pursued suspensions that closed the doors of some of these banks at least for a time, and others, perhaps, for good. The distress of many thousands of depositors who thought their money sat safely in their local bank, run by people in their community they knew well, joined in with the suffering felt by all the Americans who had lost their money in the stock market.

Bank Regulators and Examiners Order Bank Suspensions

It is to the group of suspended banks that we turn next. In 1963, Friedman and Schwartz offered their macro-level explanation that the decline in the money supply from mild in 1929 to sharp in 1930 was due to bank failures that precipitated depression conditions. But their analysis glosses over the increasingly negative micro impact on individual Americans, such as those among our Cast of Characters, immediately post-Crash. As the data confirmed, this micro level mattered hugely.

Bank suspensions were indeed increasing, and their effects had impact, though not exactly as Friedman and Schwartz depicted. *Banking and Monetary Statistics 1914-1941* starkly described the general picture of what happens when our banking system comes under the kind of threat that prevailed in late 1930. It is difficult to read this description and not reflect on how the Fed had an expectation that this sort of calamity, rather than being rare and out-of-the-blue, was an ongoing threat and inherent in the very system itself:

> The liquidation of insolvent banks is at best a slow process; and although the depositors in such banks may eventually recover a substantial amount of their deposits, they are meanwhile deprived of the use of their money. Moreover, during periods of widespread suspensions, many areas have been left wholly without banking facilities. Business concerns, farmers, and other entrepreneurs have been unable to secure bank loans, and communities have suffered from a lack of a convenient means of payment....
>
> Economic developments during and following the first World War created difficult conditions for banks. In 1921 suspensions increased sharply, while the num-

> ber of banks — which had reached the peak of over 30,000 — turned downward. For the next eight years, suspensions continued to be numerous in the agricultural regions of the country. The general economic depression of the early 1930's subjected the financial machinery of the whole country to extraordinary pressure.[2]

Throughout the 1920s and early 1930s, the U.S. had a large number of commercial banks, as the above quote states, most of which were not members of the relatively new Federal Reserve System. On December 31, 1929, for instance, there were 24,026 commercial banks of which only 35.5% or 8,522 were Fed members. Member banks were generally more urban in location, larger, had a more diverse customer base and were better capitalized than non-member banks. All of these distinctions mattered as economic conditions deteriorated. At the end of 1929, the average Fed member bank nationwide held $4.5 million in deposits while the average non-member held only $835 thousand. In contrast, the 56 member banks in New York City alone, averaged $182 million in deposits on December 31, 1929, and, interestingly, the average deposits for those member banks *rose* over the next four years to approximately $200 million.[3] However, the more concentrated a bank's lending base was, for instance, in rural areas to farmers, the more vulnerable it was in a turndown.

As to bank regulations, at both state and national levels, especially since the Civil War, the ability to suspend a bank's activities was essential in order to deter poor, possibly even fraudulent, management practices. As the Fed opened their Section 7 on bank suspensions in *Banking and Monetary Statistics, 1914-1941*:

> Bank suspensions have been a prominent and disturbing aspect of our financial history. These suspensions have been

2 *Banking and Monetary Statistics 1914-1941*, p. 281.

3 Ibid., pp. 80, 89.

> due to a variety of causes, including broad economic developments as well as certain characteristics of our banking system.[4]

At the national level, the Federal Reserve supervised and examined only member banks, although the Fed did collect certain data on nonmember banks as well. The Comptroller of the Currency in the Treasury Department focused on monitoring nationally chartered banks. State banking authorities supervised and examined state banks. Even prior to the Crash, hundreds of banks—mostly, but not entirely nonmember banks—failed federal and state examination processes each year and had their operations suspended. For example, 659 banks were suspended in 1929, of which 81 were Fed member banks and 578 were nonmembers.[5] Suspended banks were likely poorly run, often undercapitalized and located where customers in one field, like farming, predominated.

But regulators, with an eye towards protecting depositors as best they could, prioritized reopening the banks they suspended, not shutting them down. They did this by reorganizing them to ensure they operated more stably, which usually required banks to secure further capitalization and also effect a change in management before they reopened. But for depositors of a suspended bank this process could entail months-long inconvenience and possibly the loss of a small or at times larger portion of their funds. Depositors of suspended banks, got between 70% and 75% of their deposits back, as we discuss shortly. For those of us living in an FDIC-insured banking world, such insecurity is unimaginable, but it was the norm then. Understandably, enough people came to distrust banks that the image of spooked depositors hiding savings under the proverbial mattress has survived to this day.

4 Ibid., p. 281.

5 Ibid., p. 283. Throughout the 1920s, bank suspensions ranged from a low of 366 in 1922 to a decade high of 976 in 1926.

Elmus Wicker Counters Friedman and Schwartz in his "Microhistory" of the Banking Crisis of 1930

We now introduce another period expert, Indiana University economics professor Elmus "Wick" Wicker (1926-2020), whose field of concentration was the U.S. banking system and the Federal Reserve. Professor Wicker, with a pedigree that included a Rhodes Scholarship and Phi Beta Kappa key, authored six books and contributed many journal articles about the banking system and banking panics, including a history of the Federal Reserve System, 1917-1933. In his 1996 book *The Banking Panics of the Great Depression,* he published the results of a meticulous and detailed study—he called it a "microhistory"—of what was happening in the nation's banks from 1929 to 1933. In this work, which constituted a very useful narrative with a few minor statistical short-comings, Professor Wicker supplied a table, reproduced in part as our Table 10.1, (opposite) which showed the number of bank suspensions and the volume of deposits in those suspended banks, month by month, for the period from August 1929 to March 1931.[6]

Referring to the data in Table 10.1 (opposite) is useful when reading the following passage from Friedman and Schwartz's *Monetary History* describing conditions in banking as they worsened:

> Before October 1930, deposits of suspended banks had been somewhat higher than during most of 1929 but not out of line with the experience during the preceding decade. In November 1930, they were more than double the highest value recorded since the start of the monthly data in 1910. A crop of bank failures particularly in Missouri, Indiana, Illinois, Iowa, Arkansas, and North Carolina, led to widespread attempts to convert demand and time deposits into currency, and also, to a much lesser extent into postal savings deposits. A contagion of fear spread among depositors, starting from

6 Elmus R. Wicker, *The Banking Panics of the Great Depression,* Cambridge University Press, 1996, pp. 25-26.

Table 10.1		
Bank Suspensions and Deposits in Closed Banks August 1929 - March 1931 (All banks) ($ million)		
Year/month	Number of bank suspensions	Deposits in suspended banks
1929		
August	18	6.7
September	37	9.7
October	41	12.5
November	70	22.3
December	61	15.5
1930		
January	90	26.5
February	87	32.4
March	80	23.2
April	90	31.9
May	59	19.4
June	68	69.3
July	64	29.8
August	67	22.8
September	67	21.6
October	72	24.5
November	256	179.9
December	352	372.1
1931		
January	198	75.7
February	77	34.6
March	86	34.3

Source: Board of Governors of the Federal Reserve System, *Annual Report of the Federal Reserve Board 1932*, p. 154.

> the agricultural areas, which had experienced the heaviest impact of bank failures in the twenties. But such contagion knows no geographical limits. The failure of 256 banks with $180 million in deposits in November 1930 was followed by the failure of 352 with over $370 million deposits in December (all figures seasonally unadjusted), the most dramatic being the failure on December 11 of the Bank of United States with over $200 million in deposits. That failure was of especial importance. The Bank of United States was the largest commercial bank, as measured by the volume of deposits, ever to have failed up to that time in U.S. history. Moreover, though an ordinary commercial bank, its name had led many at home and abroad to regard it somehow as an official bank, hence its failure constituted more of a blow to confidence than would have been administered by the fall of a bank with a less distinctive name. In addition, it was a member of the Federal Reserve System.[7]

By contrast, investigating the situation in the banking system as it transpired in late 1930, Professor Wicker found surprisingly little awareness of any broad-scale panic at the time. As he wrote:

> The existence of a nationwide banking panic in November 1930 to January 1931 remains a matter of dispute. We can look in vain in the pages of the financial press for an event clearly designated as a banking panic; it was certainly not the name given to the accelerated bank suspensions in the final two months of 1930. The public had no difficulty in identifying the banking crises in 1873, 1884, 1893, and 1907. The passage of time should not have dulled the recognition of a banking crisis in 1930, especially if the events in those months bore a close resemblance to what had happened earlier.

7 Friedman and Schwartz (1963a), pp. 308-311.

> Friedman and Schwartz (1963) were the first to characterize the acceleration of bank suspensions in November-January as a banking crisis or banking panic.[8] They assigned a causal role to those bank failures to explain why the money stock fell and why the depression deepened, thereby giving dramatic emphasis to the significance of what had happened during those three months. The banking situation in 1930 took on a new relevance.[9]

Wicker continued with his careful analysis, referring readers to his Table 2.1.[10] (Our Table 10.1 shows the numbers of suspended banks and the deposits they hold but not the statistics related to hoarding presented in Wicker's table.[11]) Referring to his table and its statistics, Wicker stated:

> We begin by reviewing the records of bank suspensions, deposits in failed banks, and currency hoarding seasonally adjusted from the onset of the Great Depression in August 1929 to March 1931. Monthly data are set out in Table 10.1. Although the number of bank suspensions and deposits in suspended banks increased perceptibly in November 1929 and January 1930 there was no banking panic. Nor was there an increase in hoarding defined as an increase in currency held by the public seasonally adjusted.... Considering pre-1914 banking crisis experience, it is indeed surprising that the external shock of the magnitude of the stock market collapse did not result in a banking panic. And the credit for this non-event belongs to the Federal Reserve.... [T]here

8 Schumpeter used the term "epidemic." See under "Bank, assets, quality of," on page 1080 in the index of Schumpeter (1939).

9 Wicker (1996), p. 24.

10 Ibid., p. 26.

11 Ibid. Wicker's table also revealed that the numbers estimated as Currency in Circulation Seasonally adjusted shown by Friedman and Schwartz in *Monetary History* were generally about $500 million less that those shown in *BMS 1914-41*.

> was no panic in the central money market [in New York] in each of the four banking crises of the Great Depression.
>
> The first banking crisis of the Great Depression can be easily identified by the aggregate data in Table 10.1. There was a sharp escalation in the number of bank suspensions and deposits in failed banks in both November and December 1930 and a deceleration in January with total deposit *losses* of $628 million.[12] (emphasis ours)

We italicized the word "losses" in the above passage because what Wicker was labeling as losses here was actually the sum of the deposits *suspended* in the three months of November and December 1930 and January 1931. But, the records of the Federal Reserve indicated that depositors were estimated ultimately to lose 28.3% of their deposited funds in 1930 and 23.1% in 1931.[13] On this basis, the estimated losses for the deposits suspended in November 1930 through January 1931 would actually have been approximately $218 million.

Wicker was clearly questioning the scope of the banking panic from November 1930 to January 1931, when he stated, "The conclusion to which we are inevitably drawn from the diverse data on bank suspensions, deposits in closed banks, and hoarding, is that the 1930 banking crisis was region specific; it was not a national crisis."[14] This observation certainly comports with the data. In his analysis, Professor Wicker continued:

> [T]he primary concern of Friedman and Schwartz was macroeconomic; that is, they focused on the behavior of reserve and monetary aggregates and how they might have

12 Ibid., pp. 25-27.

13 *BMS,* p. 283.

14 Wicker (1996), p. 30.

> affected total output. They were only peripherally interested in the microhistory of the banking crisis ...[15]

Taking up the challenge in his book, Wicker began his microhistory of the banking crisis by observing:

> The Federal Reserve has never given an official account of what it thought happened during the 1930 banking crisis. The only reference to the events of the crisis period appeared in the Federal Reserve Bulletin in [December]1937 (p. 1205) with the publication of revised estimates for bank suspensions and deposits in failed banks between 1921-36. On that occasion Reserve officials wrote:
>
>> In these months [November-December 1930] nine large banks in different sections of the country suspended. The closing of these large banks resulted in the closing of many other banks, partly because of affiliate and correspondent relationships, and partly because of the spread of fear among depositors, particularly in territory near the location of the banks.
>
> The nine banks were never identified, but what they thought were the two main characteristics of the crisis emerged: (1) the high correlation of bank suspensions in a few large urban banks and (2) the "local" nature, the effects confined as they were to the "territory near the location of the bank."[16]

Wicker's microhistory dug deeper and investigated the cases of two infamous financial enterprises, in particular. (Peter Temin described these, broadly speaking, as cases where the decline in the

15 Ibid., p. 24.

16 Ibid., p. 32.

monetary value of bank assets collided with poor management and outright illegal activity.[17]) The two were Caldwell and Company, an investment banking firm headquartered in Nashville, which failed in November 1930, and Bank of United States in New York City that failed in December. Nothing we have seen suggests the two were related to each other except that they both took place in the same time period. We should note, of course, that given the dramatically falling short-term interest rates and declining volume of bank borrowing, it could not have been an easy time to be a banker.

Wicker described the regional house-of-cards effects when Caldwell and Company failed:

> The high concentration of bank closings in November in the St. Louis District can be traced to the failure of the investment banking firm of Caldwell and Company of Nashville Tennessee. The firm controlled the largest chain of banks in the South with assets in excess of $200 million and also the largest insurance group in the region with assets totaling $230 million. When expanded to include the interests of other enterprises, the total equaled at least half a billion dollars. The failure of Caldwell and Company had immediate repercussions in four states namely Tennessee, Kentucky, Arkansas, and North Carolina in the Atlanta, St. Louis, in Richmond Federal Reserve districts. Seventy banks failed in Arkansas of which forty-five belonged to the A.B. Banks chain, the stock of which was owned by the Home Insurance Company, a Caldwell affiliate. The fifteen or more banks that closed their doors in Kentucky were either correspondent banks or were directly affiliated with Banco Kentucky, a bank holding company that merged with Caldwell in June 1930. Similarly, at least ten bank failures in Tennessee and fifteen in North Carolina can also be traced directly to relationships between Rogers Caldwell and

17 Temin (1976), pp. 90-94.

individuals connected with the suspended banks in these states. The collapse of Caldwell and Co's financial empire raised expectations of deposit losses in the surrounding region and contributed to bank suspensions in December and January as well.[18]

As we see next, Bank of United States engaged in illegal practices that sent its president to prison, but Caldwell and Company management was also not above skirting the law. Wicker wrote unambiguously, "Managerial ineptness encompassing both poor loans and investments in the twenties and questionable legal practices deserve a fair share of the blame for the demise of both Caldwell and Company and Bank of United States."[19]

Peter Temin offered an illuminating history of Bank of United States and its inevitable failure due to substantial illegal activity:

> The Bank of United States was formed in 1913 by Joseph S. Marcus with an initial capital of $100,000. It grew slowly until Joseph Marcus's death in late 1928, when it had a capital of $6 million and six branches in New York City. Despite the grandiose name, the bank was throughout this period a small local bank, serving a predominately Jewish clientele in Manhattan. All this changed when the founder's son, Bernard K. Marcus, succeeded to the presidency of the bank upon his father's death. Bernard Marcus embarked on a vigorous program of expansion and fraud that ended with the bank's failure in 1930.
>
> It is clear that the Bank of United States under Bernard Marcus was a very different bank than it had been under his father. In two years, Bernard Marcus had quadrupled

18 Ibid., pp. 32-33.

19 Ibid., p. 51.

> the bank's capital stock and increased the number of its branches by a factor of ten. He had also formed the Bankus Corporation, which was investing in New York real estate and indulging in a variety of questionable—and it turned out—illegal activity. Problems with the Bank of United States apparently surfaced with a bank examiner's report in 1930 that wiped out $17 millions of the bank's surplus and undivided profits. After the sale, over $50 million of other assets were cited as also "impaired." These included $25 million in loans to the bank's subsidiaries (of which almost $20 million were to the Bankus Corporation, City Financial Corporation, and their subsidiaries), $17 million in mortgages and frozen real-estate loans (of which over $8 million were second or third mortgages which were frozen due to the Depression), and $13 million of other "slow" loans. Almost all of these "impaired" assets were direct or indirect claims on real estate.
>
> It should not be inferred that this was simply a bank that was dragged down by the general decline in the monetary value of assets during the Depression, because many of these real-estate investments were not simply illiquid, they were also illegal. Banks in New York are forbidden to own land in names other than their own. Yet the Bank of United States had several landowning subsidiaries.[20]

Temin went on to say that, in the financial wreckage, at least some received deserved punishment. Bernard Marcus and two other officers of Bank of United States were "indicted for this illegal activity, convicted and imprisoned."[21]

As Bank of United States collapsed, the New York State Superintendent of Banks and officials of the Federal Reserve Bank of

20 Temin (1976), p. 91-92.

21 Ibid., p. 92.

New York, with the support of some clearinghouse banks, sought to negotiate a merger of the failing bank with three other New York banks. At the last moment the merger talks fell through when the clearinghouse banks collectively rejected the terms of the proposed merger agreement. Friedman and Schwartz wrote that Bank of United States, which failed on December 11, 1930, "ultimately paid off 83.5 per cent of its adjusted liabilities at its closing," and "four-fifths of the total recovered by depositors and other creditors was paid out within two years of the bank's closing."[22] This outcome is not to excuse bad management practices but rather to show how the teeth in bank regulation effectively helped the unfortunate depositors and other creditors regain the bulk of their losses even in the pre-FDIC era.

Bank Failures in Only Five U.S. Cities in the First Banking Crisis

According to Wicker's thorough microhistory, geography clearly mattered at this time with regards to bank performance and suspensions in the U.S. Wicker pointed out, "[T]he incidence of bank failures and hoarding was greatest in the three Reserve Districts of St. Louis, Richmond, and Atlanta."[23] He identified the five most impacted cities as Little Rock, Louisville, Nashville, Memphis and Asheville. In each of these cities one or more banks failed as a result of the Caldwell and Company collapse, and Wicker concluded, "Together these five cities absorbed the urban impact of the banking panic."[24] (We suggest Wicker did not include New York City in this list because he found no "incidence of banking panic" there.[25]) So much for the notion of a nationwide banking panic which Friedman and Schwartz implied when they wrote:

22 Friedman and Schwartz (1963a), p. 311.

23 Wicker (1996), p. 53.

24 Ibid., p. 45.

25 Ibid. See his Table 2.10 on p. 47.

> A contagion of fear spread among depositors starting from the agricultural areas, which had experienced the heaviest impact of bank failures in the twenties. *But such contagion knows no geographical limits.*"[26] (emphasis ours)

Contagion, according to Wicker, did have geographical limits, the root sources of the difficulties were traceable and the crisis was not automatically a panic, certainly not a nationwide panic. On the contrary, as Wicker's microhistory found, the urban impact of the banking crises of 1930 was limited to the aforementioned five cities, all of which were in what were then relatively rural states. Wicker also warned that following only the money was deceptive as to not only the geographical extent of the panics, but also to specific and identifiable causes of the bank suspensions. Of the 608 banks suspended in November and December 1930, Bank of United States accounted for a third of their aggregate deposits and also skewed the data with regards to New York State statistics for the period. According to Wicker, deposits tell a different story:

> Forty-five percent of the deposits of failed banks were in the Federal Reserve districts of St. Louis and New York. The number of suspensions in New York was negligible (eight), but the closing of the Bank of United States in New York City with $160 million of deposits at the time of suspension explains why New York ranks first [in deposits in suspended banks].[27]

Wicker also gave ample credit to action by the New York Fed for staving off panic and for attempting, as described above, to save Fed member Bank of United States:

> [The Fed] was successful in maintaining stability in the central money market; there was no banking panic in New

26 Friedman and Schwartz (1963a), p. 308.

27 Wicker (1996), p. 28.

Table 10.2				
Changes in M-1 and M-2, August 1929 - April 1931 (Seasonally adjusted) ($ million)				
	Wicker's Table 2.11		TGD Authors	
1929	M-1	M-2	M-1	M-2
Aug	-212	-122	-212	-122
Sept	-56	-41[1]	-56	49
Oct	2,000[1]	1918[1]	1,849	1,828
Nov	-2,761	-3,117	-2,761	-3,117
Dec	931	839[1]	931	829
1930				
Jan	-757	-572	-757	-572
Feb	-261[1]	163	261	163
Mar	398	695	398	695
Apr	-401	-513	-401	-513
May	-610	-467	-610	-467
Jun	-32	30[1]	-32	130
Jul	107	40	107	40
Aug	-339	-249	-339	-249
Sept	-19	-14	-19	-14
Oct	-56	-26	-56	-26
Nov	41	-314	41	-314
Dec	-105	-686	-105	-686
1931				
Jan	-361	-401	-361	-401
Feb	152	289	152	289
Mar	45	-110[1]	45	-60
Apr	-508	-422	-508	-422

[1]Months in which Wicker made calculation errors based on his reference to Freidman & Schwartz's *Monetary History*, 1963. Corrected numbers are shown in TGD Authors' columns.

Sources: F&S; *Monetary Statistics of the United States: Estimates, Sources, Methods*, Columbia Univ. Press, 1970, pp. 409-10 & 508-9. Wicker, *The Banking Panics of the Great Depression*, Cambridge University Press, 1996, p. 50.

> York City for which Federal Reserve officials deserve full credit. The New York Fed displayed leadership and initiative in attempting to obtain merger agreement which, if successful, would have saved [Bank of United States].[28]

Was the Banking "Crisis" a Cause of the Great Depression?

Given the enormous influence of Friedman and Schwartz on accepted explanations for the Great Depression, it was bold, even brave, of Wicker to take on such eminence, but his view was the result of his own deep research into the data. Facing the likely backlash head on, Wicker began his analysis forthrightly:

> The banking crisis of 1930 has special significance among the four banking crises of the great depression because of the causal role assigned to it by Friedman and Schwartz. They maintained that... a rash of bank suspensions that decreased the money stock... *converted a mild downturn into a major depression.*[29] (emphasis ours)

In the prior chapter, we examined differences between M-1 and M-2 before what Friedman and Schwartz labeled above as the "first banking crisis"[30] began. Friedman and Schwartz informed us that M-2 had fallen -2.645% from August 1929 to October 1930. We responded that M-1 had fallen -5.610% from August 1929 to October 1930.

Table 10.2 (previous page) addresses Changes in M-1 and M-2 based on statistics found in *Monetary History* and shows monthly changes in these monetary aggregates from the beginning of the Great Depression in August 1929 to April 1931. In its left two col-

---

28 Ibid., p. 57.

29 Ibid., p. 46.

30 Friedman & Schwartz (1963a), p. 308.

umns, Table 10.2 provides statistics presented by Wicker in his Table 2.11. Referring to these statistics, Wicker raised questions regarding Friedman and Schwartz's thinking about events that happened *before* the 1930 banking crisis:

> Between November [1930] and January 1931 M-1 declined by $425 million and M-2 by $1,400 million. But the $425million decline in M-1 when compared with similar declines earlier in 1930 was not especially large. For example, … between April and June 1930 [M-1 declined] by *$1 billion,* and between August and October [by] $414 million dollars. Why, we might ask, attribute serious output effects solely to the banking crisis quarter when the changes in M-1 were either of the same magnitude or greater in earlier quarterly episodes?[31] (emphasis ours)

Then Wicker questioned the impact of the banking crisis on M-1 in the first two months—November and December—when Table 10.1 (page 287) shows the great majority of the actual suspensions—75.4% or 806—took place. Meanwhile, of the $627.7 million deposits suspended in the crisis as a whole, 87.9% were suspended during the first two months. Wicker goes on:

> Moreover, the decrease in M-1 during the two most serious crisis months is only $-64 million; it rose in November by $41 million and fell by $-105 million in December. It remains a puzzle why the 608 bank suspensions with $552 million of deposit losses in November and December failed to have a greater effect on M-1.[32]

---

31 Wicker (1996), p. 49.

32 Ibid.

Wicker then questioned the role of M-2 in the first banking crisis:

> The Friedman and Schwartz inference about the serious output effects of the first banking crisis derives solely from the behavior of M-2. Total deposits declined by $1.2 billion, $900 million of which was time deposits and only $279 million demand deposits. We may raise the same question about the behavior of M-2 that were raised about M-1. M-2 had declined by $959 million in the second quarter of 1930. Why did Friedman and Schwartz fail to attribute output effects to the decrease earlier in 1930?[33]

Wicker's Table 2.11 statistics as shown in Table 10.2 and his corresponding analyses offer powerful support for his direct queries.[34]

Why Bank Loan Repayments Matter

Beginning economics students learn that the quantity of outstanding bank loans matters as to the size of the money supply. When studying the "bank credit multiplier," they learn that an infusion by the Fed of what Friedman and Schwartz called "high-powered money"—that is, reserves—into the banking systems enables growth in loans that is considerably greater than the amount of the reserves, and that in the process of loan growth, the money supply also grows.[35] But for the Fed to grow the money supply in this manner, bank customers must *actively borrow.* If bank customers don't borrow, no matter how high-powered those available reserves, the money supply won't grow. In fact, if instead of borrowing, bor-

33 Ibid.

34 As stated above, Friedman and Schwartz's estimates of the monthly amounts of M-1 and M-2 published in their 1963 *Monetary History* are the sources for Wicker's Table 2.11 statistics.

35 Friedman and Schwartz (1963a), p. 50. See p. 50 for their definition of "high-powered money."

rowers in aggregate repay their loans, the money supply will actually shrink. A borrower repaying a bank loan writes a check payable to the bank on his or her checking account—a demand deposit—in the amount the borrower wants to repay. When the bank receives the check in repayment of the loan, the banker deducts the amount of the borrower's repayment from the borrower's outstanding loan *and* the bank's stock of loan assets and deducts the amount of the check from the borrower's checking account *and* the bank's stock of demand deposits, thereby reducing the amount of M-1. In other words, the amount of the bank's checking account deposits and the amount of its bank loans both shrink by the same amount.

Of course, if loan repayments occur during a period of widespread liquidity panic—such as what took place in the period of months after the Crash—the amount of the shrinkage of M-1 by the loan repayments may, at least temporarily, be offset by other customers who are actively converting longer-term assets into cash and depositing that cash *into* their own bank accounts, again, at least temporarily. But such periods of liquidity panic pass, and, since some of that newly liquidated cash may then be used to repay bank loans, ultimately the money stock will shrink.

Wicker's Summary and Our Response

Summarizing his considerable evidence, Wicker wrote:

> The principal conclusion to emerge from our description and analysis of the accelerated bank suspensions in November 1930-January 1931 is that there was no national banking crisis. The banking difficulties were region specific, that is, of some local and regional concern but without national importance. There was no panic in the New York money market as revealed by the number of bank suspensions or the behavior of interest rates. Bank debits outside New York City do not show significant effects on final product expenditures

except in those areas where the impact of bank suspensions was the highest. Nor would Friedman and Schwartz (1963, p. 313) disagree; they concluded that the first banking crisis 'left no clear imprint on the broad economic series' (shown here in Chart 10.1) such as personal income and industrial production.[36]

Chart 10.1

Prices, Personal Income, and Industrial Production, Monthly, 1929–March 1933

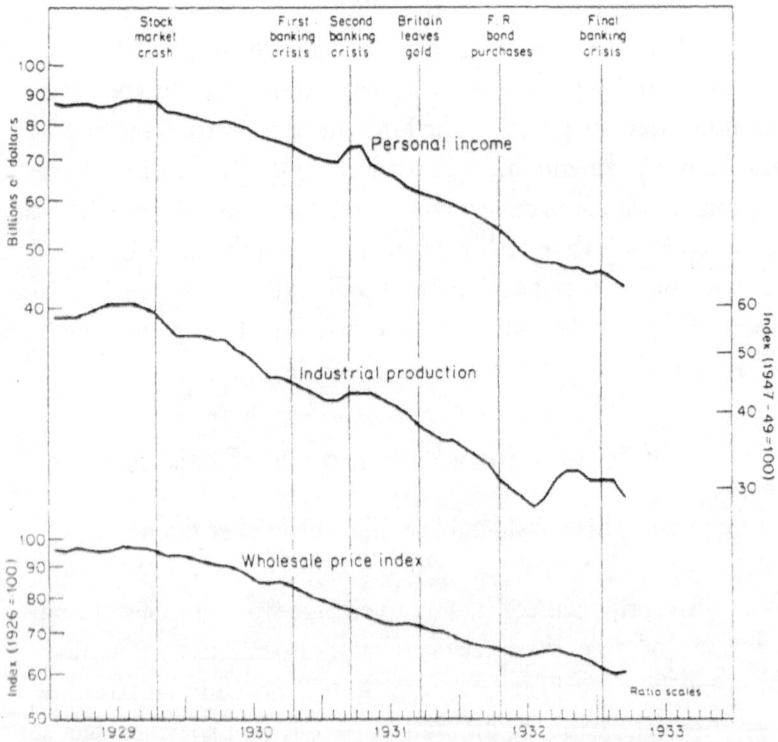

SOURCE: Industrial production, same as for Chart 16. Wholesale price index, same as for Chart 62. Personal income, *Business Cycle Indicators* (Princeton for NBER, G. H. Moore, ed., 1961), Vol. II, p. 139.

However, we posit that, even if that first banking crisis in

36 Wicker (1996), p. 58.

late 1930 was location-specific and didn't leave a "clear imprint" on, say, nationwide personal income or industrial production data, the documentable shrinkage of the (nationwide) money stock occurred instead because of debt repayments *everywhere,* and this, over time, led to continued and growing bank distress. In other words, loan repayments were an *a priori cause* of the money supply shrinking, rather than an effect.

Wicker expressed his puzzlement as to why 608 bank suspensions with $552 million of deposit suspensions in November and December failed to have a greater effect on M-1. To address that mystery, we should also consider the impact of loan repayments because loan repayments also affect M-1. Deposit suspensions should reduce the volume of deposits and, hence, of M-1, and, like Wicker, we are using Friedman and Schwartz's estimates of M-1 and M-2 here. But deposit suspensions definitely do not constitute loan repayments although the deposit checks used to make loan reductions are eliminated from deposits and thus also reduce M-1.

To address fully this mystery regarding the impact on M-1 in the period of the first banking crisis, we use the figures in our Table 5.2 (page 142) when the total loan portfolios of All U.S. Commercial Banks shrank by -$3,932 million in 1930 of which 63.7%, or -$2,505 million, occurred in the second half of 1930. Clearly the volume of loan repayment was accelerating in 1930, which is confirmed by the quarterly figures for All member banks. The amount of All Fed *member bank* loans shrank a total of $-1,344 million in the second half of 1930 with 64.6% of the decline occurring in the fourth quarter. If we extrapolate on the basis of these numbers to estimate the fall in the fourth quarter 1930 bank loans at All U.S. Commercial Banks, we find a decline of approximately $-1,618 million in the last quarter of 1930.

Unfortunately, we find that the mystery has deepened rather than moved toward a solution. Wicker asked why $552 million of deposit suspensions in November and December failed to have a greater effect on M-1. (For purposes of comparison, we suggest Wicker's figure be stated as $-552 million since that amount is "suspended" from circulation, i.e., "chasing goods." If we assume two thirds of the decline of $-1,618 million in the last quarter of 1930 were made in November and December, we find the decline is $-1,079 million, which is almost twice the amount suspended. Of course, these two amounts are additive with respect to each other.

In order to give a proper response to Wicker's conclusion, we need to observe that what we were commenting on in Chapter 9 and what Wicker was focusing on with respect of changes in M-1 were hardly evidences of "mild" decline. They were results of 1) the commencement of the Great Depression at full bore in May 1930 and 2) the pivot from increasing borrowing that ended in late October 1930 to monthly debt repayments beginning in November 1929 as described in Chapter 12 of *How the Crash Caused.* This pivot is seen most clearly in the installment sales statistics in Tables 12.4A and 12.4B in that volume.

The Crash made even those who had not participated in stock market speculation nervous. As we have discussed, such people—autonomously—took various forms of financial defensive action. They hunkered down, lowering or eliminating discretionary spending. They may have saved more for the rainy days that they felt were now upon them. They might even have hoarded cash as discussed in Chapter 3 if they were unsure about the condition of their local bank, based on rumor and proximity to places where they knew banks were in trouble, or just in an abundance of caution. However, the data clearly shows that they also did something else. They repaid debt.

Together the M-2 statistics and the IRS data confirm that people were, at least initially, repaying debts out of time deposits—their savings—at a greater rate than out of demand deposits. M-2, as we have seen, fell more than demand deposits in the first banking crisis. Only once they had depleted savings did indebted consumers try to liquidate whatever assets they could—i.e., only when they had to. It made sense to get out of debt so that they didn't lose what they'd been paying for in installments—the automobile, radio, refrigerator, furniture, piano; last of all to hold onto, the house. These were all obligations with specified payment amounts—including varyingly onerous interest charges—due by certain dates over a set period of time. Not only was the impact of deflation concerning, borrowers knew that nonpayment led to repossession of the item and loss of all prior payments. In 1930, no one imagined the Depression would go on and on into the seemingly endless future. When people repaid debt out of savings, they didn't know the risks ahead of using up those savings. And who knew that, if their bank got suspended, they might even lose some portion—or all—of whatever savings they had left or lose access to it for an indeterminate period of time? With debts repaid, at least they fully owned their purchases. As the months went on and more people became laid off or their work hours and wages cut, personal financial decision-making took on new urgency and their actions had considerably greater impact.

The Thinking of the Fed and of Friedman and Schwartz

Moving from the micro level of individual behavior to the macro level, Friedman and Schwartz summed up aspects of the thinking and approach of the Federal Reserve System (and of themselves) in the following fashion:

> **FEDERAL RESERVE SYSTEM'S ATTITUDE**
>
> The failure of the Bank of United States provoked much soul-searching by the directors of the New York Reserve Bank. They devoted meeting after meeting from mid-December 1930 to April 1931 to discussions of the responsibilities of the Reserve Bank with regard to member bank suspensions and of the actions it could take to prevent them.... Repeatedly during the next two years, the problem of bank failures and bank supervision was discussed at meetings within the System....
>
> The general tenor of System comments, both inside and out, was defensive, stressing the bank failures were a problem of

bank management which was not the System's responsibility.

> The major reason the system was so belated in showing concern about bank failures and so inactive in responding to them was undoubtedly limited understanding of the connection between bank failures, runs on banks, contraction of deposits, and weakness of the bond markets.... The technical personnel of the New York Bank understood these connections, as undoubtedly many other individuals in the system did also; but most of the governors of the Banks, members of the Board, and other administrative officials of the System did not. They tended to regard bank failures as regrettable consequences of bad management and ... regarded the banking situation as something different from the credit situation.[37]

Four additional circumstances may help to explain the System's failure both to develop concern over bank closings at an earlier date and to undertake more positive measures when concern did develop. (1) Federal Reserve officials had no feeling of responsibility for non-member banks. In 1921-29 and the first 10 months of 1930, most failed banks were nonmembers, and nonmembers held a high percentage of the deposits involved. (2). The failures for that period were concentrated among smaller banks and, since the most influential figures in the system were big-city bankers who deplored the existence of smaller banks, their disappearance may have been viewed with complacency. (3) even in November and December 1930, when the number of failures increased sharply, over 80 per cent were nonmembers. (4) The relatively few large member banks that failed at the end of 1930 were regarded by many Reserve officials as unfortunate cases of bad management and therefore not subject

37 Friedman and Schwartz (1963a), pp. 357-8.

to correction by central bank action.[38]

The Thinking of Barrie Wigmore

Barrie Wigmore also addressed the subject of the focus and inactions of the Federal Reserve System:

> Several factors account for the Federal Reserve's inactivity as a lender of last resort. For one, the Federal Reserve Board in Washington was inert. Hoover had forced Governor Young to move to the Boston Federal Reserve Bank, and Vice Governor Platt, a New Yorker, to retire, in order to make way for Eugene Meyer as the new Governor. But having forced the resignations in August, Hoover took until November to announce the replacements, which left the organization of the Board in limbo during a crucial period. Meyer was not confirmed in the job until February 25, 1931.
>
> A second factor accounting for Federal Reserve inactivity was that banks in the major cities across the nation did not appear to be in trouble.... The banks in trouble were the small, country banks which seemed to merit their demise because of their lack of capital and poor investments in real estate, agriculture, foreign bonds, and railroad bonds. Some 502 of the 608 banks which failed in November and December 1930, were non-member banks, and deposits in the 608 banks averaged less than $1 million per bank. There was no sense of responsibility for these banks at any level of the financial community.[39] (emphasis ours)

38 Ibid., pp. 358-9. In a footnote, Friedman and Schwartz stated, "We are indebted to Clark Warburton for this paragraph.

39 Wigmore (1985), p. 127.

We now transition to several chapters in which we consider the overall impact that 1930 had on life in America. In the next chapter we consider the impact on Americans as individuals. In Chapter 12 we consider the impact on American corporations and business broadly.

Summary and Conclusions

According to Elmus Wicker, "The principal conclusion … is that there was no national banking crisis." Wicker added, "the banking difficulties were … of some local and regional concern but without national importance."[40]

According to Friedman and Schwartz, "The first banking crisis left no clear imprint on the broad economic series shown in Chart 28," which is our Chart 10.1 on page 302. [41]

As we stated at the end of Chapter 9, our view of the market-propelling forces that were underway at the end of 1930 is that deflation as measured by WPI became an inexorable force by July 1930 and as measured by the CPI was well along by the end of 1930 to becoming an inexorable force itself having risen to an annual rate of -6.4% in December .

40 Wicker (1996), p. 58.

41 Ibid., and Freidman and Schwartz (1963), p. 313.

Table 10.3

Statistics of U.S. Economic Activity

($ billion)

	Aug. '30	Sep. '30	Oct. '30	Nov. '30	Dec. '30
Annualized personal income	$74.3	$73.7	$72.4	$70.6	$69.5
Index of factory employment	89.0	87.7	86.7	85.3	83.8
Index of industrial production	86	85	83	81	79
Index of wholesale prices	84.3	84.4	83.0	81.3	79.6
Friedman & Schwartz demand deposits	$21.4	$21.4	$21.4	$21.4	$21.1
Fed member bank loans		$24.7			$23.9

Sources: *HSUS* 1789-1945, pp. 328-330, 344; *Monetary History*, p.713; *BMS*, p.74.

CHAPTER 11

Retrospective & Look Forward for Americans as Individuals

With the end of 1930, we reach a point where data from both NIPA and our evidentiary Rembrandt, the IRS, come to the forefront once more. This time we focus on Americans as individuals—tax return filers in particular. Our intent is to examine data from individual tax returns for 1930, including data on loan repayments, as individuals continued to eschew consumption in order to pay off their own major over-indebtedness.[1] After a look at financial markets at the end of 1930, we offer a short review of the post-World War I period. We then consider the painful, new problem of what came to be known later as "involuntary unemployment" and make use of IRS and NIPA data to show how life in the first year of the Great Depression was hardly a bed of roses, even for those Americans who had thought of themselves (if briefly) as well-to-do. Especially with regard to unemployment, we look ahead to 1931 and beyond, examining the significant effects of the decisions people made during these challenging economic times.

Financial Markets at the End of 1930

According to Barrie Wigmore, after a flurry of optimism, the rest of 1930 showed alarming drops in stock prices, while a pall spread over the bond markets:

1 We introduced Irving Fisher's concept of over-indebtedness in Chapter 1 and discussed it further in Chapter 3.

> The optimism of spring 1930 gave way to a severe decline in stock prices in June which pushed many stocks back to their lowest prices in 1929. Stocks declined less severely, but steadily, from September through December as well, so that by year end they were 25% lower than they had been at the worst point in the Crash. Bond prices dropped $5-$10 at same time....The tone of the bond markets was more of a problem than actual prices, for very few bond prices were lower than their lowest levels in 1929.[2]

Looking Back with the Benefit of Informed Hindsight

Our retrospective begins with a look at the comprehensive National Income and Product Accounts (NIPA) prepared by the Bureau of Economic Analysis (BEA) within the Commerce Department. Their mammoth *National Income & Product Accounts of the United States, 1929-76 Statistical Tables*, published in September 1981, plus the IRS's *Statement of Income* annual reports were clearly two of our "gold standard" primary data sources.

Though NIPA only began collecting data in 1929, the BEA made an important contribution — its estimations of Gross National Product (GNP) before 1929, filling in gaps in earlier statistical series. GNP as a measure wasn't introduced until early in World War II when it served a valuable role in war production planning. Its usefulness in research and planning, even policymaking, proved great enough that the BEA made the effort decades later to estimate GNP for 1909 to 1928 and also the value of the GNP Price Deflator, the two aggregate measures of highest value to economists, historians, sociologists and others. The NIPA's GNP measures for those earlier years were significant in our research and helped us shape our narrative.

---

2 Wigmore (1985), p. 530.

Table 11.1

Gross National Product & Aggregate Price Indexes Re: 1929

1919-1939

Year	Current dollar GNP	July 1 U.S. population	Aggragate price indexes restated for 1929=100		
	($ billion)	($ million)	WPI	CPI	GNP deflator
1919	84.2	104.5	145.6	100.9	106
1920	91.5	106.5	162.0	116.9	121
1921	69.6	108.5	102.4	104.2	103
1922	74.2	110.0	101.5	97.7	98
1923	85.3	111.9	105.7	99.5	100
1924	84.9	114.9	103.1	99.7	99
1925	93.3	115.8	108.7	102.3	101
1926	97.2	117.4	105.0	103.1	101
1927	95.1	119.0	100.2	101.1	99
1928	97.1	120.5	101.6	100.0	100
1929	103.4	121.8	100.0	100.0	100
1930	90.7	123.1	90.6	97.4	96
1931	76.1	124.0	76.6	88.7	85
1932	58.3	124.8	68.0	79.7	77
1933	55.8	125.6	69.1	75.4	75
1934	65.3	126.4	78.7	78.0	80
1935	72.5	127.3	84.0	80.1	79
1936	82.7	128.1	84.8	80.9	82
1937	90.9	128.8	90.6	83.8	83
1938	85.0	129.8	82.5	82.3	83
1939	90.9	130.9	80.9	81.0	82

Source: *HSUS: Colonial Times to 1957*, Series E25, E113, F5, pp.117, 125, 139.

This table-abundant chapter commences with some basics for the twenty years from 1919-1939, then gets increasingly fine-tuned and more focused on late 1929 and early 1930 as one table of data after another leads to a more in-depth look at who was doing what in the stock market. To begin this unfolding process, Table 11.1 (above) starts at the most aggregate of levels, showing NIPA's estimated GNP for those years along with three Aggregate Price Indexes: Wholesale Price Index (WPI), Consumer Price Index (CPI) and GNP Price Deflator.

A brief historical overview provides context for what the table illuminates about events just ahead. As 1919 began, the First World War had ended. In 1920, all three price indexes were considerably higher than they had been in 1919 as the price inflation that occurred during the war continued. This especially affected agricultural prices and prices of agricultural land, since American farmers had substantially expanded their growing capacity in order to feed our allies. To end the high inflation, the Fed raised interest rates but that action initiated a short, severe period of deflation in 1920-21 (to be discussed in Chapter 12). By then European agricultural output had recovered. Unfortunately, American farmers overproduced, running up against the lower post-war demand. As a result, supply exceeded demand for U.S. commodities and prices fell. Financial difficulties for millions of farmers led to over five hundred bank failures in 1921,[3] mostly impacting smaller banks serving rural communities especially in agricultural parts of the U.S.[4]

By 1922, the Fed had reduced interest rates to encourage the economy to grow and prices to stabilize. After that, in a tiny and tidy nutshell, the U.S. then enjoyed what must have seemed like permanent prosperity in the 1920s, despite mild recessions occurring in 1924 and 1927. Strong growth continued through mid-year 1929. However, there was a darkening shadow that few were even looking at. Prosperity, both individual and corporate, as Charles Persons had claimed, was propped up by ready credit availability that swelled demand by enabling willing individuals to purchase—in installments—a home, a car, a radio and the many new inventions and conveniences that grew out of electrification—leaving millions increasingly indebted. Along with carrying installment debt, many also bought stock on margin with the same eagerness and lack of concern for possible ramifications. Then the Crash occurred and the

3 Of the 28,885 banks in the U.S. operating on June 30, 1920, two-thirds were in towns with fewer than 2500 people, according to the Federal Reserve Board, 1937, p. 906.

4 H. Parker Willis, "Who Caused the Panic of 1929?" *The North American Review,* Vol. 229, February 1930, p. 175

economy began a long downward spiral, initiating serious deflation and a dramatic and rapid shift in priority for the indebted away from consumption and towards solvency. Already, by year-end 1930, GNP in current dollars fell 12.4%, and all three price indexes, most especially the Wholesale Price Index, showed significant deflation. This was just the beginning.

The Unemployment Picture

Today we can track unemployment statistics six ways to Sunday: by location (national, state, city, county, even household); within demographics such as age, sex and/or sexual identity, ethnicity or education level; by industries, or by sector, whether public, private or nonprofit. Unemployment statistics are indeed one of the most closely watched indicators of the economy's health by policymakers, politicians, global leaders, Wall Street and Main Street. One of the Fed's major objectives, at least now, is for the economy to maintain low unemployment. This was not always the case. Just as there was no such thing as an unemployed farmer, economists before the Crash assumed there was a job for every willing worker. In other words, there was basically no unwilling unemployment in a *laissez faire* world. Therefore, there was no need to define it, much less measure it, track it, report on it or effectively to worry about it. During robust times, this topic remained in the background. As we learned from Charles Persons, only in 1930 did the reality of unemployment—specifically, involuntary unemployment—and its repercussions begin to be obvious to anyone anywhere simply walking down the street. In 1937, in his capacity as Administrator of the Works Progress Administration (WPA), Franklin Roosevelt's close friend Harry Hopkins wrote *The Realities of Unemployment,* in which he lamented not only the dire estimates of the evidence in front of everyone's face but also the lack of reliable data sources:

> How many Americans were unemployed in March 1933? Call it 18 millions or 13 millions—the smallest figure is bad enough. How many today? Eleven millions or eight millions? In any case it is nearly one employable worker out of five and at the lowest point of this depression it was almost one out of three. One major obstacle in the path of meeting the problem of unemployment has been the absence of really adequate unemployment figures.[5]

Almost a decade later, economic historian Broadus Mitchell, in his 1947 *Depression Decade; From New Era through New Deal 1929-1941,* wrote of the complex challenges of finding reliable and usable data and offered a list of the varied data sources that were available during the 1930s:

> Chief estimates by responsible agencies were those of the National Industrial Conference Board, the American Federation of Labor, the Congress of Industrial Organizations, Robert Nathan for the President's Committee on Economic Security, and the Alexander Hamilton Institute. Though these estimates differed at times by several millions, all showed the same turning points.... The peak of unemployment was reached in the first quarter 1933 and the lowest point in the third quarter of 1937. Significant features were the increase in unemployment, between the last of 1929 and the beginning of 1933, of about 4 million a year.[6]

---

5 Harry Hopkins, *The Realities of Unemployment*, BiblioGov, 1937, p. 3.

6 Broadus Mitchell, *Depression Decade; From New Era through New Deal 1929-1941*, Holt, Rinehart and Winston, 1947, p. 93.

Table 11.2

Preliminary Estimates of Labor Force, Employment, and Unemployment In The U.S., 1929 to 1940

(in thousands)

Year	Total labor force	Armed forces	Civilian labor force	Unemployment	Employment							Unemplyment as a percentage of the civilian labor force
					Total	Agricultural	Nonagricultural			Employees in nonagricultural establishments	Adjustment for duplication and incomparabilities	
							Employment	Employees	Self employed			
1929	48,065	262	47,803	1,499	46,304	9,972	36,332	29,343	6,989	30,502	-1,177	3.1
1930	48,683	263	48,420	4,248	44,172	9,869	34,303	27,551	6,752	28,655	-1,104	8.8
1931	49,270	260	49,010	7,911	41,099	9,829	31,270	24,867	6,403	25,864	-997	16.1
1932	49,830	254	49,576	11,901	37,675	9,725	27,950	21,958	5,992	22,837	-879	24.0
1933	50,403	252	50,151	12,634	37,517	9,658	27,859	22,013	5,846	22,904	-891	25.2
1934	51,032	258	50,774	10,968	39,806	9,484	30,322	24,247	6,075	25,246	-999	21.6
1935	51,663	269	51,394	10,208	41,186	9,698	31,488	25,264	6,224	26,317	-1,053	19.9
1936	52,273	301	51,972	8,598	43,374	9,598	33,776	27,183	6,593	28,328	-1,145	16.5
1937	52,849	322	52,527	7,273	45,254	9,437	35,817	28,940	6,877	30,170	-1,230	13.8
1938	53,465	335	53,130	9,910	43,220	9,322	33,898	27,213	6,685	28,377	-1,164	18.7
1939	54,095	369	53,726	8,842	44,884	9,252	35,632	28,633	6,999	29,869	-1,236	16.5
1940	54,479	535	53,944	7,476	46,468	9,192	37,276	30,051	7,225	31,388	-1,337	13.9

1929-1940: Total Labor Force: Armed Forces (from BLS) plus Civilian Labor Force (Census interpolated by BLS). Unemployment: Civilian Labor Force minus Total Employment. Total Employment: Agricultural Employment (Census interpolated by BAE) plus Nonagricultural Employment (Census interpolated by adjusted BLS). Employees: MRLF level estimates fluctuated by BLS. Self-employed: Preliminary BLS Employees in Nonagricultural Establishments:Preliminary BLS not comparable with MRLF level employees because of duplication and statistical incomparabilities.

Source: *U. S. Department of Labor, Bureau of Labor Statistics, Employment and Occupational Outlook Branch, Occupational Outlook Division, June 29, 1945. Technical Memorandum No. 20, July 4, 1945.*

Table 11.3

Estimates Of Unemployment In The U. S., 1929 to 1940

(in thousands)

Year	Preliminary BLS	A.F.L.	C.I.O.	N.I.C.B.	Robert Nathan	Alexander Hamilton Institute	Corington Gill	Daniel Carson	National Research League *	Labor Research Association	Cleveland Trust
1929	1,499	1,864	1,831	429	1,752	3,456	1,850	1,910	2,473	....	....
1930	4,248	4,735	4,710	2,896	4,646	6,929	4,750	4,825	5,325	....	4,124
1931	7,911	8,568	8,322	7,037	8,118	10,939	8,410	8,725	9,539	....	8,777
1932	11,901	12,870	12,120	11,385	11,639	14,728	12,480	13,100	14,220	16,783	13,416
1933	12,634	13,271	12,643	11,842	11,942	14,394	12,840	13,700	14,723	16,138	14,098
1934	10,968	11,424	10,845	9,761	9,998	12,419	11,130	12,115	13,288	16,824	12,130
1935	10,208	10,652	10,050	9,092	9,102	11,629	11,140	11,240	13,073	16,658	12,372
1936	8,598	9,395	8,756	7,386	7,723	10,008	9,780	10,200	12,614	14,751	....
1937	7,273	8,282	8,109	6,403	6,856	8,366	8,860	9,235	....	14,825	....
1938	9,910	10,836	11,030	9,796	9,865	11,934	11,870	....	....	16,368	....
1939	8,842	9,979	10,813	8,786	9,835	10,696	....	....	....	....	....
1940	7,476	9,104	10,276	7,607	9,552	9,379	....	....	....	....	....

* Estimates as of November except 1938, which is as of April.

Source: *U. S. Department of Labor, Bureau of Labor Statistics, Employment and Occupational Outlook Branch, Occupational Outlook Division, June 29, 1945. Technical Memorandum No. 20, July 4, 1945.*

In the appendix to Mitchell's book, he offered two tables reproduced here as Table 11.2 (opposite) and Table 11.3. (above) Table 11.2 shows a series of approximations made in 1945 by the Bureau of Labor Statistics (BLS) in the Labor Department, leading to their estimate for "Unemployment as a percentage of the civilian labor force" for 1929 through 1940. Table 11.3 compares other estimates of unemployment made by organizations cited by Mitchell and several others. These tables provide a rare, if incomplete, picture of unemployment from sources as reliable as then existed, though many of these estimates were made well after the period. To us in an era of big, bigger and biggest data, we may find it hard to believe that accurate and/or timely statistics were simply unavailable, making clear policy recommendations and timely decisions imprecise at best, if not impossible.

In terms of data collection as an asset, people had to come to recognize the value of knowing how large a problem, such as unemployment, was in order to solve it, and that required having the right information. Only once the Depression led to a large and growing number of involuntarily unemployed Americans, for instance, did the data on that phenomenon become a priority. Indeed, John

Maynard Keynes coined the term in his *General Theory:*

> We must now define the third category of unemployment, namely 'involuntary' unemployment in the strict sense, the possibility of which the classical theory does not admit.[7]

Further, only when there was the public will to have information would we fund the public sector to engage in creating collection parameters and methodologies for such data-gathering activities. However, in our period of focus we must constantly remind ourselves to picture green eyeshades, sleeve protectors and ink wells as well as gigantic mechanical adding machines ("tabulators"), and far fewer people asking important questions about the issues of the times. Working with data then, if data were collected at all, required countless tedious hours in libraries if the data were available. Now we have 24/7 access to governmental and other databases to explore, as well as the benefit of a lot of prior research.

Not everyone, of course, was unemployed. In his thoughtful 1987 book *The Great Depression,* historian John A. Garraty opened his chapter on "Workers and Unions" by illuminating an important additional aspect of the employment picture during the Depression, namely about how those still employed were faring:

> It is important to keep in mind that during the Great Depression people who had full-time jobs were usually better off, at least economically, than they had been before 1929. This was because... the cost of living fell faster and further than wages fell. It is also worth noting that at all times, a large majority of the workforce was employed. Put the other way around, the unemployed, although unprecedentedly

7 John Maynard Keynes, *The General Theory of Employment, Interest and Money,* Palgrave Macmillan, 1936, p. 15 in the Royal Economic Society edition.

numerous, were always a minority.... Another important fact to remember is that unemployment, for a majority of those who suffered the experience, tended to be a temporary condition....

On the other hand ... the hours of many workers were severely reduced. People on short time were not counted as being out of work, although in some cases they were idle for more time than workers who were without a job for substantial periods.... Few workers could feel safe when ever-larger numbers of their colleagues were out of work, and no end of the hard times was in sight.[8]

Who Did and Didn't Pay Taxes?

We need to keep in mind that income tax codes in 1928, 1929 and 1930 cast a far paler shadow on American workers then than now. Surely, in this uneasy environment, full of trepidation about the odds of continued employment, thoughts of tax obligations took a back seat as most citizens earned too little even to file. Understanding that reality while working with the available data, we concluded that our focus in our research would be on taxfilers, not the broader labor force. Statistics, estimations though some may be, support that decision.

First and foremost, given IRS rules then, most Americans did not file tax returns because they earned under the minimum income requirement for filing. The instructions on the Form 1040A for 1930 stipulated several levels of income, the first of which was "a

8 John A. Garraty, *The Great Depression*, Anchor Book Doubleday, 1987, pp. 86-87.

gross income ... of $5,000 or over."[9] Looking back from the 1940s on 1929 and 1930 in particular, Table 11.2 shows that the BLS estimated a Total U.S. Labor Force of 48.1 million in 1929 and 48.7 million in 1930. Based on our research, however, we knew these aggregate workforce numbers needed to be looked at more closely. All 3.7 million taxfilers in 1930 were at least income-earners. Of course, we cannot say that all 3.7 million filers thought of themselves as—nor were they—part of the BLS's "official" estimated 48.7 million U.S. labor force. Taxfilers also had income from sources other than wages or salaries, some in substantial amounts. As we shall see, this reported income from non-wage sources commanded our attention early on as being particularly significant.

American Individuals as Seen by the IRS in 1930

We continue here our discussion begun in Chapter 4, where we first considered American taxfilers as speculators and investors through looking at their annual tax returns as compiled, examined and presented in the IRS annual *Statistics of Income* reports. In *SOI for 1930*, the IRS began the section on individual income tax returns with the following no-frills summary:

> The number of returns of individuals for 1930 was 3,707,509, of which 2,037,645 were taxable and 1,669,864 nontaxable. The aggregate net income was $18,118,634,941;

9 The 2022 equivalent of $5,000 is approximately $87,000. The instructions on the Form 1040 A for 1930 stated: "An income tax return must be filed by every citizen of the United States whether residing at home or abroad, and every person residing in the United States, though not a citizen thereof, having a gross income for the calendar year 1930 of $5,000, or over, or a net income for the same period of (a) $1,500 or over, if single, or if married and not living with husband or wife, or (b) $3,500 or over, if married and filing with husband or wife, or (c) more than the personal exemption if the status of the taxpayer changes." This statement together with the instructions for personal exemptions appears in *SOI for 1930*, p. 335.

the net income on taxable returns was $13,692,584,305, on which the tax liability was $476,714,808.[10]

What these large and exact numbers meant in terms of telling our story required a lot of dissection, something the IRS archives allow for those of us willing to explore how the IRS sliced and diced the data.

Table 11.4 **Summary Statistics** Individual Filers			
	1929	1930	Rate of change
Returns filed	4,044,327	3,707,509	-8.33%
Taxable returns	2,458,049	2,037,645	-17.10%
(The following amounts are in $ million.)			
Aggregate net income	24,801	18,119	-26.95%
Net income on taxable returns	20,493	13,693	-33.19%
Tax liability	1,002	476.7	-52.42%

Source: *SOI for 1929 & 1930: 1929* p.5, *1930* pp.5-6.

Viewing events from a fifty-thousand-foot level, Table 11.4 (above) distributes Returns Filed, Aggregate Net Income and Tax Liability for 1929 and 1930. Every rate-of-change statistic in 1930 is down from 1929, some quite dramatically, and it would be difficult to rank-order them by their import as each measure spoke loudly about what was happening:

- Returns Filed in 1930 down more than -8%

- Taxable Returns down more than -17%

- Aggregate Net Income down nearly -27%

10 *SOI for 1930*, p.4. For those struggling to get their minds around amounts expressed in eleven digits, we give great credit to the IRS Statistical Unit for accuracy. The preparers of *Statistics of Income for 1930* took pride in their data's accuracy and likely felt they had compromised by giving up accuracy to-the-penny. Now, of course, we round to the nearest dollar when preparing our returns.

- Net Income on Taxable Returns down more than -33%
- Tax Liability down more than -52%[11]

The bottom line was that American taxfilers were fewer in number, earned less income and had a smaller tax liability in 1930 than in 1929.

All Sources of Income Declined Significantly in 1930

Table 11.5

Sources of Income and Deductions

($ million)

	1929	1930	(%) Change
Income:			
Wages & salaries	11,199	9,922	-11.4
Business	3,379	2,628	-22.2
Partnership	1,853	1,090	-41.2
Profit from short-term gains	2,338	637	-72.8
Net long-term gains	2,346	556	-76.3
Rents & royalties	1,286	974	-24.3
Interest on govt. securities	40	38	-5.0
Dividends	4,786	4,197	-12.3
Fiduciary	508	429	-15.6
Interest & other	2,211	1,940	-12.3
Total income	29,946	22,411	-25.2
Deductions:			
Loss from short-term assets	996	1,233	23.8
Net loss from business and partnerships	n.a.	173	n.a.
Contributions	529	425	-19.7
All others	3,621	2,464	-32.0
Total deductions	5146	4,295	-16.5
Net income	24,800	18,116	-27.0

Source: *SOI for 1929 & 1930: 1929* p.8, 1930 p.9.

11 *SOI for1930* observed that part of the drop in tax liability was due to a temporary drop in tax rates (startlingly low by today's standards) for 1930.

Our next level of concern has to do with the types of income taxfilers earned and which of those income categories pointed towards stock market participation. Table 11.5 (opposite) shows aggregate sources of income and deductions of all filed individual returns—filers and taxpayers—for 1929 and 1930. The first statistic that jumps out, however, is at the aggregate level. Whereas gross or total income rose 3.5% from $28,937 million in 1928 to $29,947 million in 1929, in Table 11.5 we see a dramatic 25.2% fall in total income in 1930 to $22,411 million.[12]

With that large decline in mind, for taxation purposes, the IRS divided taxpayer income into either earned (wages, salaries or business endeavors) or unearned (investments, interest, dividends, etc.) before breaking down that income into ten possible sources. Today we deal with a tax code of over four thousand pages and tens of thousands of additional explanatory and interpretive pages. Several hundred thousand skilled and accredited professionals spend their careers dealing only with tax matters, but times were simpler in the late 1920s and early 1930s and not just in terms of who had to file. By the end of 1913, when the 16th Amendment was ratified, the IRS code was 27 pages plus 400 additional pages to elaborate on the 27. Despite the enormous changes since, however, some income source descriptions have remained the same over the years and are familiar to us today, while a few have changed or been merged into another category. The list of IRS income sources with a brief definition of each category follows:

• *Wages and salaries* constituted pay for blue-collar or white-collar work.

• *Business* constituted sole proprietors' profits from unincorporated business enterprises such as local shops or small restaurants.

• *Partnership* constituted the profits from unincorporated enterprises such as law offices, family doctors, accountants, advertising,

12 See Table 4.1 (page 97) for 1928 to 1929 data.

some banking and investment banking, and asset brokerage firms that operated then and were taxed as partnerships.

• *Profit from real estate, stocks, bonds, etc., other than …* today we call "short-term capital gains" or "Profit from short-term asset sales (all classes)."

• *Capital net gain from sale of assets held more than 2 years* we call today "Long-term capital gains" or "Capital net long asset gains (all classes)."

Still familiar today are:

• *Rents and royalties*
• *Dividends on the stock of domestic corporations*
• *Fiduciary* (fees paid for the management of trusts and estates)
and • *Interest and other income* (includes what used to be a separate category *Interest on government securities*)

Income from every one of the above sources fell from 1929 to 1930, listed below in order of magnitude of the drop:

• *Profit from short-term asset sales (all classes)* and *Capital net long asset gains (all classes)* each fell more than *-70%*

• *Partnership* income down *-41.2%*, reflecting significant drops in the profitability of financial industry partnerships

• *Rents and royalties* down *-24.3%*

• *Business* (sole proprietors' profits from unincorporated business enterprises) down -22.2%.

• *Dividends on the stock of domestic corporations* down *-12.2%*

• *Wages and salaries* down *-11.4%*

• The categories *Fiduciary, Interest and other income, and Interest on Government obligations not wholly exempt from tax* all had losses and registered declines.

It is also illuminating to look at the data on what deductions the IRS allowed taxfilers to take against their incomes. The "Total deductions" figure came directly from the tax filings prepared, taxpayer-by-taxpayer, in accordance with the schedules of allowable deductions. Present-day taxfilers will recognize many of the same deductions, although the labels may have changed. For instance, what the table lists as "Loss from Short Assets" we now call "short-term capital losses," although assets then were considered short-term for two years, not one, which changed in the early 1960s. However, "Contributions," "Net loss from business and partnership," and "all other" are still familiar as tax-deductible expenses to this day.

Changes in allowable deductions, not just in income, told a similar story of losses between 1929 and 1930. The biggest change was in the category Table 11.5 (page 322) calls "Loss from Short Assets" which increased by 23.8%, reflecting the demise of the Little Bull Market. Also, a newly important category, "Net loss from business and partnership," appeared in *SOI for 1930* showing a loss of $172.5 million. The size and downward movement of both of these categories contributed to our understanding of the period.

Evidence of a New Form of Speculation in 1930

In Chapter 4, we considered the "game of speculation" as it was played in 1928 and 1929 and concluded that speculation was a game of quick profits focused on individual stocks that were "in play." There is clear evidence that speculators continued to play the game in 1930, but a significant portion of those who purchased and owned stocks at the end of 1929 and the beginning of 1930 started to engage in a second form of speculation. Instead of betting on individual stocks that were suddenly rising, then selling them quickly before the stocks went back down, this new way of speculating entailed betting on the overall market. Those who engaged in this form bought portfolios of stocks, planning to hold them as long as it took for the stock market to rise back to the level they expected the market to reach. As quoted in Chapter 6 (page 160), Alexander Dana Noyes wrote of what he called "professional speculators" who reentered the stock market on borrowed money to participate in the Little Bull Market, which he deemed a "most unfortunate experiment." Barrie Wigmore added his own observation about this ill-fated strategy:

> Old hands in the securities business remember vividly the optimism that prevailed in the early months of 1930, because many investors were enticed back into the stock market only to be wiped out in the drawn-out market decline which followed. The smart money was lost in this aftermath.[13]

Table 11.6

Speculation in 1930

Net income classes ($ thousand)	Profit on short-term sales: Amount ($ million)	Profit on short-term sales: Percent of class income (%)	Net loss from short-term sales: Amount ($ million)	Net loss from short-term sales: Percent of class income (%)
<5	109.1	1.18	-285.7	3.10
5<10	135.3	3.00	-198.1	4.39
10<25	191.5	5.15	-287.9	7.75
25<50	116.7	6.50	-154.2	8.71
50<100	42.8	3.58	-116.3	9.73
100<150	11.5	2.37	-50.0	10.33
150<300	10.5	1.89	-65.5	11.82
300<500	5.3	1.99	-26.6	10.02
500<1,000	4.0	1.44	-34.2	12.21
1,000 & over	10.2	2.38	-14.2	3.34
Total	636.9		-1,232.7	

Source: *SOI 1930*, pp.10-11.

13 Wigmore (1985), p. 128

Table 11.6 (opposite) provides evidence of both the conventional "game of speculation" as played in earlier years and the new form of speculation entered into at the end of 1929 and the beginning of 1930. We see data on the conventional form of speculation under the heading "Profit on short-term sales." Here the net income class percentage dispersion looked very much as it did in 1928 and 1929, though at a lower level of financial reward. While the data makes it clear that every net income class engaged in this familiar form of speculation, the level of commitment (as measured by what per cent of income each income class derived from Profit on short-term sales) rose from the lowest net income class to the 25<50 class.[14] Then, from the 25<50 net income class upwards, the level of income derived from Profit on short-term sales fell consistently to the highest net income class. We regard this as the "let's-make-quick-profits" school of speculation.

Table 11.6 also includes data under the heading "Net loss from short-term sales" that bears discussing because it reveals the newer form of speculation that appeared in late 1929 and early 1930. First, we see how different the net income class percentage dispersion is between the profit and loss columns. Whereas Profit on short-term sales peaked in the 25<50 net income class and thereafter fell, Net loss from short-term sales peaked in the 500<1,000 net income class. Furthermore, for the net income classes 100<1,000, their income from Net losses from short-term sales was notably high. We consider this new, longer-term form of speculation the "let's-bet-on-the-revival-of-the-stock-market" school.

This second form of post-Crash speculation when speculators were betting that the market in general would rebound on a more long-term basis was a very different "experiment," to use Noyes's word. Table 11.6 also shows us that the average affluent investors in the 100<1000 categories placed and kept appreciable sums of money at risk until they concluded that the market was not going to rebound, at which point their bets turned into losses, some of which were considerable.

14 A reminder that $25,000 in 1929 = approximately $450,000 in 2024.

These were the "professional speculators" that Noyes referred to above, and the "investors … the smart money" that Wigmore referred to, who were back in the game. Adding to the damage inflicted by the losses, Noyes and Wigmore both suggested that these players were operating on margin. Noyes said explicitly that his professional speculators were "buying stocks with borrowed money on a very substantial scale." Wigmore stated that his smart-money investors were "wiped out." We need to add Noyes's professional speculators and Wigmore's smart-money investors to our cast of characters of Repentant Ex-Speculators (post-Crash) as people who were very unhappy and highly desirous of getting out of debt as fast as possible.

Sources of Income Shed Light on Speculation in 1929 and 1930

Table 11.7 (opposite) draws on the same source materials used to produce Table 4.7 (page 111), adds 1930 statistics and provides clear evidence of both forms of speculation among taxfilers in 1930. The 1930 statistics for "Profit from short-term assets sales" confirmed the losses experienced in the course of the two forms of speculation shown in Table 11.6. These losses comprised the sums, by net income class, of 1) the positive numbers realized by conventional speculators engaged in the game of the let's-make-quick-profits school focused on stocks in play plus 2) the mounting losses from the new form of speculation—the let's-bet-on-the-revival-of-the-stock-market school—as the overall market levels expected by the new speculators failed to materialize.

Two examples should make this process clear. In the <$5,000 Net income class, when the Amount of Profit on short-term sales—$109.1 million—is added to the Amount of the Net loss from short-term sales—$-285.7 million, the total is -$ 176.6 million, the same quantity in Table 11.7 for the two forms of speculation combined in 1930. When the Total for Profit on short-term

Table 11.7			
Sources of Income Displayed by Net Income Class ($ million)			
Net income classes ($ thousand)	1928	1929	1930
	Profit from short-term asset sales (all classes)		
<5	227.6	168.6	-176.6
5<10	364.0	187.0	-62.8
10<25	711.4	355.2	-96.4
25<50	547.4	264.4	-37.5
50<100	355.4	142.5	-73.5
100<150	166.6	46.5	-38.5
150<300	199.9	63.3	-55.0
300<500	107.9	27.7	-21.3
500<1,000	109.4	29.7	-30.2
1,000 & over	148.5	56.8	-4.0
Total	2,938.1	1,341.7	-595.8
	Capital net long asset gains (all classes)		
<5	----------	----------	----------
5<10	----------	----------	----------
10<25	----------	----------	----------
25<50	46.5	28.5	13.6
50<100	248.5	257.9	87.8
100<150	185.0	223.5	63.9
150<300	332.5	422.6	108.8
300<500	219.9	301.4	67.2
500<1,000	267.1	352.5	78.4
1,000 & over	580.3	760.3	136.8
Total	1,879.8	2,346.7	556.5

Source: *SOI 1928-1930.*

sales—$636.9 million—is added to the Total of the Net loss form short-term sales— $-1,232.7 million, the sum— $-595.8 million—is the quantity reported in Table 11.7 (previous page) for the two forms of speculation together in 1930.

The lower part of Table 11.7 shows the return to investors from the sale of long-term assets in 1930. These assets—held for at least two years before they were sold—were acquired before the end of 1928, and, of note, no one with a net income <25 participated in these long asset sales. We suspect that a meaningful portion of the proceeds from these long asset sales was devoted to reducing sellers' debts and that some of those proceeds funded the speculation of the professionals and smart money.

Table 11.8

Returns from Assets by Net Income Class

($ million)

Net income classes	Short-term asset sales		Short total	Long asset gains	All asset sales
	Profits	Losses			
<5	109.1	-285.7	-176.6	-	-176.6
5<10	135.3	-198.1	-62.8	-	-62.8
10<25	191.5	-287.9	-96.4	-	-96.4
25<50	116.7	-154.2	-37.5	13.6	-23.9
50<100	42.8	-116.3	-73.5	87.8	14.3
100<150	11.5	-50.0	-38.5	63.9	25.4
150<300	10.5	-65.5	-55.0	108.8	53.8
300<500	5.3	-26.6	-21.3	67.2	45.9
500<1,000	4.0	-34.2	-30.2	78.4	48.2
1,000 & over	10.2	-14.2	-4.0	136.8	132.8
Total	636.9	-1,232.7	-595.8	556.5	-39.3

Source: *SOI for 1930*, pp.10, 11, 14.

Table 11.8 (above) refines the statistics in the prior two tables and displays by net income class the 1930 Returns from asset sales. Under Short-term asset sales are the Profit and Net Loss figures from Table 11.6. (page 326) The Short total and Long asset gains from Table 11.7 are combined into All asset sales, showing a loss of -$39.3 million in 1930.

On the basis of the statistics in Tables 11.6, 11.7 and 11.8, we concluded that speculators likely no longer saw speculation as profitable by the end of June 1930, when Noyes's professionals and Wigmore's smart money had lost their bets.

Percentage Data for 1930 Reveal the Demographic Impact of the Crash

We now turn to percentages in Table 11.9 (following page) to give us a demographic picture of the income statistics for 1929 and 1930 (echoing Table 4.6 on page 104) where the percentage entries in each net income class add horizontally to 100% in the Total income column.[15] We offer a breakdown of income sources and their significance during the period:

• In the speculation category "Profit on short gains" (or "Profit from short-term asset sales (all classes)"), we see that while all net income classes included some speculation in 1929 and 1930, it was concentrated in net income classes of 10<100, with all 1930 percentages substantially less than in 1929. Comparing Table 11.9 to Table 4.6 (page 104) shows the shift in speculation results by income class.

• In the category Net long-term gains (or "Capital net long asset gains (all classes)"), the focus was on investors, and we see the same patterns that prevailed in 1929 also in 1930 but at lower amounts. In each year, we first see a small amount of Net long gains in the 25<50 net income class. The percentages grew significantly as net income rose but at roughly two thirds the level in 1930 as the 1929 percentages.

---

15 The $ amount associated with any column can be calculated by multiplying the total $ sum in the appropriate Income categories in Table 11.5 by the percentage numbers, rendered in decimal form.

Table 11.9

Percentage distribution of total income in individual returns for 1929 and 1930, by net income classes, showing sources of income in detail

Net income classes (Thousands of dollars)	Wages and salaries		Business (sole-proprietorships)		Partnership	
	1929	1930	1929	1930	1929	1930
Under 5 (estimated)	58.81	59.90	15.07	15.34	3.47	3.29
5 under 10	45.86	49.48	17.55	14.51	6.92	5.87
10 under 25	32.64	35.74	11.96	9.96	7.52	6.56
25 under 50	22.61	24.81	6.84	6.18	7.22	6.67
50 under 100	15.46	17.99	4.17	4.04	7.44	6.98
100 under 150	11.36	13.51	3.25	3.24	8.41	5.84
150 under 300	8.48	10.83	2.25	2.05	9.82	5.58
300 under 500	5.87	8.75	1.69	1.09	9.43	3.97
500 under 1,000	3.75	7.48	0.94	0.86	9.46	1.18
1,000 and over	1.83	5.17	0.13	0.08	6.82	0.45
Total	37.40	44.27	11.28	11.73	6.19	4.86

Net income classes (Thousands of dollars)	Profit on short gains (all asset classes)		Net long-term gains (all asset classes)		Dividends on stock of domestic corporations		Rents and royalties	
	1929	1930	1929	1930	1929	1930	1929	1930
Under 5 (estimated)	2.87	1.18	----------	----------	5.27	5.31	6.22	5.38
5 under 10	6.22	3.00	----------	----------	9.65	12.70	4.93	4.43
10 under 25	12.84	5.15	----------	----------	19.30	25.09	4.21	4.12
25 under 50	17.75	6.59	1.10	0.77	28.36	36.68	3.30	3.54
50 under 100	12.66	3.58	13.15	7.35	32.92	44.20	2.47	2.62
100 under 150	8.83	2.37	24.34	13.19	33.23	49.16	1.81	2.09
150 under 300	8.63	1.89	33.05	19.62	29.53	49.83	1.27	1.78
300 under 500	6.59	1.99	41.21	25.31	27.50	50.20	0.76	1.87
500 under 1,000	6.71	1.44	45.71	27.96	27.66	52.96	0.80	1.36
1,000 and over	7.14	2.38	54.76	32.05	23.85	53.80	0.66	0.87
Total	7.81	2.84	7.84	2.48	15.98	18.73	4.29	4.35

Net income classes (Thousands of dollars)	Interest on gov't obligations not wholly exempt from tax		Fiduciary		Interest and other income		Percent of total income	
	1929	1930	1929	1930	1929	1930	1929	1930
Under 5 (estimated)	----------	----------	0.84	0.99	7.45	8.61	100.0	100.0
5 under 10	----------	----------	1.55	1.86	7.32	8.15	100.0	100.0
10 under 25	0.31	0.44	2.55	2.99	8.67	9.95	100.0	100.0
25 under 50	0.35	0.54	3.59	4.07	8.88	10.15	100.0	100.0
50 under 100	0.33	0.46	3.20	3.47	8.20	9.31	100.0	100.0
100 under 150	0.27	0.35	2.09	2.46	6.41	7.79	100.0	100.0
150 under 300	0.20	0.54	1.45	1.51	5.32	6.37	100.0	100.0
300 under 500	0.18	0.18	1.60	1.22	5.17	5.42	100.0	100.0
500 under 1,000	0.15	0.14	0.53	1.34	4.29	4.65	100.0	100.0
1,000 and over	0.15	0.21	0.57	0.53	4.09	4.46	100.0	100.0
Total	0.13	0.17	1.70	1.92	7.38	8.65	100.0	100.0

Source: *SOI for 1929 & 1930: 1929* p.10, 1930 pp.11-12.

- Wages and salaries comprised a higher percentage of total income in 1930 than in 1929, and, as net income rose, the importance of wages and salaries in 1930 rose over 1929.

- Business income in 1930 was close to the level of importance in 1929, but fell gradually with respect to 1929 in terms of relative importance as net income rose.

• Partnership income in 1930 was below its percentage importance in 1929, and its relative importance also fell as net income rose.

• Dividends were important to all net income classes in both 1929 in 1930. In 1929, dividends comprised only 5.27% of income for the lowest net income class and rose to 23.85% of income for the highest net income class. In 1930, dividends started at 5.31% of income for the lowest net income class and rose to 18.73% of income for the highest net income class. This suggests that all net income classes may have moved in the direction of buying and holding stocks in 1930 based on their dividend yields.

• As a source of income, Rents and Royalties had very similar profiles in 1929 and 1930. Starting at 6.22% and 5.38% respectively in the lowest income class, they fell as net income classes rose. In the highest net income class they were 0.66% and 0.87% respectively.

• Fiduciary was a small component of income in both years but was consistently higher in 1930 over 1929 in all but one net income class. In both years its highest value occurred in the 25<50 income class, having risen as a percentage to that class from the lower net income classes and then falling as a percentage from that class to the higher classes.

• Interest on Government obligations not wholly exempt from tax was a very small component of income for all net income classes in 1929 and 1930.

• The category "Interest and other income" was a significant component of income in 1929 and rose in importance in 1930. In both years, its highest value occurred in the 25<50 income class, rising to that percentage from the lower classes and then falling thereafter as a percentage from that class to the higher income classes.

What Happened to the Unearned Income of Individuals in the Crash Period?

Table 11.10

Demographic Ups & Downs

	1928	1929	1930
1	Wages & Salaries	Same	Same
2	Dividends	Same	Same
3	Business	Same	Same
4	Short profits	Long Gains	Interest
5	Interest	Same	Partnership
6	Partnership	Same	Rents
7	Long gains	Short Profits	Long gains
8	Rents	Same	Fiduciary
9	Fiduciary	Same	Int. on govt. securities
10	Int. on govt. securities	Same	Short losses

Source: Created by authors.

Updating Table 4.8 (page 113), Table 11.10 shows changes that occurred over the period 1928 to 1930 as to the rankings of sources of income. Of note was the change in the significance of Long-term gains which went from 7th in 1928 to 4th in 1929 then back to 7th in 1930. Almost as obvious was Short-term profits which went from 4th in 1928 to 8th in 1929 to 10th in 1930. The change in the rankings of these sources of income over these three years highlights the economic impact of what actually happened.

Table 11.11

Short-Term Profits

($ million)

Net income class	1928	% of Total	1929	% of Total	1930	% of Total
Under $100,000	2,205.8	75.3	1,947.4	83.3	595.4	93.5
$100,00 and over	722.3	24.7	390.2	16.7	41.4	6.5
Total	2,928.1		2,337.6		636.8	
Short-Term Losses	-171.7		-995.9		-1,232.8	
Revised Total	2,756.4		1,341.7		-596.0	

Long-Term Net Gains

($ million)

Net income class	1928	% of Total	1929	% of Total	1930	% of Total
Under $100,000	295.0	15.7	286.4	12.2	101.4	18.2
$100,00 and over	1,584.8	84.3	2,060.3	87.8	455.0	81.8
Grand total	1,879.8		2,346.7		556.4	

Source: Calculated by athors from Table 11.7.

In terms of which income classes were speculating, Table 11.11 (above) has condensed the net income classes into two— over and under $100,000[16]—and shows a clear trend in the changing involvement in speculation as measured by Short-term profits from 1928 to 1930. The percentage participation in speculation of the net income classes <100 grew consistently from 75.3% in 1928 to 83.3% in 1929 to 93.5% in 1930. In contrast, the percentage participation in speculation of net income classes of >100 consistently shrank from 24.7% in 1928 to 16.7% in 1929 and further to 6.5% in 1930. *As the lower net income classes became more involved in speculation, the higher net income classes became less involved.*

The Dwindling Wealth Effect: What a Difference a Year Made to Taxpayers

As we learned in Table 11.4 (page 321), 2,458,049 taxable returns were filed in 1929, and 2,037,645—17.1% fewer—were filed in 1930. Table 11.12, (following page) working with averages, suggests how those who

16 $100,000 in 1930 equals approximately $1.8 million now.

Table 11.12

Average Income by Net Income Class

Net income classes ($ thousand)	1929		1930	
	Number of returns	Average class member	Number of returns	Average class member
<5	3,012,256	$3,356	2,897,078	$3,056
5<10	658,039	7,756	550,977	7,786
10<25	271,454	16,873	198,762	17,111
25<50	63,689	37,683	40,845	39,197
50<100	24,073	77,099	13,645	78,051
100<150	6,376	138,488	3,111	137,897
150<300	5,310	232,015	2,071	232,738
300<500	1,641	432,663	552	427,536
500<1,000	976	767,418	318	764,151
1,000 & over	513	2,623,816	150	2,726,666

Source: Calculated by authors from *SOI for 1929 & 1930: 1929* pp.5 & 9, 1930 pp.5 & 10.

paid taxes in 1929 might have fared by the end of 1930 by showing how many tax return filers were in each net income class for 1929 and 1930 and the average income of each net income class member. As it turned out, the Average class member's income for 1930 and 1929 was, somewhat surprisingly, quite similar. Six average income classes went up, and four went down. But Table 11.12 (above) tells only a partial story. The real questions have to do with the dwindling wealth effect on the many taxpayers whose incomes declined. To tackle this question, we created yet another table that interprets the meaning of statistics in Table 11.12.

Table 11.13 (opposite) presents the percentage decline in the number of taxpayers in each net income class from 1929 to 1930. At first glance, we easily see that the higher the net income class, the larger the decline in the number of taxpayers in that class between the two years. This in and of itself says plenty about the dwindling wealth effect. However, to go any deeper, we bump into another data roadblock since the *SOI* series worked only with aggregate figures and did not provide detail about the circumstances of individual taxpayers. In other words, we know nothing officially about taxpayer A or B in terms of his or her specific situation. While

Table 11.13					
Downward Movement of Net Income Class Members in 1930					
Net income classes ($ thousand)	**In the year** 1929	1930			
1,000 & over	513	150			
500 < 1,000	976	318			
300 < 500	1,641	552	507	45	
150 < 300	5,310	2,071	1,602	469	
100 < 150	6,376	3,111	3,072	39	
50 < 100	24,073	13,645	6,376	2,238	5,031
25 < 50	63,689	40,845	19,042	21,803	
10 < 25	271,454	198,762	41,886	156,876	
5 < 10	658,039	550,977	114,578	436,399	
< 5	3,012,256	2,897,078	221,640	2,675,438	

Source: As shown by authors from Table 11.12.

the available statistics show the dramatic fall from 1929 of 1930 in the number of taxpayers—in aggregate—in the highest net income classes straight through to the lowest net income classes, we have no way of knowing how many taxpayers stayed in the same class, fell one income class, two income classes or even more.[17] There may have been the rare taxpayers whose net income managed to increase, thus putting them in a higher net income class, even the top class. The 150 taxpayers who were in the highest net income class in 1930 had likely been in that class in 1929. However, while we can only make guesses about this, we can say with confidence that, *in terms of numbers of taxpayers, every income class contracted in size in 1930 from 1929.*

Fortunately, Table 11.14 (following page) assists us in taking our story a bit further as it relates to the dwindling wealth effect. Since well before 1929, the IRS has published the total income statistics reported annually by filers, separated into the ten net income classes we have discussed. Using the statistics in the 1930 net income dispersions shown in Table 11.13, we can estimate total income statistics in 1930 by 1929 net income class groups to give us an idea of how

17 The statistics also do not account for changes such as removal from the analysis of taxpayers who died.

Table 11.14				
Results of Downward Movement Found by Average Class Members In their Wallets				
Net income classes ($ thousand)	1929		Average income of 1929 class members In 1930	Percent (%) change in 1930
	Number of returns	Average class member		
<5	3,012,256	$3,356	$2,735	-18.5
5<10	658,039	7,756	6,203	-20.0
10<25	271,454	16,873	14,055	-16.7
25<50	63,689	37,683	24,956	-33.8
50<100	24,073	77,099	47,814	-38.0
100<150	6,376	138,488	78,996	-43.0
150<300	5,310	232,015	113,929	-50.9
300<500	1,641	432,663	233,729	-46.0
500<1,000	976	767,418	338,048	-55.9
1,000 & over	513	2,623,816	1,321,932	-49.6

Source: Calculated by authors from *SOI for 1929 & 1930: 1929* pp.5 & 9, 1930 pp.5 & 10.

much the average net income fell by income class between the two years. These figures show us how the members of each net income class, on average, *saw their incomes decline,* causing, undoubtedly, adjustments in lifestyle and financial and spending decisions.

For example, we estimate that the 513 individuals in the wealthiest 1929 net class income, >$1 million, had collective incomes in the neighborhood of $678.2 million. 18 Thus the estimated income of the average member of the wealthiest net income class was $1,321,932($678.2 million divided by the 513 individuals in the class in 1929).

Table 11.14 shows the results of our exercise in estimation. The third column shows the estimated 1930 incomes of the average members of 1929's net income classes. Each class declined substantially from 1929 as both the figures and the rates of decline show. Collectively the rates of decline for the four highest net income

18 We make this estimate by adding all the income in 1930 reported for the 1,000 & over class—$412.6 million—plus the income reported for the 500<1,000 class—$246.1 million—plus the portion of the income reported for the 300<500 class received by 45 of the 552 individuals in that class in 1930—$19.5 million.

classes comfortably exceeded -40%. The next three net income classes—50<150—declined at rates of more than -30%. The next lower income class—25<50— a group we determined was definitely speculating, declined by -28%. The three lowest net income classes—<25—declined at rates above -15%. As we know, there are wealthy people and then there are *the* wealthy who, though still affluent, had nonetheless suffered losses.

How did taxpayers feel at the end of 1930? Among the possible feelings, frightened is certainly one. Many were becoming much more cautious about spending money. As regards the well-being of their families, businesses and communities, they also must have felt extremely apprehensive. Perhaps Joseph Schumpeter gave the most evocative answer: "[P]eople felt the ground under their feet was giving way."[19]

How Did Investors Feel at the End of 1930?

In the last of this chapter's informative tables, Table 11.15 (following page) updates the Table 6.1 (p. 166) statistics through the beginning of 1931. Over the course of 1930, the market value of all listed stocks on the New York Stock Exchange declined -24.3% from $64.7 billion on January 1, 1930, to $49.0 billion on January 1, 1931. Although $2.8 billion was lost in 1929 as a whole (as Table 6.1 on page 166 shows), over $15.7 billion in value was lost in 1930, larger than the $15.3 billion lost in October 1929, but far less than the $26.1 billion lost in September, October and November combined.

Table 11.15 (following page) also updates our statistics on Call Market Loans and presents the clearest monthly statistic on the ongoing drop in the Demand for borrowed money to spend. Over the course of 1930 the demand for Call Market Loans dropped from $4.0 billion on January 1, 1930, to $1.9 billion on January 1, 1931, a decline of -52.5%. Thus, while the market value of listed stocks fell -32.0% in 1930, the demand by brokers for call loans (and most

19 Schumpeter (1939), p. 911.

Table 11.15			
Percent of New York Stock Exchange Loans to Total Market Values of Listed Shares			
The appended table shows the ratio of total Stock Exchange member borrowings on security collateral to total listed share values ($ million)			
	Brokers' loans	Market value all listed stocks	Ratio %
1930			
Jan. 1	$3,989.5	$64,707.9	6.16
Feb. 1	3,984.8	69,008.8	5.77
Mar. 1	4,167.6	70,806.7	5.89
Apr. 1	4,656.3	76,075.4	6.12
May 1	5,063.1	75,304.6	6.72
June 1	4,747.8	75,018.9	6.33
July 1	3,727.7	63,892.3	5.83
Aug. 1	3,689.5	67,221.3	5.49
Sept. 1	3,598.6	67,721.1	5.31
Oct. 1	3,481.5	60,143.2	5.79
Nov. 1	2,556.1	55,025.7	4.65
Dec. 1	2,162.2	53,311.9	4.06
1931			
Jan. 1	$1,893.6	$49,019.9	3.86

Source: *NYSE*.

importantly, by their clients for brokers' loans) fell much faster, and the ratio of the demand for Call Market Loans to the Market Value of All Listed Stocks fell from 6.16% on January 1, 1930 to 3.86% on January 1, 1931.

How did investors feel at the end of 1930? Certainly not optimistic. For one thing, they were probably extremely reluctant to sell the stocks they held at what they considered to be bargain basement prices. Overall, they probably felt a need to tighten their alligator belts, forego looking for houses to build or buy and, along with Americans in general, to decrease their spending on consumer durables, consumption goods and services. Above all, investors, along with other Americans, wanted to pay back any indebtedness.

CHAPTER 12

Retrospective & A Brief Look Forward American Corporations & Business (Year-End 1930)

Having examined the IRS archive for useful information about the economic behavior of individuals, we shift our perspective to American business. Business involves, at its essence, an individual or a group of individuals—small or large— assembled to make and sell something of value. In order for businesses to achieve viability, what they supply needs to inspire consumer demand. Even before the Crash, business activity showed signs of falling off, and it certainly fell significantly thereafter. And, since every business entity was supposed to file tax returns, the actual figures businesses reported to the IRS in our time period revealed information that told the story of the contraction in detail. Particularly telling are statistics on both gross income (also called "gross revenues") and net income (indicating profitability). These data reveal the fall in commerce in all its scope and depth as broken down by IRS statisticians.

We call it the Great Depression for good reason. The cumulative impact of our examination is indeed profound as table after table lays bare the panoramic breadth of the economic crisis that befell the country. In conducting our research, the data engaged our emotions and our imaginations because the numbers so clearly conveyed what was actually going on in the economic lives of real people.

In recent years and decades, we have seen specific industries hit hard by one recession after another—airlines, leisure, hospitality, the motion picture and music industries around 2020; banking, finance, construction, real estate and the automotive industry in 2008-2009; the savings and loan industry between 1986 and 1995; steel in the early 1980s and from 1973-75. But the 1929-33 Great Depression affected commerce almost *everywhere throughout the U.S. economy from its very start in 1930* and without the cushion of any of the overarching governmental protections, regulations and interventions of today. Industry after industry, sector after sector, faced declines once unimaginable and certainly not anticipated. In this chapter's tables we present the IRS data in ways that allow us to give witness to what owners, management and the financial officers, accountants and bookkeepers of that time were experiencing as they prepared their income statements and reported their increasingly grim performance to the tax authorities. Through the lens of the data, we can imagine the distress and concern throughout corporate offices, large and small, where workers at all levels struggled with sharp and sudden declines in sales and revenues. We hear the silence of their sales department telephones and see the shrinking pile of orders. We hear accountants' urgent pleas to renegotiate terms with their companies' creditors as well as to pressure customers in order to collect their companies' receivables faster.

The story includes only a very few outliers to the otherwise inexorable downward spiral revealed in IRS corporate filings—insurance, for instance, and petroleum refining, providing fuel for the vehicles that had become such an essential part of American life. For almost everyone else running businesses in 1930 there were painfully difficult decisions to make as to what to do or stop doing; whom to pay or not pay; whose workers' hours to reduce or how many to furlough, all in the attempt to keep the doors open. These micro-level decisions reflected the best assessment of each owner and manager as to what was going on within their own specific industry, with their customer base and in their location in the face of challenging macro-level factors and uncertainties as to how long the bad times would last.

Fresh in the minds of decision-makers in business, as well as in Washington, was the depression of 1920-21 and the alacrity with which the economy bounced back to fuel the prosperity of the Twenties. Examining the statistics, we found clear reasons why conditions in 1930 went quite another way and did not bounce back with alacrity. We compare the depression of 1920-21 with 1930 in the pages ahead.

Keynes's Thoughts Regarding "Effective Demand"

We step back from our overview of business life in America in 1930 to offer some theoretical context and weight to the potent IRS statistics to come. Important is Keynes's concept of "effective demand." To define "effective demand," Keynes began by postulating, using mathematical notation and italics for emphasis, that "the aggregate supply price of the output from employing N men ... can be called the *aggregate supply function.*" (Keynes's emphasis) Then Keynes proposed a second hypothesis "[s]imilarly let D be the proceeds which entrepreneurs expect to receive from the employment of N men ... which can be called the *aggregate demand function.*" (Keynes's emphasis) Using this theoretical framework, Keynes then defined "effective demand"[1]:

> The value of D at the point of the aggregate demand function, where it is intersected by the aggregate supply function, will be called *the effective demand.*[2] (Keynes's emphasis)

We see the focal importance to Keynes of his concept of effective demand in the clear and effective way in which he brought it to his readers' attention. Keynes chose to express his *General Theory* in a single bound-volume of six "Books." Book I was entitled

1 Keynes (1936), p. 25.

2 Ibid.

"Introduction" and comprised three chapters whose objective was to prepare readers for his *magnum opus.*

Keynes's one-paragraph-long Chapter 1 of his Book I had the title "The General Theory" and began:

> I have called this book the *General Theory of Employment, Interest and Money,* placing the emphasis on the prefix *general.* The object of such a title is to contrast the character of my arguments and conclusions with those of the *classical* theory of the subject, upon which I was brought up and which dominates the economic thought, both practical and theoretical, of the governing and academic classes of this generation, as it has for a hundred years past.[3] (Keynes's emphasis.)

The paragraph continues from there:

> ...I shall argue that the postulates of the classical theory are applicable to a special case *only* and not to the general case.... Moreover, the characteristics of the special case assumed by the classical theory happen *not to be those of the economic society in which we actually live,* with the results that its teaching is misleading and disastrous if we attempt to apply it to *the facts of experience.*[4] (emphasis ours)

Keynes's title for Chapter 2 of Book I was "The Postulates of the Classical Economics" and Keynes elaborated on the postulates that, in his opinion, limited classical economics to the "special case only." At the risk of some oversimplification, it is our view that he started Chapter 2 by considering what he labeled "the real wage of an employed person." Very early in the chapter Keynes stated:

> The classical theory of employment—supposedly simple

3 Ibid., p. 3.

4 Ibid.

and obvious—has been based, I think, on two fundamental postulates, though practically without discussion, namely:

I. The wage is equal to the marginal product of labor …

II. The utility of the wage when a given volume of labor is employed is equal to the marginal disutility of that amount of employment.

That is to say, the *real wage of an employed person* is that which is just sufficient (in the estimation of the employed persons themselves) to induce the volume of labor actually employed to be forthcoming…. *Disutility* must be understood to cover every kind of reason which might lead a man, or a body of men, to withhold their labor rather than accept a wage which had to them a utility below a certain minimum.[5] (our emphasis)

Having begun Chapter 2 in this fashion, Keynes ended the chapter with the following summary of the chapter's conclusions:

At different points in this chapter we have made the classical theory to depend in succession on the assumptions:

(1) that the real wage is equal to the marginal disutility of the existing employment;

(2) that there is no such thing as involuntary unemployment in the strict sense;

(3) that supply creates its own demand in the sense that the aggregate demand price is equal to the aggregate supply price for all levels of output and employment.

5 Ibid., pp. 5-6.

> These three assumptions, however, all amount to the same thing in the sense that they all stand and fall together, any one of them logically involving the other two.[6]

Keynes set up the end of Book I, Chapter 3, entitled "The Principle of Effective Demand," to launch his readers fully into his core thinking in *General Theory*:

> This analysis supplies us with an explanation of the paradox of poverty in the midst of plenty. For the mere existence of an *insufficiency of effective demand* may, and often will, bring the increase of employment to a standstill before a level of full employment has been reached.[7]

In other words, effective demand—full aggregate demand—can be insufficient to produce full employment. And as we know from Table TI.1 (page 3), a major insufficiency of effective demand developed in 1930 and would worsen year-by-year until the end of Hoover's presidency in 1933, causing unemployment as a percentage of the civilian labor force to worsen very painfully from 3.1% in 1929 to 25.2% in 1933 as shown in Table 11.2 (page 316).

IRS Gross Income Data Serve as Statistics of Keynesian Effective Demand

Table 12.1 (opposite) presents Gross Income reported annually to the IRS for all sectors of the American corporate economy for the years 1918-1930 and what Keynes called "the effective demand" for each year, for the corporate sector specifically, in the righthand column labeled, "Aggregate gross income." The lower portion of Table 12.1, headlined "Percentage Change of Gross Income from Prior Year 1928–1930," shows the last years of prosperity moving into the Great Depression. Altogether we see in Table 12.1 the

6 Ibid., pp. 21-22.

7 Ibid., pp. 30-31.

Table 12.1

All Sectors: Gross Income 1918-1930

($-billion)

Year	Agriculture	Mining and quarrying	Manufacturing	Construction	Transportation and utilities	Trade	Service	Finance	Aggregate gross income
1918	0.52	4.00	44.17	1.95	3.72	21.66	1.10	5.89	83.0
1919	0.79	4.68	52.29	2.01	5.15	25.44	1.47	6.46	98.3
1920	0.73	6.15	56.65	2.24	9.15	31.51	1.95	8.39	116.8
1921	0.68	3.89	38.44	1.77	9.00	27.34	1.76	7.55	90.4
1922	0.71	3.70	44.68	1.77	9.75	28.68	2.22	8.93	100.4
1923	0.77	4.86	56.92	2.22	10.53	32.28	2.42	8.46	118.5
1924	0.81	4.85	53.91	2.21	10.18	35.12	2.63	9.07	118.8
1925	0.79	4.92	60.83	2.31	11.88	39.85	2.84	12.45	135.9
1926	0.86	4.55	62.49	2.82	14.77	40.94	3.36	12.30	142.1
1927	0.82	3.84	63.72	3.06	15.14	40.94	3.59	13.20	144.3
1928	0.83	3.59	67.27	2.98	15.80	43.20	3.83	19.71	157.2
1929	0.88	4.05	72.13	3.08	17.08	43.49	4.19	15.66	160.6
1930	0.67	3.00	60.90	3.04	16.00	37.21	4.16	13.30	138.3

All Sectors: Percentage Change of Gross Income from Prior Year 1928-1930

(% Percent)

Year	Agriculture	Mining and quarrying	Manufacturing	Construction	Transportation and utilities	Trade	Service	Finance	Aggregate % change in gross income
1928	0.4	-6.5	5.6	-2.5	4.4	5.5	6.7	49.3	8.9
1929	6.8	12.8	7.2	3.5	8.1	0.7	9.5	-20.5	2.1
1930	-23.9	-25.9	-15.6	-1.3	-6.4	-14.5	-0.7	-15.1	-13.9

Source: *SOI 1918-1930.*

overall composition of our economy—in the IRS's eight corporate business sectors—as we experienced burgeoning prosperity in the 1920s. Then, for the critical years 1928-1930, we see how each sector's performance changed from the prior year, as we moved, after an abrupt reversal in 1928-29, into the Great Depression. Notably, just as there was no precipitating event for the Great Crash, *we see that there was no specific industrial or commercial sector (or sectors) that led the way into the Great Depression.* As regards Keynesian effective demand, we see it falling for corporations from $160.6 billion in 1929 to $138.3 billion in 1930, resulting in the aggregate % change dropping -13.9% over the year 1930.

Even a cursory glance shows how dramatically gross income dropped in almost all sectors of American corporations in 1930. The smallest drop—the roughly -$40 million drop in the Construction sector—perhaps reflected Hoover's $2 billion commitment in infrastructure stimulus funds. Overall, however, Aggregate corporate Gross Income fell from $160.6 billion in 1929 to $138.3 billion in 1930, a -13.88% decline of -$22.3 billion in 1930. In the early 1920s' depression, there was a -22.6% decline of -$26.4 billion in 1921, from $116.8 billion in 1920 to $90.4 billion in 1921. A decade later, the hope, not-unreasonable but ultimately unfounded, that the economy would begin to return to prosperity in 1931 as it had in 1922 influenced decision-making in 1930.[8] We will look into the statistics for 1920-22 in greater detail shortly.

Table 12.2 (opposite) delves into the same 13 years of aggregate corporate gross income statistics in Table 12.1 by focusing on the twelve Manufacturing subsectors in 1918-1930 and the year-over-year percentage changes for 1928-1930. The 1930 data readily show the dramatic drop in almost every manufacturing subsector of American corporate business. The only notable exception was within Chemicals and Allied Substances, specifically, "Petroleum

8 Friedman and Schwartz later suggested that if the banking crises hadn't begun at the end of 1930, prosperity would have returned more quickly.

Table 12.2

All Manufacturing, Gross Income 1918-1930

($-billion)

Year	Food products, beverages and tobacco	Textiles and textile products	Leather and leather products	Rubber and rubber goods	Lumber and wood products	Paper, pulp, and products	Printing and publishing	Chemicals and allied substances	Stone, clay, and glass products	Metal and metal products	All other metal industries	Aggregate gross income
1918	9.43	6.76	1.73	1.05	2.00	1.01	0.97	4.08	0.69	13.36	3.10	44.17
1919	14.04	7.14	2.20	1.17	2.47	1.19	1.28	4.56	0.84	13.51	3.89	52.29
1920	12.29	8.21	1.89	1.04	3.31	1.80	1.76	5.57	1.32	15.10	4.37	56.65
1921	8.27	5.69	1.42	0.64	1.85	1.00	1.72	3.88	0.95	9.81	3.22	38.44
1922	8.87	6.80	1.46	0.94	2.40	1.16	1.85	5.71	1.17	9.98	4.34	44.68
1923	10.08	7.86	1.60	1.08	2.97	1.44	2.69	6.11	1.36	16.60	5.13	56.92
1924	11.85	7.19	1.51	1.12	2.83	1.36	2.17	5.89	1.38	15.94	2.67	53.91
1925	13.40	7.72	1.51	1.47	2.97	1.49	2.28	7.07	1.50	19.11	2.31	60.83
1926	13.48	7.75	1.66	1.60	3.07	1.65	2.55	8.09	1.66	18.45	2.53	62.49
1927	13.91	7.81	1.73	1.45	2.80	1.67	2.57	8.77	1.60	19.19	2.23	63.72
1928	14.25	7.84	1.72	1.39	2.84	1.73	2.68	9.55	1.65	21.17	2.45	67.27
1929	14.77	8.23	1.74	1.43	2.79	1.80	2.87	10.29	1.66	24.09	2.47	72.13
1930	13.19	6.42	1.39	1.10	1.99	1.58	2.66	11.98	1.41	17.20	1.99	60.90

Manufacturing Sector, Percentage Change of Gross Income from Prior Year 1928-1930

(%-Percent)

Year	Food products, beverages and tobacco	Textiles and textile products	Leather and leather products	Rubber and rubber goods	Lumber and wood products	Paper, pulp, and products	Printing and publishing	Chemicals and allied substances	Stone, clay, and glass products	Metal and metal products	All other metal industries	Aggregate % change in gross income
1928	2.4	0.4	-0.5	-4.2	1.4	3.5	4.4	8.9	3.4	10.4	9.9	5.6
1929	3.6	5.1	1.1	3.0	-1.7	4.0	7.1	7.7	0.0	13.8	0.7	7.2
1930	-10.7	-22.1	-20.2	-22.9	-28.9	-12.1	-7.2	16.4	-14.8	-28.6	-19.1	-15.6

Source: *SOI 1918-1930.*

and other mineral oil refining," which rose 38.1%, or $2.3 billion, from a gross income of $6.04 billion to $8.34 billion. That robust performance reflected America's embrace of cars and trucks that was sufficient to lead to an overall growth rate of 16.4% for the entire Chemicals subsector in 1930. On the downside, however, weakness in the various components of Metal and Metal Products (called by the IRS the "Metal products and processes" subsector), indicated the decline in demand by end users of steel, including in automobile production.

Business Cycles in the Period 1918-1930

In point of fact, the historical statistics show that the Roaring Twenties were not consistently roaring and bullish. Looking back, the Hoover administration and others viewed the decade of the 1920s as beginning with a severe depression which passed quickly and almost without lasting effect. However, several other business cycles occurred in the 1920s, as those in business knew all too well. To give a statistical picture of when those cycles began and ended, it was—and still is—the non-profit, non-partisan research organization, National Bureau of Economic Research (NBER), specifically their Business Cycle Dating Committee, that pinpoints the American economy's peaks and troughs. [9] They measure cycles from trough to peak for expansionary phases and from peak to trough for contractionary phases.

The NBER's reference numbers for business cycles between 1918-1930 give useful perspective on the period. We offer a verbal précis here of these business cycles starting with 1918 following the end of World War I. NBER's researchers designated a peak in August 1918 and a trough in March 1919 as the economy recovered from wartime. Then the economy expanded to a peak in January 1920 before reaching a trough in July 1921 as the economy contracted. But, because the economy takes time to return to profitability from the bottom of a trough, most of the losses in profitability were re-

---

9 NBER cycles can be found at https://www.nber.org/research/data/us-business-cycle-expansions-and-contractions.

corded in 1921. This overall period is usually called the Depression of 1920-21.

Differing Elements Result in Very Different Outcomes

Irving Fisher weighed in after the fact:

> I venture the opinion, subject to correction on submission of future evidence, that, in the great booms and depressions, each of the above-named factors has played a subordinate role as compared with two dominant factors, namely *over-indebtedness* to start with and *deflation* following soon after; also that where any of the other factors do become conspicuous, they are often merely effects or symptoms of these two. In short, the big bad actors are debt disturbances and price-level disturbances.
>
> While quite ready to change my opinion, I have, at present, a strong conviction that these two economic maladies, the debt disease and the price-level disease (or dollar disease), are, in the great booms and depressions, more important cause than all others put together.[10]

It wasn't until 1933 that Professor Fisher's flurry of papers delving into the Crash and the Great Depression began appearing. He didn't specifically focus on 1920-21, likely for a reason that we discuss below. One key aspect of his explorations led him to connect over-indebtedness with deflation as the two causal steps that brought the country deep into depression and into deflation territory with no end in sight. He saw them coupled, but carefully connected the word "great" with booms and depressions as only "great" booms and "great" depressions were relevant. This implies that Fisher, well

10 Irving Fisher, "The Debt-Deflation Theory of Great Depressions", *Econometrica*, Vol, 1, No. 4 (Oct., 1933), pp. 337-357.

familiar with what happened in 1920-1921, did not regard that period as "great." For one thing, he knew that there was no over-indebtedness at that at time, and there were other components that set the two periods apart as well. In 1965, the Fed referred to the period as a recession, an albeit "severe" one, but not deserving of a small-d depression designation.

How else did the two depression periods differ? Further discussion follows, but in relation to 1920-21, the Fed raised interest rates (on commercial paper) from 5% to 6% in January 1920 and to 7% in July to curb the inflation that had been fueled by several things related to the end of World War I. For one, there had been various restrictions on consumption goods, such as rationing, and prices during the war. "Doing without" led to pent up demand, and, when restrictions were lifted, prices rose, the very definition of inflation. Secondly, the country was still on the gold standard, and the gold supply had risen because some purchasers of munitions and other war-related goods had paid in gold, thus causing an increase in the gold supply which, necessarily, translated into an increase in the money supply as the money supply only grew in relation to gold supply growth. Again, this was inflationary—more money chasing fewer goods.

Another distinction between the two depressions has to do with electrification. At the start of the 1920s only 35% of American homes were even electrified. Over the course of the decade, especially with the development of the suburbs, that figure grew to 70%, implying a huge built-in demand for newly designed electrical appliances and other goods—most of it acquired on installment debt terms stimulated by the increasingly nuanced advertising industry. By the time of the Crash, all forms of indebtedness had exploded and met much of that pent-up demand. Making the shift from acquisition to debt repayment became the much smarter personal choice in a punitive deflationary environment even though that individual action, collectively, had a disastrous effect on the economy overall.

Moving further into the decade, NBER recorded two moderate cycles. The first involved an expansionary phase from the July 1921 trough until its peak in May 1923, followed by a contractionary phase until its trough in July 1924. In the second cycle, an expansionary phase from July 1924 until its peak in October 1926, preceded a contractionary phase to a trough in November 1927 when the expansion that followed constituted the legendary Great Bull Market, although signs of the Great Bull Market were visible even before November 1927. (See Chapter 6. page 186, for H. Parker Willis' view that speculation began in 1925.[11]) This next expansionary phase lasted until the August 1929 peak pinpointed by NBER. The lengthy, and severe, contractionary phase that began just preceding the Crash clearly constituted what we know as the Great Depression. Per NBER, it didn't end until the March 1933 trough, the very month Herbert Hoover left office and Franklin Roosevelt becade President.

Comparing the Depression of 1920-21 with the Great Depression's Start

Given the economic fluctuations of the post-Great War decade, optimism prevailed on Wall Street and in Washington that the downturn following the Crash of 1929 would also presumably be milder than the depression of 1920-21 and, like that earlier depression, pass quickly. Was this hopeful thinking at the time so unrealistic?

Though Paul Warburg's warning was far more dire, events proved him right. But why? It is useful to go to the data to compare the two deflations coming in such close succession, in order to derive observations about deflation in general. Having obtained from the IRS archives the statistics of gross income from 1918-1930 shown in Tables 12.1 (page 347) and 12.2 (page 349), we were curious to see what these statistics told us about similarities and differences between the two major depression events.

Highlighting Friedman and Schwartz's View in *Monetary History*, as we have seen, they focused on the period of 1929-1933 in Chapter 7 of *Monetary History* entitled "The Great Contraction, 1929-33." There they related that the behavior of the U.S. econo-

11 Willis (1930), pp. 174-183.

my up to the last months of 1930 was due to nonmonetary forces and might indeed have improved, as occurred in the downturn of 1920-21, had a "wave of bank crises" not taken place. In a section of *Monetary History* discussing "Wartime and Postwar Inflation," they offered their "Chart 16" that we have reproduced here as Chart 12.1.

Chart 12.1 presents seven horizontal depictions of historical statistics displayed over the years 1914 through 1933 with Reference Cycle Expansions and Contractions. The Cycle Expansions are por-

Chart 12.1

EARLY YEARS OF FEDERAL RESERVE SYSTEM

CHART 16
Money Stock, Income, Prices, and Velocity, in Reference Cycle Expansions and Contractions, 1914–33

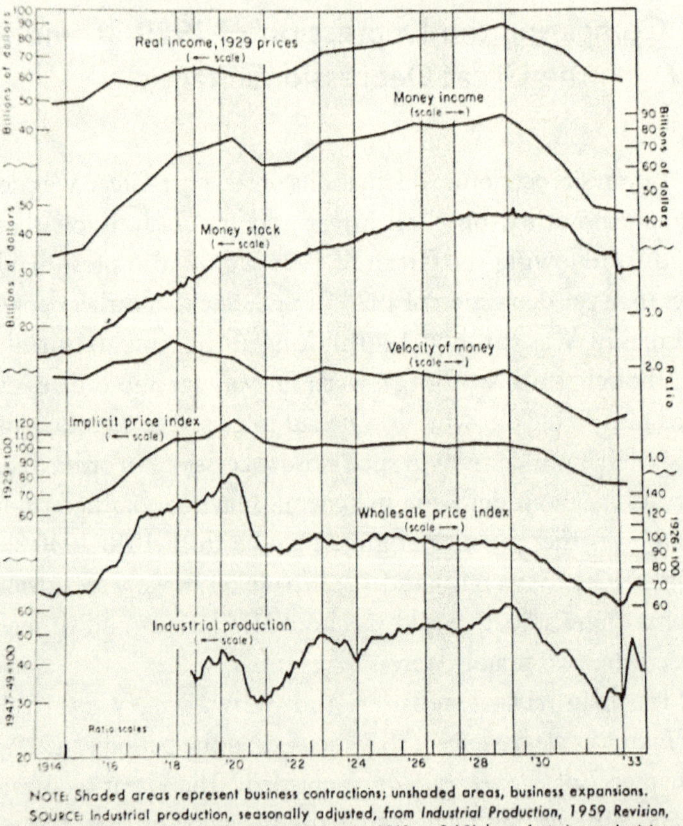

NOTE: Shaded areas represent business contractions; unshaded areas, business expansions.

SOURCE: Industrial production, seasonally adjusted, from *Industrial Production, 1959 Revision*, Board of Governors of the Federal Reserve System, 1960, p. S-151 (manufacturing and mining production only). Other data, same as for Chart 62.

trayed on white vertical backgrounds, and the Cycle Contractions are shown on lightly shaded backgrounds. Friedman and Schwartz began their consideration of Wartime and Postwar Inflation by calling attention to the set of historical statistics labeled "Wholesale price index," a key index likely chosen because it related most closely to wartime production, especially of manufactured and agricultural goods. Describing what the chart maps for this key index, Friedman and Schwartz wrote:

> As Chart [12.1] shows, wholesale prices were roughly constant until the final quarter of 1915. Then they began a rapid climb that was to continue with only minor interruptions until May 1920, when wholesale prices stood at nearly 2½ times their level in the first half of 1917, before the entry of the United States into the war; and again from mid-1919 on. The only appreciable decline—from September 1918 to February 1919—corresponds with the August 1918–March 1919 business cycle contraction and that decline was only 5½ per cent.[12]

We compare what happened in the depression of 1920-21 with the Great Depression as represented also in Chart 12.1 to see if doing so helps us understand what occurs in depression and what causes and results from deflation.

As an initial matter, the period of 1919-1922 represented the transition from a wartime economy to the consumer economy that followed. As we look at the lowest set of historical statistics in Chart 12.1 entitled "Industrial production," we use the well-known analogy of guns and butter to wonder how the wartime production of guns declined over this period and was replaced by the peace-time production of butter. The Industrial production statistics do not actually help answer this question because they do not inform us as to *what* was produced. But other statistics provide clues. For example, we associate the Wholesale price index (WPI) more with the guns and the Consumer price index (CPI) with butter. In considering

12 Friedman and Schwartz (1963a), p. 196.

the years around 1920-21, we found that both averages fell, but the WPI dropped earlier and at a precipitous rate, while the CPI declined later at a slower rate, which, as we will see, served as a basis for the dramatic climb in industrial production of consumer goods during the expansion that followed 1920-21.

Before considering what Friedman and Schwartz related regarding the Depression of 1920-21, we address historical considerations that include wartime financing.[13] First, the financial activities of both the Treasury Department and the Federal Reserve showed federal debt management functions of the Treasury Department as taking priority in the period of the First World War. Secondly, the Federal Reserve was a new institution with no history of established policy practices to fall back on. Moreover, unlike the Treasury Department with an established hierarchy, the Fed consisted of twelve regional banks that reported to a central Board in Washington, D.C., but operated separately from the Board and from each other in terms, for instance, of setting interest rates. Furthermore, among these separate Reserve Banks one stood out: the Federal Reserve Bank of New York, because it had, within its region, the nation's central "money market," giving it both national and international focuses, status and influence. The New York Fed included, among its members, the largest banks in the country. But, within the Fed's diverse group of "financial entities," at a time when prices were changing dramatically, there was no consensus on what caused prices to change—more specifically, what caused inflation and what caused deflation.

Friedman and Schwartz revealed that there were strong views held by other parties outside the Treasury Department and Federal Reserve. For example:

> Federal Reserve policy during 1919 gave rise to much controversy, both at the time and since, and has been severely criticized. The Joint Congressional Commission of Agriculture Inquiry, established in 1921 in response to the sharp break in prices in 1920, concluded, and in our view,

13 See their Chapter 5 in *Monetary History*, section 2, "Wartime and Postwar Inflation," p. 196.

correctly:

> The commission believes that a policy of sharp advances in discount rates should have been inaugurated in the first six months of 1919, and cannot excuse the action of the Federal Reserve Board and the Federal reserve banks in this period in failing to take measures to restrict the expansion, inflation, speculation, and extravagance, which characterized the period.

Governor [of the Federal Reserve Board] Harding's reply, as recorded in his memoirs, was characteristic:

> [T]he Board felt that it was its duty to cooperate with the Treasury authorities. Failure to cooperate would have been tantamount to an undertaking by the Board to dictate the policies of the Treasury.

> It seems clear that personal weakness, not mistaken principle, was the major explanation for the Board's inaction.[14]

Friedman and Schwartz wrote specifically about the Depression of 1920-21 in the last section of their Chapter 5, "The Contraction of 1920-21":

> The rise in discount rates in January was not only too late but also probably too much. The National Bureau dates the peak of the expansion as occurring in January 1920, simultaneously with the rise in rates and before the higher rates could have taken affect. The contraction, at first mild, became extremely severe in its later stages when it was characterized by an unprecedented collapse in prices.

> There [was] little sign of any severe decline until past the middle of the year. Indeed, it was not until early fall that

14 Ibid., p. 228.

> contemporary observers were in substantial agreement that a sizable contraction was under way....
>
> Beginning sometime about the middle of the year, the contraction changed its character. From a mild decline or sideways movement, it became one of the most rapid declines on record. From their peak in May, wholesale prices declined moderately for a couple of months, and then collapsed [Chart 12.1 page 354]. By June 1921, [wholesale prices] had fallen to 56% of their level in May 1920.... This [was], by all odds, the sharpest price decline in the period covered by our money series, either before or since that date and perhaps also in the whole history of the United States....
>
> What was true of prices was true also of many physical magnitudes. Industrial production, employment in manufacturing, and similar series show a precipitous increase in the rate of decline in the autumn of 1920. The result is that although *the contraction* was relatively brief—the National Bureau dates the trough in July 1921—it *ranks as one of the severest on record.* Its brevity makes annual data misleading guides to its severity.[15] (emphasis ours)

Friedman and Schwartz were, of course, referring to the contraction of the money supply. Using their own money supply estimates for years 1920-21, from January 1920 to January 1921, M-1 contracted -3.4%, and from January 1921 to January 1922, the money supply as measured by M-1 contracted -9.0%. (Measured slightly differently—from December 1920 to December 1921—covering the second year of the Depression of 1920-21, the M-1 money supply contracted -10.8%.) By contrast, in the Great Depression, from January 1929 to January 1930, M-1 contracted -1.7%, and from January 1930 to January 1931, M-1 contracted -4.3%. Whenever f of 1920-21 ended, whether after 18 months, or two years, or perhaps

15 Friedman and Schwartz (1963a), pp. 231-2.

even more, there is no question that the contraction of the money supply was *breathtakingly severe!*

We make one further observation regarding Friedman and Schwartz's view of what they called the Contraction of 1920-21. Through their lens shown above in Chart 12.1, we see that the astonishing drop in wholesale prices and the awesome (but brief) contraction of the money supply set the country up to emerge into a period of remarkably stable prices. In Chart 12.1 we see this most clearly in the Implicit price index which is shown immediately above the Wholesale price index. This evolving price stability was a key ingredient of the prosperity of the 1920s. As we continue our comparison and analysis of the depressions and deflations that were bookends to the 1920s, we will achieve a deeper understanding of the period.

The Vigorous Federal Reserve Rate Policy of 1920-22

The discount rate policy pursued by the Federal Reserve System in 1920-21 and also in 1922 was consequential. *BMS* reported that at the end of 1919 all but two of the Federal Reserve banks maintained their discount rates at 4.75%, and the two exceptions, Kansas City and Dallas, maintained theirs at 5%. In January 1920, with what we interpret as the clear objective of curbing inflation, all but two of the twelve Federal Reserve banks, managing rates independently at that time, *began raising their discount rates,* initially to 6%. The two holdouts raised their rates to 6% in early February.[16] In June 1920, four Federal Reserve banks, including New York, raised their rates to 7%, and a fifth bank joined them in November. Then, in the spring of 1921, the banks, including New York, then at 7%, *began cutting their rates.* In July 1921, four Federal Reserve banks, including New York, cut their discount rates to 5.5%. By September only six Federal Reserve banks remained at 6% and one at 6.5%. By December 1921, three Federal Reserve banks (including New

16 *BMS 1914-1941,* p. 439.

York) were at 4.5%, seven were at 5%, and two were at 5.5%. By December 1922, three Federal Reserve banks (including New York) were down to 4%, and nine were at 4.5%.

H. Parker Willis (his potent 1930 article attributing blame for the Crash is discussed in Chapter 6.), who had worked as Congressman Carter Glass's "chief advisor" on the formulation and passage of the Federal Reserve Act of 1913 and was chairman of the committee that planned and organized the twelve new Federal Reserve banks, added another important objective of the Fed's interventions. From the perspective of his diverse experiences—Willis also served as Secretary of the Federal Reserve System from 1914 to 1918 and was Director of Research for the Board of the Fed for several years in the early 1920s—he wrote:

> Experience shows how dangerous it is for banks which carry demand deposits to have their resources to any great extent in bonds. It was, therefore, the effort of the Treasury Department as well as of our banking authorities during the years 1920-21 to drive this great volume of bonds out of the banks and into the hands of the public. By the end of 1921 two thirds of the securities they held had been driven out of Reserve banks and one-half out of member banks.[17]

We know that NBER designated a cycle of expansion that began in March 1919 as peaking in January 1920 when all but two of the twelve Federal Reserve banks aggressively raised their discount rates to 6%. But a comparison of the statistics for 1919 and 1920 in Tables 12.1 (page 347) and 12.2 (page 349) does not appear to suggest that, even with these rate hikes, 1920 was a year of contraction.

17 Willis (1930), p. 178.

Table 12.3

Comparing the Depression Downturns of 1920-22 and 1930

Percentage Change from Prior Year

All Business Sectors

(% Percent)

Year	Agriculture	Mining & Quarrying	Manufacturing	Construction	Transportation & Utilities	Trade	Service	Finance	Aggregate Gross Income
1920	-7.59	+31.41	+8.34	+11.44	+77.67	+23.86	+32.65	+29.88	+18.80
1921	-6.85	-36.75	-32.14	-20.98	-1.64	-13.23	-9.74	-10.01	-22.56
1922	+4.41	-4.88	+16.23	0	+8.33	+4.90	+26.14	+18.28	+11.06
1930	-23.92	-25.90	-15.57	-1.30	-6.37	-14.45	-0.67	-15.08	-13.88

All Manufacturing Sub-Sectors

(% Percent)

Year	Food products, beverages and tobacco	Textiles and textile products	Leather and leather products	Rubber and rubber goods	Lumber and wood products	Paper, pulp, and products	Printing and publishing	Chemicals and allied substances	Stone, clay, and glass products	Metal and metal products	All other metal industries	Aggregate gross income
1920	-12.46	+14.99	-14.09	-11.11	+34.01	+51.26	+37.50	+22.15	+57.14	+11.77	+12.39	+8.34
1921	-32.71	-30.69	-24.87	-38.46	-44.11	-44.44	-2.27	-30.34	-28.03	-35.06	-26.32	-30.14
1922	+7.26	+19.51	+2.82	+46.88	+29.73	+16.00	+7.56	+47.16	+23.16	+1.73	+34.78	+16.23
1930	-10.71	-22.07	-20.22	-22.90	-28.88	-12.10	-7.23	+16.42	-14.82	-28.62	-19.13	-15.57

Source: Calculated by authors from *SOI for 1920-22* and *1930*.

Examining Closely the IRS Gross Income Statistics for 1920-1922

Indeed, the statistics in Table 12.3 (previous page) show that despite the Federal Reserve Banks' actions, 1920 was a year of *robust growth.* Aggregate Gross Income was up 18.80% in 1919, having risen 18.41% from 1918, even though the growth of the Manufacturing Sector had slowed from the robust 18.38% growth rate experienced in 1919 to still-strong 8.34% growth in 1920 as Tables 12.1 and 12.2 indicate.

Regardless, there is no question that the statistics in Table 12.3 reveal 1921 as a year of depression (which, with no monthly or quarterly statistics available from the IRS, can look like a sudden reversal) with Aggregate Gross Income down more than -20%. All across Table 12.3, sectors and subsectors turned down, some dramatically. In two Manufacturing subsectors (Lumber and wood products and Paper, pulp and products), the turndowns were more than -40%. Six others declined more than -30%. (Interestingly, counter to trend, printing and publishing only turned down just over -2%.) The overall picture for All Business Sectors was not quite as grim as within Manufacturing (in aggregate), though Mining and Quarrying both turned down more than -30%, the Construction sector was down more than -20%, Trade and Finance declined more than -10% and even the remaining three sectors, corporate Agriculture, Transportation and Utilities and Service, all turned down, though under -10%.

Then in 1922, after the Federal Reserve banks had lowered discount rates to more normal levels, business activity revived across all sectors, except Mining & Quarrying, and across All Manufacturing Sub-Sectors with Aggregate Gross Income for All Business Sectors growing 11.06% in 1922 and for Manufacturing 16.23%.

One statistic that deserves particular attention is the 18.28% rebound in Finance, the second highest growth rate of any sector in 1922, which points out two crucial differences between the two depressions. First, unlike the time leading up to the 1929 Crash, no speculation was apparent at the beginning of the 1920s, and, second, nothing analogous to the Great Crash occurred in 1920-1922.

To illuminate what happened in 1920-1922 further, we have brought monthly statistics regarding price changes to bear in Tables 12.3A and 12.3B. Table 12.3A (based on the Prices Indexes in Table 2.1A (page 52) shows that double-digit price increases occurred in the WPI, the CPI and the Implicit GNP Price Deflator for 1920, clear signs of inflation. They were replaced by double-digit price *decreases*

Table 12.3A

Change in Price Indexes from Year Earlier

Year	Wholesale Price Index (WPI)	Consumer Price Index (CPI)	Implicit GNP Price Deflator
1919	5.6%	15.1%	n/a
1920	11.3%	15.8%	14.2%
1921	-36.8%	-10.9%	-14.9%
1922	-0.9%	-6.3%	-4.9%
1923	4.1%	1.8%	2.0%

Source: Authors' calculations, based on Table 2.1A and it's source.

Table 12.3B

Consumer Price Index: All Urban Consumers 1919-1923

Monthly Percentage Change, Annualized

(% percent)

Year	Jan	Feb	Mar	Apr	May	Jun	Jul	Aug	Sep	Oct	Nov	Dec
1919	17.9	14.9	17.1	17.6	16.6	15.0	15.2	14.9	13.4	13.1	13.5	14.5
1920	17.0	20.4	20.1	21.6	21.9	23.7	19.5	14.7	12.4	9.9	7.0	2.6
1921	-1.6	-5.6	-7.1	-10.8	-14.1	-15.8	-14.9	-12.8	-12.5	-12.1	-12.1	-10.8
1922	-11.1	-8.2	-8.7	-7.7	-5.6	-5.1	-5.1	-6.2	-5.1	-4.6	-3.4	-2.3
1923	-0.6	-0.6	0.6	1.2	1.2	1.8	2.4	3.0	3.6	3.6	3.0	2.4

Source: (CPI): Bureau of Labor Statistics (BLS), all items in U.S city average, 1913-2017.

in all three measures in 1921, of which the WPI was by far the most dramatic and severe at -36.8%. Then in 1922, all three indicators experienced single-digit decreases, with WPI very close to unchanged for the year. Finally, all three increased by single-digits in 1923, although the WPI suggested a resurgence (which appeared only as a small up-tick in Chart 12.1). Table 12.3B (previous page) shows Monthly Percentage Change in the Consumer Price Index Annualized for 1919-1923. The table shows 1919 as a year of double-digit inflation, suggesting that the objective of the Federal Reserve Banks as they raised discount rates in 1920 was to reduce the rate of inflation. But, did they want to bring about deflation?

Table 12.3B shows that double-digit inflation actually rose in 1920 for the first seven months of 1920 over those of 1919 to a high of 23.7% in June before starting to fall and becoming single-digit numbers of annualized inflation in the last three months of 1920. (Chart 12.1 reveals the WPI was plummeting at a very high deflationary rate from roughly the spring 1920 to mid-year 1921.) Throughout 1921, the Consumer Price Index Annualized fell at deflationary rates. The rates were single-digit for the first three months of 1921 and became double-digit for the rest of the year, accelerating to -15.8% in June 1921 then diminishing to -11.1% in January 1922. The remaining eleven months of 1922 and the first two months of 1923 generally showed falling annualized CPI rates of deflation. The remainder of 1923 reflected low and slightly rising inflation.

Tables 12.3C (opposite) and 12.3D (page 366) demonstrate that the deflation of 1921 did not occur during a period of credit stringency. Commercial paper rates provided important measures of the short-term interest costs of corporate borrowers. Table 12.3C shows that the highest commercial paper rates occurred after the Federal Reserve raised discount rates in early 1920, but that before the end of that year they had begun to fall. In fact, commercial paper rates were falling from November 1920 until September 1922. Table 12.3D shows that, as commercial paper rates fell, bank borrowers were simultaneously repaying bank loans from the final quarter of 1920 through the first quarter of 1922. The data show that one important similarity between the two deflations was that,

Table 12.3C												
Commercial Paper Rates 1919-1923[1] **New York City Banks** (% Percent)												
Year	Jan	Feb	Mar	Apr	May	Jun	Jul	Aug	Sep	Oct	Nov	Dec
1919	5.26	5.13	5.50	5.44	5.23	5.32	5.38	5.38	5.38	5.25	5.30	5.91
1920	6.00	6.44	6.91	6.91	7.33	7.91	8.08	8.13	8.13	8.13	8.10	7.97
1921	7.85	7.66	7.63	7.58	6.94	6.72	6.35	6.16	6.10	5.85	5.44	5.13
1922	5.03	4.88	4.82	4.60	4.38	4.38	4.13	4.13	4.13	4.44	4.82	4.88
1923	4.63	4.66	5.10	5.38	5.03	5.00	5.07	5.19	5.35	5.38	5.16	5.03

[1]Monthly average of weekly figures.
Source: *BMS* pp. 452-453.

in both periods, deflation developed as borrowers began repaying their bank loans. (See Table TI.1 on page 3)

When compared, both depressions exhibited the same pattern with regards to interest rates, the price indices and bank loan repayments. In the 1920-21 depression, commercial paper rates began falling in the fourth quarter of 1920, and borrowers began repaying bank loans that same quarter. The consumer price index began falling in January 1921, reached its maximum rate of deflation, -15.8%, in June 1921 and continued to fall into early 1923. In 1929-1930, short-term rates began falling before the end of 1929 and fell throughout 1930 (Table 8.4, page 258). Borrowers were repaying bank loans throughout 1930 (Table 5.2, page 142). And deflation, which Professor Kindleberger assured us in Chapter 3 began in the fourth quarter of 1929, developed and grew (Table 8.1, page 232).

In addition, it should come as no surprise that, as shown in Friedman and Schwartz's *Monetary History* section "The Contraction of 1920-21," the size of the money stock was falling as also occurred later in the "Great Contraction." Friedman and Schwartz reported the peak of the earlier expansion in M-1 was $23,906 million in March 1920 followed by a -16.7% decline in M-1 over 22 months to the $20,450 million trough in January 1922. Using their preferred base—M-2—the peak was $34,776 million in September 1920 followed by a decline of -8.9% over 16 months to the trough in

Table 12.3D			
Quarters of Member Bank Borrowing Change 1919-1923 ($ million)			
Date	Bank loans	Change from prior peroid	% Change
1919			
Mar 4	$13,877	-$347	-2.4%
Jun 30	15,414	1,537	+11.1
Nov 17	17,423	2,009	+13.0
Dec 31	18,149	726	+4.2
1920			
May 4	19,198	1,049	+5.8
Jun 30	19,533	335	+1.7
Nov 15	19,852	319	+1.6
Dec 29	19,555	-297	-1.5
1921			
Apr 28	18,487	-1,068	-5.5
Jun 30	18,119	-368	-2.0
Dec 31	17,394	-725	-4.0
1922			
Mar 10	17,080	-314	-1.8
Jun 30	17,165	85	+0.5
Dec 29	17,930	765	+4.5
1923			
Apr 3	18,419	489	+2.7
Jun 30	18,750	331	+1.8
Sep 14	18,719	-31	-0.2
Dec 31	18,842	123	+0.7

Source: *BMS*, p.72.

January 1922 of $31,663 million.[18] *Sic transit gloria mundi!*

1920-22 in summary:

•The IRS gross income statistics show that 1920 was a year of robust expansion despite the aggressively raised Federal Reserve discount rates early in the year. In fact, NBER declared January 1920 as a "peak," which indicates commencement of a contraction. Chart 12.1 shows the WPI rising slightly into the spring of 1920 then plummeting at a very high deflationary rate from roughly spring 1920 to about mid-year 1921. The annualized monthly CPI statistics for 1920 show that inflation rose to 23.7% in June, then, while declining, remained inflationary for the remainder of the year.

•The IRS statistics show 1921 as a year of significant contraction. Chart 12.1 shows the WPI dropping significantly from spring 1920 to mid-year 1921. Table 12.3B shows the CPI Annualized first becoming deflationary in January 1921, reaching a high of -15.8% in June 1921, then beginning to decline at double-digit rates until January 1922.

•The IRS statistics show 1922 as a year of quite respectable expansion. Chart 12.1 and Table 12.3A both show the WPI as rising slightly in an inflationary fashion in 1922. On the consumer side, Table 12.3B shows the CPI falling in a deflationary fashion throughout 1922, and Table 12.3A shows -6.2% deflation for 1922.

• Statistics support revision of the dates NBER called the peak and trough in 1920. The peak was more accurately sometime closer to mid-year. As for the trough, NBER should probably have called the point at which expansion resumed

---

18 Friedman and Schwartz (1963a), p. 710.

in 1921 as sometime that year later than July.

Insights into Evolving Policies at the Treasury and the Fed in 1914-1921

In *Federal Reserve Monetary Policy, 1917-1933,* Elmus Wicker set the scene for the early years of the Federal Reserve:

> When the United States entered the war in April 1917, the Federal Reserve System had been in existence for barely more than two years. Yet within that short time the reserve officials had made an impressive record of organizational achievement....
>
> Initially both the Secretary of the Treasury and the Comptroller of the Currency were *ex officio* members of the Federal Reserve Board....
>
> Treasury decisions concerning ... the composition of the Federal debt not only challenged the alleged independence of the Federal Reserve but severely weakened it.
>
> The key to World War I financial policy and its aftermath is Secretary McAdoo's decision to finance war borrowing at rates below those prevailing in the open market.[19]

Wicker explained how the Treasury Department and the Federal Reserve Board held contrasting views regarding the causes of inflation:

> The Treasury had no official theory about the wartime rise in prices. However, the papers of Russell C. Leffingwell offer the views of the Assistant Secretary of Treasury who was

19 Elmus Wicker, *Federal Reserve Monetary Policy, 1917-1933,* Random House, 1996, pp. 3-8.

> responsible primarily for financial affairs. Leffingwell was a brilliant and articulate spokesman for the Treasury policy. He was fully as intelligent, persuasive, and strong-willed as his arch-rival in the Federal Reserve System, Benjamin Strong....
>
> Leffingwell defined the goal of Treasury policy during World War I as having been to finance the war so that it could be won without "avoidable inflation." To Leffingwell "avoidable inflation" meant first and foremost the maintenance of the gold convertibility of the dollar.... Leffingwell denied that the rapid increase of wartime government expenditures was inflationary.
>
> That expansion was accomplished without depreciation of our currency. There never was at any time a premium on gold in the United States.[20]
>
> In this instance, Leffingwell completely divorced inflation from the rise in prices. In sharp contrast to the Leffingwell approach to an explanation of price inflation [was] the position of the Federal Reserve Board. The foundation of the Board's inflation theory was the quantity theory of money, while recognizing the existence as well as the importance of the "cost–push" explanation. Unlike the Treasury, the Board confined its use of the term inflation to a rise in prices.[21]

In *A History of the Federal Reserve; Volume I, 1913-1951,* professor of political economy at Carnegie Mellon, Allan H. Meltzer, focused on the last days of the presidency of Woodrow Wilson:

> Glass left the Treasury early in 1920 and was elected to the Senate.... The Treasury intervened in the Board's policy much less. For the first time in its brief history, the System

20 Ibid., p. 19 and Leffingwell Papers (Library of Congress), Letterbooks, XXXIII, 65-66.

21 Ibid., pp. 18-22.

> had control of its policy and sufficient resources to carry it out. But it lacked enough determination and coherence of views to act....
>
> In its annual report for 1920, the board defended the sharp rise in discount rates as necessary to "maintain the strength of the Federal Reserve Banks, which are the custodians of the lawful reserves of the member banks," a reference to the gold reserve ratio.... Federal reserve officials defended the deflationary policy as a means of reversing the effects of the previous inflation and restoring the gold standard to its pre-war gold price....[22]
>
> President [Warren G.] Harding's administration had a different attitude than its predecessor. Pressure for lower discount rates came from farmers, Congress, the Treasury, and particularly Andrew Mellon, who had become secretary of the treasury in the new administration and was therefore ex officio chairman of the Federal Reserve Board. Mellon favored a reduction in the discount rate from the time he took office, March 1921.[23]

We know that, in the spring of 1921, Reserve Banks that were at 7%, including New York, began cutting their rates. In July 1921, four Federal Reserve banks, including New York, cut their discount rates to 5.5%. By September only six Federal Reserve banks remained at 6% and one at 6.5%. By December 1921, three Federal Reserve banks (including New York) were at 4.5%, seven were at 5%, and two were at 5.5%. By December 1922, three Federal Reserve banks (including New York) were at 4%, and nine were at 4.5%.

Meltzer recognized that the Depression of 1920-21 brought a

22 Allan H. Meltzer, *A History of the Federal Reserve: 1913-1951,* University of Chicago Press, 2003, pp. 107-109.

23 Ibid., p. 112.

myriad of problems for farmers in particular, but he also observed:

> The NBER dates the trough of the business cycle at July 1921.... Industrial production turned in August and rose strongly. By March 1922 production was more than 20% above the previous year.[24]

Comparing Vital Sectors in 1921-22 with their Counterparts in 1930

Beginning with the Finance sector, it was much stronger in the Depression of 1920-21 than in 1929-30. Table 12.3 reveals that gross revenue in the Finance sector fell -10.01% in 1921 by comparison with 1920, whereas it fell -15.08% in 1930 compared to 1929.

Furthermore, just ahead, Table 12.4 (page 373) will show that the Finance sector earned $1,015.5 million in the two-year period 1920-1921 but only $686.8 million in the two years 1929-1930. While we noted earlier the 18.28% rebound in the Finance sector in 1922, we haven't introduced 1931 IRS numbers yet to compare to 1922, but we know the corresponding comparison will not produce a positive number for the second year of the Great Depression. Moreover, in 1929-30 as Table 12.1 shows, the gross income of the Finance sector fell two years in a row from 1928, a drop of -32.5% or -$6.41 billion. In the depression of 1920-21, the drop was 10%, amounted to -$0.84 billion and lasted only one year.

Perhaps the most telling comparison of the two periods of depression and deflation is qualitative and relates to the financial situations and motivations of consumers. The 1920-21 depression was prompted by economic adjustments following the end of the First World War. During the war much advertising was directed to consumers to act patriotically and buy war bonds and to practice frugality in consumption. Indeed, as we have just seen, the actions

24 Ibid., p. 117.

of the Fed in raising discount rates was also directed to adjusting to the end of the war. Specifically, its objective was ending the high inflation that was the outgrowth of war-related Treasury financing practices. Furthermore, H. Parker Willis told us that the joint policy of the Treasury and the Fed in 1920-21 was to compel the public to engage in even further saving—in his words, to "drive this great volume of bonds out of the banks and into the hands of the public."

By the end of the Depression of 1920-21, American citizens had *saved* growing amounts of money for multiple years purchasing war bonds—called Liberty Bonds— and other forms of federal debt. They had engaged in frugality even to the point of acquiring "this great volume of bonds [from] the banks." Looking at the end of the depression (or contraction) of 1920-21 through the lens of Friedman and Schwartz's Chart 12.1, it is our contention that American business had adjusted output away from supplying wartime purchasers to offering innovations to fulfill peacetime demand from savings-flushed potential purchasers. Prosperity ensued!

By contrast, in 1930, the first year of the Great Depression, and throughout the remainder, the American public was *in debt* and facing the reality of having dramatically increased borrowing between 1922 and October 1929. At first, the borrowing funded the acquisition of homes using mortgages, as well as automobiles, radios and other household goods, using installment credit. But, somewhere in 1925-27, stock speculation developed using readily offered margin accounts to acquire stocks, commodity futures, etc. By March 1929, the speculation had become unstoppable, though, in point of fact, no serious effort was made to apply brakes. The Crash of 1929 resulted, causing the Great Depression to commence at full throttle in May 1930, with a specific cause-and-effect linkage, as explained in *How the Crash Caused*. Americans quickly realized they had become, as Irving Fisher labeled it, over-indebted, or if imprudent, deeply in debt, and therefore they began repaying those debts by reducing consumption (Table 5.2, page 142). Repaying bank loans resulted in deflation. Just as critical, reduced consumption, along with a

The IRS Statistics of Profitability for 1918-1930: Net Income Less Deficit

Table 12.4

All Sectors: Net Income Less Deficit 1918-1930

($ million)

Year	Agriculture	Mining and quarrying	Manufacturing	Construction	Transportation and utilities	Trade	Service	Finance	Aggregate net income	Change from previous year (% Percent)
1918	30.3	496.3	4,534.1	118.2	679.5	1,001.6	45.0	478.7	7,383.8	-27.1
1919	64.2	251.7	4,852.6	140.6	879.0	1,379.3	102.8	703.1	8,373.3	13.4
1920	5.3	525.6	3,282.3	85.3	678.6	571.7	116.3	639.4	5,904.5	-29.5
1921	-47.8	-229.4	-121.0	15.8	498.5	-54.9	58.9	376.1	496.3	-91.6
1922	6.8	6.0	2,641.0	39.2	782.8	695.3	88.8	490.2	4,750.0	857.2
1923	42.3	-50.7	3,570.9	69.2	1,131.8	933.1	129.2	457.3	6,283.1	32.3
1924	1.7	-66.9	2,763.5	90.7	1,094.3	802.1	135.5	534.5	5,355.3	-14.8
1925	17.6	243.6	3,701.1	113.1	1,333.9	966.5	174.2	1,067.6	7,617.8	42.2
1926	15.1	272.3	3,708.1	108.9	1,603.2	834.6	157.2	808.9	7,508.4	-1.4
1927	16.7	29.4	3,087.6	111.7	1,391.4	794.5	127.4	956.7	6,515.4	-13.2
1928	30.4	125.3	3,910.5	99.5	1,639.9	891.3	127.5	1,405.1	8,229.6	26.3
1929	19.3	232.1	4,405.8	108.3	1,902.0	729.8	160.2	1,188.7	8,746.1	6.3
1930	-45.9	-44.3	1,117.7	68.1	1,000.7	-87.6	55.0	-501.9	1,561.7	-82.1

Source: *SOI 1918-1930.*

major drop in fixed investment by American businesses, caused unemployment. Altogether, a major years-long downward spiral of dissaving, deflation and depression had begun.

To explore conditions during the two downturns within specific business segments, we now return to the extensive IRS statistics on net income that take us from the macro-level NBER business cycle numbers to a more micro level. Table 12.4(previous page) shows Aggregate Corporate Net Income less Deficit for each of the eight IRS corporate business sectors for 1918-1930, then aggregates them and offers the percent change from the prior year. In its *SOI* series, the IRS displayed statistics of Net Income (of profitable corporations) separately from those with Deficits (of unprofitable corporations). The statistics in Table 12.4 take both into account by deducting the losses reported by the non-profitable companies from the income reported by the profitable ones to arrive at Aggregate Net Income less Deficit.

As Table 12.4 shows, there were critical differences between the two time periods. We look first at the Finance sector because of its outsized role in what was taking place in both downturns, but especially in 1929 forward. At first glance, clearly the various components of the Finance sector experienced the two depressions differently. In 1921, the sector as a whole still earned $376 million in aggregate profits (although that was well below the 1920 level of $639 million) and, in fact, still *earned more than $1 billion in profits during the whole contractionary period of 1920-1921.* As the sector was flush from World War I, there had been no noteworthy or protracted speculation, or borrowing for it, and there certainly was no stock market crash. By contrast, throughout 1930-33, banks, brokerages and other entities in the Finance sector *experienced momentous losses, including over half a billion dollars in 1930 alone.* Tellingly, the Finance sector in aggregate did not return to profitability until 1936.

As further statistical evidence of the differences between the Depression of 1920-21 and the Great Depression post-Crash, Table 12.5 (opposite) shows Aggregate Corporate Net Income less

Manufacturing Subsectors

Table 12.5

Manufacturing Subsectors: Net Income Less Deficit 1918-1930

($-million)

Year	Food products, beverages and tobacco	Textiles and textile products	Leather and leather products	Rubber and rubber goods	Lumber and wood products	Paper, pulp, and products	Printing and publishing	Chemicals and allied substances	Stone, clay, and glass products	Metal and metal products	All other metal industries	Aggregate net income
1918	498.5	757.6	113.6	99.8	158.2	92.7	56.1	379.5	75.3	2,009.1	294.8	4,535.1
1919	528.4	903.5	239.4	122.1	264.9	124.6	120.0	423.7	95.9	1,669.4	360.8	4,852.6
1920	221.0	292.0	-42.9	-4.9	294.1	237.6	149.5	344.9	142.9	1,274.9	373.3	3,282.3
1921	10.0	137.9	-48.8	-96.5	-49.7	-4.3	97.5	25.3	43.5	-228.6	-7.3	-121.0
1922	297.4	456.8	63.8	17.4	159.7	61.6	161.7	395.1	109.1	634.9	283.5	2,641.0
1923	382.7	491.6	36.3	24.4	266.5	95.0	142.3	325.4	173.5	1,249.4	383.9	3,570.9
1924	441.1	128.8	38.4	41.6	121.1	74.3	147.5	389.9	144.5	1,095.8	140.4	2,763.5
1925	442.0	298.3	47.1	109.0	147.2	99.0	161.4	540.9	163.7	1,555.3	137.1	3,701.1
1926	497.1	119.5	46.4	12.7	103.8	106.1	172.5	715.9	173.1	1,610.9	150.2	3,708.1
1927	477.6	296.7	77.4	50.9	31.1	110.4	163.7	384.5	128.9	1,260.0	105.5	3,086.6
1928	559.8	196.1	49.4	-1.3	70.7	103.6	219.5	788.3	139.5	1,655.0	139.8	3,920.5
1929	580.2	160.9	40.4	17.1	67.1	104.5	223.1	854.5	130.2	2,121.7	106.1	4,405.8
1930	445.1	-264.1	-25.4	-51.6	-116.6	37.3	121.6	358.6	39.4	602.6	-29.2	1,117.7

Source: *SOI 1918-1930.*

Deficit from 1918-1930 for companies in each of the eleven IRS Manufacturing sub-sectors. Data, of course, gain meaning by examining real-world events. For example, the -$121 million loss in 1921 in the Manufacturing sector as a whole was attributable to the end of war-related manufacturing and the requirements for factory retooling to ramp up peacetime production. In 1930, as we saw in Table 12.2, all sub-sectors of Manufacturing except Chemicals and Allied Substances experienced significant drops in *gross* income. In terms of *net* income, however, likely as a continuing reflection of the prosperity of the late 1920s, 1930 saw six of the eleven subsectors remaining sufficiently profitable for the Manufacturing sector as a whole still to operate in the black to the tune $1.12 billion.

Continuing to compare statistics for American business between 1920-21 and 1930, we again turn to Table 12.3 (page 361). The last row in Table 12.3 shows that in most cases, sharper downturns occurred in 1921 than in 1930. Aggregate Gross Income for All Business Sectors turned down -13.9% in 1930 as compared with a downturn of -22.6% in 1921, and All Manufacturing Sub-Sectors fell -15.6% in 1930 versus -32.1% in 1921. Not surprisingly, the Finance sector showed particular weakness in 1930. In 1921, the gross income of the Finance sector dropped -10.0%, having fallen from a very high rate of growth—29.9%—in 1920. This made the rebound of 18.3% in 1922 less unexpected. But in 1930, the Finance sector was significantly weaker, having already fallen -20.5%, in 1929, as Table 12.1 (page 347) shows, when the Crash took place. Certainly, the Statistics of Economic Activity tables offered at the ends of Chapters 3 and 6-10 showing the declining pace of business month-by-month throughout 1930 make it clear that the likelihood of business picking up in 1931 as it had in 1922 was exceedingly slim. It is an important reminder that such helpful data were either not available at all or not available in a timely enough manner to be usable by business and government policymakers.

Detailed Sectoral Reports on Corporations in 1930

We now focus on 1930 and consider both gross and net income results, first within the Finance sector, then in one bellwether subsector of Manufacturing. Net versus gross income figures give us a picture of profitability, which is, of course, the critical indicator of the health of a business, an industrial sector or, indeed, an entire economy.[25]

The story within the Finance sector pre- and post-Crash is predictably dramatic. Table 12.6 shows Net Income Less Deficit for the various business components of the Finance sector from 1928 to 1930.

Table 12.6

Finance Net Income Less Deficit from 1928 to 1930

($ million)

Industrial groups	1928 Net income less deficit	1929 Net income less deficit	% Change from 1928	1930 Net income less deficit	% Change from 1929
Finance:					
Banking and related industries:					
National Banks	162.9	154.5	-5.1	37.3	-75.9
State and private banks, savings banks, loan and trust companies	273.2	261.1	-4.4	93.0	-64.4
Joint-stock land banks	-7.7	-10.4	35.5	-8.8	-15.8
Stock and bond brokers, investment brokers, investment bankers, and investment trusts.	233.0	56.0	-76.0	-441.5	-888.5
Real estate and realty holding companies—Realty development, holding, or leasing; realty trust, etc.	257.2	76.8	-70.1	-96.5	-225.6
Total banking and related industries	918.6	538.0	-41.4	-416.6	-177.4
Insurance companies:					
Life insurance—Mutual or stock companies	111.7	104.7	-6.3	94.3	-9.9
Other insurance—Accident, casualty, fire, marine, title, etc.	130.9	91.8	-29.8	-73.1	-179.6
Total insurance companies	242.5	196.5	-19.0	21.2	-89.2
Other finance:					
Loan companies—Building and loan associations; mortgage, note, or pawn brokers; insurance agents, promoters, stock syndicates, foreign exchange, and finance n.e.c.	229.1	432.8	88.9	-106.5	-124.6
Total finance	1,390.2	1,167.3	-16.0	-501.9	-143.0

Source: *SOI for 1928-30*: 1928 p.339, 1929 p.293, 1930 p.237.

The most eye-catching earnings numbers, though certainly not unexpected, were those for Stock and bond brokers, investment brokers, investment bankers and investment trusts. In the robust year of 1928, this subgroup earned $233 million. In the year of the Crash, earnings dropped by almost -76% to $56 million. Then in

25 Chapter 13 deals with a third sector, Agriculture.

Table 12.7			
Finance Gross Income Less Deficit from 1929 to 1930 ($ million)			
Industrial groups	1929 Gross income	1930 Gross income	Percent change (%)
Finance:			
Banking and related industries:			
National Banks	$1,252.0	$1,081.5	-13.6
State and private banks, savings banks, loan and trust companies	1,972.0	1,728.7	-12.3
Joint stock land banks	3.7	4.5	22.5
Stock and bond brokers, investment brokers, investment bankers, and investment trusts.	3,912.7	3,150.1	-19.5
Real estate and realty holding companies—Realty development, holding, or leasing; realty trust, etc.	2,448.5	2,256.9	-7.8
Total banking and related industries	9,588.8	8,221.8	-14.3
Insurance companies:			
Life insurance—Mutual or stock companies	772.4	932.7	20.8
Other insurance—Accident, casualty, fire, marine, title, etc.	1,992.0	1,903.1	-4.5
Total insurance companies	2,764.4	2,835.8	2.6
Other finance:			
Loan companies—Building and loan associations; mortgage, note, or pawnbrokers; insurance agents, promoters, stock syndicates, foreign exchange, and finance n.e.c.	3,212.7	2,239.6	-30.3
Total finance	15,565.9	13,297.2	-14.6

Source: *SOI for 1929 & 1930*: 1929 p.293, 1930 p.237.

1930, this single subgroup lost $442 million, the lion's share of the entire Finance sector's $502 million loss. While the change in fortunes for the companies in this subgroup was substantial—it is important to bear in mind that because, at the time, most Wall Street entities were partnerships, not corporations—these dire results gave only a partial view of the damage on Wall Street. Later in this chapter, we will discuss IRS partnership income statistics in detail.

Gross Income figures are also telling. Table 12.7 (above) shows how Gross Income for the Finance sector fell -14.6% from 1929 to 1930, but its various subgroups experienced different results. For instance, gross income of the Banking and related industries subgroup fell by -14.3%, slightly less than the sector as a whole. Gross income of the Insurance subgroup, however, rose 2.6%, likely due to increased use of automobiles and trucks requiring insurance as reflected in the increased demand for petroleum in 1930 noted above.

Gross income of the Finance subgroup Other, whose components included building and loan associations and stock syndicates, fell by a concerning -30.3% as activity within those businesses slowed. None of these drops in 1930 come as a surprise, because, as we have posited, borrowers were focused on one thing—paying off debt. Borrowers were, in fact, as our overall analysis has shown, rapidly repaying their debt obligations, across a broad spectrum, including their accounts payable. This collective action brought short-term interest rates down significantly as demand for loans fell. Thus, as 1930 progressed, banking institutions earned less interest on a diminishing quantity of outstanding loans, a double hit to their bottom lines that caused their -14.3% drop in gross income.

The figures in Tables 12.6 (page 377) and 12.7 (opposite) provide us with a better understanding of what Friedman and Schwartz called the banking crisis of 1930, which began in November and continued with lingering effects into January 1931. As we have described in Chapter 10, the "crisis" can for the most part be traced to the failure of one large corporate finance entity, Caldwell and Company, a regional investment banking firm headquartered in Nashville, Tennessee. In *The Banking Panics of the Great Depression,* Elmus Wicker (on whom we drew heavily in our account of banking in 1930 in Chapter 10) wrote that Caldwell and Company "controlled the largest chain of banks in the South … and also the largest insurance entity in the region."[26] The insurance part of their business may have helped, but with bank earnings hit hard and fast by the rush to reduce debt and the interest rate decline that followed the Crash, any entity, such as Caldwell and Company, that owned a chain of banks, especially those that were principally local, smaller in size, not members of the Federal Reserve System and with lending heavily concentrated in one or two industries, such as agriculture, was necessarily in deep trouble. Add in malfeasance by senior management and Caldwell and Company's failure was assured.

We also focus on the gross income of various components of the Metal products and processes subsector of the Manufacturing

26 Wicker (1996), pp. 32-3.

Table 12.8

Metal Products and Processes Change in Gross Income, 1929 to 1930

($ million)

Industrial groups	1929 Aggregate gross income	1930 Aggregate gross income	Percent change (%)
Metal and its products:			
Iron and steel-products of blast furnances, rolling mills, foundries, etc.	6,160.4	4,264.8	-30.8
Locomotives and railroad equipment	540.2	409.4	-24.2
Motor vehicles, complete or parts	6,247.6	3,993.9	-36.1
Factory machinery-food-production machinery; leather, metal, paper, printing, textile, and woodworking machinery.	813.3	621.1	-23.6
Agricultural machinery and equipment	813.5	649.6	-20.1
Electrical machinery and equipment	1,467.3	1,108.9	-24.4
Miscellaneous machinery-building, construction, gas, and mining machinery and equipment.	1,781.9	1,437.2	-19.3
Household machinery and equipment, etc.	796.6	586.0	-26.4
Office equipment, etc.	484.3	376.0	-22.4
Metal building material and supplies	902.7	744.0	-17.6
Hardware, tools, etc.	1,338.1	976.6	-27.0
Precious-metal products and processes; jewelry, etc.	399.7	289.0	-27.7
Other metals, products, and processes; combinations of foundry and machine shop	2,347.1	1,741.5	-25.8
Total metal and its products	24,092.6	17,197.9	-28.6

Source: *SOI for 1929 & 1930*: 1929 pp.290-291, 1930 pp.233-234.

sector, as presented in Table 12.8. (above) We zero in on this large subsector because within it were major industries that carried unusual weight when assessing the overall condition of American business at the time. A quick scan of the subsector's component entities confirms its importance.

As a whole, the gross income of the thirteen categories in the Metal products and processes subsector fell by -28.6%. Unsurprisingly, Iron and steel products experienced the largest percentage drop of -30.8%. Even the smallest percentage decline, -17.6%, in Metal building materials and supplies, was significant. With slowdowns in construction and automobile production and belt-tightening measures by indebted households, these gross income declines were inevitable.

In order to dig further into how business decision-makers were looking at their current realities, it became useful to compare contemporary IRS data with the later-aggregated NIPA numbers. Clearly, one management strategy was cutting back on fixed investments that depended upon having confidence in the future climate for their businesses. Statistics from NIPA confirmed this shift in strategy. Of particular relevance is the -26.8% decline in Gross Domestic Fixed Investment, which was from $14,483 million in 1929 to $10,601 million in 1930 as businesses cut back budgeted expansion plans.

Using the IRS's gross income figures for the Metal products and process subsector as our "rough cut" example for comparing the IRS figures and the NIPA figures, we see that this subsector's 1930 gross income fell -28.6% from $24,093 million in 1929 to $17,198 million. Although the IRS numbers were considerably larger than the corresponding NIPA numbers for Gross Domestic Fixed Investment, the rates of decline were similar. Despite the fact that the two agencies gathered data and defined variables differently, the trend was the same in both data sets and confirmed that the same forces were impacting fixed investments spending.

Showing net income figures indicating profitability, Table 12.9 (following page) offers the IRS figures for Net Income less Deficit for each Industrial group of the Metal Products and Processes subsector in 1929 and 1930. The table reveals that Net Income less Deficit for the subsector as a whole dropped almost -72% from $2,121 million to $603 million. It also shows that the profitability of each of the thirteen industrial components of the subsector dropped dramatically from 1929 to 1930, as two industrial groups, Building material and equipment and Precious metal products and processes, went into the red, highlighting the declines in construction and luxury goods purchases such as jewelry.

Table 12.9

Metal Products and Processes Net Income Less Deficit, from 1929 to 1930

($ million)

Industrial groups	1929 Net income less deficit	1930 Net income less deficit	Percent change (%)
Metal and its products:			
Iron and steel-Products of blast furnances, rolling mills, foundries, etc.	491.2	134.9	-72.5
Locomotives and railroad equipment	52.0	27.4	-47.3
Motor vehicles, complete or parts	473.7	158.4	-66.6
Factory machinery-Food-production machinery; leather, metal, paper, printing, textile, and woodworking machinery.	81.8	18.8	-77.1
Agricultural machinery and equipment	107.9	44.2	-59.0
Electrical machinery and equipment	201.8	84.9	-57.9
Miscellaneous machinery-Building, construction, gas, and mining machinery and equipment.	150.2	24.2	-83.9
Household machinery and equipment, etc.	59.4	24.3	-59.1
Office equipment, etc.	68.0	31.5	-53.7
Metal building material and supplies	64.9	-0.4	-100.6
Hardware, tools, etc.	170.0	21.7	-87.2
Precious-metal products and processes; jewelry, etc.	18.3	-9.4	-151.4
Other metals, products, and processes; combinations of foundry and machine shop	182.5	42.2	-76.9
Total metal and its products	2,121.7	602.6	-71.6

Source: *SOI for 1929 & 1930*: 1929 pp.290-291, 1930 pp.233-234.

Business and Partnership Data Filed on Individual Returns

To create an overall picture of American business in 1930, we must add into our account sole-proprietorships and partnerships. As we discussed in Chapter 11, individuals were required to file tax returns that reported income from these important revenue-generating activities—including lawyers, doctors, small local businesses, farmers, and, as we said earlier, many brokerage firms. We must turn to the Business (i.e., sole-proprietorships) and the Partnership statistics submitted to the IRS on individual income tax filings and then add these numbers to the corporate statistics in order to arrive at the Total Gross Income reported to the IRS on all American business regardless of type of ownership.

Though perseverance wins in the end, there were caveats to consider when making this calculation. First, the information reported on individual tax returns by taxfilers who had Business and Partnership income to report was *net, not gross, income.* Taxpayers who had privately-owned businesses and/or individual shares in any partnership paid taxes on profits—and profits were net of allowable operating expenses. Second, since the IRS collected taxes only on profitable sole proprietorships and partnerships, unprofitable business activities and many minimally profitable businesses (such as subsistence farms, as we will in see the next chapter) lay outside consideration. These business activities that presumably generated at least some revenue were ubiquitous in America at the time, though they seemed to operate, in military parlance, "under the radar" as to the taxing authorities.

The IRS statistics for 1929 and 1930 told a mixed story as regards Business and Partnerships. In 1929, Table 11.5 (page 322) shows that 4.04 million individual taxfilers reported $3,379 million of Business net income and $1,853 million of Partnership net income, a combined 21.1% of the total $24.8 billion of Net income reported by individuals in 1929.[27] One year later, as *SOI for 1930* reports, 3.71 million individual taxfilers (down -8.1% from 1929) reported reduced amounts of $2,628 million of Business net income and $1,090 million of Partnership net income.[28] With $18.1 billion of net income reported in 1930 by individual American income taxfilers down -27.0% from 1929, these two categories accounted for -22.7% of the decline. Notably, Partnership net income fell much more significantly than Business net income on individual tax filings for the simple reason that most brokerage business was done in 1930 by partnerships. As Table 12.6 (page 377) shows, the Finance sector corporate brokerage business lost $-442 million in 1930, and Table 11.5 (page 322) shows that individual filings of Part-

27 *SOI for 1929,* pp. 4 & 8.
28 *SOI for 1930,* pp. 4 & 9.

nership net income also suffered a punishing decline from 1929 to 1930. Meanwhile, the Business net income of individuals reporting $5,000+ incomes fell -22.2%, a significant decline, if not as stark.

Comparing Business Net Income of Individuals with Corporate Net Income

How did the individual filers' Business net income numbers compare to overall corporate results? Sole proprietorships, including lawyers, doctors, tradesmen and small retailers, clearly constituted an important part of aggregate American business activity in 1929. It turns out that individual profitability (i.e., just Business net income of sole proprietors, not Partnership net income) reported by individual taxfilers in 1929—$3,379 million—comprised a full 38.63% of the $8,746 million in overall corporate profitability (Aggregate Corporate Net Income Less Deficit) shown in Table 12.4 (page 373). In fact, by the end of 1929, individual filers' businesses, despite any post-Crash belt-tightening, were performing better than corporations in general, though we suspect that as 1929 wore on, corporations in many business segments had already begun belt-tightening a notch or two.

More notable is that individual profitability fell much more slowly from 1929 to 1930 than corporate profitability did. [29] Table 12.4 (page 373) shows a dramatic fall of -82.1% in corporate profitability in 1930, from $8,746.15 million in 1929 to $1,562 million in 1930. But as we noted in Table 11.5 (page 322), Business profitability of all individual taxfilers— 38.63% of total corporate profitability in 1929 ($3,379 million vs. $8,746 million)— fell only -22.2% to $2,628 million in 1930.

---

29 Individual profitability includes both business and partnership income. Table 12.9 shows only business net profits on individual returns over $5,000.

What Cushioned the Drop in Individual Business Profitability?

Before returning to IRS archive statistics, we feel the need to give a tentative answer to this question. We believe that sole-proprietors were close enough to their customers or clients to have immediate and concrete understanding of what their motivations were. For example, when attorneys lost clients or store owners lost customers, as sole proprietors they could adjust decisively in order to stay solvent. Naturally this scenario only applied to sole-proprietors who had not succumbed to the lure of speculation and encumbered tthemselves (and their businesses) with too much unserviceable debt.

To explore one example of a sole-proprietorship, let us imagine a hypothetical automobile dealer who was not in debt and had not speculated. At the beginning of 1928, he was principal salesman of his sole-proprietorship and let us suppose he had an additional sales force of four. In early 1929, to meet the car manufacturer's optimistic dealer quota of 76% more vehicles to sell, he hired three more salesmen. But with production slowing as he knew from reading *Automobile Trade Journal and Motor Age* and with his unsold vehicle inventory visibly growing, perhaps by May 1929, he might have laid off one or two salesmen. By August or September, a third salesman might be gone. After the Crash, he might have laid off one or two more. Close to his customers and his community, our automobile dealer had considerable latitude in managing the expenses of his sole-proprietorship, difficult as it may have been to lay off his salesforce. Then, as 1930 progressed, he might have continued to reduce the size of his salesforce as slower sales warranted, ultimately becoming the only salesman on the increasingly quiet lot. From there he could rehire only as demand for automobiles returned.

Widening our view of the overall business picture in America, Table 12.10 (following page) shows Net Profit from Business (i.e., sole proprietorships and partnerships) based on IRS filings by individuals, comparable to the format that the IRS used in upcoming Table 12.11

(page 387)) on Net Income of Profitable Corporate Corporations for 1930. These tables break individual Business income into IRS business sectors, enabling us to compare, within an industry, how corporations and individuals involved within an industry experienced what was happening.

One problem we encountered was that the IRS only worked with individual filers with net income of $5,000 or more, resulting in an unfortunate data gap. How much did the unmeasured group of lower income business income earn? To measure that gap, at least we know from *SOI for 1930* (Table 11.5 page 322) that of the $2,628 million of total business income reported by all American taxfilers, $1,216 million was reported by the IRS as shown in Table 12.10's Net profit from business column as coming from individuals with incomes of $5,000 and over. Thus, business income from taxfilers earning less than $5,000 reported $1,412 million in business income, 53.7% of total Business profits of individuals.

Table 12.10
Net Profit from Business for 1929 and 1930, Reported
IRS Individual Returns of $5,000 and Over

Industrial groups	1929			1930		
	Number of businesses	Net profit from business ($ million)	Percent (%)	Number of businesses	Net profit from business ($ million)	Percent (%)
Agriculture and related industries	19,306	113.3	6.2	9,708	51.4	4.2
Mining and quarrying	1,558	16.1	0.9	915	9.6	0.8
Manufacturing:						
Food products, beverages, and tobacco	3,181	26.1	1.4	2,314	19.1	1.6
Textiles and textile products	2,522	24.8	1.4	1,430	12.9	1.1
Leather and leather products	219	2.4	0.1	119	1.1	0.1
Rubber and related products	96	1.2	0.1	47	0.4	0.0
Lumber and wood products	778	6.9	0.4	375	3.1	0.3
Paper, pulp, and products	160	1.7	0.1	100	0.9	0.1
Printing, publishing, and allied industries	2,332	19.7	1.1	1,733	13.9	1.1
Chemicals and allied products	484	5.7	0.3	282	3.4	0.3
Stone, clay, and glass products	485	4.0	0.2	314	2.7	0.2
Metals and metal products	2,165	22.2	1.2	1,133	10.5	0.9
All other manufacturing industries	1,233	15.7	0.9	716	7.6	0.6
Total manufacturing	13,655	130.4	7.1	8,563	75.4	6.2
Construction	11,551	102.0	5.6	7,128	65.5	5.4
Transportation and other public utilities	2,567	19.7	1.1	1,800	14.0	1.1
Trade	62,665	458.6	25.0	36,863	253.5	20.9
Service-professional, amusements, hotels, etc.	91,587	762.5	41.5	72,431	607.8	50.0
Finance-banking, insurance, real estate, stock and bond brokers, etc.	12,695	140.6	7.7	8,864	80.0	6.6
Business not suffciently defined to be classed with other division	12,891	93.0	5.1	8,368	58.2	4.8
Grand total	228,475	1,836.3	100.0	154,640	1,215.5	100.0

Source: *SOI for 1930*, p.15.

Table 12.11

Net Income of Profitable Corporations for 1930

($ million)

Industrial groups	Total number of returns	Corporate net profit	Percent of total (%)
Agriculture and related industries	10,961	40.5	0.63
Mining and quarrying	17,635	194.1	3.02
Manufacturing:			
Food products, beverages, and tobacco	15,252	580.2	9.03
Textiles and textile products	14,692	105.6	1.64
Leather and leather products	2,461	38.7	0.60
Rubber products	607	12.2	0.19
Forest products	7,501	35.8	0.56
Paper, pulp, and products	2,113	73.6	1.15
Printing, publishing, and allied industries	11,736	176.1	2.74
Chemicals and allied products	7,380	534.1	8.31
Stone, clay, and glass products	4,724	92.8	1.44
Metals and metal products	20,831	1,003.0	15.60
All other manufacturing industries	7,801	105.2	1.64
Total manufacturing	95,098	2,757.5	42.89
Construction	20,035	150.6	2.34
Transportation and other public utilities	23,662	1,334.2	20.75
Trade	134,769	651.1	10.13
Service-professional, amusements, hotels, etc.	42,064	234.2	3.64
Finance-banking, insurance, real estate, stock and bond brokers, etc.	153,182	1,064.8	16.56
Nature of business not given	21,330	1.8	0.03
Grand total	518,736	6,428.8	100.0

Source: *SOI for 1930*, p.21.

The breakdowns for individual and corporate filings by business sector allowed us to fine-tune comparisons. Table 12.11 (above), again broken down by business sector, compares corporations with the individual filing statistics from Table 12.10. Percentages are the proportional relationship of the various business sector statistics with total corporate net profits of $6,429 million. When comparing Tables 12.10 and 12.11, it is worth noting that in occupations that likely involved significant personal interactions between business owners and their customers such as those in the Construction, Trade and Service sectors, individual filers reported appreciably higher proportions of their incomes as profits—5.38%, 20.86%, and 50.01%

respectively—than applied to profitable corporate income in those categories—2.3%, 10.1%, and 3.6% respectively. Within these three business sectors in particular, community was key. Sole-proprietors who were providing an essential service in a community and had an established local customer base gave the sole-proprietor the ability to reduce expenses more quickly than corporations to stay profitable.

The standout on the corporate side is the Manufacturing sector where individual filers, with good reason, reported much less net income proportionately to corporations, depending on the subsector specifics. This makes sense since a high proportion of business entities in certain industries in subsectors of the Manufacturing sector require corporate structures to enable fundraising with stock and bond offerings. For example, Corporations reported 1.6% of their 1930 income in Textiles and their products while individual filers reported 1.1%. Corporations reported 1.6% of their income in Printing, publishing, and allied industries while individual filers reported 1.1%.

We turn now to one particular business sector—Agriculture—and to the large population of 6.2 million American farmers in 1930 to see how this important and essential economic group—almost all operating farms as individuals, not corporations—was faring as the Depression set in.

CHAPTER 13

American Farmers: Speculation, Indebtedness and the Shrugged-off IRS

(Year-End 1930)

Now that we have addressed the economic behavior of both incorporated entities and individuals in America, we turn to an important subset of individuals, as broken down by the IRS, engaged in a critical unincorporated business activity—farming. As we learned in the prior chapter, individuals who operated an unincorporated business, regardless of their overall net income, were required to file a tax return and report that business income (or loss). This large group included America's professionals like doctors, dentists, lawyers and accountants and partners in partnerships, as well as local merchants, tradesmen and almost all of the nation's farmers. We also saw that while individuals with net profits from unincorporated businesses experienced declines, they were actually faring better than corporations in 1930. What about America's farmers?

First, some demographics are in order. According to the Department of Agriculture's 1930 census, there were 6,288,648 farms in the U.S.[1] Eager to explore this material group of 6.3 million American farmers with an additional 24 million or so people residing with them — nearly a quarter of America's population lived on farms in 1930—we encountered a surprising statistical anomaly. Regarding

1 U. S. Department of Commerce, Census Bureau, *Fifteenth Census of the United States: 1930, Agriculture*, Vol. 1, p. 13. This census was taken April 1, 1930, by U.S. Department of Agriculture enumerators.

the vital contributions of that particular segment to the nation's collective wellbeing, the IRS archives, so rich in information about taxfilers, proved uncharacteristically lacking. In fact, our research revealed that only 9,708 farmers filed tax returns for 1930 as individuals with unincorporated business income from farming, and another 9,618 farmers filed as incorporated businesses.[2] That meant almost 6,270,000 American farmers in 1930 apparently *failed to file tax returns.*

This anomaly, of course led us to wonder why farmers failed to file in 1930, but we also wanted to understand how farmers' experiences fit in with what was going on in the country economically. This chapter explores how farmers, so important to the nation's very health, left little statistical footprint, despite sharing similar pressures with many nonfarming Americans.

Risk-takers Created the Country

Risk tolerance is a familiar aspect of the American psyche. In many ways, America's evolution as a nation has relied on risk-takers. Risk and the idea of speculation go hand in hand. The truly risk-averse do not speculate. They don't like the odds and stay on the sidelines. Farming, however, takes some level of risk tolerance given so many unknowns from weather to soil conditions to commodities prices to health and beyond. The intrepid settlers who spread out all over the continent and became farmers—autonomously and in aggregate—were no exception.

Did farmers speculate in the stock market? Unlikely more than a handful did, but they definitely speculated in other ways in their daily decision-making. As an inherently risky endeavor, each farm at the time seemed like a tiny kingdom of its own, isolated and relatively self-sufficient. Farmers were inclined to a basic distrust of governmental oversight. While they might not have viewed themselves as akin to stock speculators, farmers historically definitely

2 *SOI for 1930*, p. 15.

speculated when they accepted the challenge of a land grant to settle on a piece of land that, if they worked the land for a certain number of years, they would then own. They speculated when they planted their first crop and then every crop after that. They speculated when they decided to grow a different crop. Farmers speculated when they took on debt to buy more land, as they did during World War I in order to increase production to feed war-torn Europe. When the war ended, they also speculated by continuing to grow too much. Farmers speculated on livestock, farm equipment, seeds and growing practices. In deciding not to file required tax returns, they speculated—and were right—that there would be no repercussions.

This chapter is the product of some considerable head scratching about this material group of Americans in 1930. Farming was too significant a sector of the population to ignore since, as we said, approximately 25% of the 1930 population lived on farms, and yet the IRS was pretty much a data dead end due to farmers' failure to file. In fact, the IRS offered us only a passing glance at this sizable group of Americans engaged in the crucial activity of feeding the nation.

Questions arose. Why didn't farmers file their tax returns? What was the economic condition of these more than six million farmers who didn't file? Was their failure to file costly to the Federal government in terms of tax revenue?

Given the absence of comprehensive IRS data on farming, we needed to do some creative research to seek answers to our questions. Looking for relevant data and possible explanations, we consulted various government sources that included the IRS, specifically its *SOI for 1930* and *SOI for 1929*, but also the US Department of Agriculture, the US Census Bureau and even the Works Progress Administration, though not operational in 1930. We attempted—and failed— to find scholars who had focused specifically on the missing tax returns, although several intrepid economic historians and others approached farming in 1930 from angles that were helpful in understanding the stressors confronting farmers.

As we dug further, we came to understand that, though their farms were located in distinctly rural environments and the heart and soul of their lives were formed in ways that were distinct from urbanites and suburbanites, farmers still meshed with non-farming Americans in several important ways. This chapter discusses our conjectures based on the information and the data we found and comes to the conclusion that farmers, although dealing with multiple challenging forces in 1930, shared one big pressure with many of their nonfarming fellow citizens —their debt level.

Clear IRS Codes About Filing

It was certainly the objective of the IRS codes to capture all unincorporated and incorporated commercial activities in the country. As to individuals, wage or salary earners did not have to file if their net income was under $5,000 and earned solely from those wages or salaries or from an unearned source like dividends or interest. However, commerce of any kind by an individual triggered a filing requirement. As we have seen, unincorporated commercial endeavors were extremely common in the America of 1930 and covered a wide range of work efforts. For IRS purposes, these sole proprietors reported their commercial activities as individuals under the income and expense category that the IRS simply called Business. Partners in partnerships, such as most Wall Street brokerages or the larger law firms at the time, reported their share of partnership income as individuals under the income and expense category called Partnership.

With regards to the obligations of individuals in such unincorporated business activities as farming—included in the industrial group Agriculture—the income tax form instructions for 1930 were straightforward. To quote directly from those instructions:

> If you owned a business, or practiced a profession on your own account, fill in Schedule A on page 2 of the return, and enter the net income (or loss) as Item 2 on page 1 of the return.

> This Schedule should include income from: (a) Sale of merchandise or products of manufacturing, mining, construction, and agriculture; (b) Business service, such as hotel, restaurant, and garage service, amusements, laundering, storage, transportations, etc.; and (c) Professional service, such as dentistry, law, or medicine. In general, report any income in the earning of which you incurred expenses of material, labor, supplies, etc. [3]

The 1930 IRS tax form instructions led us to the very Form 1040 Schedule of Farm Income and Expenses—Schedule F—that would have confronted any of the over six million unincorporated farmers in 1930 who, as individuals reporting earnings from farm activities, were required to file. The intentions of the Form 1040 instructions could not have been more direct:

> If you are a farmer and keep no books of account, or keep books on a cash basis, obtain from the Collector, and attach to this return Form 1040F, Schedule of Farm Income and Expense, and enter the net farm income as Item 2 on page 1 of this return. If your farm books of account are kept on an accrual basis, the filing of Form 1040F is optional.[4]

We will discuss how these instructions, despite their intentions, may have misled farmers into thinking they didn't have to file.

Putting the Data in Perspective

The statistics in *SOI for 1930* and *SOI for 1929* revealed the downward economic trend among all taxfilers in the U.S. Those with business income were no exception. In aggregate, the 3.7 million

---

3 Internal Revenue Service, Individual Income Tax Return for calendar year 1930.

4 Instructions for Form 1040 1930 from the Internal Revenue Service at https://www.irs.gov/pub/irs-prior/f1040f--1930.pdf

individual taxfilers in 1930 generated $22.4 billion in total income, down -25.2% from 1929's total income of $29.4 billion generated by 4.04 million taxfilers. As to those with business income (including the few farmers who did file), the IRS data for 1930 showed that 154,640 of those 3.7 million filers earned $2.6 billion in income from an unincorporated business, comprising a relatively small 11.7% of total individual filer net income. Aggregate numbers are telling. The number of filers with unincorporated business income in 1930 was down -32% from the 1929 peak of 228,475 filers who generated $3.4 billion from an unincorporated business. Furthermore, in 1930, of the 154,640 filers reporting business income of any kind, about one-third or 48,329 earned under $5,000 so, though required to file, they paid no tax.

In terms of the big picture regarding the 3.7 million total taxfilers earning $5,000 or more, two income categories accounted for the most taxable income in 1930. There were 515,718 individuals who reported income from salaries and commissions, and 494,916 filers who reported dividend income.[5] (More than a few filers clearly earned in both categories.) In contrast are the 154,640 individual filers—filing farmers included—who reported business income.[6] While business income filers were spread among all net income classes, a significant majority—64% or 99,252—were in the $5,000 under $20,000 net income categories.

Because the IRS divided business income of $5,000 or more into industrial groups, we know that the two dominant groups in this income range were "Service—professional, amusements, hotels, etc." comprising 46.8% and "Trade" comprising 23.8%, and these two groups in aggregate earned 71% of total net profits from business sources. The IRS industrial group of Agriculture comprised

5 *SOI for 1930*, p. 10. In contrast, wages and salaries comprised 44.3% of total filer income with 78.1% of that income earned by filers in the three lowest net income categories, under $10,000.

6 Ibid., p. 13. Of course, many individuals reported multiple sources of income, such as salaries and dividends.

only 6.3% of the number of filers with net income of $5,000 and over who earned a mere 4.2% of total net profit from business. Since farming is a subset within Agriculture, we see farming's relative insignificance in terms of taxable income, at least among those few farmers reporting profits of $5,000 or more. But, what about the millions of farmers who likely made much less money and didn't even bother filing?

What the IRS Does Tell Us About Farmers in 1930

As stated earlier, according to *SOI for 1930*, there were only 9,708 returns from individuals with net income of $5,000 and over from "Agriculture and related industries." Since the IRS Statistical Unit only sampled taxfilers earning under $5,000 and did not break down that sampled data into industrial groups and certainly not into "farmers," we had no way of determining how many additional farmers filed but didn't make the statistical sampling cut. Our assessment remains that it would have been a small number of lower-income farmers to add to that 9,708 figure, and they would have had a minimal tax obligation, if any.

What about incorporated farms? The few farms that were incorporated were included within the *SOI for 1930* corporation breakdown of "Agriculture and related industries." As we stated, the IRS reported only 9,618 such corporate farming returns, another modest number. Adding the farmers who filed as individuals with unincorporated business income to those who were incorporated and filed as corporations, the IRS archives accounted for 19,326 of the 1930 agricultural-census-reported 6.3 million farms, a mere 0.3%.[7] Both extremely low farmer filing figures highlight two facts about farming in 1930 America: how few farms were then incorporated, and, equally important, how few farmers earned enough to show

---

7 *SOI for 1930*, p. 231.

up in *SOI for 1930* statistics that focused on individuals with net income of $5,000 and over.

Farmers and Their Failure to File

Returning to the 1040 filing instructions, there are several ways they may have confused many farmers, if—and this is a big if—they even saw a 1040 in the first place, much less the Form 1040F. It would have been easy, and perhaps even logical, for farmers to make the assumption that their net income was too low to bother getting Forms 1040 or 1040F at all.[8] But then there was that final sentence: "If your farm books of account are kept on an accrual basis, the filing of Form 1040F is optional."

It is widely known that Henry Ford grew up on a Michigan farm and had only a sixth-grade education. Clearly that didn't stop him from astounding success by any measure. Many farmers in rural areas may have had limited access to schools or time to attend them, yet, in the world of their farms, lack of education didn't stop them either. It's not a stretch, however, to question their accounting skills. Farmers in 1930 may not have understood, much less used, "accrual" accounting. Data on how many farmers kept what kinds of books was outside the scope of this project and certainly did not present themselves in the resources we explored.

On the other hand, farmers certainly would have understood the word "optional." The IRS's choice of the word "optional" raised our eyebrows as perhaps one key rationale farmers opted out of filing. We don't know what the word-of-mouth about filing taxes might have been (not to mention the typical farmer's attitude towards taxation) or how news passed around in the pre-social-media era. Farming communities certainly had the local Grange, other organized agricultural groups, church socials or gatherings of farm

8 We use both "farmers" and "many farmers," which would be more accurate and are aware that some farmers did well during this period.

neighbors around kitchen tables. We can't help but wonder if the few time-constrained farmers who actually got their hands on the 1040F, read the word "optional" and fed the form to their pigs.

We learned from the *IRS Historical Fact Book: A Chronology 1646-1992* that in 1930 the IRS had only 11,979 employees charged with collecting over $3 billion in revenue.[9] Our research efforts to find data on how many tax collectors there were, where they were located or how—and how many—1040F forms got into actual farmers' hands gleaned no results. We do know that many farmers would have had to make a journey of some considerable distance to reach their nearest IRS Collector to pick up that daunting Schedule F. In any case, based on our research, there seemed to be no repercussions for farmers who didn't file, an idea that that might have been circulating around farm communities.

The American Farm: Where Dream Might Turn to Nightmare

Farming was indeed a commercial activity as every farmer had the expectation of selling their principal crops, but more than that, farmers farmed in "the America where dreams were linked with land, where hope was defined by the shape of clouds and the smell of rain in the wind," as environmental historian T. H. Watkins wrote in *The Hungry Years,* his 1999 book about the Great Depression.[10]

It's worth taking a moment to appreciate the dominance of farming in American life. The country's dreams historically were intricately interwoven with farm life. In 1840, 70% of the workforce

9 U.S. Department of the Treasury, *IRS Historical Fact Book: A Chronology 1646-1992,* p. 249. At its peak in 1991, the IRS had 117,017 employees who were responsible for collecting $1.1 trillion in revenue.) The IRS had 74,454 employees in 2022. Automation improved productivity, but the level of IRS funding has always been polarizing.

10 T. H. Watkins, *The Hungry Years*, Henry Holt and Company, 1999, p. 335.

was engaged in agriculture.[11] But things were changing. According to Watkins, in 1900, more than 41 percent of America's people lived on farms.[12] The U.S. Department of Agriculture's 1930 farm census reported that 24.8% of the total U.S. population of 122,775,046, or 30,445,350 people lived on farms: the farmer, the families of farmers and any hired hands. From this census we know there were 6,288,648 farms in 1930. In contrast, by 2020—when the family farm was increasingly endangered—there were 2 million farms, with less than 2% of the country's population of almost 330 million living on farms. In addition, now almost all farms are incorporated, and it's a good bet that they all file tax returns.

In the 1920s, some farmers had benefitted from the various technological advances that were expanding across the country. As University of North Texas professor Steve Craig described in an article in *Agricultural History*:

> [B]y 1930 over half of farms in the United States had automobiles, about a third had telephones, and smaller percentages had electricity and radio. However, the coming of the Great Depression altered adoption patterns considerably. Throughout the 1930s the percentage of farm homes with automobiles remained flat, while the number with telephones substantially declined. Yet during the same period, the number of rural families owning radios nearly tripled...[13]

By the end of 1930, many farmers, along with many other unincorporated entrepreneurs, had declining incomes. Economic historian Giovanni Federico, author of *Feeding the World: An Economic History of World Agriculture, 1800-2000*, explored in a separate

11 All data from the 1920 or 1930 agriculture census.

12 Watkins (1999), p. 341.

13 Steve Craig, "The More They Listen, the More They Buy" Radio and the Modernizing of Rural America, 1930-1939," *Agricultural History*, Vol. 80, No. 1 (Winter, 2006), p. 2. As a point of interest, radios before electrification were battery-powered.

article the veracity of a long-held view that the condition of farming brought on the Great Depression:

> On the eve of the depression, the condition of American farmers was not terrible, although surely not very good. The 1920s had been quite an eventful decade (to say the least) for them. Farmers had profited handsomely from the war-time boom and were hard hit by the fall in prices. From 1917 to 1921, their real income fell by 55 percent—i.e., as much as from 1929 to 1932. In the 1920s it crawled back, and at the end of the decade it was back to its prewar level. However, farmers had lost ground relative to the rest of the economy and also relative to their own employees. GDP per capita was 30 percent higher than before the war and agricultural wages were some 10 percent higher. This difference with their own employees may have affected the farmers' status and self-perception more than the comparison with far-away city dwellers....[14]

The statistics bear this out. *SOI for 1930* reports, for example, that, of that small number of 9,618 incorporated farms that filed, 5,753 or almost 60% of those returns showed no net income, and another almost 9% filed as inactive corporations with no income data. This picture even for those farmers who took the step to incorporate, though "not terrible" as Federico claims, was "surely not very good."

By year-end 1930, many farms in much of the nation were operating under duress. As Watkins explained it, "In probably no other area of national concern was the difference greater between the theories being shaped into policy in late-night Washington offices and the actual experience of real people suffering the consequences of a dream become nightmare."[15]

---

14 Giovanni Federico, "Not Guilty? Agriculture in the 1920s and the Great Depression," *The Journal of Economic History*, December 2005, Vol. 65, No. 4, p. 962.

15 Watkins (1999), p. 342.

Watkins offered these additional observations about farm life in America and how the demographics had already changed prior to 1930:

> The number of individuals who owned their own farms had declined by nearly half a million between 1910 and 1930, while those who lived on and worked land owned by others—renters, or tenant farmers, as they were called—increased by more than 300,000 in those same twenty years. In the Deep South, tenant farmers and sharecroppers outnumbered farm owners by more than a million, while in California and other parts of the Far West, wage laborers, most of them migrants, accounted for nearly 50 percent of the total farm population of nearly a million. With few exceptions, the remaining family farmers, brutally overworked, their numbers and importance declining, the fate of their farms and families vulnerable to whatever providence might bring them in the way of weather and what politicians and the financial community might bring them in the way of economic insecurity, had little time and less energy to devote to the finer points of democratic tradition.[16]

Perhaps one of those "finer points of democratic tradition" pertained to filing taxes. Regardless, it is worthwhile to look back to the 1920s to see the forces that became the nightmares Watkins spoke of confronting farmers by the end of that decade. We turn to historian John A. Garraty's *The Great Depression* and his informative chapter, "What It Did to Farmers":

> How important the perilous state of agriculture in the late 1920s was in causing the Great Depression is a subject of some debate. But it is beyond dispute that agriculture

16 Ibid., pp. 341-342.

was generally depressed in those years. Between 1925 and 1929, nearly every agricultural commodity traded in world markets fell in price. Enormous stocks of grain, coffee, tea, cotton, and other crops piled up in warehouses and elevators. As a result, farmers by the millions suffered heavy losses.[17]

The Debt Factor for Farmers

Garraty's reference to these losses comports with many Great Depression scholars who attributed agriculture's condition to farm indebtedness incurred during World War I in order to expand acreage and output to feed Europe. But then, as stated earlier, American farmers failed to cut back on planting once European farmers were able to grow crops again. Moreover, comparisons between farming in 1920 and in 1930 highlight the role that debt continued to play.

Fortunately, given the scant input from the IRS, we have other governmental data to draw from to get a fuller picture of the farm economy. We have mentioned data from the agricultural census. Every ten years from 1840 to 1920, then every five years after that, the National Agriculture Statistics Service of the U.S. Department of Agriculture conducted special censuses under the auspices of the Bureau of the Census in the Department of Commerce. (In June 1929, Congress called for a census of agriculture to take place on April 1, 1930, along with the general census.) These agricultural censuses, described as "a complete count of U.S. farms and ranches and the people who operate them," looked "at land use and ownership, operator characteristics, production practices, income and expenditures, and many other areas."[18] This source seemed promising.

The Introduction to the first post-World War I census report stated, "In 1920, six principal causes were offered to explain the decrease in number of farms between 1910 and 1920." These causes were:

---

17 John Garraty, *The Great Depression*, Anchor Book Doubleday, 1987, p. 52.

18 https://agcensus.library.cornell.edu/census_year/1930-census/

• *scarcity of labor*: Farm labor which was difficult to secure and expensive in 1920, though it would become fairly plentiful and reasonably cheap in 1930 and beyond.

• *consolidation of farms*: While there was a decrease in the number of farms, there was an actual increase in the average acreage of farms. This was closely related to the increased use of improved heavy farm machinery.

• *oil and mining development*: The development of new oil fields and mining areas resulted in reduction of farms in such areas, as in the new oil sections of Oklahoma, Louisiana, and Texas.

• *extension of city areas*: The growth of cities required land formerly devoted to farms.

• *abandonment of low-grade farms*: The rural farm population decreased by approximately 1,200,000 (425,000 in Georgia and South Carolina alone).

• *cotton boll weevil making cotton farming unprofitable*: Between 1920 and 1930, following the invasion of the weevil, there was a decrease in Georgia of about 55,000 farms due almost exclusively to this cause, and in South Carolina of about 34,000 farms due primarily to this cause.[19]

It is easy to understand why the condition of farmers in many locations became widely known by city and town folk alike as being serious, whether or not that opinion had been influenced by, as Federico wrote, "disadvantaged farmers [who] complained loudly, and their plight looms large in the traditional account of the crisis."[20]

---

19 Census Bureau (1931), pp.11-12.

20 Federico (2005), p. 962.

The 1920s, pre-Crash, may have been booming for many in urban areas, but the decade did not shorten the list of issues farmers were dealing with, even before "dust bowl" conditions.

Why wasn't bankruptcy risk on the list of issues? Contrary to the conventional wisdom, the number of farmers who filed for bankruptcy, relative to how many millions of farms there were, was remarkably low throughout the 1920s and even during the entire Great Depression. According to a Department of Agriculture historical report, in 1920, 997 farmers filed for bankruptcy, the lowest level since 1913. Throughout the 1920s, filings gradually increased to a high of 7,872 in 1925, gradually declined to 4,464 in 1930 and further to 4,025 in 1931 before heading up slightly until 1935.[21] Even in the mid-1920s, bankruptcy filings per 10,000 farms were in the 13.5 range. In 1930, the figure was 8.44. The reality, as the report authors wrote in their Summary, confirmed the insignificance of bankruptcies compared with other factors:

> A comparison of historic data indicates that bankruptcy has played only a small role in the over-all decline in farm numbers over the past 70 years....There were 51,863 farm bankruptcies...filed during 1920-29, as the farm economy collapsed following the economic boom induced by World War I, up from 12,001 for the 1910-19 decade. There were 37,814 farmer bankruptcies filed from 1930-39 during the Great Depression.[22]

With farm bankruptcy filings dismissed as playing only a minor role among farmers' woes, we flash forward to June 1937, when the

---

21 Jerome M. Stam and Bruce L. Dixon, U.S. Department of Agriculture, Economic Research Service, "Farmer Bankruptcies and Farm Exits in the United States, 1899-2002," March 2004, p. 33. Statistics excluded farmers who were sharecroppers.

22 Ibid.

Division of Social Research in the Works Progress Administration (WPA) under the administration of Harry Hopkins published a research monograph called *Farmers on Relief and Rehabilitation*. The report's Letter of Transmittal gave a dismal summation of the state of agriculture in the U.S. in the Depression years. Adding to the reasons from the Agriculture Census for the sorry state of farming was the WPA's grim list of problems already confronting farmers at the end of the 1920s that may well have contributed to the low farmer tax return filing rate in 1930. The WPA report emphasized the fact that the depression in agriculture began long before 1929 and that the distress of the early 1930s "merely accentuated farm problems of long standing." Chief among these problems were rural birth rates burdening family and work life on farms and creating inheritance issues as multiple heirs inherited plots too small for profitable farming. There were submarginal farmlands, including land over-farmed and contending with soil erosion that would contribute to the Dust Bowl of the 1930s. More farms were run by tenants rather than by owners. Most significantly, debt burdened many farmers, including those leading to foreclosures. Each of these problems merited serious attention, which disgruntled farmers let their elected representatives know. However, governmental efforts to help farmers were spotty at best in the early 1930s because, as historian John Garraty offered, "of [Hoover's] distaste for government interference in the marketing of goods. He believed that the federal government should help farmers to help themselves, not treat them as some special type of ideal citizen."[23] Ironically, one thing farmers could have done to help themselves would have been to cut back on growing, but they evidently did not do this in significant numbers.[24]

23 Garraty (1987), p. 57.

24 Besta Asch and A. R. Mangus, *Farmers on Relief and Rehabilitation*, Research Monograph VIII, Works Progress Administration, Division of Social Research, 1937, p. iii.

Farm Indebtedness Adds to the Woes of Farming

Due to the low farmer filing numbers, the IRS archives did not record a factor impacting farmers that other sources clearly showed—debt. For many farmers, like many of their fellow Americans, indebtedness was a major dampener and weighed heavily. While we found no evidence that farmers were speculating in the stock market, many had mortgaged their farms to acquire additional land during World War I. According to Federico, some farmers speculated on purebred livestock, while others borrowed to purchase tractors and other farm equipment to improve productivity.[25]

For many farmers, not unlike their urban and suburban neighbors, debt service obligations came to govern their purchasing decisions. Focusing primarily on the Corn Belt states, University of Texas, Austin history professor Sally H. Clarke explored issues farmers in those states faced in 1930. [26] In a 1991 article in the *Journal of Economic History*, Clarke looked in particular at the factors that impacted whether or not a farmer chose to purchase a tractor between 1920-1940.[27] Regardless of the positive impact a tractor would have on farm productivity, current indebtedness played a big role in that decision.[28] Clarke's research showed that for farmers who carried debt from World War I land purchases, the need for cash to carry that debt, much less to pay the loan off, deterred them from

25 Federico (2005), p. 965. Farmers borrowed mostly from local banks, and this debt load came to put stress on those banks as we have covered elsewhere.

26 The Corn Belt included farms in many states, but the focus of Clarke's research was Illinois, Indiana, Iowa, Missouri and Ohio.

27 Sally H. Clarke, "New Deal Regulation and the Revolution in American Farm Productivity: A Case Study of the Diffusion of the Tractor in the Corn Belt, 1920-1940, *The Journal of Economic History*, March 1991, Vol. 51, No. 1, pp. 101-123.

28 The extent of Clarke's careful research into farm productivity measures is beyond the scope of this work. Suffice it to say, Clarke was thorough and used familiar data sources (including Census Bureau and USDA) and much prior work by other academics. Clarke also observed that the older the farmer, the less likely he was to buy a tractor.

purchasing a tractor— even, or especially, on time. Land prices had begun to fall in 1922 and continued to fall throughout the 1930s, thus raising their debt-to-land ratio. Using the 1930 Census for her data, Clarke observed the unevenness of debt burdens among the 6.3 million farmers:

> The burden of debts...was not shared equally among farmers but instead affected a significant minority. As of 1920, 60 percent of owner-operator farmers carried no debts; this figure slipped to 55 percent by 1929....But a significant number, perhaps one-third of indebted farmers, were saddled with large debts relative to their assets. Many of these farmers would eventually fail in the Great Depression.[29]

Clarke summed up her research as to farmers' conservative financial behavior:

> [O]n the eve of the Great Depression farmers had contended with two financial barriers to investment [in a tractor]. First, where farmers were prone to favoring resources that saved cash, the quantitative tests indicated that as their cash income shrank, proportionally fewer farmers invested in tractors. Second, quantitative tests reflected the consequences of the credit crisis in which the lag in the tractor's adoption varied systematically with the ratio of debts to land values or the percentage of farmers who were mortgaged....[I]t is noteworthy that these financial variables, especially the cash margin and indebtedness, were statistically significant.

After 1929 the market for corn collapsed; by 1932 corn prices averaged just a third of their 1929 level. Farmers immediately curtailed investments. Sales of tractors dropped slightly from 1929 to 1930, then skidded 50 percent to

29 Clarke (1991), p. 110.

> 58,000 units in 1931, and another 57% to just 25,000 in 1932 and 1933. Farmers also fell behind in their debt payments, prompting creditors to foreclose. Foreclosures nearly tripled from 1929 to 1933.[30]

Although there was much about the average farmer's life that was different from life in urban environments, farmers had, like so many other Americans, speculated by taking on debt, whether it was for more land, a tractor or a purebred bull. We might, in fact, add farmers to our cast of characters of Repentant Ex-Speculators. They simply had speculated on livestock rather than shares of stocks.

The USDA's Quinquennial 1930 Census Proves Revealing

In April 1930, the U. S. Department of Agriculture conducted its quinquennial census of farms across the country. The scale of this operation was impressive. The directive for the census and the enumerators who conducted it was straightforward: "[E]ach enumerator must personally visit each dwelling in his subdivision and secure each and every item of information required" on the date of the census, April 1, 1930, so that, "All farm information was secured by a personal interview with the farmer, a member of his family, or other responsible individual." In other words, every farmer in America was to be personally visited on April 1, 1930, an accomplishment that is hard to visualize. In point of fact, the notes accompanying the 1930 Census of Agriculture report did include this curiously insightful caveat: "The omissions or mistakes of the enumerator, or misunderstanding on the part of the farmer or unwillingness to answer certain questions on debts, taxes, or other personal matters,

30 Ibid., pp. 114-5. Statistics on tractor sales are U.S. totals.

add to the list of unsatisfactory returns due to human frailties."[31] Such frailties might also have applied to a farmer's failure to file a tax return. Nonetheless, the agricultural censuses enumerated uniquely valuable information about America's farms.

The 1930 census data confirm that not only was the U.S. farm population gradually declining but the average value of farms was also declining—unless the property had certain advantages due to location (near urban area), soil quality, weather conditions, licensing of oil, gas or mineral rights or simply luck. In addition, farmers' equity was declining and, while farm debt went down a little, the loss in farm value for the indebted still meant the debt-to-equity ratio was increasing.

Comparing the 1920 and 1930 agricultural census reports offered some overall data about declining farm value, declining farmers' equity and farm indebtedness. Average farm value January 1, 1920 was $80,327. A decade later, farm value had declined -27.4% to $58,378 only to decline another -7.3% by January 1, 1931. Farmers' equity had a similar downward trajectory. It was down -31.8% from January 1, 1920, to January 1, 1930 and another -8% to January 1, 1931 ($68,006 to $40,879). Although farm indebtedness declined over the same eleven-year period, the debt-to-equity ratio increased as farm value declined.

With the ongoing decrease in corn and other commodities prices, farm revenues were also dropping. In 1920 cash receipts for American farmers were $12,608 million. By 1930 cash revenues dropped over 28% to $9,021 million. One data source, the Bureau of Agricultural Economics, reported that realized net income of farm operations declined -39% from $7,126 million in 1920 to $4,340 million in 1930, well before the full effects of the Depression. Shockingly, average realized net income of farm operators dropped -53% over the decade, from $1,298 per farm to $688 per farm.

---

31 *1930 Census of Agriculture*, p. 11.

One Nebraska Farmer's Story

Oral histories can provide rich anecdotal evidence of nationwide issues by putting a human face on the statistical story of farming at this time. In 2003, for instance, Nebraska writer Bill Ganzel posted "One Farmer's 1930s Balance Sheet" on a website of local history called lhf.org. In his post, we caught a glimpse of farm life during two years in particular—1928 and 1932—as seen through the eyes of farmer Otto Opitz who kept carefully detailed account books (laudable, if rudimentary by accounting standards) that his family held onto and then shared.[32] For impact, we have recreated his entries here as Table 13.1.

Table 13.1			
Farmer Otto Opitz's Balance Sheet, 1928 and 1932			
1928 Income		1932 Income	
Cream sales for full year	$ 105.90	Cream sales for full year	$ 6.45
Egg sales for full year	161.07	Egg sales for full year	1.85
Wheat, in March sold 614 bushels @ $1.21/bu. & Sept. 205 bu @ .84/bu.	920.24	Wheat, in May sold 226 bushels @ $.42/bu.	68.75
Corn, in August sold 435.5 bushels @ .83/bu.	361.80	Corn, in August sold 901 bushels @ .25 and .26/bu.	231.50
Livestock, throughout the year he sold a steer, 26 hogs, an "old cow" and bull calf.	608.74	Livestock, in July he sold one bull	25.00
"Western land rent" on wheat land Otto owned near Hayes Center, Nebraska, in Dec.	238.50	"Western land rent" in March	68.75
Total	$ 2,290.35	Total	$ 402.30
1928 Major farm expenses		1932 Major farm expenses	
Total taxes on "Home Place," Hayes Co. land, & personal property.	$ 260.42	Total taxes on Hayes Co. land, "town property," and home place.	$ 137.97
Equipment, in Feb. a wagon and "evener" probably a grader.	52.00	Two teams of horses, in Jan., plus harness and "covers."	227.00
In Aug. "New Whippet car."	576.00	In Aug. "Paid Machinery Note, and on Horse Note."	196.75
In July, threshing bill	35.70	(No threshing bill indicated.)	
Various expenses including posts, woven wire, barrel, coal tar, railroad fares and roofing	202.64	In April, "Lister Share" (plow) from Montgomery Ward catalog	2.73
Total	$ 1,126.76	Total	$ 564.45

Source: *LivingHistoryFarm.org*, Bill Ganzel, 2003.

It is apparent in Opitz's accounts that farm life went from comfortable to very tight over the four years. In 1928, Opitz earned $2,500; by 1933, his income dropped to $430, *before* costs. Ganzel stated that there were three months in 1932 when Opitz earned no

32 Bill Ganzel, "One Farmer's 1930s Balance Sheet," http://lhf.org.

income. By 1932, cash was scarce and carefully reserved to pay real estate taxes or a "machinery note" and a "horse note." The Opitz farm was doing all it could to keep up with repaying its debts.

No Returns? No Repercussions

Because not filing income tax returns bears considerable consequences today, it is a remarkable fact that millions of America's farmers fell through the cracks of accountability to the federal government via the tax return in 1930. But from all our research, we came to sympathize with those millions of farmers who faced such intractable, unpredictable and difficult forces of both nature and markets and who, with one or likely more of those natural and market factors dogging them daily, chose not to bother filing their taxes. It is not difficult to imagine that, along with farmers' supporters in Congress, those employed at all levels of the IRS may, in point of fact, have been empathetic towards farmers as a group. Might there have been an unofficial position that farmers, though technically unincorporated businesses, wouldn't suffer consequences for not filing? Research neither supported nor contradicted such imaginings.

How much income tax revenue from farms actually failed to be collected for 1930? Upon examining data from the USDA Census of 1930, *SOI for 1930* and *SOI for 1929*, we concluded that certainly very little tax revenue was lost. In this era before monoculture, by all accounts most farms were fairly self-contained economic units. Farms grew enough diverse produce to feed the farm family and any farmhands. Livestock and poultry provided milk, meat and eggs. Barter was common, either between farmers or between farmers and tradesmen or professionals like doctors. It was common for farms to be richer than many urbanites and even than nearby town dwellers in the essentials, like food, but most farmers were definitely cash poor. As any revenues went right back into the farm, their net cash income, as with farmer Opitz, was low, and, therefore, would not have been taxed, if a tax return had even been filed.

Our speculations in this chapter as to why farmers didn't file add a curious side story to our generally data-rich narrative, though it is clear that by 1930, despite their failure to file tax returns which put them out of range of IRS statisticians, America's farmers shared the same compelling burden of indebtedness as so many other Americans. This burden led to careful spending decisions. But when debt obligations combined with declines in revenue from their farming activities and in the value of their assets, particularly land, the downturn for farmers, in particular, had begun well in advance of the rest of the country.

The next chapter turns to 1931, a full year of deflation that left fewer and fewer Americans unaffected.

CHAPTER 14

An Overview of 1931 in the U.S. Repayments of Over-Indebtedness Accelerate

As with prior chapters, the overall intent of this last narrative chapter of *The Deflation of 1930* is to offer detailed explanations, based on thorough and careful analysis of statistics from reliable sources using widely accepted financial analysis techniques— what we might call data forensics or forensic financial management. As our focus in this chapter shifts to 1931, we show how weaknesses throughout the economy became even more prevalent, persistent and, in fact, growing, with debt repayment accelerating, adding to, and even determining the downward trajectory.

The year 1931 further confirmed the power and direction of the dynamics that developed following the Crash in late-autumn 1929, as conditions deteriorated and solutions continued to elude those who were in positions to tackle them. Seeing no end in sight, without any form of governmental safety net and so literally left to their own devices, individuals did what they could to deal with their own constraints, be they unemployment, underemployment and, likely, onerous debt obligations. Increasingly, the personal plight of one individual was common to neighbors, reflecting how local enterprises that provided jobs were doing, how their community was doing, and so, too, the nation, as Irving Fisher's theory of over-indebtedness played itself out daily in the real lives of millions of Americans.

To assess the nation's true condition in both the business world and among still-indebted households in 1931, we turned to the aggregate corporate balance sheets found in the IRS archives once again to provide us with the necessary statistical insights.

Could Americans Tighten Their Belts Even More?

In this volume's Introduction, we referred to Gilbert Seldes' description of the tenor of the times as having the "general attitude which is called 'deflation.'" What behaviors did that attitude imply for the average American whose understanding about deflation derived, not from an academic approach, but rather from their own situation within their neighborhood, their town, their state? The well-understood idiom "tighten our belts" applied even more in 1931 to individual actions, and by year end, many people, by punching new holes in their fraying belts, had reduced their consumption spending even further — with the primary objective of continuing to pay off their debts to banks and other corporations for obligations taken on during better days. As in 1930, those many autonomous individual decisions led to further slowdowns in most manufacturing sectors and in most commodity sales, added to unemployment, as well as the growing deflation and shrinkage of the money supply. The average American could not have been expected to understand that their autonomous actions, although seeming to be beneficial to their family situation, in aggregate made the situation worse, and deflation and what it caused became a millstone around everyone's neck.

The Painful Costs of Deflation: Repaying Prior Debt with Ever Harder-to-Earn Dollars

Deflation, so important in the developing Depression period, has been a far rarer condition in our country's recent history than inflation, so we likely have a less clear idea of what it means for deflation to become an economy-wide condition and a prevailing attitude, as Seldes described it. From 1929 onward, however, it impacted individuals and businesses profoundly. The impact of deflation depended on whether an entity (corporate or individual) owed money or was owed money, as well as on whether an entity had cash or needed cash and, like most, had to earn it in order to repay debt. As the 1931 diary entries by Youngstown, Ohio, attorney Ben Roth will show, in Roth's world, cash was scarce, and those few with cash were able to buy, for instance, real estate at greatly reduced, post-Crash prices. Indeed, for those enviable few with cash, deflation brought an expanded ability to purchase more with less because prices for goods and services had declined. Growing debt repayment by individuals to corporations (including banks) in the deflationary environment of the early 1930s affected both those who were also still in the position to buy and those who increasingly were not. Our emphasis here is on deflation's impact on the latter.

As we have seen, deflation began in late 1929 and accelerated throughout 1930. In 1931, it accelerated, or worsened, further, raising the real cost of repaying debt when determined debtors faced even greater obstacles to repayment because of the swelling dollar and shrinking incomes. Deflation—and, equally important, the expectation of further deflation—heightened the incentive for debtors to repay debt faster as the cost of that debt increased.

Deflation essentially means falling prices, and two price indices, the Wholesale Price Index, most relevant to corporations, and the Consumer Price Index, most relevant to individuals, showed deflation's impact on both segments. The WPI relates, generally speaking, to goods and services businesses buy to finish the products they sell to customers. For example, sparkplugs go into automobiles, copper goes into electrical wiring and electrical power drives machinery. The CPI relates to goods and services consumers buy. Examples include milk, clothing and electrical power that illuminates homes and keeps hot water warm. On the corporate side, the WPI was deflation's indicator. Measured at 93.3 in December 1929, it plunged -14.7% to 79.6 in December 1930. In the last two months of 1930 alone, the WPI fell 1.9%. By December 1931, it had further dropped to 68.6. 1

1 *HSUS 1789-1945*, p. 344.

Debt repayments were fixed monthly amounts determined at the time of purchase. So, every month the same amount was due, but the dollars to repay that debt had required more work time than when the loan agreement was signed. As the real worth of the dollar swelled, by comparison with the end of 1929, a dollar spent repaying debt in December 1930 had grown to cost the equivalent of $1.17 in December 1930 dollars and by the end of 1931, the cost of repaying that debt was $1.36 in 1931 dollars, having risen even further and faster as the burden of the Great Depression progressed. Corporations (including banks) who were creditors, were being repaid in increasingly more expensive, and valuable, deflation-period dollars.t Meanwhile, corporations who were debtors were repaying debts with cash that had taken more revenue to make as prices dropped and demand softened. Of course, as the dollar was worth more in what it could buy, creditors of any kind—when they could collect—were the winners.

Table 14.Deflation

Consumer Price Index: All Urban Consumers 1931

Monthly Percentage Change, Annualized

(% percent)

Jan	Feb	Mar	Apr	May	Jun	Jul	Aug	Sep	Oct	Nov	Dec
-7.0	-7.6	-7.7	-8.8	-9.5	-10.1	-9.0	-8.5	-9.6	-9.7	-10.4	-9.3

Wholesale Prices for the United States 1931

Monthly Percentage Change, Annualized

(% percent)

Jan	Feb	Mar	Apr	May	Jun	Jul	Aug	Sep	Oct	Nov	Dec
-15.4	-16.0	-15.6	-17.0	-17.5	-16.8	-14.5	-14.3	-15.6	-15.2	-13.7	-13.6

Source: (CPI): Bureau of Labor Statistics (BLS), all items in U.S city average, 1913-2017. (WPI): Index of Wholesale Prices for the United States, Federal Reserve Bank of St. Louis, Economic Research Division, 1913-1968.

The Consumer Price Index or CPI also impacted the most indebted individuals, such as our class of Repentant Ex-Speculators (post-Crash) who had visualized getting rich in pre-Crash times. Table 14.Deflation, (above) when compared with Table 8.1 (page 232), shows that deflation in the CPI worsened from -6.4% in December 1930 to -7.0% in January 1931, and deflation in the WPI worsened from -14.7% in December 1930 to -15.4% in January 1931. CPI then rose some over the year, still ending 1931 at -9.3%. The WPI mostly fell over 1931, ending down -13.6% in December 1931. Neither was encouraging news.

The Great Depression: A Diary by Youngstown Attorney Benjamin Roth

The publication, during the Great Recession year of 2009, of *The Great Depression: A Diary* by Youngstown attorney Benjamin Roth (1894-1978) was timely. His son, attorney Daniel B. Roth, whose family had retained the diary, got it into the capable hands of *Slate* magazine business and finance website editor James Ledbetter who, particularly at a time when parallels to the Great Depression were frequently made, immediately sensed the diary's value. As he wrote in the book's Introduction, "Here is history told from the point of view of the Depression's dramatically affected, but not its thoroughly trampled." [2]

As one of the dramatically affected but not thoroughly trampled, Benjamin Roth began his journal on June 5, 1931, when he wrote the following observation about the "great school of experience" the times afforded him:

> For the first time in my personal business life I am witnessing a major financial crisis. I am anxious to learn the lessons of this depression. To the man past middle life it spells tragedy and disaster but to those of us in the middle thirties it may be a great school of experience out of which some worthwhile lessons may be salvaged.

2 Benjamin Roth, *The Great Depression: A Diary,* PublicAffairs (Perseus Books Group), 2009, various pp 1-46 . Introduction by James Ledbetter, editor, p. xxi. Rather than footnote each quote, all diary entries appear from pages 1-46, when Roth's 1931 entries ended.

With this thought in mind I am going to write down brief accounts of developments as they occur from time to time.

While Roth's diary covers a decade, we chose to quote from what he wrote in 1931, our year of focus in this volume's final chapter. To bring an authentic, contemporary voice into our data-dominant discussion, we place thematically-linked selections from his entries into three places in this chapter, beginning with the following:

- August 9: Most professional men for the past two years have been living on money borrowed on insurance policies, etc. The only work that comes in now are impossible collections on a contingent fee basis. Everybody is digging up old claims and trying to realize on them. Tempers are short and people are distrustful and suspicious. There is nothing to do but work harder for less money and cut expenses to the bone.

- August 18: There is no money in circulation and all business is at a standstill.

- September 1: Prices are falling rapidly. The 1929 dollar buys $1.40 in merchandise….It is almost bad taste to give a big party or to drive a new car.

- October 6: Stocks have been going down, down, down for over a month now. The latest explanation is that English investors are selling their U.S. investments in order to get U.S. dollars which are worth about 25% more in depreciated English currency.

- December 30: Stocks and bonds are going down. Even U.S. gov'ts are selling as low as 82.

Deflation's Impact on Our Cast of Characters

In 1931, three of our Cast of Characters were most affected in terms of deflationary Depression-era financial realities.

Corporate Financial Executives. This group was tuned into the implications of deflation. By 1931, many Corporate Financial Executives, seeking cash and reduced fixed costs, were anxiously identifying and selling, if they could, idle or unnecessary corporate assets, despite having to do so at distressed sale prices. Executives could use write-offs to reduce corporate taxes. They also did stock buy-backs at low per share prices. This enabled them to maintain dividends by spreading dividends over fewer outstanding shares. This strategy also made earnings-per-share statistics look more favorable.

Repentant Ex-Speculators (post-Crash). By mid-1930 the ranks of Repentant Ex-Speculators had grown as Noyes's "professionals" and Wigmore's "smart money" lost their bets when the Little Bull Market dropped significantly in May then ended in June. Recognizing as they did that the real cost of repaying loans was rising in 1931, Repentant Ex-Speculators (post-Crash) were even more motivated to get out of debt as fast as possible. For some this was an increasingly humiliating experience. Bernard Baruch wrote of the sad state of old friends, wiped out in the Crash, soliciting ever smaller amounts of money as their prospects dwindled in the early 1930s.

Debtors (in general). Along with monthly statements of amounts due from bankers, finance companies, mortgage lenders and even loan sharks if things had gotten really bad, many debtors were starting to receive high-pressure dunning letters in 1931 or even house calls demanding payments. Like Repentant Ex-Speculators, Debtors (in general) were subject to rising real costs of debts being repaid with more costly dollars. Furthermore, repayment terms bore high fixed interest rates established in earlier, more prosperous times. In this era of rising unemployment, it became frequent practice for debtors to develop strategies to keep the bill collector from the door. One strategy was to develop plans for borrowing money from second lenders to pay off first lenders or even third lenders to pay off second lenders. Others were on a constant and dizzying carousel of rotating whom they made payments to. For many debtors, the pressure only intensified in 1931 as income dropped or even stopped.

We now return to the view of 1931 from the standpoint of corporate balance sheets. Despite falling revenue as sales declined, companies also received revenue from debt repayments, some just from other corporations, some from individuals and some from both.

U.S. Corporate Sources and Uses of Funds in 1931

Table 14.1, (following page) a Sources and Uses of Funds Analysis for 1931 based on the Aggregate Corporate Balance Sheets reported in the IRS's *Statistics of Income for 1930* and *for 1931,* enables us to identify in what direction each asset and liability class changed over the course of 1931 and by how much.[3] The data show that, as conditions deteriorated, companies, attempting to keep their doors open, were raising operating funds by "liquidating"—i.e., selling—whatever they could. At the top of the list of liquid assets is, of course, cash and inventory. These are relatively tangible assets that corporations usually have control over. For example, corporations can reduce their cash by spending it which, in 1931 they did. The aggregate quantity of cash that corporations held dropped 24.4% or -$5,132 million.

Corporations can reduce the aggregate value of their inventories by cutting production and selling those inventories rather than investing in making new goods. In 1931, the aggregate value of inventory held by corporations dropped -19.3% or -$3,632 million. Elsewhere on their balance sheets, they can raise operating funds by selling—if possible—assets such as "excess" land, redundant facilities, idle equipment, etc.

By contrast, most corporations had much less control over

3 *SOI for 1929*, p. 25: *SOI for 1930*, p.27.

Table 14.1			
1931 Aggregate U.S. Corporate Sources & Uses of Funds ($ million)			
Assets:	1930	1931	Difference
Cash	21,012	15,880	-5,132
Notes & accounts rec.	59,675	48,667	-11,008
Inventory	18,771	15,140	-3,632
Tax exempts	10,228	10,667	439
Investments other	83,809	74,305	-9,504
Capital assets	120,994	115,303	-5,692
Miscellaneous	19,511	16,534	-2,977
Total assets	334,002	296,497	-37,505
Liabilities:			
Notes & accounts pay.	26,870	23,251	-3,618
Bonded debt & mortgages	50,282	48,101	-2,181
Miscellaneous	95,768	81,882	-13,887
Capital stock:			
Preferred	19,117	19,117	0
Common	87,067	79,794	-7,273
Total capital stock	106,184	98,911	-7,273
Surplus	61,632	51,976	-9,656
Less deficit	6,734	7,624	890
Net surplus	54,898	44,352	-10,546
Total liabilities	334,002	296,497	-37,505

Source: *SOI for 1930 & 31*: 1930, p.27, 1931, p.30.

Notes and accounts receivable. It is certainly true that banks call loans, thus exercising what looks like a measure of control over this category of assets. But the Great Depression was a time when we have found little or no evidence that banks were calling loans. Rather, the evidence we have found is that debtors were choosing to repay their bank loans as fast as they could. In 1931, the category Notes and accounts payable of corporations (including banks) declined

-$11,008 million, meaning that parties who were not corporations repaid 18.4% of the debts they owed corporations at the end of 1930. (Given the tenor of the times we are confident that few banks and other corporations "forgave" debtors in 1931 in any material way by writing them off.)

The dramatic funds flows revealed in the numbers in Table 14.1 (opposite)— sources and uses using balance sheets reflecting profits and losses—evidence the very real struggles of America's corporations (including banks) to keep their heads above water in order to survive the depression conditions and to emerge, sometime in the future—hopefully— into prosperity once more.

U.S. Corporations Shrank in 1931 as Aggregate Total Assets and Liabilities Dropped 11.2%.

The most startling and dramatic statistics shown in Table 14.1 are the differences between the Total Assets and Total Liabilities for 1930 and 1931 (and, it is in the nature of balance sheets that these two sums are the same): $296,497 million in 1931, down 11.2% or -$37,505 million from $334,002 million in 1930.

We can wrap our minds around the magnitude of this shrinkage over one year by comparing it with the fall in 1931 GNP. The -$37,505 loss in 1931caused by the shrinkage of aggregate corporate Total assets and liabilities equaled *-49.3% of the total GNP of 1931 of $76,073 million.* With Total assets and liabilities of unincorporated business accounted for approximately 11.15%, or -$4,182 million, of total *corporate* shrinkage, the aggregate decline of American business (including banks) in 1931 rose to *-54.8% of that year's GNP.*

A sizeable portion of these declines was due to deflation. Table 2.1B (page 53) is perhaps the best table to show the impact of deflation in any given year of the Great Depression. Each of the three measures of price changes reflects a different "market basket" of goods and services available for purchase in the year under consideration. We are familiar with the WPI and CPI, and the GNP deflator relates to components of Gross National Product.

To evaluate the impact of deflation on the changes of Total assets and liabilities of American businesses, the WPI shows a -15.5% decline, nearly 25% of the shrinkage of Total assets and liabilities of American businesses in 1931. However, using the GNP deflator, -11.5% approaches one fifth of the decline in the value of American business, a number greater than -$8 billion.

Comparing Sources and Uses Table for 1931 with 1930

The sources and uses table for 1931, Table 14.1, looks quite different from the 1930 corresponding table in Chapter 5, Table 5.1 (page 139). In 1930, most line items slowly declined. Most important, Total assets and liabilities dropped -0.5% or -$1,776 million from 1929. By contrast, in 1931, as we saw, virtually all line items declined from 1930 by -11.2%, or -$37,505 million. A future volume of *The Great Deleverage Series*, will show what a hard year 1931 was for corporations, banks, sole proprietorships and certainly workers and their families.

As to the national economy, today we have difficulty imagining not having ready access to a considered view of the size of the United States economy or its directionality, and we expect, even demand, indicators in as current time as possible for decision-making. Are things going up or down? Expanding or contracting? But as we know, in 1931 (or earlier) there was no such measurement as Gross National (now Domestic) Product. However, although Depression-era contemporaries did not have such data to assess and possibly help formulate policy, ever since GNP was conceived of and calculated years later by Stanley Kuznets and NIPA, we know that the 1930 Gross National Product was $90.7 billion, down -12.3% from $103.4 billion in 1929. GNP for 1931 shrank another -16.1% to $76.1 billion.

In Chapter 5, our analysis showed that in 1930, over $7 billion of Notes and accounts receivable was repaid by all types of borrowers—individuals; other corporations; Federal, state, and local governments; even foreign entities—to lender corporations (including banks). That $7 billion in repayments comprised 7.9% of 1930 GNP.

In 1931, as Table 14.1 shows, debtors, corporate as well as individual, repaid the remarkable *additional sum of $11 billion* in Notes and accounts receivable to lender corporations (including banks). Debts repaid to corporate lenders in 1931 equaled 14.5% of GNP, a 54.9% increase from 1930 to 1931 and a staggering detour of cash away from consumption.

The data show unambiguously that in the U.S. in 1931, most corporate financial executives, business owners dealing with ever slower sales or financially strapped homeowners, became increasingly determined in their attempts to repay debt. Indeed, as Seldes said, the "general attitude which is called 'deflation'" changed behavior.

What Portion of the $11 Billion Was Repaid to Banks in 1931?

We have kept up the reminder that corporations also included banks, not just manufacturers or service providers, because of the banks' critical and unique impact on the size of the money supply through lending and the mechanism of the bank multiplier effect. Our objective now is to determine how much of the $11 billion repayment in 1931 was made to banks, because that measure goes a long way towards explaining what was going on in the banking sector where the money supply was shrinking. As we reported in Chapter 5, bank loan repayments to All (Fed) Member Banks commenced in the *first quarter* of 1930 with a net repayment of $1,031 million in loans, causing a -4.3% decline in loan volume. Further, over the full year 1930, while All Member Banks were repaid 32% or $2,280 million of all notes and accounts receivable that were repaid, the broader category of All Commercial Banks accounted for 55% of the $7,135 million in notes and accounts receivable repaid. It is clear borrowers were paying down loans and not taking out new loans.

Beyond that, we ask if banks tightening lending standards and not lending to weakened borrowers? Certainly we found evidence of foreclosures by mortgagees in 1930, but we also found mortgagees were often willing to continue past-due mortgages in open status rather than foreclose and have to deal with more property ownership. These demand-and-supply factors for credit, contributed to a much weaker bottom line for the banks as they entered 1931, especially banks with lending concentrated in troubled business segments such as farming.

Table 14.2 (opposite) shows the corresponding statistics on bank loan repayments for 1931. All Commercial Banks accounted for 62% or $6.8 billion of the $11 billion in notes and accounts receivable repaid in 1931, a significant 73% greater than the $3.9 billion in loan repayments made in 1930. As for the subsector of All Member Banks, in 1931, they were repaid 42% or $4.6 billion of the $11 billion, and 15.2% more than the $3.9 billion in repayments to All Commercial Banks in 1930. This was, indeed, the "great contraction" in banking that Friedman and Schwartz focused on in *Monetary History*, and the contraction only grew. With regards to the timing of repayments over 1931, we found mid-year statistics indicating a rising trend in repayments for All Commercial Banks from 42.1% of the $11 billion total over the first half of 1931 to 57.9% over the second half. Similarly, All Member Banks received 44.5% of repayments over the first half and 55.5% over the second half.

We turn from this grim picture to the other component of notes and accounts receivables, to find out what was going on in the non-banking portion of the corporate world as corporations did business with each other.

Table 14.2 **Spreading the Repayments of $11,008 Million Over 1931 on the Basis of Bank Loan Repayments** ($ million)				
All comercial banks				
	Total loans	Change in loans	Period %	Change in notes & accounts receivable
12/31/30	32,034			
6/30/31	29,166	-2,868	42.1%	-4,634
12/31/31	25,226	-3,940	57.9%	-6,374
Total Change	-6,808	-6,808	100.0%	-11,008
All member banks				
	Total loans	Change in loans	Period %	Change in notes & accounts receivable
12/31/30	23,870			
3/25/31	22,840	-1,030	22.3%	-2,455
6/30/31	21,816	-1,024	22.2%	-2,444
9/29/31	20,874	-942	20.4%	-2,246
12/31/31	19,261	-1,613	35.1%	-3,863
Total Change	-4,609	-4,609	100.0%	-11,008

Source: *BMS*, pp.19 & 74.

The Great Depression: A Diary by Youngstown Attorney Benjamin Roth (continued)

• July 30: "The trouble is that nobody has any money. On account of numerous bank failures, the few people who have money are afraid to spend it and are buying government securities. From the extreme of speculation in 1929 people have now turned to the extreme of caution. In my own case I find it a problem to take in enough to pay expenses and there is nothing left for investment.

• August 17: ...[F]our of the largest commercial banks in Toledo, Ohio closed their doors (total deposits over $100 million). Also that eleven Savings & Loan companies in

Toledo stopped paying out money. The conclusion seems clear that savings and loan companies are not good places to deposit money even tho they pay a high rate of interest… the City of Toledo is completely tied up for lack of money…. Foreclosure does not help much because there is no re-sale market. The bank simply becomes the owner of the real estate. Moratoriums of one year are being considered on mortgage payments in many states.

• August 21: People seem to have lost all confidence in banks and are quietly withdrawing their funds and putting it in safety vaults….Government and postal savings are popular today.

• August 22: Things are happening fast and the people are getting more demoralized each day….The closing of a bank in a city seems to drag down banks in the small communities nearby…. distrust of all banks is growing like a cancer.

• August 29: People who have savings accounts in the Home Savings & Loan Co. are willing to sell them at a discount. They are also being accepted as payments on real estate, autos, and merchandise but the buyer always suffers a loss. If necessary I will accept them in fees and apply them on my mortgage.

• September 29: I am really afraid for at least two of our big banks here. It would be a calamity. My emotions tell me it just can't happen and yet—my logic says it *must* happen unless some drastic solution is found at once. Last night's paper listed further bank failures in Philadelphia, Detroit and Pittsburgh. This means additional failures in the small surrounding towns. In a great many instances fraud is shown on the part of bank officials who used bank funds to play the stock market. The whole banking fraternity is in public disfavor and many of them face prison.

- October 7: The bank closing movement started in the mid-west and now seems to be penetrating the east.

- October 22: Something is wrong with our banking system yet in spite of the Federal Reserve.

- November 12: Things remain at a standstill. There is no money in circulation, the stores and business places are deserted and everybody seems to have given up their initiative. The banks are still closed, school teachers are unpaid and there is no money to pay salaries of county and city officials. There is some talk about issuing scrip against bank deposits.

Repayments From Corporations to Other Corporations

Corporations conduct a lot of business with each other. Many corporations, in fact, only sell their products or services to other corporations, who, in turn, use those goods in the manufacturing of finished goods to sell to consumers. Accounts payable and accounts receivable are standard accounting terms that corporate financial managers are always addressing. As to receivables: Who owes us, how long have they owed us and when are they likely to pay? As to payables: Whom do we owe, how long have we owed and when are we obligated to pay? In 1931, due to the very nature of business, many corporations owed a high proportion of their (short-term) Accounts payable and also of their (long-term) Notes payable to other corporations, not to banks.

Table 14.3			
Repayment of Notes & Accounts Receivable in 1931 by U.S. Corporations, U.S. Individuals and Others ($ million)			
	1930	1931	Differences
Notes & accounts receivable	59,675	48,667	-11,008
100% of payables of corporations	-26,870	-23,251	-3,618
Payables of individuals & others	32,806	25,416	-14,626
Notes & accounts receivable	59,675	48,667	-11,008
95% of payables of corporations	-25,526	-22,089	-3,437
Payables of individuals & others	34,149	26,578	-14,445
Notes & accounts receivable	59,675	48,667	-11,008
90% of payables of corporations	-24,183	-20,926	-3,256
Payables of individuals & others	35,493	27,741	-14,264

Source: *SOI for 1930 & 31*.

Remembering that one corporation's receivables are other corporations' payables (and vice versa), we present in Table 14.3 (above) three alternative ways to compare the 1931 statistics with 1930 with regards to the change in Aggregate corporate Notes and accounts receivable and the change in Aggregate corporate notes and accounts payable. As in Chapter 5's discussion comparing repayments in 1929 to 1930, Table 14.3 offers three alternative assumptions as to what percentage of payables—100%, 95% or 90%—that corporations repaid to corporations as opposed to the percentage repaid by others (such as individuals, state, local and federal governments and foreigners). Our primary interest once again is looking at specifically how much individuals were repaying to corporations. But first we must look at corporation-to-corporation transactions in order to back into the significance of repayments by individuals.

The top section of the table assumes U.S. corporations paid all of the net change in their Notes and accounts payable in 1931 to other U.S. corporations. Under that assumption, the difference between 1930 and 1931 was $3,618 million of the total $11 billion change in Notes and accounts payable. Since our main interest, as we have said, was the non-corporation entities—Individuals and others—this 100% assumption suggests that Individuals and others owed the residual $7,390 million in payables to U.S. corporations in 1931:

- *100% Assumption:*

1930: $7,135 million – $2,583 million = $4,552 million

1931: $11,008 million – $3,618 million = $7,390 million

The second alternative assumption is that U.S. corporations paid 95% of their net change in Notes & accounts payable in 1931 to other U.S. corporations. Under the 95% assumption, we subtracted 95% of $3,618 million in payables, or $3,437 million, from the net change Notes & accounts receivable of $11,008 million, to arrive at the slightly larger sum of $7,571 million that Individuals and others paid to U.S. Corporations:

- 95% Assumption:

1931: $11,008 million – $3,437 million = $7,571 million

The third alternative assumption is that U.S. corporations paid 90% of their net change Notes and accounts payable in 1931 to other U.S. corporations. Under our 90% assumption, we subtracted 90% of $3,618 million, or $3,256 million from the net change in Notes nd accounts receivable of $11,008 million, to arrive at a still higher sum of $7,752 million that Individuals and Others must have repaid to U.S. Corporations:

- 90% Assumption:

1931: $11,008 million – $3,256 million = $7,752 million

Inevitably, as we stated in Chapter 5 concerning 1930, adjusting the U.S. corporation-to-U.S. corporation statistics downwards initially from 100% to 95%, then to 90%, *raised* the residual amount that Individuals and others must have paid to U.S. corporations. The initial 5% decline caused payables by Individuals and others to increase by $181 million in 1931. The further -5% decline to 90% caused payables by Individuals and Others to increase by $362 million. The size of the downward adjustment in U.S. corporate Notes and accounts payable from 100% to 95% to 90% only served to increase the amounts Individuals and others repaid. As it is likely that less than 100% of U.S. corporate payables went to other U.S. corporations, the significant sums repaid by individual debtors in 1931 would have added to the dampening of the economy even further. After careful consideration of the alternatives presented in Table 14.3, we chose the second alternative, that U.S. corporations paid 95% of their Notes and accounts payable due in 1931 to other U.S. corporations, thereby arriving at $7,571 million as the sum Individuals and others paid to U.S. corporations (hereafter called "the 95% assumption").

Individuals' Financial Decisions in 1931: Reaching Our Conclusions

Assessing the debt repayments made by U.S. individuals—autonomously and in aggregate—has, from the beginning, stood front and center in terms of our research objectives. We knew there were definitely important questions we needed to answer in order to prove our case, but sometimes we encountered impediments to finding those answers directly or accurately.

Table 14A.Results (page 432) shows the conclusions we drew in our extended estimation process. Under the 95% assumption, U.S. individuals and other entities repaid $7,571 millions to U.S. corporations (including banks). However, since our main focus is on U.S. individuals, first we went through the precursor step of estimating payments by the "others" component of individuals and others—specifically the Federal government, State and local governments and Foreigners, plus the bankruptcies attributable to individuals in the U.S.—so that we could arrive at figures for U.S. individuals only. As Table 14A.Results (following page) shows, U.S. individuals' repayments aggregated to $2.1 million, thus reducing the $7,571 million from Table 14.3 (page 428) based on the 95% assumption to *$7,569 million repaid by U.S. individuals alone in 1931.*

Because we strongly prefer to exercise caution in estimation, we will refer to our estimate for 1931 henceforth as a "$7+ billion" debt repayment by individuals, including mainly and importantly, consumers.[4] In addition, we note that included in this repayment estimate is the reduction of -$447.3 million in outstanding debt obligation owed to the Five Retail Establishments Combined in 1930 as presented in Tables TI.2A and B (pages 52-53). That sum constituted more than 6.3% of the $7+ billion repayment.

$7+ Billion Repaid by U.S. Individuals in 1931

Again, exercising caution in our estimation process, we offer, over and above the $4+ billion repaid in 1930, the estimate of *$7+ billion* in additional debt repayment in 1931, a significant amount that served to deepen the Depression. We arrived at $7+ billion as a *conservative* estimate of debt repayment by individuals, though it is nonetheless in the neighborhood of an impactful one-tenth of GNP being redirected from consumption to debt repayment.

Still, obviously consumption did not cease altogether in 1931. According to the NIPA statistics (see Table TI.2., page 4), individuals

4 As discussed in Chapter 12 (page 339), some individuals went into debt, not as individual consumers, but for their businesses, as sole proprietors or partners in partnerships. In general, throughout this book use of "individuals" covers both. However, when appropriate, particularly as it relates to indebtedness, we specifically include "and consumers" to make it clear that there can be a difference. Not all individuals were indebted due to individual consumption, whereas all indebted consumers went into debt due to consumption.

Table 14A.Results			
Estimated Assignment of "Others" at the End of 1931 to U.S. Corporations and Individuals ($ million)			
"Others"	Amount	U.S. corporations	Individuals in the U.S.
Federal govt.			
Notes payable	$-43		$-43.0
Accounts payable	+68		+68.0
State & local govt.			
Notes payable	+173		+173.0
Accounts payable	+62		+62.0
Foreigners	-215[1]		-215.0
Bankruptcies			
Personal	-24.9[2]		-24.9
Private banks	-4.9[3]		-4.9
Business failure	-170.1[4]	-152.8	-17.3
Total	-154.9	-152.8	-2.1

Source: Authors' estimates.

Note: "Others" include federal, state and local governments which are removed from the individual column by subtraction, but, if positive, are interpreted as causing individuals to maintain additional sums on deposit to offset their added effect.

[1] Assigned entirely to individuals on the grounds that foreigners are not U.S. corporations.

[2] Personal bankruptcies are all attributable to individuals.

[3] Private banks are unincorporated institutions.

[4] Individuals get 10.14% based on statistics in Table 14A.5. Corporations receive the remainder of the amount in the first column.

continued to purchase all kinds of goods and services to the tune of $60.5 billion in 1931. It is important to keep in mind that most workers were still employed (at least to some extent) at the end of 1931. This is not to minimize the impactful reality that unemployment ended the year at almost 16%—though such a measurement was not well articulated at the time—and it would grow worse in 1932 and into 1933 before New Deal programs began to filter some workers' wages back into the economy.

Concluding Thoughts on 1931 (and Forensic Accounting)

Although, as we have described previously, unemployment was not well understood as either a concept or a reality of nationwide significance, almost three-quarters of the workforce remained employed in some fashion throughout the period. However, the dampening impact of job losses, as part of the general attitude of deflation, was widespread and visible, and by the end of 1931, everything had changed psychologically regardless of employment status. For the employed, some may have felt lucky or even secure, but many worked fewer hours, had taken a pay cut or two, or, if commission-based, were making less due to lower demand for their wares. Regardless, although they still had at least some income, they knew people who were unemployed—relatives, colleagues, neighbors, from the news or local gossip. This made the attitude shift that had taken place since the Crash almost society-wide.

The shock of the Crash in terms of the immediate losses it engendered, on top of the debt burden those losses placed on many speculators across all income lines, changed consumption habits pretty much overnight. Many employed workers felt increasingly insecure about their ongoing employment prospects as they watched assembly lines sit idle and sales fall at their companies. That insecurity led to changes in their spending habits especially because, over the 1920s, many, again at all levels of income, had become accustomed to buying on installment and had built up sizable levels of installment debt. Whether or not they understood accounting, they sensed their debt level was already too high relative to their income and boded much worse at possibly a lower income level— or, much worse, no income—in the near future. Consuming less in order to discharge debts as quickly as possible became top priority. This dual, autonomous action by individual Americans—in aggregate—created a collective force that took corporate America (always remembering corporations included banks) with them.

True to the American character, people figured out non-cash

ways to acquire what they needed most. For instance, a barter economy developed for those who lacked cash but had items or skills of value that they could trade, such as exchanging laundry services or sewing for eggs or plumbing services. Physicians in rural communities, for example, might have been paid in produce or other goods of value. A 1930s ophthalmologist in New Mexico frequently received payment for treatment in Native American pottery, rugs and jewelry. As Benjamin's Roth's diary entries in 1931 indicated, people also sold their savings passbooks in suspended banks at a discount to get cash.

Continuing to put a human face to our data, we begin to bring this chapter to a close with a third set of quotes from Benjamin Roth's 1931 diary entries before presenting our final set of Statistics of U.S. Economic Activity for this difficult year and offering some Concluding Thoughts.

The Great Depression: A Diary
by Youngstown Attorney Benjamin Roth
(continued)

Roth's diary quotes about general conditions in Youngstown and beyond:

- August 10: I note in today's Legal News that the Kirsch home on Coronado Ave. is being foreclosed by the bank on a $7,500 mortgage. It can be bought for the price of the mortgage and is worth $10000. This and many other bargains are being offered today. The Legal News carries advertisements today of 78 sheriff sales to be held within the next 30 days. In almost every case, the properties will be bought back by the bank for the 1st mortgage plus taxes and court costs. There are no bona fide bidders.

• Roth offered an update on August 26, 1936: The Kirsch property was bought eventually by the U— family for about $7500 but instead of using cash they used Home Savings & Loan Co. pass books which were selling at 50¢ on the dollar. This family has bought much real estate this way and in the next few years will reap a harvest.

• August 20: The city is planning a bond issue to provide for relief needs this winter. Hold-ups and killings are becoming more frequent and it becomes dangerous to walk the streets after dark.

• September 2: As nearly as I can make out from a study of past panics, the cycle of business is always moving down toward a panic or up toward a boom. It rarely for long travels in a straight line. At the present time we are clearly moving down and the turn has not yet come.

• December 11: It is generally believed that good stocks and bonds can now be bought at very attractive prices. The difficulty is that nobody has the cash to buy.

• December 18: The only moral I can see is to limit investments to the highest grade issues and to diversify.

• December 23: Predictions for the new year have all been very conservative so far. A number of enterprising auto merchants and real estate dealers have been offering a bonus of 10 or more shares of common stock in Republic Steel, Continental and other low stocks with each sale made. Others are giving cheap stocks as Xmas gifts to elevator boys, etc.

As Roth made painfully evident, things were still "clearly moving down and the turn has not yet come," as his September 2, 1931, entry stated. Indeed, the bottom was still ahead. Suffice it to say that by year-end 1931, Americans were in the thick of it, and it must have seemed like they were in a thicket unable to see other than right where they were, barely able to remember the "good" times behind them nor envision days ahead when they might see open sky again.

Even in the diary entries we quoted, Roth repeatedly observed that residents of Youngstown, Ohio (and, by implication, other localities) had little or no spendable money or cash. This reality clashed with reporting in *The Chronicle* that throughout 1930, the Federal Reserve had been carrying out their easy money policy open market operations in the purchase of United States government securities and bankers' acceptances. Local banks participated in open market operations because they were in a bind. Their customers with funds on deposit were leaving those funds on deposit and weren't borrowing, even as customers with little on deposit weren't eligible for borrowing. Since they weren't earning interest from lending, local banks in this position had no other option than to send the funds back out of their localities by purchasing increasing quantities of interest-bearing government securities in money markets. Thus, the Fed's open market operations not only failed to put cash into the hands of local bank depositors, it removed cash from local markets.

To close out our look at 1931, in his Financial Markets column recapping that eventful year that he published on January 4, 1932, *New York Times* Financial editor Alexander Dana Noyes reflected on the two prevailing views as to the state of things. One view came from those who predicted that conditions would "be vastly more destructive during 1932 and will occasion general breakdown."[5] The second view was that the current conditions would prevail until

5 Alexander Dana Noyes, *New York Times,* January 4, 1932, p. 28.

"compulsory reaction, readjustment, retrenchment and liquidation have been so thorough as to indicate the eventual completion of the process."[6] Noyes failed to take sides, but as 1932 began, America was teetering in the balance between the two possibilities, both of them grave indeed.

6 Ibid.

Table 14.4

Statistics of U.S. Economic Activity

($ billion)

	Nov. '30	Dec. '30	Jan. '31	Feb. '31	Mar. '31
Annualized personal income	$70.6	$69.5	$68.5	$68.1	$72.0
Index of factory employment	85.3	83.8	82.4	81.4	81.1
Index of industrial production	81.0	79.0	78.0	79.0	80.0
Index of wholesale prices	81.3	79.6	78.2	76.8	76.0
Friedman & Schwartz demand deposits	$21.4	$21.1	$20.7	$20.9	$20.9
Fed member bank loans		$23.9			$22.8

Sources: *HSUS* 1789-1945, pp. 328-330, 344; *Monetary History*, p.713; *BMS*, p.74.

CHAPTER 15

Incipient Conclusions: Interim Thoughts about Deflation

THE DICTIONARY DEFINES "incipient" as "beginning to exist or appear."[1] While we regard the first two volumes of *The Great Deleverage Series* each as large accomplishments, we also regard our work as ongoing. For now, this means that further research and analysis is needed — even regarding 1930 as we shall see.

The Meaning of Deflation

So far, we have concluded that deflation as measured by the WPI had become an inescapable force by mid-year 1930 (see page 308). This is so because among other things nothing was done to combat it. About the deflation itself, however, previous historical analyses have been inadequate if not evasive. As Professor Temin observed:

> Neither Friedman and Schwartz nor the postwar econometric investigations of the depression payed much attention to deflation....
>
> [A]dding the deflation to the list of events to be explained has complicated the story enormously. Neither hypothesis can be said to have successfully incorporated the deflation into the resulting narrative of the depression.[2]

1 *Random House Webster's College Dictionary;* Random House, Inc.; 1997; p. 659.

2 Temin, p. 168.

Friedman and Schwartz did set the stage appropriately in the opening paragraph of Chapter 7 of *Monetary History,* which is entitled "The Great Contraction."

> The contraction from 1929 to 1933 was by far the most severe business cycle contraction during the near-century of U.S. history we cover …

And they conclude this introductory passage to Chapter 7 suitably:

> [I]t is hardly conceivable that money income could have declined by over one-half and prices by over one-third in the course of four years if there had been no decline in the stock of money.[3]

But there is much between the start and end of this two-page introductory passage that we view as polemical and hardly beyond question. For example:

> The monetary collapse was *not the inescapable consequence of other forces, but rather a largely independent factor* which exerted a powerful influence on the course of events.[4] (emphasis ours)

Having declared deflation as measured by the WPI to have become an inexorable force in July 1930 and as measured by the CPI to be well on its way to becoming an inexorable force in December 1930 when it reached -6.4% on an annualized basis, we must respectfully disagree with Friedman and Schwartz.[5] We reject their notion that monetary collapse was a "largely independent factor." Rather

---

3 Friedman and Schwartz, pp. 299-301.

4 Ibid., p. 300.

5 See page 232 in this volume.

it resulted from the autonomous decisions of myriads of indebted Americans, especially consumers, to repay their debts, especially to banks, as quickly as possible from the start of the Crash onwards. Their net repayment of debt caused the money supply to contract, which caused deflation to develop and grow contemporaneously. And as we learned, most clearly in Chapter 8, it was deflation that caused the value of American properties, especially real estate and debt instruments such as mortgages secured with real estate, to shrink in value and thus give rise to growing foreclosures or alternatively to mortgage debt carried on open account by lenders who found themselves unable to sell mortgaged properties or who chose not to liquidate them.

We also take exception with a statement by Friedman and Schwartz in this introductory passage that caused us to scratch our heads:

> True, as events unfolded, the decline in the stock of money and the near collapse of the banking system can be regarded as a consequence of *non-monetary* forces in the United States ...[6] (our emphasis)

Really? In *How the Crash Caused,* we showed that the decline of the stock of money commenced with the start of the Crash (if not shortly before then) and was most clearly reflected in the repayment to banks of $-2.781 billion during the November downside of what Friedman and Schwartz called "the sharp wiggle."[7] Are we to suppose that Friedman and Schwartz considered that this repayment was caused by *non-monetary* forces? Might they have deemed a crash or deflation as something other than a monetary force?

Lastly, Friedman and Schwartz did observe in *Monetary History* that the Treasury Department, too, had—*and still has*—monetary powers:

6 Friedman and Schwartz, p. 300.

7 Ibid., p. 305. See *How the Crash Caused* pp. 273-4.

> The Treasury's debt management powers were then *and are now* comparable to the Federal Reserve System's ability to conduct open market operations.[8] (our emphasis)

The context of this comment was the presidency of Theodore Roosevelt, but the italicized words caused us to ponder how Hoover might have used these Treasury powers most fruitfully during the Great Depression.

Dictionary Meanings of Deflation

We find that our dictionary defines the noun "deflation," along with "the erosion of soil by the wind (1890-1895)," as "a fall in the general price level or a contraction of available money (opposed to inflation)." On reflection, we are quite comfortable with this definition. It appears to us that we can interpret monetary collapse and deflation perhaps as meaning virtually the same thing. The monetary collapse was more than just the inescapable force of deflation. We view the two as appearing inextricably bound together and tied so tightly as to become a tautology. Deflation *can constitute* monetary collapse.

Furthermore, our dictionary defines the verb "to deflate" as "to reduce (currency, prices, etc.) from an inflated condition," as well as "to release the air or gas from (something inflated, as a balloon)." As to letting the air out of an inflated balloon, we can argue metaphorically that that is just what happened. But what let the air out was not some invisible hand. Rather it was the hands of many Americans acting simultaneously but autonomously in aggregate to repay outstanding debt in potent economic reaction to the Crash.

A New Benchmark History

For Christmas 2025 an old friend gave us *A History of the American People* by the eminent British historian, Paul Johnson.

8 Ibid., p. 150n.

Beginning before the landing at Plymouth Rock, this enormous volume of 1,088 pages, copyright 1997, covers American history from the age of exploration before 1620 to the late Twentieth Century. Its introduction to the Great Depression reads:

> The Wall Street crash of October 1929, and the Great Depression which followed it, lasting effectively to the beginning of World War II in 1939, remain mysterious, despite more than half a century of economic and historical analysis since.[9]

Johnson follows with his own attempt to "make historical sense of a tragic series of events for which no satisfactory explanation has yet been provided,"[10] carefully sourcing Galbraith and others. Nevertheless, he joins Kindleberger who labeled as "baffling" the second quarter of 1930, which is when our evidence clearly indicates the Great Depression reached full force. We have certainly also seen the confusion associated with explaining the rapid rise of unemployment as observed by Charles E. Persons and the Bureau of Labor Statistics, and ultimately as set forth by Broadus Mitchell and shown in Tables 11.2 and 11.3 (see pages 316-17).

As the authors of a new, quite different and straightforward account, we consider ourselves to be setting the record straight. What we have shown in our first two volumes of *The Great Deleverage Series* is that in the 1920s, consumers borrowed a lot of money, and they spent on consumption their incomes *plus* what they borrowed. Prosperity ensued! When the Crash occurred, they suddenly realized that, rather than growing wealthier with speculation and borrowing, they were deeply and precariously in debt. The statistics demonstrate that there was a dramatic pivot in November 1929, as observed above. Americans started to repay their debts aggressively and to spend on

9 Paul Johnson, *A History of the American People,* HarperCollins, 1997, p. 727.

10 Ibid.

consumption their incomes *less what they repaid.* The result was not only significant deleveraging but also tragedy and hardship for a great many American families. Unemployment developed and grew. Repaying bank loans caused deflation to occur. Deflation caused the value of real estate to fall as we saw in Chapter 8. Foreclosures rose, and we advanced in the downward spiral of the Great Depression.

Could Hoover Have Issued a Successful Call to Action in 1930 to End the Great Depression in America?

In his account of the Great Depression, Johnson makes a statement that propels us to linger in 1930 addressing Incipient Conclusions:

> The panic merely knocked out the speculative element, leaving sound stock at about their right value in relation to earnings. If the recession had been allowed to adjust itself as it would have done by the end of 1930 on any earlier analogy, confidence would have returned and the world slump need never have occurred.[11]

In 1921, significant deflation was replaced rapidly by growing consumption. War-time credit suppression ended. Credit taps opened. Consumption rebounded.

The situation in 1930 was completely different. A crash had taken place, Consumers were repaying debt. Deflation resulted and grew.

Could Hoover have done anything in 1930 to reduce the impact of deflation or even end the Great Depression?

The next volume in *The Great Deleverage Series* will include an historical novel whose story begins in the second quarter of 1930 and whose working title is currently, *Restoring Prosperity with Nearly*

11 Ibid., p. 735.

Balanced Budgets. We hope it will not surprise our readers that we have conceived a way to put the Treasury's debt management powers to work healing the Depression.

About Appendices

For interested readers, Appendices to Chapters 5, 9 and 14 are available at www.TideMillgroup.com/Publishing

References

Volumes I and II of *The Great Deleverage Series*

Allen, Frederick Lewis. *Only Yesterday: An Informal History of the 1920's.* Harper & Brothers Publishing, 1931.

Angly, Roger. *Oh Yeah?.* Viking Press, 1931.

Appelbaum, Binyamin. *The Economists' Hour.* Little, Brown and Company, 2019.

Aronson, Alex. "Here's What Things Cost 100 Years Ago." *Country Living*, July 30, 2020.

Asch, Besta and A R Mangus, *Farmers on Relief and Rehabilitation.* Research Monograph VIII. Works Progress Administration, Division of Social Research, 1937.

Automobile Trade Journal and Motor Age, February 1930.

Barber, William. *From New Era to New Deal: Herbert Hoover, the Economists, and American Economic Policy, 1921-1933.* Cambridge University Press, 1985.

Baruch, Bernard. *The Public Years.* Holt, Rinehart, and Winston, 1960.

——. *My Own Story.* Holt, Rinehart and Winston, 1957.

Bernanke, Ben S. "Bankruptcy, Liquidity, and Recession." *American Economic Review*, Vol. 71, No. 2, Papers and Proceedings of the Ninety-Third Annual Meeting of the American Economic Association, May, 1981, pp. 155-159.

Bernays, Edward L. *Public Relations.* Forgottenbooks.com, 1945.

Bordo, Michael and Hugh Rockoff. "The Influence of Irving Fisher on Milton Friedman's Monetary Economics." NBER Working Paper Series, Working Paper 17267, August 2011.

Brooks, John. *Once in Golconda: A True Drama of Wall Street 1920-1938.* Allworth Press, 1969.

Brunner, Karl, ed. *The Great Depression Revisited.* Martinus Nijhoff Publishing, 1981.

Calder, Lendol. *Financing the American Dream.* Princeton University Press, 1999.

Clark, Evans. *Financing the Consumer.* Harper & Brothers, 1930.

Clarke, Sally. "New Deal Regulation and the Revolution in American Farm Productivity: A Case Study of the Diffusion of the Tractor in the Corn Belt, 1920-1940." *The Journal of Economic History*, March 1991, Vol. 51, No. 1, pp. 101-123.

The Commercial & Financial Chronicle, Vols. 128-130, 1929-1930.

Committee on Recent Economic Changes of the President's Conference on Unemployment. *Recent Economic Changes in the United States, Volumes 1 and 2.* NBER, 1929.

Craig, Steve. ""The More They Listen, the More They Buy': Radio and the Modernizing of Rural America, 1930-1939." *Agricultural History*, Vol. 80, No. 1, Winter, 2006, p 2.

Davis, L. Ronnie. *The New Economics and the Old Economists.* The Iowa State Press, 1971.

Fabricant, Solomon. "Profits, Losses and Business Assets, 1929-1934." *Bulletin 55*. NBER, 1935.

Federico, Giovanni. *Feeding the World: An Economic History of Agriculture 1800-2000.* Princeton University Press, 2005.

——. "Not Guilty? Agriculture in the 1920s and the Great Depression." *The Journal of Economic History, Vol. 65, No. 4, December 2005, pp. 949-976.*

Felix, Edgar. *Electrical Merchandising, Vol. 43, January 1930.*

Fellner, W J, et al. *Ten Economic Studies in the Tradition of Irving Fisher.* John Wiley & Sons, Inc., 1967.

Ferderer, J. Peter. "Institutional Innovation and the Creation of Liquid Financial Markets: The Case of Bankers' Acceptances, 1914-1934." *The Journal of Economic History,* Vol. 63, No. 3, *September* 2003, pp. 666-694.

Fisher, Irving. "The Debt-Deflation Theory of Great Depressions." *Econometrica*, Vol. 1, No. 4, October 1933.

Booms and Depressions: Some First Principles. Adelphi Company, 1932.

Fisher, Irving and James P. Warburg. "Reply to Senator Elmer Thomas and Professor Irving Fisher." *The Annals of the American Academy of Political and Social Science*, Vol. 171, January 1934, pp. 337-357.

Fisher, Irving Norton. *My Father Irving Fisher*. Comet Press Books, 1956.

Friedman, Milton. "A Theoretical Framework for Monetary Analysis." *The Journal of Political Economy*, Vol. 78, No. 2, March-April 1970, pp. 193-238.

Friedman, Milton and Anna J. Schwartz. *Monetary Statistics of the United States: Estimates, Sources, Methods*. Columbia University Press, 1970.

——. *Dollars and Deficits: Inflation, Monetary Policy and the Balance of Payments*. Prentice-Hall, 1968.

——. *A Monetary History of the United States 1867-1960*. Princeton University Press, 1963.

——. "Money and Business Cycles." *The Review of Economics and Statistics*, Vol. 45, No. 1, Part 2, Supplement, February 1963, pp. 32-64.

Galbraith, John. *The Great Crash 1929*. Mariner Books, 2009.

Ganzel, Bill. "One Farmer's 1930s Balance Sheet." http://lhf.org

Garraty, John. *The Great Depression*. Anchor Book Doubleday, 1987.

Goldsmith, Raymond, Dorothy Brady and Horst Mendershausen. *A Study of Saving in The United States Vol.3*. Princeton University Press, 1956.

Goldsmith, Raymond and Robert E. Lipsey. *Studies in the National Balance Sheet of the United States, Volumes 1 and 2*. NBER and Princeton University Press, 1963.

Grant, James. *Bernard Baruch: The Adventures of a Wall Street Legend*. Axios Press, 2012.

Grebler, Leo, David M. Blank and Louis Winnick. *Capital Formation in Residential Real Estate: Trends and Prospects*. Princeton University Press, 1956.

Haberler, Gottfried. *Prosperity and Depression: A Theoretical Analysis of Cyclical Movements*. League of Nations, 1937.

Hansen, Mary Eschelbach and Bradley A. Hansen. *Bankrupt in America*. The University of Chicago Press, 2020.

——. "Crisis and Bankruptcy: The Mediating Role of State Law, 1920-1932." *The Journal of Economic History*, Vol. 72, No. 2, June 2012, pp. 448-468.

Hart, Albert Gailord and The Committee on Debt Adjustment. *Debts and Recovery: A Study of Changes in the Internal Debt Structure from 1929 to 1937 and A Program for the Future*. The Twentieth Century Fund, 1938.

Hetzel, Robert L. "The Contributions of Milton Friedman to Economics." *The Economic Quarterly*, Federal Reserve Bank of Richmond, Vol. 93, Winter 2007, pp. 1-30.

Hickock, Lorena. *One Third of a Nation: Lorena Hickok Reports on The Great Depression*. University of Chicago Press, 1981.

Holthausen, Duncan M, Malcolm L. Merriam and Rolf Nugent. *The Volume of Consumer Installment Credit, 1929-38*. NBER, 1940.

Hoover, Herbert. *The Annals of America*, Vol. 15. *Encyclopedia Brittanica*, 1968, pp. 79-82.

——. *The Memoirs of Herbert Hoover 1920-1933: The Cabinet and the Presidency, Volume 2*. The Macmillan Company, 1952.

——. "Address on the 150th Anniversary of the Battle of Kings Mountain." Public Papers of the Presidents, October 7, 1930.

Hopkins, Harry. *The Realities of Unemployment*. BiblioGov, 1937.

Huertas, Thomas and Joan Silverman. "Charles E. Mitchell: Scapegoat of the Crash." *The Business History Review*, Vol. 60, No. 1, Spring 1986, pp. 81-103.

Hyman, Louis. *Borrow: The American Way of Debt*. Vintage Books, 2012.

Irwin, Douglas. *Peddling Protectionism: Smoot-Hawley and the Great Depression*. Princeton University Press, 2011.

Johnson, Paul. *A History of the American People*. Harper Perennial. 1997

Karabell, Zachary. *The Leading Indicators: A Short History of the Numbers That Rule Our World*. Simon & Schuster, Inc., 2014.

Keynes, John Maynard. *The Collected Writings of John Maynard Keynes*, Volume XIII. The Macmillan Company, 1973.

——. *The General Theroy of Employment, Interest and Money*. Palgrave Macmillan, 1936.

——. *The Treatise on Money*, Vol. 2. The Royal Economic Society, 1930.

Kindleberger, Charles. *The World in Depression 1929-1939*. University of California Press, 1986.

Klein, Lawrence R. *The Keynesian Revolution*. The Macmillan Company, 1966.

Klein, Maury. *Rainbow's End: The Crash of 1929*. Oxford University Press, Inc, 2001.

Klingaman, William. *1929: The Year of the Great Crash*. Harper & Row, 1989.

Lawrence, Josephine. *If I Have Four Apples*. Grosset & Dunlap, 1935.

Lippmann, Walter, "The Peculiar Weakness of Mr. Hoover," *Harpers*

Magazine, Volume 161, (June, 1930)

MacKay, Charles. *Extraordinary Popular Delusions and the Madness of Crowds.* L. C. Page & Company, 1932.

Marsh, John. *The Emotional Life of the Great Depression.* Oxford University Press, 2019.

Marx, Arthur. *Life with Groucho.* Simon & Schuster, 1954.

Mazur, Paul M. *American Prosperity: Its Causes and Consequences.* Viking Press, 1928.

Meltzer, Allan H. *A History of the Federal Reserve, Volume 1: 1913-1951.* University of Chicago Press, 2003.

Mitchell, Broadus. *Depression Decade: From New Era through New Deal 1929-1941.* Holt, Rinehart, and Winston, 1947.

Mitchell, Wesley C. *Business Cycles and Their Causes.* University of California Press, 1941.

New York Stock Exchange. *New York Stock Exchange Year Book 1929-1930,* 1930.

The New York Times. January 4, 1932; October 22, 1929, et al.

Noyes, Alexander. *The Market Place: Reminiscences of a Financial Editor.* Little, Brown and Company, 1938.

———. "Financial Markets: New Year Prophesies, New Year Uncertainties, and Underlying Economic Facts." *The New York Times,* January 4, 1932, p. 28.

Olney, Martha. *Buy Now Pay Later: Advertising, Credit, and Consumer Durables in the 1920s.* The University of North Carolina Press, 1991.

———. "Avoiding Default: The Role of Credit in the Consumption Collapse of 1930." *The Quarterly Journal of Economics,* Vol. 114, No. 1, February 1999, pp. 319-335.

Ott, Julia C. "When Wall Street Met Main Street: The Quest for an Investors' Democracy and the Emergence of the Retail Investor in the United States, 1890-1930." *Enterprise & Society,* Vol. 9, No. 4, Cambridge University Press, December 2008, pp. 619-630.

———. "The Free and Open People's Market: Political Ideology and Retail Brokerage at the New York Stock Exchange, 1913-1933." *The Journal of American History,* Vol. 93, No 1, June 2009, pp. 44-71.

———. "The Free and Open People's Market: Public Relations at the New York Stock Exchange, 1913-1929." *Business and Economic History,* thebhc.org, Vol. 2, 2004.

Persons, Charles E. "Credit Expansion, 1920 to 1929, and its Lessons." *The Quarterly Journal of Economics*, Vol. 45, No. 1, November 1930, pp. 91-130.

Phillips, Chester A., Thomas F. McManus and R. W. Nelson. *Banking and the Business Cycle A Study of the Great Depression in the United States.* The Macmillan Company, 1937.

Pierce, Phyllis S., ed. *The Dow Jones Averages 1885-1995.* 4th Edition. Irwin Professional Publishing, 1996.

Roth, Benjamin. *The Great Depression: A Diary.* Public Affairs. Perseus Books Group, 2009.

Rubenzer, Steven and Thomas Faschingbauer. *Personality, Character, and Leadership in the White House: Psychologists Assess the Presidents.* Potomac Books Inc, 2004.

Samuelson, Paul. *Economics* (Seventh Edition). McGraw Hill, 1967.

——. *The Collected Scientific Papers of Paul Samuelson.* The MIT Press, 1966.

Schumpeter, Joseph. "Irving Fisher's Econometrics." *Econometrica*, Vol. 16, No. 3, July, 1948, pp. 219-231.

——. *Business Cycles: A Theoretical and Statistical Analysis of the Capitalist Process. Volumes I & II.* McGraw-Hill Book Company, 1939.

Schwartz, Anna. "Understanding 1929-1933," in Karl Brunner's *The Great Depression Revisited.* Martinus Nijhoff Publishing, 1981.

Seldes, Gilbert. *The Years of the Locust (America, 1929-1932).* Little, Brown & Company, 1933.

Shlaes, Amity. "Calvin Coolidge Revisited: New Find on 1929 Crash." *Forbes*, Vol. 193, No. 7, July 14, 2013.

——. *The Forgotten Man: A New History of The Great Depression.* Harper Collins, 2007.

Smith, Richard Norton. *An Uncommon Man: The Triumph of Herbert Hoover.* Simon & Schuster, Inc. 1984.

Stam, Jerome and Bruce Dixon. "Farmer Bankruptcies and Farm Exits in the United States, 1899-2002." U.S. Department of Agriculture, Economic Research Service. Agriculture Information Bulletin Number 788, 2004.

Steel, Ronald, *Walter Lippmann and the American Century*, Little Brown and Company, 1980.

Temin, Peter. *Did Monetary Forces Cause the Great Depression?*. W. W. Norton & Company, 1976.

Tobin, James. "Neoclassical Theory in America: J. B. Clark and Fisher." *The American Economic Review*, Vol. 75, No. 6, December

1985, pp. 28-38.
Warburg, James P. and Irving Fisher. "Reply to Senator Elmer Thomas and Professor Irving Fisher." *The Annals of the American Academy of Political and Social Science,* Vol. 171, January 1934, pp. 337-357.
Watkins, T. H. *The Hungry Years.* Henry Holt & Co, 1999.
Westerfield, Ray B. "The Balance Required by Borrowers." *The Journal of Political Economy,* Vol 33, No. 3, June 1925.
White, Eugene N. et al. *The Housing and Mortgage Markets in Historical Perspective.* University of Chicago Press, 2014.
Wickens, David L. *Residential Real Estate, Its Economic Position as shown by Values, Rents Family Incomes Financing and Construction, together with Estimates for all Real Estate.* NBER, 1941.
Wicker, Elmus R. *The Banking Panics of the Great Depression.* Cambridge University Press, 1996.
——. *Federal Reserve Monetary Policy 1917-1933.* Random House, 1966.
Wigmore, Barrie. *The Crash and Its Aftermath.* Greenwood Press, 1985.
Willis, H. Parker. "Who Caused the Panic of 1929?" *The North American Review,* Vol. 229, No. 2, February 1930, pp. 174-183.

The authors also acknowledge the importance of http://www.jstor.org to our ongoing research efforts.

Governmental Sources and References

Asch, Besta and A. R. Mangus, *Farmers on Relief and Rehabilitation.* Research Monograph VIII. Works Progress Administration, Division of Social Research, 1937.
Board of Governors of the Federal Reserve System, *Banking and Monetary Statistics 1914-1941,* 1943.
Board of Governors of the Federal Reserve System, *Annual Report of the Board of Governors of the Federal Reserve System, 1929, 1930, 1931.*
U. S. Commerce Department, Bureau of Economic Analysis. *The National Income & Product Accounts of the United States, 1929-76 Statistical Tables,* 1981.
——. U. S. Census Bureau.
Historical Review of State and Local Government Finances, 1948.
Historical Statistics of the United States, 1789-1945.
Fifteenth Census of the United States: 1930, Agriculture, Vol. 1.

Committee on Recent Economic Changes of the President's Conference on Unemployment. *Recent Economic Changes in the United States, Volumes 1 and 2.* NBER, 1929.

Hetzel, Robert L. "The Contributions of Milton Friedman to Economics." *The Economic Quarterly*, Federal Reserve Bank of Richmond, Vol. 93, Winter 2007, pp. 1-30.

Hoover, Herbert. "Address on the 150th Anniversary of the Battle of Kings Mountain." Public Papers of the Presidents, October 7, 1930.

Stam, Jerome and Bruce Dixon. "Farmer Bankruptcies and Farm Exits in the United States, 1899-2002." U.S. Department of Agriculture, Economic Research Service. Agriculture Information Bulletin Number 788, 2004.

U.S. Treasury Department. Internal Revenue Service. *Statistics of Income for 1929, 1930, 1931.*

Internal Revenue Service. *IRS Historical Fact Book: A Chronology, 1646-1992.* Forgotten Books, 2018.

In addition, the authors express their gratitude to the Federal Reserve Bank of St. Louis, FRED and FRASER in particular. Their comprehensive libraries made our research possible.

National Bureau of Economic Research (NBER) References

Bordo, Michael and Hugh Rockoff. "The Influence of Irving Fisher on Milton Friedman's Monetary Economics." NBER Working Paper Series, Working Paper 17267, August 2011.

Committee on Recent Economic Changes of the President's Conference on Unemployment. *Recent Economic Changes in the United States, Volumes 1 and 2.* NBER, 1929.

Fabricant, Solomon. "Profits, Losses and Business Assets, 1929-1934." *Bulletin 55.* NBER, 1935.

Goldsmith, Raymond and Robert E. Lipsey. *Studies in the National Balance Sheet of the United States, Volumes 1 and 2.* NBER and Princeton University Press, 1963.

Holthausen, Duncan M, Malcolm L. Merriam and Rolf Nugent. *The Volume of Consumer Installment Credit, 1929-38.* NBER, 1940.

Wickens, David L. *Residential Real Estate, Its Economic Position as Shown by Values, Rents, Family Incomes, Financing, and Construction, Together with Estimates for all Real Estate.* NBER, 1941.

Index

A

Above the line source of income, 109
Additional debt repayment, 431
Aggregate demand function, 343
Aggregate supply function, 343
Automobile industry,
  changes in, 59-60, 89, 217
  economic importance, 88
Automobile dealers, 54, 58, 60, 189, 191, 205, 208

B

Bank borrowing, 15, 144
Bank holiday, 247
Banking and Monetary Statistics (BMS), 132n, 141n, 221, 359
  bank suspensions, 283-84, 289-90
  decline in bank loans, 266, 268
  loan repayments, 143-44
  repayment estimates (authors' methodology), 158-59
  repayments ignored by Friedman and Schwartz, 155
Banking crisis, 1
  bank suspensions: viewpoints (Friedman and Schwartz), 288-91, 301
  and M-1 and M-2
  first banking crisis, 274, 276, 279
  loan repayments (importance), 300-01, 303-04, 379
  no banking crisis (Wicker), 301, 308
Banking difficulties, 301, 308
Bank failures, 265, 286, 313, 425-26
  Bank of United States, 288, 292, 295-96
  Caldwell and Company, 292, 295
  cause of decline in money stock, 156-57, 266, 279, 283,289 *see also* bank suspensions
  impact on New York Reserve Bank, 305-06

Bank of United States, 255, 266, 288, 292, 293, 294, 295, 296, 298, 305
Bank loans, 85, 131n, 143-44, 245
decline:
in demand, 266, 268
encourages hoarding, 51
results in deflation, 16
over-indebtedness leads to stampede liquidation (Fisher), 31
repayments, 143-44, 155-57
Bank loan repayments, 141, 272, 365, 423-24
deflation begins, 49
Bank suspensions, 156-57
and deposits, 286-87
impact of, 283-85, 305
New York Reserve Bank, 305
panic, 288-89, 296
Bank of United States, 296, 298
failure, 255, 266, 288, 292
impact on New York Reserve Bank, 305
fraud, 293-95
Baruch, Bernard, 132, 135, 164-65
cautious philosophy, 126, 128-30, 133
market madness, 116-17
Below the line deduction, 109
Blind spots, 193, 442
Booms and Depressions: Some First Principles, 19, 22
Budget deficit, 252
Bureau of Economic Analysis (BEA), 311
Bureau of Labor Statistics (BLS), 317, 320

C

Caldwell and Company
cause of crisis, 279
failure, 255, 265-66, 292, 295
fraud, 293

Call loans, 203, 420
about, 21
Mitchell takes action, 179, 184-85
originators of, 130, 167
volume of, 132-33, 339
Census bureau, 41, 269
decline in rural farms, 402n
farmers, 389-91
Persons' resignation, 248
questionable accuracy in 1930, 201-03
Clarke, Sally H.,
about farmers' debt 405-06
Consumer debtors, 6
Consumer debt repayment, 44, 58
Consumers, 1, 9, 142, 371
Americans become consumers, 152
credit repayments, 59-60, 138
debt repayments, 4, 6, 12, 14-16, 44n, 49, 58, 64, 150-53, 158, 194-95, 226-27, 244, 258-59, 272-73, 275, 419, 430, 441
on consumption and debt repayment (Olney), 153n, 251, 268, 270n, 272
on consumption and liquidation (Fisher), 85
drop in consumption, 55-56, 59, 272-73
Temin's comment, 152
falling demand, 190
Fed impact, 454
pivot in behavior, 304
repayment statistics, 225-27, 258-59
Consumer Price Index (CPI), 56, 440 *see also* WPI
deflation, 1929-32, 415-16
deflation accelerates, 233, 280, 308
definition, 53
price changes 1920-22, 363-64, 367

Corporate balance sheets, 23, 94
statistical insights, 413, 419
Corporate tax filings, 137-38, 139n, 141-41, 341-42, 382-84, 387 *see also* IRS
Correctives, 176, 177, 186
Countervailing forces, 10
economic decline, 253
Hoover's faults, 168
speculation grows, 447
Craig, Steve, 398
Crash, 3, 7, 313-14, 331, 334
bank loan repayments, 301
Baruch's view, 116
business activity, 341, 376
cause of the Great Depression, 84, 189, 196-97, 204, 207, 353, 372
commodity prices, 70, 85
contraction begins, 157
debts, 135, 137
debt repayment, 4, 10-11, 13-15, 18, 49, 145, 147, 151, 244, 251, 304, 352, 443
deflation, 1-3, 9-11, 16, 49, 66, 69, 90, 444
drop in bank loans, 16
falling demand, 12, 55, 57, 190-91, 223
falling production, 59, 70, 215
finance sector, 376-77, 379
Hoover, 161, 168, 173, 186, 198, 260, 262, 440
indebtedness, 229
investment trusts, 132
investors, 125, 130, 133
liquidity panic, 66, 68-69
mortgages, 234, 245
over-indebtedness, 1, 18-19, 23
leading to deflation (Fisher), 351
Willis' views, 176-77
parties responsible for the Crash, 174-75

pivot in behavior, 60
prosperity, 1928 and 1929, 122
rates of change (chart) 1929-1933, 3
rethinking priorities, 7
speculation, 91, 100, 112,
speculators, 168
stock market's temporary revival, 198-99
taxpayers affected, 110
velocity of money, 51, 78
WPI, 70
Credit granted, 189-90, 250
automobiles, 205-06
pivot, 59-60
Credit policy, 250

D

Debt disease, 43, 351
Default rate on consumer credit, 251, 269
Deflation, 25, 65, 81, 242, 305, 351, 353
comparison of 1920-21 to the Great Depression, 355-56, 364, 65, 367
key sectors, 75, 371
authors' insights, 439-44
benefit to the well-to-do, 61
Black Thursday impact, 32-33
data for CPI and WPI, 233, 279-80
Debt Deflation Theory, Irving Fisher, 19, 21-22, 42-43
debt repayment, 244, 264-64, 272, 314, 442
defined, 8, 442
detriment to the indebted, 62-63
development and impact, 9, 10-11, 14, 17, 49, 134, 411
fall in prices (Kindleberger), 86-87, 90
Federal Reserve, 57
the general attitude, 281-82, 449
hoarding, 77-78, 86

impact,
on business, 49-51, 58
on Cast of Characters, 135
on commodity prices, 70-73
on governments, 64
on loans and debts, 34, 36, 42-43
on mortgage holders and real estate, 234-35, 238, 441, 444
liquidity panic, 68-69
monetary collapse, 442
monetary event, 12-13
origin at the Crash, 1-2, 4
price levels, 66-67
statistics, 52-53, 56
Temin's observation on, 439
Deleverage, 1, 12, 244
Department of Agriculture, 391, 401, 403, *see also* Farmers
Census of 1930, 389, 407
Deposit currency,
decline in velocity, 81
meaning, 28-29
Direct action,
Hoover prevents, 261
to reduce speculation, 182, 187
Distress selling, 49
on deflation's cause, 32
en masse, 29, 33
Fisher's view, 26-28, 76
impact on mortgages, 234
liquidity panic, 68
stampede liquidation (Fisher), 28-29
leading to deflation, 32-33
Dollar disease, 35
defined by Fisher 41, 43
link to deflation, 49, 65

Downward spiral, 314, 372
due to deflation, 10, 14
mortgage exceptions, 242
liquidation, 42
Downward trendline, 225
Due and payable, 242,
consumer debt repayments, 55, 138, 147
its meaning, 243

E

Effective demand, 346, 348
defined by Keynes, 343

F

Farmers, 11, 57, 388
in American life, 397-401, 404 *see also* Giovanni Frederico
banks, 383-84
bankruptcy, 403 *see also* Department of Agriculture
debt, 392, 401, 405-408 *see also* Frederico
decrease in farms, 401-02 *see also* Frederico
demographics, 389 *see also* Department of Agriculture
depression solution, Hoover vs. Mellon, 278-79
Smoot-Hawley impact, 218, 220
taking risk, 390-91
tax filings, 390-97, 399
Federal Reserve System, 14
banks, 284, 286, 379 *see also* Elmus Wicker
Bank of United States, 288, 305 *see also* Friedman and Schwartz
call loan statistics, 131, 142-43
evolving policies, 368-69 *see also* Wicker
failure to act on speculation, 265, 307 *see also* Friedman and Schwartz and Barrie Wigmore
loan repayment, 158-60
rate policy in 1920-22, 359-60
restoring order, 90

Federico, Giovanni, 398, 399, 402, 405
Fisher, Irving, 1, 10, 58,
  Debt Factor Approach, 18, 42
  deflation, 64-65, 58, 351
  distress sales, 73, 76
  dollar disease, 41-43, 65
  economists' views on Booms and Depressions, 44-47
  equation of exchange (see also Friedman), 82-83
  hoarding, 51, 75, 77, 86, 271
  index numbers, 39-41, 222
  over-indebtedness, 21, 23, 25, 27, 62, 135, 234, 310n, 351, 372
  into depression, 26-27
  liquidation, 27-28, 75-76
  price level, 32-39
  volume of currency, 28-32
  Smoot-Hawley, 219
  Stampede liquidation, 28-29, 32-33, 68
  velocity of money, 78-81, 83-85
Foreclosures,
  data, 246-47
  debtors, 135
  farmers, 404
  impact of deflation, 56, 63, 235
  mortgages, 234, 241-42
Forensic financial management, 412
Friedman, Milton, 155
  equation of exchange (see also Fisher), 82-83
  on the Fed, 14
Friedman, Milton and Anna Schwartz, 9, 11, 44, 47, 138, 154-56, 280, 355
  about 1920-21, 355-59, 365, 367n, 372
  bank failures, 264-66, 286, 288n, 289-90, 295, 296n
  on bank suspensions, 283,

did banking crisis lead to the Great Depression, 298-300, 302-03, 308, 348n
on debt repayment, 154-56, 157n
decline of money stock, 270, 271n, 272, 274, 276, 279, 441
is deflation a monetary force, 9
direct pressure by the Fed, 187-89
Fed's failure to act, 264-65, 305-06, 307n
ignoring:
debt repayment, 272, 273n
deflation's impact on the Great Depression, 439-41
nonmonetary forces started the Great Contraction, 84
time deposits and M-2, 51
velocity of money and income, 82-83, 86

G

Ganzel, Bill, 409
Garraty, John A.,
  on employment, 318-19
  Hoover's view, 404
Great Contraction, The, 187, 264, 266, 440
  Friedman and Schwartz term, 84, 276
  caused by nonmonetary forces, 84, 156, 353
Great Depression, 17, 45, 47, 86, 94, 251, 153, 171, 186, 218n, 256, 281, 304, 310, 318, 341, 346, 351, 353, 355, 416, 444
  1930 importance, 1, 11
  bank suspensions, 286-87, 289-90, 298
  impact on business, 346, 348
  cause of the Crash, 84, 189, 196-97, 204-05, 250
  compared to depression of 1920-1921, 10, 11, 145, 353, 355, 358, 371-72, 374
  debt, 35, 243
  debt repayment, 58, 138, 155, 244-45, 273, 415, 420-21
  deflation' impact, 444 *see also* Deflation
  impact on farming, 398-400, 403, 406
  installment credit, 11, 14, 54-55, 207

falling consumption, 152, 154
mortgages, 233, 235
Gross National Product (GNP), 314 *see also* GNP Price Deflator
changes in CPI and WPI, 53, 57, 66, 312, 363
debt repayment, 423, 431
impact from decline in corporate assets and liabilities, 1931, 421-23
repayments impact, 423, 431
a valuable measure, 311
GNP Price Deflator, 53, 66, 311, 312, 363

H

Hart, Albert Gaylord, 243, 244, 245
Hoarding, 51, 77, 78, 86, 245, 271, 289, 290, 295
Hoover, Herbert, 14, 157, 161, 173, 179, 198-99, 255, 257, 348, 350, 442, 444
background, 191-93
falling production concerns, 57, 217
false optimism, 162-63
farmers, 404
full economic depression begins, 281-82
impact on the Federal Reserve, 307
short comings, 168, 185-87, 192, 231, 247, 252, 278
Smoot-Hawley pessimism, 208-09, 214, 218-20
stabilization plan, 168-72
tax cut, 97
unemployment, 281, 346
view on speculation, 179, 182-83 Hopkins, Harry, 314, 315, 404

I

Incipient Conclusions, 12, 279
Individual profitability, 384

Individual tax filings, 319, 320-21, 382-83, 385-86 *see also* IRS
Inescapable monetary force, 9, 444
Inflation, 9, 34-36, 40
    1920-1921, 359, 363-64, 367
    comparison to deflation, 16, 50-53, 56, 233, 413
    cause, 8, 352
    criticism of the Fed, 356-57
    impact on farmers, 313
    Treasury vs. the Fed, 368-70, 372 Installment credit, 1, 11, 14, 60, 197, 205, 207, 210, 215, 251, 372, 449
Installment credit, 1, 197, 210, 372
    decreasing demand, 11, 14, 60, 215, 251
    factor leading to the Great Depression, 207
Involuntary unemployment, 8, 59, 310, 314, 345
IRS, 11, 121, 343
    corporate tax filings, 137-38, 139n, 141-41, 341-42, 382-84, 387
    debt repayment, 155, 304
    business decline, 348-50
    effective demand (Keynes), 343, 346, 348
    farmers, 389-97
    debt, 401, 405
    not filing taxes, 410-11
    gross income, 362, 367, 371
    income classes, 337
    sources, 323-25
    individual tax filings, 319, 320-21, 382-83, 385-87
    methodology, 96, 109-10
    Net Income less Deficit, 373-76, 381-82
    statistics, 97, 99-100, 104, 107, 113, 126, 353, 373
    a statistical resource, 93, 102, 311
IRS Statistical Unit, 94, 96, 321, 395

J

Job losses, 248
Johnson, Paul., 442, 443, 444

K

Keynes, John Maynard,
effective demand, 343, 345-46 *see also* IRS
involuntary unemployment, 318
Keynesianism, 12
Kindleberger, Charles, 196, 207, 234
deflation, 11, 73-74, 134, 365
falling prices, 69-71, 86
Kings Mountain, North Carolina, 260

L

Leffingwell, Russell C., 368, 369
Lippmann, Walter, 219, 260
Liquidation,
call loans, 179 *see also* Charles E. Mitchell,
debt factor approach, 42 *see also* Irving Fisher
deflation, 32-34, 74
distress selling (*en masse*), 32-33
impact on stock market, 68
insolvent banks, 283
over-indebtedness result, 27-29, 31-32, 41
pessimism and depression, 75-76, 84-85, 231 *see also* Fisher and Joseph Schumpeter
security loans, 31, 157, 162
Little Bull Market, 11, 76, 197, 325-26
about, 165, 167
its end, 209, 282
its high, 253
Long-Term Gains and Losses, 109
Lord Kitchener, 192

M

M-1, *see also* M-2
 decline in money supply, 272-73, 298-99, 300n, 301, 358, 365
 defined, 51
 essential element of money supply, 271
 impact of debt repayments, 304
M-2, 51, 271, 273, 303 *see also* M-1
 decline in money supply, 298-300, 365
 defined, 51
 impact of debt repayments, 304
 nonessential element of money supply, 272
Mellon, Andrew, 183, 209, 252, 277, 278, 279, 369, 370
Meltzer, Allan H., 370-71
Mills, Ogden Livingston, 209, 278
Mitchell, Broadus, 315, 317
Mitchell, Charles E., 187m, 189
 call loan relief, 179, 183-86
Monetary force, 9, 14
Monetary phenomenon, 12, 13, 15
Money Illusion, 34, 36
Money supply, 14-15, 51, 84, 155, 352
 bank failures, 266, 279, 283
 contraction, 49, 73, 358-59, 441
 equation, 12, 276
 impact of debt liquidation and repayment, 10, 13, 29, 31, 275, 279, 300-01, 303
 importance of bank loans, 16, 30
 M-1 vs. M-2, 270-72
 non-bank corporations, 141n
Mortgage debt, 1, 237, 240, 242
Mortgage financing, 237
Mortgages, 233, 234, 235

N

National Income and Products Accounts (NIPA) 310-312, 381
Net credit change, 60, 61, 189, 190
Nominal decline, 56
Noyes, Alexander Dana, 255
  on 1932, 436-37
  end of the Little Bull Market, 207-09
  fall in commodity prices, 209
  Hoover, 161-62, 198
  on panics, 256
  on speculators, 223-24, 326-28, 418
  Wall Street's view of the Crash, 165-66
  warnings from Warburg, 13, 117-18

O

Olney, Martha L.,
  on low default rate, 251, 268, 270
  lowering consumption and repaying debt, 153n, 251, 268, 272
Opitz, Otto, 409, 410
Over-indebtedness, 11-12, 310
  absent in 1920-21, 352, 372
  a cycle, 25-26
  debt factor approach, 18-19
  distress selling, 27
  impact of maturity dates, 21-22, 23n
  link to deflation, 351,
  liquidation of debts, 28
  purchase money mortgages, 240-42 *see also* residential real estate and David L. Wickens
  mortgage debt, 234
  Schumpeter's slant on Fisher, 24
  stampede liquidation, 31
  vicious spiral downward, 41
Overview of 1931, 12

P

Peoples' expectations, 58
Persons, Charles, E., 210, 443, 251
lessons of credit expansion, 249-50, 313
resignation from Census Bureau, 202-03, 248
on unemployment, 314
Principal conclusion, 301, 308
Profit and Net Loss, 330
Public works, 161, 170, 172, 261, 440
Purchase money mortgage, 240-242 *see also* residential real estate and Wickens

R

Radio industry, 58
Real cost, 16, 58
Real decline, 56
Reflation, 24, 43, 44
Residential real estate *also* Wickens, and Urban residential properties
lack of data, 235, 238
loan durations, 236
purchase money mortgages, 240, 241n
values, 237-38
Residual losses, 229, 449
Roth, Benjamin, 12, 414
1931, diary of the times, 416-417, 425, 434-36

S

Schumpeter, Joseph, 21, 289
on nation's mood, 339
first half of 1930, 224-25, 231
praise for Fisher, 19-20, 22-24, 44n, 81
Seldes, Gilbert ,1, 2, 115-6, 228, 231, 292, 281, 413, 463
The Years of the Locust, 1, 2, 115, 282, 463
on Herbert Hoover, 262
Short-Term Gains and Losses, 109

Shrinkage over one year, 421
Significant pivot in behavior, 60
Smoot-Hawley Tariff, 208, 212
    flaws, 218-20
Sources and Uses, 46, 136, 138
Speculation, 18, 55, 212, 304, 385
    1928, speculators vs. investors, 107-08
    averting the Crash (Seldes), 116
    benefits of, 120
    cause of the Crash, 91, 281n
    consumer indebtedness, 229, 233, 251-52
    Fed's inability to curb, 90, 357
    game of speculation, 118-19, 325, 327
    Hoover's short comings, 173, 180, 183, 193
    someone in high authority (Galbraith), 177-78
    impact of, (Willis,), 176
    insider speculator instigators, 7
    investors' perspective, 125-26
    Little Bull Market, 167-68
    new form of speculation, post-Crash, 325, 327-28, 330-31, 335
    not apparent in early 1920s, 362, 374
    short-term gains and losses, 110-11
    source of income from tax filings, 99-103, 112
    ends, 224
    speculation and farming, 390
    Warburg's warnings, 12-13,
    reflection on (Noyes), 117-18
Speculators, 18, 55, 212, 304, 385
    created inflated purchasing power, 13
    distress selling, 33
    Durant, William C., 252
        Kennedy, Joseph, 199
    losses change consumer habits, 433

number of, 118, 120, 123-24
reducing debt, 282
returning to the market (1930), 164n, 165-68, 223
tax returns and income, 11, 94, 105-07, 320
vs. investors, 107-08, 114-15, 125-26, 130

Stampede liquidation (Fisher), 28-29, 32-33, 68
Statistics of Income (SOI) for 1928,
individual tax returns, 94, 107, 120, 125
Statistics of Income (SOI) for 1929,
individual tax returns, 93-97, 120, 125, 130, 138, 383
farmers, 391
Stock Exchange, 108
brief recovery in 1930, 164-67, 198
downturn, 212-14, 219, 339
wirehouse closings, 255
wirehouse growth, 121-22
Hoover's urging to curb manipulation, 180
Smoot-Hawley impact 219
Stock Market, 86, 184, 251, 253, 282, 289, 304, 312, 323
1st day of the Crash, 68-69
deflation, 74, 134
deteriorating conditions, 196, 200, 203, 207, 209, 212-13, 225
implosion leads to liquidation, 31
investors, 126, 128, 133
Hoover urges curb of manipulation, 180-81, 185-86, 193
liquidation, 31, 84-86, 90
madness and speculation, 115-18, 120, 122
optimism and Little Bull Market, 163-65
participants, 94-95
Smoot-Hawley impact, 218, 220
speculators, 223-24, 226

T

Taxpayer Demographics, 101
Temin, Peter, 45, 84, 138, 152-54, 156, 291-94, 439
    bank failures, 291, 292n, 293-94
    Booms and Depressions, 19, 21-26, 34-35, 42-44, 46, 68, 74, 80, 232, 351
    on drop in consumption, 152-54
Tobin, James, 65, 441, 442
Twentieth Century Fund, 243, 244

U

Unearned income, 103, 105, 334
Unemployment, 231, 247, 278, 310
    causes of, 10, 346, 374
    contributing to contraction, 50
    consciousness of, 281-82
    Hoover's view, 172
    impact of deflation, 56, 61
    by industry, 248
    involuntary, 8, 59, 310, 314
    Keynes' point, 345
    unemployment rising, 63, 265, 281
    workers, 318-19
Unsold vehicle inventory, 385
Urban residential properties, 237, 240, 242

V

Velocity of money,
    definition of (Friedman and Schwartz), 82
    demand deposit accounts relationship, 81
    impact of hoarding, 5, 77-78
    Schumpeter on Fisher, 81n
Vulnerable to downside reaction, 177

W

Walburg, Paul, 210, 353,
criticisms, 118
investors listen, 128
Federal Reserve System actions, 14
speculation, 12-13, 117, 179
Wall Street, 105, 116, 119, 128n, 207, 215, 443
Cast of Characters, 5, 7
distress selling, 32
investors, 125-26
optimism, 161, 164, 198, 353
partnerships, 378, 392
responsibility for the Crash, 174, 281n
speculators, 135, 179, 208, 223-24
warnings ignored, 13-14, 118
Watkins, T. H.,
on farms, 397, 398n, 399-400
White, William Allen, 57, 162, 169, 179, 181, 219, 257
Hoover, 192
Wholesale Price Index, 52, 57, 66, 312, 314, 440
Wickens, David L., 240, 242
about real estate, 235-38
Wicker, Elmus R.,
banking crisis and panic, 84, 286, 288-91
on Caldwell and Company's failure, 379
cause of bank closings, 292-93
challenging Friedman and Schwartz's explanation for the Great Depression, 298-300
commencement of the Great Depression, 304
Federal Reserve's early years, 368
geographics of bank failures, 295-96
impact on M-1, 303-04
no national banking crisis, 301, 302n, 308

Wigmore, Barrie, 67, 252, 255
  1930 decline in stock prices, 310, 311n
  concern growing, 20, 203, 220, 221n
  Crash's impact on commodities and prices, 67, 68, 69n,
  declining economic conditions, 247, 248n
  Federal Reserve inactivity, 307
  investment trust volume, 132
  smart money losses, 224, 326n, 328
Willis, H. Parker, 313, 353, 360, 372
  on bonds and banks, 1920-1921, 360, 372
  responsibility for the Crash, 174-77
Works Progress Administration (WPA)
  about farms, 391, 404
Wholesale Price Index (WPI), 312, 421 *see also* CPI and GNP
  1920-1922, measures, 363-64, 367
  defined, 52-53, 66
  deflation impact, 233, 308, 314, 422, 440
  indication of deflation, 414-416
  precedes drop in CPI and GNP, 57, 356

Regarding Permissions

The formation and very rapid growth of Amazon in recent decades have changed the publishing business radically. From our vantage as authors, who have agreed with our publisher to take responsibility for seeking and securing the necessary permissions from the copyright owners whose works we quote, the impact of these changes has been significant.

Considering our extensive use of statistical information, we count ourselves very fortunate that the federal government does not seek copyright protection on the works it produces. This includes all manner of official undertakings from congressional investigations to publications of the Federal Reserve System, the Treasury Department, the Commerce Department, the Department of Agriculture, the Bureau of the Census, etc. We made ample use of this free information requiring no permission, while also footnoting sources for readers' reference. We, as historians attempting to tell an important story with data as evidence, are grateful to all the entities we have been able to access that have fulfilled their responsibilities over the decades to make information available to the public.

Early on we consulted with copyright lawyers, literary agents and experienced industry professionals. Uniformly they responded that our work, because of its transformational nature regarding what is already known of 1929-1933, should be enough to justify fair use.

Certainly the consolidations, attrition and other changes in the publishing world over the course of many decades have made it more difficult to identify who owns what as it relates to works published in the distant past. Examples include several of our historically most insightful sources, including Alexander Dana Noyes who published *The Market Place* in 1938 and Gilbert Seldes who published *The Years of the Locust* in 1933, as to the chain of ownership of their particular publisher and their copyrights.

We hope our sincere and great respect for authors and publishers of for-profit works of economic theory and history is apparent throughout *The Great Deleverage Series.* For queries, please contact us at permissions@tidemillgroup.com.

About the Authors

John C. Harvey is an inventor/entrepreneur, videogame developer, and economic historian. With his co-inventor, Jim Cuddihy, he has received 103 U.S. patents, and licensees of their technologies have included Cisco Systems, Direct TV, and Dish Network. The videogame he and colleagues have developed is targeted to educational applications in the fields of macroeconomics, finance and investments and is called "Beat the Fed." He has degrees from Yale University in history and the University of London in economics, and an MBA in finance from the Wharton School. He served as an officer in the U.S. Navy. He and co-author Mary Keil met through Wharton and have worked together on many ventures since then.

Mary Keil worked in commercial banking at Citibank before she and John Harvey co-founded the partnership that became Personalized Media Communications. She co-authored *Enterprise in the Nonprofit Sector* and *Come Rain or Come Shine: Friendships Between Women.* Keil received a Tony nomination for producing the musical *Starmites* and executive-produced with John Harvey the independent feature film *Swing,* which she also wrote. Now living in Humboldt County, CA, she graduated with a B.A. in economics from Connecticut College and received an MBA from the Wharton School.

www.ingramcontent.com/pod-product-compliance
Lightning Source LLC
LaVergne TN
LVHW100247210926
848480LV00003B/851
* 9 7 9 8 9 9 1 0 7 3 4 1 7 *